IF MY NAME WAS PHIL JACKSON...

WOULD YOU READ THIS?

The Anonymous Adventures of an Anonymous Coach

By RICK TURNER

Published by Sepia Books

Printed in the United States of America * By Lightning Source * Cover by David Mitchell Design

A portion of the proceeds from this book will go to the Jumpball Basketball Programme in Kingston, Jamaica. To learn how you can make a personal donation, please go to www.jumpballbasketballprogramme.org

This book is dedicated to my family, who have had to put up with this "journey" for far too long, particularly my daughter Scout and the memory of her grandfather, Gary Wortman (Papa Gary), who I wish was here to read it

CONTENTS

ACKNOWLEDGEMENTS

There are a few people that I briefly need to thank, for whom without; this book would have never been written. The obvious are all the friends and family who have supported me in this process and at a minimum, kept their doubts and questions hidden behind my back and out of ear shot. But for reals… there are some specific people who made this possible.

Back in the 6th grade, a girl named Robin Kuhen moved away from Kirkland, Washington, never to be heard from again. Every boy at Ben Franklin Elementary had a small crush on the diminutive figure skater whose family stole her from us and moved her to Colorado. While I was searching for an editor for this book, my boy John Backschies was simultaneously on Facebook searching for the long, lost 6th grade beauty, Robin Kuhen and the answer to "what ever became of…".

After failed attempts by many others before him, John found the elusive, Robin Kuhen from Colorado by way of Kirkland, Washington and it turns out she is now the beautiful and talented, self-described "soccer mom", Robin Hebl from North Carolina. And, along with carting kids to and from practices everyday, Robin also happens to be an editor… just what the doctor ordered and the timing couldn't have been better. John put the two of us in touch and Robin agreed to take on the task of fixing my many, many mistakes and providing some invaluable advice and much appreciated wisdom along the way. I am so happy to get reconnected with Robin and can't thank her enough for how she has helped me with this project.

Throughout the body of this book I touch on some of the many coaches who have influenced me during my career. It really breaks down into three groups. There are those whose work I have admired from either up close or at distance for many, many years. They are too numerous to mention in this small space but I will do my best to let them know personally when I get the opportunity. There is another group of coaches who I have followed closely and even though I don't know them personally, I have attempted to "borrow" some, if not many, of their philosophies. Two in particular are Don James and Frosty Westering, who I have great admiration for and would love the opportunity to meet and tell them in person someday. Their body of work stands on its own but their reach and influence goes beyond those who they have personally coached. I thank them as well. The final group is the coaches who have helped me personally and who I really want to thank here publicly for inspiring me, believing in me, teaching me and always being supportive when called upon. They are: Mike

Cashman, George Karl, Stan Morrison, Ed Pepple, Lorenzo Romar, Bob Weiss and Ernie Woods.

Those are pretty good guys to learn the game of basketball from and even though some of them may read that and say "Huh?"... their influence in my career has been unequaled, instrumental and very much appreciated.

I'd also be remiss if I didn't acknowledge and thank the various coffee shops that let me bang this out in their stores for hours and days at a time without harassing me to buy more and hang out less. I tried many but really, there were only three where I consistently felt welcome, the staff was friendly, the wi-fi was free (and working) and the coffee was bomb. Since Howard Shultz sold the Sonics fans down the river a few years ago, I've tried my best to stay away from Starbucks when possible. In doing so, I wrote much of this book at St. James Espresso in downtown Kirkland, WA, Tully's in Issaquah (and a special shout out to the 'regular' ladies there who always shared their table with me) and the Tully's in Medina. I appreciate your willingness to put up with me.

Finally, when all was said and done, the book was finished and edited, all the t's were crossed and the final i's were dotted... I had one last thing to finish... and that was figuring out a cover for the book. I didn't know where to find a graphic designer and couldn't really afford one if I ever did. I called my longtime friend Dave Mitchell to ask him for some experienced guidance and without hesitation (and despite a challenging budget) Dave stepped up and agreed to design and format the cover himself. I can't thank him enough for putting in the last puzzle piece and finally allowing me to take out my list of things to do and cross off "write a book".

FOREWORD

In January of 1992, Sonics President/General Manager, Bob Whitsitt, offered me an opportunity to leave my job coaching the Real Madrid team in Spain and come back to the States to coach the Seattle SuperSonics. I had no idea what to expect upon returning to the NBA but I felt pretty fortunate to inherit a talented roster of players that included Gary Payton, Shawn Kemp, Derrick McKey, Michael Cage, Ricky Pierce, Nate McMillan and Eddie Johnson. From the time I touched down at Sea-Tac Airport that day in mid-January, to the time I was wheels up on the way to Milwaukee to coach the Bucks in 1998, the city of Seattle, the fans, players and staff of the Sonics were always very special to me and hold a large piece of my heart.

Our teams there in Seattle had a great deal of success, with multiple 60-win seasons, memorable playoff series and a trip to the NBA Finals in 1996. We had teams of character, as well as teams of characters but one thing that I never doubted was their passion and competitive spirit. When I reflect back on some of my former players from those teams in Seattle, even though we butted heads from time to time, I have the utmost respect for the way those men competed and the love and spirit that they played the game of basketball. That passion seemed to trickle down and seep throughout the entire front office as well, and I always felt strongly that the folks who worked for the team on the business side of things were some of the hardest working people in the league. They shared in the joy of our team's success and played a large part in the organization's overall achievement.

One of those front office people was Rick Turner.

I got to know Rick when he started showing up at our practices as part of the broadcast staff for the Sonics, early on in my time with the team. As his face became more familiar and his passion for the game became obvious, I started to give him small jobs to do during our practices. I could tell very quickly in our relationship, that Rick was what we call a "gym rat". He loved the game, soaked it up and took every opportunity that we gave him to be a part of what we were doing. At the time, I didn't know about his dreams of coaching but I could always tell that a fire burned deep.

It wasn't until he showed up in my office one day to tell me about his desire to coach, and that he was leaving the organization to pursue it, that I understood the depth of his passion. I honestly didn't know where that pursuit would take him or how serious he would get about it until after I read this book.

I have to say, reading this book brought back a flood of memories to some special times in my life. I reflected on my own coaching experiences in basketball's "minor leagues" and the various places around the world that this sport has taken me. It was a place where the basketball soul was pure and unclouded by the craziness of money. In the NBA, money and ego will sometimes get in the way of what a beautiful game basketball can be.

I was fortunate to have some success coaching in the Continental Basketball Association while I was with the Albany Patroons as well as with the Montana Golden Nuggets (a team located in Great Falls, Montana) and Rick's experiences in those two cities were fun to read about as they helped me recall some very special times and special people that I met while my own career was still taking shape.

People don't realize the quality of competition, the quality of talent and the quality of play that was found in the CBA, the ABA and can now be found in the NBDL. It can be basketball in its purest form if the situation is right; and I think Rick Turner showed that he could take some pretty challenging situations and make them right. We both found out that there is no glory to be had in basketball's minor leagues. There are no ESPN highlights, no labor disputes, no news conferences or ticker-tape parades. It's just basketball. And for hoop junkies like Rick and me… it's perfect.

You will be able to pick up right away, just as I did when we met, Coach Turner's passion, love and insight for the game of basketball. You will see for yourself, that this guy is a grinder, a survivor with a "dog-on-a-bone" type personality, along with being a pretty darn good basketball coach. This book will make you laugh, make you think and give you a real behind-the-scenes view of life on the road and the toils of those who try to live their passion in the face of people who say they can't.

I am impressed with Rick's character and perseverance as he has tried to break into a profession that can be very unforgiving. I speak from first hand experience; the coaching profession can test one's resolve and make them question themselves at every turn. I remember this when I was coaching for Real Madrid in Spain, when all I wanted to do was get back to the States, and praying that someone would give me a shot somewhere… anywhere… in college ball or back in the NBA. It can be a lonely existence and a ruthless business. I admire his ability to stay afloat.

I also admire Coach Turner's ability to tell a story and he has shared quite a few good ones in this book. You will recognize many of the names involved and some others you might not, but either way you'll be left smiling or simply shaking your head, wondering if something like that could have really happened. Believe me when I tell you that it did.

Rick Turner is a basketball coach who you've probably never heard of. As he simply states in the title, this is "the anonymous journey of an anonymous coach". But it is people like Coach Turner who remind those of us who have been lucky enough to carve out a career doing something that we love, the reasons why we do it.

This is a fun read, a crazy adventure; at times pretty inspiring, enlightening and most importantly, an honest account of one coach's pursuit of his dream. I hope you enjoy it as much as I did.

No matter what direction Rick's pursuit of basketball takes him, I know that there will always be a place in the game for people, who have the ability to teach, to lead, respect the game and make those around them better… like Coach Turner.

- George Karl

PART I:

THE SEEDS

1

Little Rock

Look… if you had one shot…
One opportunity… to seize everything you ever wanted
One moment… Would you capture it?
Or just let it slip?

- Eminem "**Lose Yourself**"

Surreal.

As we prepared for our pre-game meeting before we went out on the floor for warm ups, I looked at my two assistant coaches, Harold Wright and Russ Schoene. After all we had been through leading up to this game tonight; it was hard to believe what was happening. We couldn't really find the words to describe the moment. Instead, the three of us just shared a look… and laughed.

We weren't preparing for an NBA Finals Game 7. We weren't preparing for a Final Four match up. We weren't even preparing for a high school state championship. On the basketball Richter Scale, this would barely jiggle Jello. But for the ten guys on the roster and the 15,000 spectators that were waiting to unleash their partisan venom on us, this was a "moment".

Contain Kareem Reid, don't allow him to get to the middle. Don't let Todd Day get early confidence with his jumper and keep Oliver Miller off the offensive glass. Those were the "brilliant" instructions that we sent our charges as they went out to battle. As I looked around an unusually quiet yet determined locker room, the pride I felt was nearly overwhelming. I was so proud of the guys in front of me, so happy that I was able to share this moment with Harold and Russ and couldn't help but feel a bit of pride for myself.

Our uniforms didn't say Chico's Bail Bonds on the back but they may as well have. Undersized, unheralded and unknown; we somehow found a way to play for each other. Every cliché that you hear a coach talk about when referring to the intangibles of what makes a team great, you could apply to this group. One of the consistent themes that we pounded into them all season long was to "make the big time where you are". It was a philosophy that I stole from a legendary football coach in the Seattle area named Frosty

Westering. In fact, Coach Westering wrote a book with that same title, where he talked about the importance of respecting your current situation and treating whatever you are doing at the moment, as the most important thing happening; if to no one else but yourself. I remembered talking about that at the very first practice of the season, nearly five and a half months earlier. I remembered talking about it before we played in front of six people in Visalia, California back in December. I remembered talking about it the third time our paychecks didn't cash and everyone wanted to quit.

We put our hands together for the final time. We knew this team would never play together again. We understood that in this moment, in this game, we had somehow captured the ever elusive lightening and the Alltel Arena in Little Rock, Arkansas was the bottle. Off-guard, Matt Glynn said a quick team prayer after which, forward Dontay Harris clapped his hands and said "Let's go fellas". Co-captain and point guard Jimmy Haywood said "Together, on 3. 1-2-3…" And 13 voices joined in unison for the final time. The sound reverberated within the walls of the visitor's locker room…

"TOGETHER!"

I walked out of the vomitory in to a raucous Alltel Arena with 15,000 crazed spectators cheering loudly and bouncing to the beats of Beyonce and Jay-Z signing "Crazy In Love". I shook Arkansas coach Joe Harge's hand as I walked by the home team's bench. Then, I shook hands with the guys along the scorer's table, thanking each of them as they wished me a not so sincere "good luck, coach". I paused at our bench as our team warmed up at the opposite end of the floor. I put my hands in my pockets and fought back a wry smile. I cocked my head to see what 15,000 people looked like from the visitor's bench. I took a deep breath and couldn't help but think to myself.

"God, I'm glad I'm here"

***

The collective "they" have said that one can't look forward without first looking back. It is difficult to negotiate your direction if you don't first know where you've been. In my on-going struggle to get my own compass to point in the right direction, I decided to take an inventory of where I've been. It is my hope by writing down my experiences that this will either illuminate a path to an evolutionary road forward or at least worst-case, provide the necessary perspective to realize that my chosen pursuit has been, well, in one word… naive. As I begin the process of telling my own story, I'm not even sure which conclusion I'm rooting for. Only that there is perhaps some clarity to the decisions that I have made and new hope for the ones that are destined to follow. I'll let you know by the end if such an epiphany occurs.

If you knew me well, you would know that I cannot do anything without apologizing for it first. I am a "preface-er". In other words, before I say what I really want to, I try and prepare you for it by prefacing or softening the blow. Like saying to the waiter, "I'm really sorry, I know you're busy but could I get another Diet Coke?" or commenting to a pretty girl, "I'm sorry, I'm not trying to hit on you but could you tell me what time it is?" This paragraph is a case in point but I feel it is necessary to say that I do believe that it is incredibly self-indulgent to write a "memoir" or "auto-biography" when you've never really done anything particularly meaningful in your life. Not to say that my life has had no meaning, just that it seems kind of arrogant to think that reading this would be of any interest to anyone other than my sister, who is an incredibly easy target.

The genesis of this came about when I started to send out emails describing my basketball coaching experiences in China during the 2008/2009 season. I reported on what was happening there to about 150 people that I considered close friends and family. Not exactly an unbiased audience, but I received so much positive feedback and requests to further embellish my story, that I figured they couldn't all just be indulging my ample ego. No matter what your self-image is, if enough people at the party keep telling you that you look good, chances are that you do. In my case, so many people asked and demanded that I write this memoir, I decided... for once... to believe them instead of me. So to continue bashing that poor dead horse, it is not arrogance and ego that compel me to write this. It is acquiescence and trust in those who encouraged it...

I am a basketball coach.

That might be the first time that I've ever said that out loud.

I am a basketball coach.

It's not that I didn't know it or believe it myself. It's just that I never thought anyone else ever did. I have been embarrassed by what people would think if they heard me say that out loud. All the other basketball coaches that I know have "credentials". They played "somewhere" for "someone" or coached with "someone" or are related to "someone" or know "someone".

Not me.

Call it brash, naïve or just plain dumb. I embraced this journey without a boost up or even a point in the right direction. I leaped and then looked as I joined a business full of characters that I loathed and held in contempt. My own arrogance told me that I could succeed in the coaching business without having to rely on someone else and without an impressive pedigree. From my initial perspective, I wasn't really sure how to go about getting a coaching job or even the type of coach that I wanted to be. I did however know what kind of coach I didn't want to be and that was a place to start.

I never wanted to be one of those coaches who is always wearing sweats or who would never be seen without sporting their team's logo-ed polo shirt. Maybe some of that was my own jealousy that I didn't have my own logo to display or maybe it was me just being an ass but I knew that I didn't want to be "that guy".

For about an eight-year run in the late '90s to early 2000s a group of "my boys" and I would make the trip to the NCAA Final Four. Omar Parker, Scott Weller, Brett Schenck, Jim Koontz and I all shared a common thread. It was a connection to Quin Snyder either through childhood, high school or college. Quin grew up in the Seattle area, played basketball at Duke University, was an assistant coach at Duke and had become the head coach at the University of Missouri. Because of that connection to Quin, there was always an excuse to go to the Final Four. Along with these trips came ample opportunity to meet interesting people and see interesting places.

Quin swam in deep water within basketball circles and it wouldn't be unusual for us to be drinking chardonnay with, then Cincinnati coach, Bob Huggins at 3a.m. in some hotel bar in Tampa or playing golf with ESPN's Jay Bilas and former NBA star Sean Elliot at the Quarry in San Antonio or holding court with Rollie Massimino at Commander's Palace in New Orleans.

What I didn't know when I first started making these trips however, was that simultaneously, in conjunction to the Final Four Tournament, was the National Association of Basketball Coaches (NABC) National Convention. This convention was held every year in the same city and on the same weekend as the Final Four. Thousands of college basketball coaches from all over the country, at every level, converged once a year to pimp themselves. We found this to be a target-rich environment for our acerbic comments and holier-than-thou condemnation for all the guys in sweats and logo-ed polo shirts running around trying to "jack each other off" in effort to get the next job.

One year, Scott suggested that we should all show up wearing polo's from a fictitious school with a made up mascot and then walk around the hotel lobbies with the same self-importance and righteousness as the other lemmings that were there networking and handing out resumes to people that didn't care; going for "open" positions that were already filled. Our crappy team polo shirt would give us carte blanche to prove that we belonged there, and more importantly, give other coaches the illusion that we might have something to offer them, beyond our hilarious banter and uncanny ability to point out everyone else's flaws.

This was an idea we unabashedly threw ourselves into. We debated on names. Omar suggested the "New Hampshire State Fighting Anvils". Koontz threw out the "Utah A&M Hummin' Hebrews" but I think it was Weller whose idea we settled on with the "Florida Union at Kissimmee University Flying Sycamores". The logo would be an old Sycamore tree flying through the air, with its roots still connected at the bottom holding a basketball in one of its hand-shaped branches, snarling, as it was about to dunk on you. Of course the coup de grace would be the acronym for Florida Union – Kissimmee University printed right there below the logo. Weren't we clever?

So by this time I had figured out a few things on my list of what NOT to be. Number one, I knew that I never wanted to be a "logo guy". Number two on my list was that I never wanted to rely on someone else to advance my career. Not because I was so much more righteous than anyone else but because I didn't trust myself to hook up to the right wagon. I knew at the time (and still do) that historically, the safest way of getting promoted is by being an assistant coach for someone that has had success. It doesn't matter whether or not you are any good. As long as your boss is viewed as being good then you get promoted. One of three things happens in this scenario. 1) Either the guy you work for gets a better job and brings you along with him (with your new job now comes a more lucrative and higher profile), 2) he gets a better job and you get hired to replace him or 3) your team has a good year and you get a job somewhere else because people think that if your boss is *that* good, you must be *that* good too (the proverbial coaching tree).

The only problem with this is; what if your boss isn't that good? Who would ever know if you were a good coach and how could you prove it? Or, what if you're both good but for whatever reason have other factors preventing you from garnering success in your league or conference? Budget, facilities, ownership, management or other outside influences that are out of your control? Then where are you? As an assistant coach, you've put your career into the hands of some guy whose own myopic decisions impact your future livelihood. It has always seemed a little too optimistic for me. It is like my golf game. I step up to the tee with my driver in my hand, swing hard and hope that it goes straight. When I slice it hard into the siding of the million dollar craftsman, 80 yards up the fairway, it has to be the driver's fault… right?

No logo's, no wagon jumping and lastly, I knew that I didn't want to be consumed by basketball. I thought that there was a better way to live your life rather than spending every waking moment in the gym. I felt (and still feel) like with anything else in life; you must have balance in order to be successful. You must make time for your friends and family. Take time to sit around and do nothing or take time to do anything you want. You must make time to allow outside influences to help you gain a broader perspective which will in turn, help you become even better in your job. I think it's better to work efficiently and extremely hard for a shorter time, rather than simply trying to "out do" the guy next to you by competing to see who can put in more hours. In college, I always heard that you were better off sleeping than if you were to stay up all night cramming for a test. Either you knew the stuff or you didn't. Study long, study wrong was the motto. Obviously, these aren't the types of sentiments that go over well in a job interview but they are true for me. Everyone is wired differently, I know, but I felt like this was the best path for me.

I also liked the idea of having conversations with people that weren't just about some kid's vertical, his bad hands or his slow feet. I was confident enough in my own evaluation of player abilities to not really care what other people thought while at the same time, I was not secure enough with myself to want to give another coach my own opinions. I wanted to avoid conversations where coaches were sitting around the gym, exchanging war stories about their careers'… mostly because I didn't have any.

I couldn't talk about the time I guarded Andrew Toney or what it was like to be coached by Jud Heathcoat or the game we barely lost to Providence in the NCAA tournament. I've never thought that it made me less of a coach though. It is my belief that you don't need to have had a heart-attack in order to be a cardiologist or know how to swim in order to drive a boat. Don't get me wrong. I'm not saying that I can't or won't talk hoops. Or, that I don't like spending time in the gym… because I do. I just felt like I could be a good coach but still have interests outside of basketball.

In 1997, right before I took the final big leap into coaching full-time, I had a brief conversation with longtime NBA coach George Karl who, at the time, was coaching the Seattle SuperSonics. Coach Karl was someone that I did and still do have a ton of respect for. He was the one who showed me that it was okay to be passionate about the game of basketball. He confirmed to me that it was not only okay but necessary to demand that those around you respect the sport in a way that brought honor to everyone that preceded you in it. Some of the beliefs that I had about the game, beliefs that I felt others would feel were corny, cliché or trite… Coach Karl shared and reaffirmed. Our conversation that day was brief but for whatever reason, it made a lasting impression on me.

I had been working for the past nine years at the Seattle SuperSonics in a variety of roles. I started as an intern in 1989 in the Game Operations and Promotions Department where I scheduled National Anthem singers, halftime acts and created different contests for corporate sponsors during timeouts among many other things. By the time I left in 1997, I was the Director of Broadcasting and had oversight of all radio and television programming for the club. With any time left over, I did whatever I could to insert myself into the basketball operations side of the business.

I volunteered with the Sonics Director of Scouting, Gary Wortman, and helped him with videotaping college games, logging video and even just simple filing. I started showing up for team practices and helping out in small ways by rebounding for players or simply keeping score of scrimmages. What ever the task, however mundane, trite or trivial, it allowed me access to observe and see how things were being done at an elite level of basketball with one of the most successful teams in the league. It showed me the commitment necessary to sustain success at those levels as a player and as a team… and it gave me the confidence to know that I could do it myself.

One day, I went over to the team's practice facility to see if Coach Karl was in his office. I didn't have an appointment but just dropped by to see if he had a few minutes to talk. As I walked into Coach's office on that September day of 1997 he greeted with what he thought was my name. "How you doin' Carter?" he asked me. I didn't have the nerve to correct him. Rather, I thanked him for allowing me to take a small part in practices over the past seasons and that I was quitting my job with the team and going to try coaching full time. At that time, Coach Karl and I were kind of kindred spirits. We each shared disdain for a boss who we thought was incompetent and maybe we each felt a little betrayed by the owner of the team whom we'd given our souls to.

At the end of the conversation, I asked him if he had any advice for someone in my position. He said that he did. He started out talking about the things that were frustrating him about the job and the state of the league. Mostly he spoke about how the "tail wagged the dog" in the NBA and how coaches had no power over players because of the salary structure in the league. But then he said something that struck me between the eyes and has stayed with me ever since. It is something that I was lucky to have heard and more fortunate to have believed because many before me have learned this lesson the hard way.

Coach Karl said to me, "Carter (umm???), if you remember just one thing remember this… your players have to hate you".

After all that, I had figured out the type of coach that I didn't want to be. That was easy. The trick now was to figure out the type of coach that I did want to be.

2

Kirkland

September of '75, I was 47 inches high;
My mom said by Christmas I would have…
A bad-ass mother GI Joe, for your little minds to blow…
I still got beat up after class.

- Ben Folds Five "**One Angry Dwarf and 200 Solemn Faces**"

The Sonics came to Seattle the same year that I was born, in 1967. I don't have a lot of early childhood memories that specifically would pinpoint where my interest in the game became acute but I do remember going to my first basketball game. There is an old picture of me and my parents standing courtside at a Juanita High School basketball game which is a local high school in Kirkland, WA., the town I grew up in. I was probably about four years old. It stands out in my memories mostly because it might be the only time my parents and I ever did anything like that before or since. I have a vague memory of asking some of the high school players for their autographs after the game but I couldn't tell you who any of them were or anything about the game. As I write about it now, it strikes me as kind of funny because it is one of the few memories I have of doing something with both my parents together. Maybe because there is a picture that proves it happened but those kinds of family moments growing up were few and far between.

I also remember my first Sonics game. My dad and I went with our friends, the father/son duo of Joe and Joey Singleton, when Joey and I were seven years old. We sat in the very last row of the Seattle Center Coliseum at just about midcourt. They played the Houston Rockets with Calvin Murphy, who I would later coach against and Rudy Tomjanovich, who I would later get absolutely over-served with one night in Houston after a Seattle/Houston Western Conference Semi-Finals game (but that's another story altogether). At my first game, the Sonics beat the Rockets that night 104-103 and I was hooked.

The Sonics made the playoffs for the first time in franchise history in that year of 1975 behind Head Coach Bill Russell and they were led by the great Spencer Haywood, sharp-shooter Fred Brown, fan favorite Slick Watts and 7'2" rookie Tom Burleson. For whatever reason though, my favorite player on that team and my very first favorite basketball player ever, was not one of those Seattle area legends. My favorite was a 6'2" guard from the University of Minnesota named Archie Clark.

Why Archie Clark? I really don't know… He only played that one season in '74-'75 for the Sonics and he wasn't particularly spectacular as I remember, but as #21 in green and gold, he was my guy. It could have been as simple as the fact that I had his plastic Slurpee cup from 7-11, with his picture and bio printed on the side or maybe he had a big game that night against Houston. I'm not sure, but when you're seven years old there sometimes isn't a lot of logic behind your choices.

Unlike kids today, there were no such things as replica jerseys back then. We would just have to find what we called "number shirts" with our favorite player's number printed on each side as a way to deify our favorite athletes. My two best buddies in second grade at Benjamin Franklin Elementary were David Seno and Mike Malmin. In fact, Dave is still one of my closest friends 35 years later. Our elementary school didn't have a gymnasium, so the three of us would hook up in the outdoor "play shed" every recess where we would play "Sonics". Mike would be Slick Watts, Dave would be Fred Brown and I was Archie Clark. Mike and I would play duel roles though as he also got to be legendary Sonics radio play-by-play man Bob Blackburn, while I was the coliseum public address announcer, George Tolles. I also had the ability to imitate the coliseum's horn pretty well so I was tasked with that job also; quite a full plate for a seven year old.

We would wear our number shirts to school as often as we could. I, of course, had a #21 and a #32 (Archie Clark and Fred Brown), Mike had Slick's #13 and Dave had Spencer Haywood's #24. In fact, in our second grade class picture for Mrs. Johnson's class (I had a crush on her), you can see me in my #21 shirt and Dave in his #24 shirt (Mike's mom must have remembered that it was picture day because he had on a nice sweater vest). None of us ended up being particularly good basketball players, but we did each wind up living a piece of our second grade childhood fantasies. Both Dave and I worked for the Sonics at one point in our careers and Mike went on to have an excellent career in broadcasting as a local news anchorman.

To put it kindly, my own basketball career fell well short of approaching spectacular. I played on my first organized team when I was nine years old for the Wolfpack in the Kirkland Parks and Recreation Department. I've often talked during recruiting visits about the fact that you never really remember the games when you look back on your playing career. The teams that you beat, the teams that you lose to are insignificant. Margins of victory, the "butt whoopin's" you took and the final scores usually fade quicker than the Seattle Mariners in August. What is really important though, are the friendships that you make and the memories you collect as you spend an extraordinary amount of time with your teammates throughout the course of a season. Chances are that you can't remember the final score of the "big game" against your rival in any one year but I'll bet you can name almost every guy that played on your team. That is part of what makes participation in team sports special and important. People that have never competed as part of a team don't get that and it is very difficult to help make them understand.

That dynamic, coupled with 30 years of distance, makes it especially difficult for me as I try to recall the seeds of my basketball genesis. However, three things come to mind immediately as I search for recollections of that early stage of my basketball life. Two are trivial but kind of funny and one possibly played a more significant role when I was growing up.

One of my first memories of my basketball career is getting to go to the record store after one of our games with my good friend John Backschies and his dad Frank (or as I like to call him, Mr. Backschies). I have always been a big music junkie, even as a kid and my mom gave me some money to buy a record. But, I had a problem. Making big decisions has never been easy for me and even the purchase of a $3.00 record was no different.

Would it be Manfred Mann and "**Blinded by the Light**"? *"Racked up like a deuce, you know the roaner in the night"* (or something like that…)

Maybe I should get "**Lorelei**" by Styx? *"When I think of Lorelei, my head spins all aroooouuund. She frightens every butterfly; she moves without a sooouuund…"*

I finally settled on the 45rpm record of "**Rubberband Man**" by The Spinners. *"Uh Rubberband, uh Rubberband Man. Doodoo do- do- do- do doodoo. Doodoodoo doodoodoo!"*

That purchase made me think that I was the coolest guy in the fifth grade. As it turned out, I wasn't.

That went to Darren Roark who was the closest thing to Fonzie in the greater Seattle area. At least that's what we thought. He walked around with the big huge GOODY comb in his back pocket so he could get his hair feathered properly at any time and he was most known (and possibly revered) among my friends for taking two girls to the movies at the same time. I know because I was there and saw it with my own two eyes. I don't remember the movie, probably something like **Benji**, but we were sitting there waiting for the movie to start when Darren strutted in like John Travolta in **Saturday Night Fever** (comb in one back pocket and Velcro wallet chained to his Toughskins in the other). He was flanked by Julie Tachibana AND Signe Christensen (two hotties). Not only were they on each side of him as the three of them slinked down the theater aisle to find their seats, but the capper was Darren's s*** eating grin as he had each of his hands in each of their back pockets!!!

Unbelievable!

Don't get me wrong, Darren wasn't a kid that I wanted to be like. That was as far from the truth as Tom Cruise and Katie's marriage. That kid terrorized me growing up. Not only was he "cool" but he was a bit of a bully too. A bad combination which gave him carte blanche at Ben Franklin Elementary as well as the territory between NE 65th and NE 70th streets on Rose Hill in Kirkland. One day he grabbed me on the playground, put me in a headlock and bashed my head into the soccer goal post just because he felt like it. Another time he convinced the other kids in the neighborhood to start calling me Ricky Retardo as they buzzed by me on their bikes, and I'm not even Latin.

My second memory from that time is the only one that actually involves thoughts of playing in a basketball game. My neighborhood buddy Lance Gatter played hoops with me all through elementary school before he figured out that there wasn't a lot of room for 4-foot-nothing post players at the junior high level. So, he switched to hockey until he found out that there wasn't a lot of use for 5-foot-nothing defensemen in the NHL. As a 10 and 11 year old "baller", Lance never met a shot he didn't like. I mean literally. Lance would shoot it ANYTIME and EVERYTIME he had the ball. One specific game stands out however, as I remember dribbling up the floor and passing to Lance just over the midcourt stripe. Lance never hesitated. He turned and fired a 45-foot hook shot from just about midcourt (not a jump shot, not a set shot but a HOOK shot). And let's be clear, time was NOT running out on the clock. In his defense, he could have been under a tiny bit of duress from the defense but lets face it; at that age, aren't you always under defensive duress? The answer to the obvious next question is no, he didn't make the shot. But when you are shooter, you have to have a short memory and my boy Lance's memory must have been the size of Kid Rock's buddy, Joe C (RIP). Of all the games that I played from age nine until I got to high school, the image of Lance's midcourt hook shot with ten and a half minutes left on the shot clock stands out more than any other play that I can remember.

The third early basketball memory from that time for me wasn't an on-the-floor memory. I've thought about it quite often over the ensuing years and have always wondered if any other kids experienced the same feelings at that age. We played our games back then at the Juanita High School Fieldhouse. It had four full courts and on the weekends would be ground zero for youth basketball in our area. Right down the street from Juanita was a McDonald's. I LOVED McDonald's. What kid doesn't? After my games, I would be another one of the begging 10 year-olds, pleading with their parents to take them to McDonald's. It was especially great after early morning games, when they were still serving breakfast because I wanted to marry the Mickey D's pancakes. Usually, my parents indulged me and we'd go in, sit with some teammates or other friends from school, and power down a cheeseburger, fry and orange drink.

There was an exception to this though.

Once in a while, either because my dad was out of town (usually on a hunting trip) or if my parents drove to the game in separate cars... I never wanted to go in. We'd drive up to the McDonald's and my mom would ask if I wanted to eat inside. I'd say no. She knew that I loved McD's and yet couldn't understand why I didn't want to go in. I would just say that I wasn't hungry or didn't feel like eating.

What was actually going through this 10 year-olds mind was the fear that if I walked into the restaurant with just my mom or just my dad, everyone in the restaurant would look at us and think that my parents were... d-i-v-o-r-c-e-d.

This was a devastating thought as a 10 or 11 year-old and it was a fear that gripped me my entire childhood. I only bring it up here because by the time that it actually happened when I was 16 years old, it was no longer a fear but a relief. How does it relate to basketball? When my mom finally left or was kicked out of our house (just a matter of semantics depending on who you talk to) on Mother's Day in 1984… I wasn't there to say goodbye or worry where she was going or to convince her to take me with her. I was at the elementary school up the street. Shooting baskets and working on my game.

I came home to find that she was gone.

***

1979 – 1982 at Rose Hill Junior High are known to me as the "Dark Ages". Ben Franklin, Benjamin Rush and Rose Hill Elementary Schools all fed into RHJH and the transition for this kid was, in a word… insurmountable.

Awkward.

Miriam-Webster's Online Dictionary defines Awkward as: *lacking social grace and assurance. Causing embarrassment.*

I'm actually somewhat surprised that my seventh grade ASB card photo isn't attached to the page as a more complete testimony to enhance the definition. To my credit, escaping from the "Dark Ages" relatively unscathed could be used as proof for any future beautification that the Pope may have in mind for me because it was nothing short of a miracle. Some major factors were not working in my favor for any real hopes of social success at RHJH.

First, I was living in a house with parents that couldn't stand each other. The sadness of that was washed away by that time but the stress that it creates on a pre-pubescent kid is overwhelming. Second, most of my friends from Ben Franklin were going in a direction that I didn't want to follow; by experimenting with cigarettes, alcohol and even more serious substances. My fear and reluctance to part take in their youthful expression was looked upon by them as weak, which pretty much ostracized me from "the group". Third, I was slow in maturing and the boys' version of "aunt flo" wouldn't smack me in the Adam's apple for quite some time. And as if that wasn't enough, I was forced to walk the halls of Rose Hill JH not only with braces on my teeth… but also a two-piece headgear set as well.

I was Geek, squared. My braces, with remnants of Ding Dongs, Pop Rocks and Pringles lodged in various crevasses should have been enough… but it wasn't. In what I thought was a diabolical effort to shine the Klieg lights on my already glaring buck teeth… the dentist prescribed headgear.

But this wasn't your father's headgear. Just in case the one strap around my neck, yanking my upper jaw to my spine didn't completely humiliate me enough… they gave me the full-on skull cap strap as well, that simultaneously pulled your teeth up into your eyes.

It was part yarmulke and part 1930's football helmet, I didn't know whether I should wear an inappropriate large number as a skill position player or slit my wrists with an Izmel. The really attractive sight was when I got to finally begin the 27-step procedure to undo that metal monstrosity. The awsomenisity of the cool pattern that the straps left on my incredibly huge, bowl-cut blonde hair-do was impossible to describe and I can only imagine how even more disconcerting it was to witness. Those moments were priceless. It was only to be outdone by my mom giving me a home perm when I was 14 years old to add the proverbial cherry.

As you can see, I had no chance.

In the movie **Animal House**, Dean Wormer told Flounder that "Fat, drunk and stupid is no way to go through life, son". Just as "short, skinny and without confidence", is no way to go through junior high. I had been playing every sport, in every season up until this point, but in junior high, things started getting serious and the boys were being separated from the, uh… other boys. I was too small to play football in junior high because previously I had been playing down to my weight. This meant that teams were selected by weight of the players instead of their class and age, so I always played with the younger kids. It was just like in **Seinfeld**, when Kramer took karate class with the 12-year olds.

When basketball season came, I had to "tryout" for the first time ever and both my seventh grade and eighth grade tryouts ended up with me not seeing my name posted on the PE office window for kids to report to the first practice. Baseball was no better. I was cut in seventh grade and again in eighth grade, even though I always thought baseball was my best sport. I was still able to play baseball in the summer for Hilton Products in Kirkland's Pony League as a 13 and 14 year old, but that too would soon come to an end.

My dad was a baseball coach and he headed up the elite select baseball program in the area for high school kids. I loved going to their games in Kirkland and at the time, they were a well-attended community event. It's important to realize that during this time in the late 70's and early 80's, Kirkland baseball was experiencing unprecedented success and competing nationally in baseball events at all age groups. In fact, in 1980 and 1982, Kirkland sent teams to Williamsport, PA for the Little League World Series. In 1982 they won the world championship and Kirkland was thrust onto the national stage for baseball while their top player, 12year-old Cody Webster's image became the "thrill of victory" on **ABC's Wide World of Sports**.

I remember going to watch my dad's baseball teams play in various tournaments around the Northwest during the summer months. They competed against teams with players named Strawberry, Stottlemeyer and a tall skinny kid from Southern California named Randy Johnson. I couldn't wait for the day that I would (hopefully) be able to play on his team.

Then, one day when I was 14, my dad told me that he wanted to have a "talk" with me. He and I didn't have many "talks" at that time so I smelled something fishy. He sat me down in the living room and told me that what he was going to say was very difficult. He paused for a moment and I wondered what it could be. He took a deep breath and spoke.

He said, "Son, you're just not a very good baseball player…"

He told me he thought that I would be better off choosing one sport and concentrating on being good at that instead of being just average in everything. He suggested that basketball would be my best sport. Funny, because I thought that it was my worst. In fact, the last two years I had been cut from the junior high team and hadn't played at all since.

Then I started to get suspicious. I started thinking that maybe my dad was embarrassed of me not being a good baseball player and wanted me to stop before I was at the age where he would be forced to keep a player (me) on the team that didn't belong.

I was devastated by this talk with my dad. I loved playing baseball but didn't feel like I could go against his pretty straight-forward and blunt request. So, I did what I was told and just started focusing on basketball.

In 1981, the Lake Washington School District in which Rose Hill Junior High was part of, adopted a new rule. I hated the new rule at the time. It felt like another evasive encroachment of ever-expanding political correctness and an attempt to over-protect kids by not hurting feelings. It seemed "soft" to me. In hindsight however, I have to believe that I might be one of the students most positively affected by that rule, even to this day. Without it, you certainly wouldn't be reading this.

That year, as I entered the ninth grade, the district adopted a rule which stated that no student trying out for a varsity sport could be cut from the program entirely. In other words, everyone would make the team and for the first time ever, ninth graders could play on the junior varsity team.

How humiliating, I thought.

Nonetheless, I tried out for the varsity basketball team again in the ninth grade; but this time, instead of being cut; I was placed on the JV.

I had no idea at the time, how that one small rule would change my future indelibly. Playing on the JV team, I was able to experience individual success for the first time in my athletic life. My confidence grew and it didn't seem to matter that I was schooling

Spazzy Spaserton and Physically Challenged Midgets. I was like Anthony Michael Hall in **Sixteen Candles**; I was "King of the Dipshits". The season ended with me getting "called up" to varsity for the final two games of the year against Redmond and Finn Hill and earning my first varsity letter. I was invited to the end-of-season party over at Coach Thornley's house and for the first time in a long time, I started to make some new friends. I am quite certain that had it not been for that new rule in 1981, I would have never played sports again.

With a new fire lit in my belly, along with the help of a mini-growth spurt, I heeded my dad's directive and worked hard on my basketball game during the summer before my sophomore year as I prepared to enter high school. The confidence that I gained from my end-of-year call up was the springboard that I needed to start feeling accepted on the basketball court. No longer was I the last pick in a "second captain, first choose" scenario. I started attending various basketball camps around the area and my dad even got me a personal trainer, which at that time was unheard of.

I went to the first day of tryouts at Lake Washington High School filled with excitement, anxiousness and nerves. All the familiar faces from Rose Hill Junior High were there along with all the kids from Kirkland Junior High as well, which was the other school that fed into Lake Washington. I tried to do the numbers in my head. I made lists of who I thought would make the sophomore team, which guys were good enough for JV and those sophomores that could possibly make varsity. I knew that I was on the bubble to either make the sophomore team or to be cut from the basketball program entirely. The tryouts lasted three days and they were the toughest practices that I had ever been through. Tough was good though for me because I knew that what I lacked in talent, I made up for by out-working guys; so the tougher the better for me. Anyone that couldn't handle it and quit, would be one less guy for me to compete against. The tryouts were Monday, Tuesday, Wednesday and the list would be posted Thursday morning with the names of those players who were to report to practice Thursday afternoon.

I had to see for myself. I didn't want to hear the news from someone else. I didn't want anyone to give it away by looking at their face and seeing a look of condolence or congratulations; so I wouldn't look at anyone until I went to the coaches' office to see the list for myself. I walked up to the door and looked first at the varsity list. There were two sophomores that made the team, Scott Rolfness and Chris Davis. This was good. Rolfness was a lock but I wasn't sure about Chris. This meant maybe another opening. Then, I looked at the junior varsity list. Jim Jackson and Kevin Kent were the only sophomores on that list. Not so good. I figured there could be 4 sophomores listed there. It was going to be close… As I looked at the 1982-83 Lake Washington High School Sophomore Basketball Team roster my heart jumped up into my mouth. It would be everything I ever wanted or a terribly crushing blow. The list was in alphabetical order.

Brad Fridell…

Emmet Haggerty…

Gary Holzer…

Steve Jacobson…

John Jones…

Kenny Long…

Troy McCabe…

Willie Myers…

Kevin Putz…

John Starkel…

Then it happened. Sandwiched between Bob Taplett and Paul Wedeberg, there it was. I had never made any team before in my life; at least not one where you had to tryout and where other kids got cut. It was, at that point, the single greatest accomplishment of my life. I doubled checked the list again, just to be sure. And there it was, in beautiful, bold, 12-point font…

Rick Turner

***

For a guy that is attempting to tell his life story, it would help if I had a more clear memory or least faked it a little better. I think because of the melodrama taking place inside my house at the time, I have blocked out many of my own thoughts and feelings during this point of my adolescence and specifically my final year of high school. Or maybe it's my own superficiality that prevented me from having any real feelings. Nevertheless, I cannot for the life of me, remember why I chose to go to Bellevue Community College after high school. I have some theories. First is that we had money issues and that was the only school that we could afford. Another is that I wanted to continue playing basketball and the coach at Bellevue Community College at the time, Ernie Woods, invited me (and my buddy Jim Jackson) to play there. The other scenario which seems most plausible is that I waited too long to fill out any other college applications and it was too late to go somewhere else. It is probably a combination of all three but Bellevue Community College is where I ended up after high school.

For whatever reason, I was always a good student even though I didn't put a lot of effort into it. A's and B's were pretty routine and the occasional C was the exception. I graduated from high school with a 3.4 GPA and although I didn't have a great SAT score, I could have been accepted into many schools. My basketball game was getting better and better but being a "late bloomer", I wasn't really recruited by many schools. By the time classes started at BCC in the fall of 1985, I knew that I wanted to play at a four-year school and not a junior college. However, I had a couple things that were working against me by this time. First, I had no one around me that I trusted to advise me on what I should do about basketball. And two, I was so single-minded as to my goal of playing at a four-year university that I was unable to objectively look at my situation.

The basketball season came and went without me at BCC. Like most 18-year olds, all I could think about was moving out of my house. I wanted to go to the University of Washington but my dad told me that if I went there, I would have to live at home.

I was a Washington Husky fan my entire life. Going back to the 70's with players like James Edwards and Chet "The Jet" Dorsey, my dream would have been to play for the Huskies just like they did. The Husky basketball program was pretty mediocre at that time, in the mid 80's, and I felt like I was good enough to get a walk-on spot.

My "inspiration", if that's what you want to call it, was a guy named Clay Damon. He inspired me, not by how good he was, but to my thinking; how good he wasn't. I remember not being particularly impressed with Clay Damon, who was a starter for the Huskies at that time. I put his name up on my bedroom wall as a way to inspire me to work harder. My flawed thought process was that if Clay Damon can play there, then I can too. I thought I was at least as bad as him… It wouldn't matter though because as I said earlier, there was no way that I was going to live at home so attending Washington was out of the question.

On a side note, as I look back on it now, I know that I wasn't even close to being as good as Clay Damon (teenage testosterone will play tricks on your mind).

After one year of classes and sitting out the basketball season at BCC, I applied to and was accepted at Western Washington University in Bellingham, Washington; about 90 miles from Kirkland. I had a bunch of friends who were going to school there, it had in-state tuition so it was cheap (-ish) and it was the perfect distance away from home yet still close enough to where I could come back without problem when I wanted.

I didn't know anything about the basketball team at Western. I didn't know the coach, didn't know any of the players and in general just had no connection. I was either too cocky or just too stupid to understand what a monumental uphill battle that I would have to try and get onto that basketball team. That, coupled with a continuous three-year battle with injuries would prevent me from ever putting on a uniform for the WWU Vikings.

In a lot of ways, I feel like karmic justice was delivered to me at that time. I reaped what I had sown. I had a chance to play at BCC and I more or less took a big dump in the coach's mouth. My own arrogance and uncanny ability to over-think the situation got in the way of me playing there; and who knows what might have happened if I did.

As I said, I was just coming into my own as a player and all I needed was more coaching and game experience. BCC's Coach Woods was one of the best coaches in the area and I could have benefited immensely from his tutelage. Who knows why we do the things we do but I look back at that as one decision where I'd like to have a do-over.

A dislocated thumb, plantar-fasciitis, a detached retina and an over-all lack of ability were the only things standing in the way of me and a great basketball career at Western Washington University. It seemed to be one thing after another; and after a while, I had just lost all my fight. Basketball was now out of the picture and I needed to figure out what was next; but I had no clue.

3

Seattle

So take it as a song, or a lesson to learn;
and sometime soon, be better than you were.
If you say you're gonna go, then be careful;
and watch how you treat every living soul

- Band of Horses "**Detlef Schrempf**"

The Seattle Sonics played their home games at the Seattle Center Coliseum. 14,099 seats, it was home to Michael Jordan's "Free Throw Line Dunk" during the 1987 NBA All-Star weekend. It was a great place to watch a game without a bad seat and the crowd was right on top of the action. But in the late 80s, the Sonics played a handful of their games in Seattle's Kingdome. The Kingdome sat nearly 70,000 people for football and would seat up to 40,000 for basketball. The Sonics would target their top attended games before the season and schedule them for the Kingdome. Tickets for these games were not hard to get and in 1989 the hand of fate sent me from school in Bellingham to the Kingdome to watch a game between the Sonics and the Milwaukee Bucks.

There were six of us that made the trip down to Seattle for the game and our friend Phil Mazzaferro, got the tickets through his parents Entertainment '89 coupon book. The only problem was that our seats were way up in the 300 level. Unlike the coliseum, there <u>was</u> a bad seat in the house at the Kingdome. Actually, there were many of them, most of which you could find up on the 300 level. So, I started thinking about ways to scam us down to some good seats. It would be easy to sneak myself down there. The fact is, I had snuck into many of games in my brief game-sneaking into career but it would be much more difficult to sneak six guys in. If I could figure it out, I'd be the hero of the night. So I started planning my strategy on about my third Mickey's Big Mouth Malt Liquor as we drove through Marysville, still an hour away from downtown Seattle.

My roommate Jeff, had a friend named Michelle whose parents both worked for the Sonics. I couldn't think of her last name so I asked Phil, who took her out on a date once, if he knew her last name.

"Wortman" he told me.

"Michelle Wortman" I repeated to myself, trying to cement it in my mind for future use.

I had an idea.

We got to the game. By now I had sufficiently made Mickey shut his Big Mouth and was walking across the Kingdome parking lot with a light head and enough liquid courage to invigorate Bert Lahr. The "fellas" went up to find their seats while I quietly broke off in the opposite direction. I got to the "Arena Level" entrance door just north of the Sonics locker room and I walked right by the Kingdome usher like my name was Rick Kingdome. I got about five paces past before I heard her.

"Uh… Sir! Can I see your ticket?"

I acted like I didn't hear her. "Just keep walking" I whispered to myself.

"Sir…!"

Obviously, she doesn't know who I am.

There were enough people to follow in behind me that the usher got sidetracked with checking everyone else's tickets and forgot about trying to pursue me and my ticket. The first obstacle was out of the way. "What now?" I thought as my heart pounded and adrenaline rushed through me. I was standing on the floor of the Kingdome. My buddies were a zip code away, in the nosebleed section while I stood along the railing that led from the locker rooms to the court, waiting to see Tom Chambers, Dale Ellis and Xavier McDaniels walk by.

I searched for a friendly looking usher, finally spotting one standing near the court. I walked up and asked if she knew where I could find Mrs. Wortman, who worked for the Sonics. I picked the right usher because she quickly walked over to a team employee standing near the scorer's table, pointed over at me and said something to her. The woman she spoke to came right over.

My plan was perfect. I'd meet Michelle Wortman's mom, talk for a few minutes and hold my hand out as she would magically upgrade our tickets to something south of the 300 level. However, my courage was quickly wearing off.

"Can I help you?" the woman asked.

"I'm looking for Mrs. Wortman. I'm a friend of her daughter's. Do you know where I can find her?"

"If you can wait right here, I'll go try and get her for you"

So I waited. And waited. And waited. I was starting to feel some trepidation about this whole thing but I stuck it out.

Finally she showed up.

She stuck her had out to shake, "Hi, I'm Sharon" she said hurriedly. Obviously, she had better things to do than talk to some strange kid that she's never met who claims to be friends with her daughter.

I told her that I was friends with Michelle from WWU and that I was down here from Bellingham with some buddies.

To say that I was friends with Michelle was a major stretch. My roommate was friends with her but I had only met her a couple of times. I'm pretty sure she didn't even know who I was. But I had an agenda and I wouldn't be stopped.

Sharon Wortman's reaction was underwhelming to say the least. She thanked me for saying hi but then the conversation came to a lull. "Do something" I thought to myself.

In my mind, Mrs. Wortman would have said "Where are you guys sitting?" I would tell her that we were up in the 300 level and she would say "Oh, way up there? Why don't I move you guys down here where you can see the game better…" I'd go find "the fellas'" back at our seats, whip out the ticket upgrades and be the hero for the rest of the night. It would be the beginning of my reign as our version of "Red, the guy that can get things" (aka Morgan Freeman in **The Shawshank Redemption**).

All I needed was for Sharon Wortman to catch on to the plan.

But she didn't.

I had to say something quick.

"Uh, I was wondering if you guys offer any internships?" I asked meekly as I searched for a way to prolong the conversation.

She said "Yes, sometimes, but there isn't anything right now. Why don't I take your number and let you know if I hear of anything"

"Great!" I said through a fake smile as I tried to hide the disappointment of having to be banished back to the nosebleed section. I didn't really want an internship; I just needed to keep the conversation going, so I threw that out there. I gave her my number and never thought about it again… until my phone rang two months later.

When the phone rang at 11:30a.m., I was still sleeping. Who could be calling so early I grumbled to myself. My roommate, Jeff, answered the phone.

"Hey, Jackass, it's for you" his scratchy throat bellowed as he banged on my bedroom door.

I rose from the dead, whipped on a t-shirt and stumbled to the phone.

"Hello?"

It was Sharon Wortman at the other end of the line. I scrambled to try and remember who Sharon Wortman was and how she got my number. I vamped until it started to come back to me, but I was still confused as to why she would be calling. She asked me if I was still looking for an internship. I hadn't really thought about it since the game a couple months earlier. I thought for minute as she talked.

"Why not?" I wondered to myself.

I was just about to graduate and had nothing else going on or even immediately planned for that matter. She told me that I should call the Director of the Game Operations and Promotions Department, tell him that we spoke and ask about the opening; which is what I did.

Todd Eley hired me in September of 1989 as his assistant and the two of us made up the entire Game Ops/ Promotions Department for the Seattle SuperSonics. My salary for this 40-hour a week plus job was exactly zero dollars. We worked everyday from 9a.m to 6p.m. including all home games and I loved every minute of it. My main focus was to schedule all of the in-game entertainment during the Sonics' games. That included National Anthem singers, halftime entertainment, sponsorship contests during timeouts, all-star balloting and any pre-game or post-game events.

This turned out to be a windfall for all of my buddies because I soon found out that it was a good idea to have a modicum of control when doing different promotions. My friends ended up as the benefactors as I included them in many of the contests and various promotions that we staged throughout the game. Not only were they getting free tickets to the Sonics game from me but they would usually also get to compete somehow for prizes. My friend Omar was a free-throw away from winning a car one time, an Isuzu Rodeo; he missed the shot and instead, was awarded the consolation prize of a giant chocolate bar. My boy Phil hit a half-court shot at one of the games to win a trip to Sweden (courtesy of Northwest Airlines). I was always surprised that no one ever noticed that the same guys kept showing up in these contests over and over throughout the season.

One thing that Todd Eley and this job did for me though, was provide an appreciation for how important preparation can be when performing your duties. The lessons in preparation that I was taught during this internship made a significant impact on the rest of my career. Todd was meticulous in having us (me) be prepared for any contingency. I had to carry a back-up note card with the lyrics to the Star-Spangled Banner in case our singer forgot the words. I needed to have mops at the ready, in case a fraternity guy threw up on the floor during our "Bat Races" contest (which actually happened one time at the feet of the team owner). I carried batteries in my pockets in case the wireless microphone that we used crapped out. And we stashed away extra give-away items for those fans who complained that they didn't get there in time to receive their freebie.

For each thing we did, we tried to come up with every possible scenario that could go wrong and have a plan for it.

Although I loved working for the Sonics and looked forward to going into work everyday, I had a problem. I needed a job. Even though I was working well over 40 hours a week, I was doing it for free. I actually earned my final eight college credits there but I think you get my point. I needed some income. I tried to think of places where I could work part-time and at night. I thought about the airport. I had always wanted to work for an airline because of the flight benefits, so I thought I'd give that a shot. I went down to Sea-Tac Airport and got an application from every airline that had a desk inside. I filled one out for each one of them and waited.

The first response that I received was a letter from Northwest Airlines. It was a form letter which thanked me for applying and that my information would be kept on file. You know what I'm talking about; we've all got them at one time or another. The next one came from Alaska Air. It was basically the same form letter but with a different signature. The next came from United Airlines. Again, "thanks but no thanks, xoxo United". The next one came from Delta. It said the same thing but there was something different about this letter. It didn't have a generic, typed signature at the bottom from some faceless, heartless HR computer template. This one was actually signed by someone. Upon further examination, the ink was real. It still said thanks but no thanks but at the bottom was signed,

Sincerely,

Larry Bauer
Station Manager
Delta Cargo – SeaTac Airport

…with his real signature on the letter. This was all I needed. I called Delta's toll-free number. I tracked down the direct number to the cargo office in Seattle. I dialed the number. The phone rang. A voice at the other end said…

"Delta Air Cargo this is Cathy, can I help you?"

"Hi Cathy, I'm trying to get a hold of Mr. Bauer. Is he available?"

"He's in a meeting right now. Can I leave a message for him?"

"Yes, could you let him know that Rick Turner called?"

"Does he have your number, Mr. Turner?"

"I don't think so, just in case, here it is…"

He didn't call back. The next day I called again.

"Delta Air Cargo this is Cathy, can I help you?"

"Hi Cathy, I'm trying to get a hold of Mr. Bauer. Is he available?"

"Can I tell him who is calling?"

"Yes, this is Rick Turner."

"Just a moment Mr. Turner…"

I waited on hold listening to all the beautiful destinations that I could go to on my next Delta Vacation. She's back.

"I'm sorry Mr. Turner but Mr. Bauer is in a meeting right now. Can he call you back?"

This went on for nearly two weeks. I called back everyday until it got to the point where Cathy recognized my voice.

"Delta Air Cargo this is Cathy, can I help you?"

"Hi Cathy, I'm trying to get a hold of Mr. Bauer. Is he available?"

"Oh, Hi Rick. How are you today?" by now she recognized my voice and would ask like she actually cared.

The routine of me calling and Cathy coming up with a reason to not put me through to Mr. Bauer continued daily.

Then one day it changed and she finally put me through.

"You're a persistent bugger, aren't you?" the man's voice said at the other end.

I told him that I wanted to sit down with him and talk about a job. Even if he didn't have one, I wanted to meet him face-to-face and learn more about the company. He agreed, or should I say acquiesced.

I met Larry Bauer in his office a couple days later at Sea-Tac Airport. I nervously sat in front of him and told him that I would do anything for a foot in the door and a chance to work at Delta even if that meant coming into his office to empty his trash every night until something opened up. He looked me over a few times and asked some questions. Then he picked up the phone and made a call. He asked the guy at the other end if they were still looking for a part-timer to work various shifts for people who went on vacation or called in sick. He hung up the phone and wrote down a name.

"Go see Jack over at Gate B-2, he's expecting you."

For the next 4-5 months, I worked for the Sonics and Delta Airlines. I was putting in over 80 hours a week and having a blast doing it. The job at Delta was loading baggage onto the planes before they left and unloading them when they came in. As I look back on it now, it was the most fun job that I have ever had. We would work HARD for an hour and a half or so and then wait around for another hour until the next plane came in. In between we'd watch TV, play cards and tell stories. It was like being in a locker room as part of a team. Lots of "guys being guys" type of stuff.

***

As my internship with the Sonics came to an end in May of 1990, I heard about the sale of the minor league baseball team where I went to school in Bellingham. The Bellingham Mariner's were a Single A affiliate for the Seattle Mariner's and a couple of years earlier was the professional jumping off point for the Mariner's first round pick in 1987, Ken Griffey Jr.

I had dabbled in some radio and television while I was in college and had always wanted to scratch that play-by-play itch. With confidence from my recent experience stalking Larry Bauer at Delta, I decided to call the new owner of the "Baby M's", ask him for a radio job and refuse to take no for an answer. I had the added advantage this time of being able to add "from the Seattle SuperSonics" to my name as the secretary attempted to screen my call.

This time I got right through.

I met Jerry Walker for lunch in Bellingham just a few days after reaching him by phone. It was immediately obvious that he was extremely excited about his new purchase of the baseball team but simultaneously totally overwhelmed with the work ahead to get ready for the season; which started in mid-June.

I cut right to the chase.

I told him about my interest working in the broadcast booth and that my experience with the Sonics could be of help in other areas for the organization. He told me that the team only had three paid positions. The rest were volunteers. One was a groundskeeper, and the city was taking care of that. Second was a concession stand manager and he just hired a woman for that job yesterday. And the third was bus driver.

"Do you know how to drive a bus?" he asked

"Oh yeah, of course. I used to drive my dad's dump truck all the time"

The fact was I had driven my dad's dump truck once. He owned a landscaping company and had a big 16-ton dump truck with the hydraulic lifts and the whole nine yards (can you tell by my description that I have no real clue about dump trucks). I had driven it only one time and that was when I convinced him that it would be a fun idea to take my date to the senior prom in his dump truck. While other kids were driving up in limos and other fancy cars, we'd come rolling in with this beast. What girl wouldn't appreciate the creativity in that? Actually, its all part of my next book titled, **"30 Years of Bad Relationships With Women: What's Their Problem?"** I practiced driving it for a couple hours before arriving at her house behind the wheel of this big, monster truck, wearing my black tuxedo, waiting to pin that corsage on her boo... I mean dress. She was understandably horrified as I pulled up to her house.

Back to Jerry Walker though.

"I'd love to be your bus driver" I told him enthusiastically while thinking to myself... "How do I learn to drive a bus?"

I studied for and passed the written part of the Commercial Driver's License test with relative ease. The next part was the driving portion. I showed up to practice with the actual bus that I would be driving and immediately noticed that it was exactly what you would expect a minor league baseball team's bus to look like.

It was a 1958 former Greyhound bus with peeling paint and a partly scratched-off team logo on each side. The heads (whatever they are) were cracked so the entire backend of the bus was caked in black, gritty oil. Upon walking inside it, after soaking in the damp, musty smell; I noticed that many of the seat backs were either broken or broken off entirely. This bus was straight out of central casting.

The first game of the season was on June 16th. It was a home game at beautiful Joe Martin Stadium, just east of downtown Bellingham and across the street from Haggen's Supermarket. Jerry had promised his 70-some year old father Ivan, the play-by-play gig. It was a great gesture by a son who was helping his father to live a lifelong dream.

As a fan listening on the radio, it fell a little short of that.

Ivan had no radio experience, didn't have a particularly rich background in baseball and he didn't have a "hip" bone in his body. Actually he had a bad hip but that's not the type of "hip" that I'm talking about. You don't need a strong baseball background if you have a good on-air personality, just as easily you can get away with less of a personality if you have some prior experience to draw upon. Unfortunately, God love him, Ivan had neither. He felt like he needed a signature home run call but what he came up with was so contrived and over thought that its delivery had the spontaneity of a Catholic Church service.

"And you can color it gone…!" he would drone on in monotonous exalt as the ball cleared the fence.

I walked up to the press box where I could watch the home opener with some of the other team employees. What happens next still has me scratching my head.

Someone walked up to me and asked if I'd be willing to do the Public Address announcements because the regular PA announcer called in at the last minute saying that he couldn't make it. I said, sure. As the game approached, the owner got nervous about the PA because it was opening night and he wanted someone that he knew a little better and trusted more to perform the duties. So, he pulled the guy who was supposed to be Ivan's "partner" off the broadcast and inserted him into the PA announcer's spot. Ivan didn't want to do the game by himself and he knew that I had some radio background, so he asked me if I'd jump on the air with him. He let me do innings 4-6 of the play-by-play that night (I think because that's how the Seattle Mariners broadcast team did it) and the rest as they say is history.

I Wally Pip'd the other guy. He was only scheduled to do home games anyway so they made him the permanent PA announcer. Since I was driving the team bus I was the only other person that traveled with the team… thus, I was at every game and became Ivan's sidekick on the road as well.

I worked that first year with Ivan and then became the main play-by-play voice for four more years. We had some great players come through Bellingham during that time, both on our team and as visitors. Derek Lowe, Raul Ibanez, Paul Konerko, Gary Matthews Jr, Troy Percival and Mike Sweeney are just a few that immediately come to mind who played in the Northwest League during those years. After that first year, I was also able to shed my bus driving duties after an eventful full season behind the wheel which included:

Getting lost on our first road trip to Everett and having to turn the bus around in a parking lot. It was the first time I had ever needed to put the bus in reverse and didn't know how…

Having the entire team out behind the bus trying to "push start" it one time after a game in Yakima when it wouldn't start…

Fearing for our lives when the brakes went out on a hill in Seattle before the one game we played each year at the Kingdome.

Good times with that bus… good times.

***

Just as the Bellingham Mariners job came together at the end of my Sonics internship, I caught another lucky break at the end of that baseball season. Out of the blue, I received a call from the Sonics Director of Broadcasting, Kim Ackerley. Kim was the daughter of the Sonics owner Barry Ackerley and she was leaving the team. Her Network Producer was being promoted to take her position. She called to ask if I'd be interested in taking his position as Network Producer for the Sonics. As a way to make the position more attractive and pay more money they also assigned me with duties at one of the radio stations that the team owned.

This was an amazing opportunity for me and I didn't hesitate to take Kim up on her offer. It would be my first "real" job. It was a career builder as opposed to something to do to just make some money. I had always wanted to pursue a broadcasting career and now it was pursuing me. I didn't know a lot about it at the time but both Kim and my new boss, Dave Guyer, said that it would be easy to pick up and they would help train me. Beyond the chance to return to the Sonics and actually get paid, I also would get to work downstairs at KJR.

KJR-AM radio had been one of the most popular stations in the Seattle area for the past 40 years. I listened to it religiously growing up in the '70s. They played pop hits and also carried America's Top 40 starring Casey Kasem on weekends (I always wanted to do a long distance dedication). They had great local personalities like Pat O'Day (a Rock and Roll Hall of Famer), Gary Lockwood, Jerry Kaye, Charlie Brown and traffic beauty, Debbie Deutch just to name a few. But AM radio was going through a transitional period at that time. More and more people were tuning in to the FM band to listen to music and AM radio was dying. In 1988, WFAN in New York became the first radio station in the country to switch to an "all sports" format. The Ackerley family, who owned KJR, was thinking about doing the same.

I happened to be the right guy, in the right place, at the right time. I was hired to be the Sonics Network Producer which essentially meant that on the radio, during games, I inserted the commercials and cued the announcers after timeouts. There was a little more to it but not much. I also became the producer for the two-hour sports talk show that aired from 6p.m.-8p.m. on Tuesday and Thursday nights on KJR. The show was called "Callin' All Sports" and Sonics play-by-play announcer, Bob Blackburn was the host.

It was great for me because Bob was one of my idols growing up and now I got the chance to work with him. It was good for KJR because although they didn't know it at the time they hired me… I was a total talk-radio geek. I'm confident in saying that I was probably one of the few 23-year olds who had been listening to Larry King every night on the radio since I was 15.

In hindsight, I was the perfect guy for KJR to hire at that time. In spite of my young age, I knew how good radio was supposed to sound because I had been listening to talk-radio for a long time. I was a first generation Seattle sports fan and had closely followed the Sonics, Mariners and Seahawks closely since their inceptions. I knew the histories of the teams and the right people to talk to. My internship a year earlier had taught me how to aggressively "work the phones". I had a strong work ethic and my age brought youthfulness to a traditionally older format.

In a very short amount of time we grew the sports presence on KJR. We quickly went from twice a week to every night. Then we hired a news guy from Los Angeles named Dave Grosby who became "The Groz" and expanded our show from two hours to four hours. Not too long after that we brought in Mike Gastinaeu (The Gas Man) as another producer and expanded again from noon to 8p.m. In less than a year, we had taken our format to a 24 hour, all-sports network just like WFAN in New York City. I think we were just the third or fourth station in the country to switch to this format.

As you can imagine, during this expansion there were many new people hired to work throughout the various day parts. By now we had about five full-time producers and a handful of board operators. We had a great on-air staff including a woman from Florida who immediately made headlines with her abrasive style and demanding personality. She was the "Fabulous Sports Babe" aka Nancy Donnellan, who didn't take any crap and bullied her way into a male dominated profession. She knew that there was nothing worse than a host without an opinion and she never shied away from confrontation. She was difficult to get along with on and off the air when she was "The Babe" but when she wanted to be Nancy she was great to be around. Usually however, she was "The Babe".

The University of Washington football team was one of the top programs in the country during the late '80s and early '90s. There was an on-going debate within the listenership of the station as well as in KJR's halls as to whether the Pac-10 was the best conference in college football. "The Babe" was waving the SEC banner around to whoever would listen, claiming that it was the best conference. I have always been a "Pac-10 guy" so I decided to spend some time researching the numbers along with head-to-head comparisons of the two conferences. Anyone can skew numbers so they will support their argument and I put together a huge report which outlined and documented the virtues of the Pac-10 conference as it compared to the SEC. I presented this report to "The Babe"… it didn't go over well.

"You always have to be right, don't you?" she berated me, "You just can't let it go…" she bitched as she stormed away.

I had done it halfheartedly as a joke. The fact was that I didn't really care who was better but I didn't like the way she just dismissed the Pac-10/SEC argument. So, I put the report together trying to be kind of funny while also giving her a good-natured jab. That jab seemed to be perceived more like an upper-cut to the solar plexus.

The recession of the early '90s had a substantial impact on the radio business. KJR, along with sister stations, KUBE and KTLX (now KJR-FM) found themselves looking for ways to cut costs and trim the fat. Everyone knew that layoffs were coming and did their best to prepare for the worst. I was called into Program Director Rick Scott's office in the spring of 1991 expecting the worst.

He told me to sit down. I was pretty nervous and could feel my face getting red and blotchy just to prove it to everyone else. He explained that he was in a position where he had to make some difficult decisions. He said that we were cutting back and had to let some people go. I was readying myself for the big blow. He said that he was letting go of the board operators and the producers would have to pull double duty. From now on, we'd have to "run the board" (push the buttons and answer phone calls) during the various shows as well as produce them. He asked me if I'd be okay with this.

I paused.

I'm not getting fired? He's just telling me that I need to run the board?

"Yeah, of course I am" my shaking voice said, still full of nervous anxiety.

I was running through the names of my co-workers through my head. Jay Garza who produced Gas' show would be okay. Jon Hunter, who did mornings, would be okay. Pat Haller and Rick Dupree were safe…

"What about Chris Martin?" I asked Rick, but I was afraid that I already knew the answer. Chris was the low man on the totem pole.

"Well, unfortunately, we're going to have to let Chris go" surprisingly he told me this even before he told Chris. He asked that I keep it to myself so he could talk to him first.

I walked out of the office with mixed feelings. I felt relief for myself as I got reprieve from the guillotine but at the same time I felt awful for my friends including Chris Martin who had to be let go.

This brush with The Turk had properly motivated me to get in early the next day and prepare for the show. It's funny what a good motivator fear can be. As I walked into the Sports Pit, which is what we called the area of cubicles and desks shared by the entire sports staff, I got a call from Rick Scott's assistant who asked that I come down to Rick's office. Just like the day before, I walked into his office and sat down but this time without all the nerves and trepidation of the day before. My neck and face had its regular pinkish hue, absent of any signs of distress and I was actually somewhat distracted by all the things that I needed to get done later that day.

"Close the door" Rick told me as I remained oblivious.

"What's up?" I asked

"We decided to keep Chris and let you go" he said as cold and blunt as a process server

Not a sliver of compassion or regret.

He handed me a check and said "I need to get your keys from you"

Ouch.

I attempted to put a sentence together to ask why he changed his mind but I couldn't. My own mind was spinning as I tried to collect and re-compose myself. Then it occurred to me. Although Chris was new, he was only working for one person. All his time was spent producing one show and taking Chris away from that show would force the host out of their comfort zone. Not that it would be very difficult but the radio business is all about ego and one's ability to flex their muscle when they can. I learned first hand that you have to be careful about whom you take friendly jabs at when you're dealing with prima donnas and their egos. I learned that there can be consequences to "always having to be right". It became clear to me when I remembered whose show Chris produced...

The Fabulous Sports Babe.

***

Jobless and with nothing to do but spend my severance check, I started on two things. First, I looked for a new job and two, I worked on improving my social calendar. One of the ways I would go about accomplishing number two was by putting a basketball team together to compete in a local men's league with a bunch of my boys. I called a few guys and got some commitments from those who wanted to play. On my way to sign us up for the league, I decided to swing by the apartment of two of my buddies, Phil and John, to see if one of them wanted to come with me to sign us up.

As usual, I simultaneously knocked and walked in.

Oops, bad idea.

As I walked in the door, I could see the living room of the apartment clearly. There was John, on the couch. I got only as far as the "Hhh" of "Hey, what's up?" when I saw what was up. It was John. He was "up". Not only was he up, but he was "up and down" as well. The beautiful blonde was straddling him as they both writhed, naked and sweating on the disgusting beer and tobacco spit-stained couch of the apartment.

"Uh-oh... sorry" I muttered before they both turned to look at me startled.

I caught eyes with the girl as her long, golden blonde hair was now dark with sweat as it stuck to her forehead. Her fair skin was flushed and her unusually rosy cheeks, in respite from the impending rapture, burned an image into my memory that will last forever.

It was my naked girlfriend Stacy.

We had been dating since my junior year of college. We had gone through more than our share of ups and downs over the previous four years, but with maturity I blindly felt a sense of stability encroaching on our relationship. So much so, that I was considering a plan to propose marriage at some point in the near future. I can't say that I was completely surprised by what I saw that afternoon in John's apartment but the blow was no less devastating.

In truth, I was never really upset with John about what happened. It obviously strained our relationship but I couldn't really blame him. Besides, he wasn't my girlfriend, she was.

I turned back around and silently shut the door. I suppose they "finished" after I left.

Double ouch.

***

I spent the next few weeks feeling sorry for myself. I figured that I was officially depressed one afternoon as I sat on my couch watching **The People's Court**. With a blanket wrapped around me and my chin figuratively in my soup, there was a knock on the door. It was my friend Phil. He saw my car in the driveway and stopped by to say hi.

He walked in, only to witness me doing my best Debbie Downer impression, before there ever even was a Debbie Downer. He listened to me belly ache for a while and complain about all of the "why's and how comes" that were happening in my life. Then he spoke.

"Dude" he said, because that's what guys say before they're about to be really profound.

"What are you doing?" he simply asked me with an incredulous indignation that seemed to slap my insides silly.

That was all it took.

Maybe it was the perfect thing to say. Maybe I was just ready to be "over it". Or maybe it was just coincidence. But I experienced something at that moment which was tangible. I could actually physically feel something lift off of me and the only word that I can use to describe it would be a real, honest to goodness epiphany. Not some mental comprehension but the strangest physical realization that you could imagine. It is something that I've never experienced since.

What was I doing, I thought. Why was I really upset? Was this really "the girl" that I wanted to spend my life with?

Of course she wasn't.

Was KJR the only job out there?

Of course it wasn't.

And just like that... the hurt was gone. I never thought about her again, at least in a way that stirred any emotional response. And my job search, which had been put on indefinite hiatus, was back on.

As I thought about things that I wanted to do, something kept coming back to mind. I still had not had the chance to finish scratching my personal itch to play basketball. By now I was 24 years old and just reaching my athletic prime. I was still playing a lot of ball and was better than I had ever been. I had a couple of friends that were playing overseas and I thought this would be a great time for me to get away for a while, do something I loved and grow up a little. I thought about where I'd like to go and more than anywhere else, I kept coming back to Australia.

I looked into what it would take and how much it would cost. Maybe I over-romanticized it in my mind but my plan was to just get a backpack together and go. I would worry about details once I got there but my problem was the expense of a plane ticket. I thought about trying to work on a freighter that was going there or even working as a deckhand with someone who was sailing a boat Down Under. I went down to one of the local marinas in Seattle to ask around. I had no luck. I could find enough money to get to Australia but I was worried about how to get back. The cost of an open-ended ticket was much more expensive than a regular round trip. So I got a job as a bartender at Anthony's Homeport in Kirkland to try and make enough money to get my plane ticket.

Everything was good by the spring of 1992 and I had just about had all the money that I needed to buy my ticket to Australia. I was working out every morning; getting shots up, lifting and conditioning myself before the trip. I was about one paycheck away from making the plane ticket purchase when I got a phone call one afternoon before work. It was Gary Spinnell, the Vice President of Sales and Broadcasting for the Sonics. I didn't know Gary all that well when I was with the team so it was surprising to hear his voice at the other end of the line. He asked me if I could join him for lunch the next day. I wondered what was up but I agreed to meet him at Duke's Restaurant on Queen Anne just down the street from the Sonics' office.

It was good to see him. Since I had been laid off by KJR, I decided not to stay on at the Sonics as the Network Producer. It had been a while since I had seen anyone from the office. I had lost touch with many coworkers and was looking forward to catching up. It was early April of 1992 and the Sonics were fighting for a playoff spot in the toughest division in basketball the Western Conference's, Pacific Division.

Gary didn't waste any time exchanging pleasantries.

"Dave Guyer is leaving and I want to know if you would be interested in taking his position?"

"WHAT?" I thought to myself as I was completely blindsided by his revelation. Dave was the Director of Broadcasting for the Sonics and my boss while I was with the team.

"Dave says that you are the only guy to consider, that you can step in right away and not skip a beat"

Flattering words but not entirely true. I had worked closely with Dave while I was with the team but the bulk of my knowledge was based in radio and not television. They were in a bind however because the playoffs would be starting in a couple of weeks and the Sonics had decided to televise their home playoff games on pay-per-view television. I think they were the first team in the league to attempt pay-per-view and they needed someone that had knowledge of the department to replace Dave immediately as they tackled this controversial endeavor. Timing and familiarity made me the most logical choice.

Australia would have to wait.

***

The years that I spent at the Sonics were special in many ways. It allowed me to play an integral part of a unique and successful organization. Time and distance has given me the appropriate perspective to realize that the staff we had assembled during those years was incredibly talented and special. It was true on the basketball operations side as well as on the business side. It was easy to measure the success of the team on the basketball side of things. The Sonics won 486 games and lost only 252 in the nine seasons that I was with the team. It was the best nine- year period in the team's history. Don't get me wrong, I'm not claiming to have had anything to do with that success but winning was the culture and it infiltrated the business side of the operation as well.

My job description fell within the Sponsorship Sales and Broadcast Department which was the revenue engine for the team but it also gave me the ability to work cross-departmentally. I was involved in many projects that included marketing, ticket sales, game operations and promotions. I had oversight of the largest budget (outside of player salaries) in the office and our department was smashing our revenue goals year in and year out.

Our staff, and particularly our Sponsorship and Sales Department, worked hard and "relaxed" even harder. Part of our duties on the sponsorship side of things was providing hospitality for our clients. In this area we never disappointed. It started with our department head, Scott Patrick.

Scott took over for Gary Spinnell (the guy who hired me) in 1993. His title was Vice President of Sponsor Sales and Broadcasting. Scott's ability to take care of clients was only surpassed by his ability to take care of his staff. From around 1994 to 1997 we had an unbelievably tight group who worked for each other and together we worked hard for Scott.

Doug Ramsey, Dave Perry, Giles Dowden and Joe Schafbuch were the sales team. Anne Mastor, Hannah Hensel and Warren Dowd worked in support and Bridget Billig, Dave Seno and I focused on the broadcast end. In hindsight, we may have been a little cliquish within the overall office dynamics and in fairness, there were others who contributed to our department's success throughout that time; but the group I mentioned was the original core group.

We hosted parties, took clients on road trips and did everything we could to show our clients a good time. It was our hope that in doing so, we could depend on their continued support and grease the skids to charge increased advertising rates. In the process, we created what I felt was a very unique bond among us that is difficult to replicate. It is like chemistry on a basketball team. You don't know why it happens or how it happens and you can't do anything to force it to happen. There is no formula that you can use to create this kind of chemistry and there really isn't anything you can do to create it if it's just not there.

Chemistry is borne through leadership. If you look historically at teams with great chemistry, you can invariably point to tremendous leaders within that group. Coaches can be great leaders but they can't force chemistry. It has to come from leadership within the roster. Sometimes it is the best player on the team that provides that leadership which produces great chemistry but many times it is someone that plays a lesser role on the field or court who does it away from the public eye.

You could come up with many examples of this from your own favorite teams but I like to look at the 1996 Sonics as an example.

In 1996, the Sonics lost to Michael Jordan's Chicago Bulls in the NBA Finals. The Sonics were led by Gary Payton and Shawn Kemp, two all-stars at the time and among the best players in the league as well as in Sonics team history. But behind the scenes, the Sonics had great leaders like Sam Perkins and Nate McMillan who understood their roles and provided stability within the locker room which manifested into team chemistry. Head Coach George Karl did what was necessary to promote that chemistry, but ultimately it had to come from within the players themselves.

It is interesting to see how subtle changes in team chemistry can have such a major impact on a team's performance. The only change in the Sonics roster from 1995 to 1996 was the departures of Kendall Gill and Sarunas Marciulionis, two very good NBA players. They were essentially replaced by the additions of Hersey Hawkins and David Wingate, who were considered more "jouneymen-like" in their careers. I'm not saying that either Kendall or Sarunas were the reason the Sonics didn't play in the NBA Finals in 1995. There is also a large "luck" factor that is involved in advancing through the playoffs but it is fascinating to me how a seemingly small change in a team's roster can produce significantly, if not dramatically different results... both positively and negatively.

Our own little sponsorship group within the office was a microcosm of that chemistry dynamic. Scott Patrick became our touchstone as we spent more time with each other than we ever did with our own families.

We took clients to the old Boston Garden before it was torn down. We brought them to the old Chicago Stadium before it was replaced by the United Center. We saw Madison Square Garden and the Forum in Los Angeles. We partied in the upscale Buckhead neighborhood on our trip to Atlanta and golfed in Phoenix when we were there to play the Suns. Playoff games, the 1996 NBA Finals and All-Star Weekend parties were just a sample of the events that we attended to show clients our appreciation as well as enhance our own experience within the workplace. We pushed the boundaries of taste and professionalism on occasion but usually came away unscathed. We loved each other at times and hated each other at times. We ate together, drank together, fought each other and cheered each other. As I reflect on that time, I realized that we were a team in every way as the Sonics who played on the floor were... and our leader was Scott.

On November 1, 2008 Scott Patrick passed away at the age of 51 from a brain tumor. Needless to say, he was way too young. I was living in China when it happened and while he had been deteriorating for a while, the news still hit me like a punch in the stomach. I reached out to that team of co-workers who I had spent so much time working together with and playing together with under Scott. Even though we had all gone in different directions, we each shared in the grief of his passing and for one last moment, we came together for each other. Upon hearing the news, I sent an email to my former "teammates" and tried to express my thoughts about his loss...

> ----- Original Message -----
> **From:** Rick Turner
> **To:** 'Poll, Mitch ; gilesdowden ; hjhensel ; 'Mitsakos, Anne' ; Bridget Billig
> **Cc:** mford ; voiceofthesonics ; D.Henderson ; brianr.henderson ; mwade ; David Seno ; Doug Ramsey
> **Sent:** Sunday, November 02, 2008 5:26 PM
> **Subject:** Re: Scott
>
> It's funny how time and distance can change someone's perspective in such a seemingly short span.
>
> If you recall a particularly challenging situation in your life, time and distance can render it almost trivial.
>
> Today, under the worst circumstances, we are forced to reflect on a time that we all shared together. It was often times stressful (especially for a group of young 20-somethings). It was, many times frustrating (because someone in that stupid office, pissed us off). And maybe we found ourselves in over our heads from time to time

(or was it just me?). But the one thing that never wavered was our ability to count on, lean on and rely on Scott Patrick.

Words don't seem adequate. Saying that words don't seem adequate, doesn't seem adequate.

If you can allow me to use a 'double-negative'... no one didn't like Scott. We've all had our list of "haters" at one time or another. Maybe even at one time, each other. But I have never met anyone who EVER had a negative word to say about Scott. Giles mentioned that he was his "best boss ever". I couldn't agree more... but I'd have to add that it was because he was uniquely more than a boss. Most of us have gone on to be "bosses" at one time or another since we left Scott's nest and speaking for myself, I know that I have fallen short of the standard that he set.

Firm while remaining flexible, never prideful, always spreading the credit around... working hard, playing hard. He was definitely my "boss". Not my "friend", not "like a dad" nor "like a brother". He was just Scott which, I guess, was really all of them put together. He was so many things to so many people. There was Dad Scott, Husband Scott, Husky Scott, Seahawk Scott, Ellensburg Scott, Golf Scott, Cigar Scott and more... I'm just so glad that I got to know him.

As I read Rhonda's posting this morning, a rush of memories came flooding in. Bridget's "cartwheel episode" was one of the first. A trip to Houston when KC and Scott hit golf balls off the hotel balcony on to the freeway below. The years that he and Anne spent working together before I got there and after I left. The interns, the road trips, the Barry and Ginger's, the games and especially the post-games... through all of you I had the opportunity to share Scott.

This blesses us with a bond that through time and distance, like it or not... will never be trivial nor ever be forgotten. Much like none of us will ever forget Scott.

Whether we find ourselves in Seattle, New York, Chicago, Michigan, Hawaii or Taiyuan, China... I hope at some point in the next few days we can each raise a glass (preferably scotch) to our friend Scott; we'll smile and think about one of our shared memories of a guy that had such an impactful life in too short an amount of time.

Cheers Scott

✳ ✳ ✳

By the summer of 1997, I was eager to expand my role with the Sonics and try to take on some new challenges. I spoke with my boss Scott Patrick, the Sonics broadcast team of Kevin Calabro and Marques Johnson as well as KJR Program Director Tom Lee who had replaced Rick Scott a few years earlier. We had decided that I would join the on-air team and work as the courtside reporter for radio and television. I wouldn't make any more money for doing this and in fact I would save the team money by not having to pay somebody else. More than anything, I felt stagnant in my job and needed to move my career forward and this was a great way of doing it. With all the interested parties on-board, Scott wanted to keep the team's president in the loop as to my new expanded role.

John Dresel had rarely gotten involved with any broadcast decisions, usually leaving them up to Scott and Tom with input from me. I knew that Dresel never really warmed-up to me after he stepped into his position as team president in 1994. In fact, Scott flatly told me that John didn't like me because I didn't obey the company dress code and he thought that I was "weird" after an introductory meeting we had shortly after he took over.

When he became Team President, Dresel went around the office having meetings with directors and department heads as a way to learn what was going on in the office. One afternoon he knocked on my office door and asked if we could meet. I wanted to impress him and tried my best to be enthusiastic about getting to know him. Even though I worked more hours than others in the office (because I was the only one required to work during away games) I told him that I would meet him at any time and any place. He suggested 7:00 a.m. the next morning. We played Golden State that night who tipped-off their games at 7:30 p.m. After the game, post-game show, call-in show and post production work, I'd get home sometime after midnight. Instead of suggesting a later time, I thought... ugh... but said "Yeah, seven sounds great, I'll be there" feigning an eagerness that I hoped wasn't too transparent.

Nevertheless, I showed up at John's office early the next morning at 6:45 a.m. I was armed with coffee, milk, tea, donuts and bagels for him to choose from and the extras would be put in the lunchroom for everyone else to enjoy when the office opened later at 8:30. When John showed up shortly after seven, I was waiting with my bounty, enthusiastically offering my gifts with a brown-nosing effort that would be the envy of Dwight Schrute. We spoke in his office for about 30 minutes and I actually thought that it went well, which is unusual for me because I often don't perform well in meetings where I have to promote myself. I never thought about that meeting again until a couple years later when Scott told me that John came away from it thinking I was "weird". I didn't think that bringing in coffee and donuts could be seen as weird??? But hey, I don't know... like I said, I've never been a good ass-kisser anyway.

When Scott told John Dresel that I would be doing the courtside reporting for the team broadcast during the 1997 season, John personally inserted himself for one of the only times that I can remember before or since.

He flatly said no.

Scott broke the news to me as only he could. He acted pissed off at John and empathetic toward me. He apologized and tried to come up with some conciliatory solutions but ultimately I knew that if I wanted this to happen, I'd have to convince Dresel myself.

I called John's assistant Lorna and asked if she would put me on John's calendar. She told me that she'd check with him but then, she never got back to me. I knew that he was avoiding me. I saw him in the hall one day and confronted him about a meeting. Not in an aggressive way but very politely and respectfully I asked if I could get together with him to discuss the broadcast. He acquiesced and agreed to sit down with me a couple days later.

I practiced my pitch, put together some air-check tapes and redid my resume as I prepared for our meeting. Because of what Scott had told me, I knew I was going into the meeting at a considerable disadvantage. I would have to try and change his perception of me and show him who I was and what I had done. I sat down with him in his office and my plan to do just that came spilling out.

I explained to Dresel that I had already been working on air at KJR as well as on the Sonics broadcast in a lesser role; this would just be an expansion of that. I let him know that I had done play-by-play for the Bellingham Mariners for five seasons with tremendously positive feedback. I gave him a cassette tape of sample work that I had done as a reporter on KJR, on the Sonic broadcasts and with the baseball team. I re-emphasized how all the pertinent parties involved were on-board with me joining the broadcast team. And finally, I appealed to his sense of loyalty.

"John, I've been here for nine years. I started as an intern and worked for free. I consistently put in over 400 hours of unpaid overtime every year because I have pride in what I do and I care about the quality of the broadcast and this company. I have helped the department to grow and helped give us the best ratings in team history. I'm not looking for more money and in fact will end up saving the company money by doing this. All I'm asking for is an opportunity to show you what I can do. If you want, I will audition on preseason games and if you don't like it, we'll change direction… I'm just looking for an opportunity to grow in my position and grow professionally…"

He leaned back in his chair, crossed his legs and smugly looked me straight in the eye. I'll never forget what he said: verbatim.

Incredulously, making sure I heard every syllable he slowly replied with excruciating precision.

"This is the Seattle SuperSonics. We're not in the BUSINESS of giving people opportunities."

Those words rang in my ears. I sat there dumbfounded, as if I had been blindly slapped in the face. What was left to say? How could you respond to a comment like that? You're not in the business of giving opportunities, I thought to myself. You're not in the business of giving opportunities to someone that has given his entire life to this company over the past nine years? You're not in the business of giving opportunities to someone who has worked his ass off to make you look good everyday since you arrived? You're not in the business of giving opportunities to someone who has done everything that he could to deserve one?

Was it because I didn't wear a tie? Was it because I was "weird" enough to bring you coffee and donuts for a morning meeting? Or was it because you really are the total jackass that everyone in the office thought you were? It was a good thing that the

Ackerley's were in the business of giving people opportunities when they hired John Dresel because he was WAY in over his head and did nothing to ever disprove it…

…but I'm not bitter.

It was as if I had an out-of-body experience at that moment. I looked at myself sitting there in front of his desk from up above. I was wounded and defeated like someone who had just caught his girlfriend screwing his buddy on a dirty living room couch. Then the room brightened and I swear that I could see a light bulb go off over the top of my head just like you would see on a cartoon.

I knew immediately that my time with the Seattle SuperSonics was over.

PART II:

THE SEEDLINGS

4

Bellevue

And there's always another point of view,
A better way to do the things we do
And how can you know me and I know you?
If nothing is true?

- The Raconteurs "**You Don't Understand Me**"

Even though my "real" job was working in the Sonics front office, I did everything that I could during those nine years to remain in the basketball part of basketball. I coached and scouted at Mercer Island High School under one of the most successful coaches in the history of high school basketball, Ed Pepple. I volunteered after hours to help Sonics Director of Scouting, Gary Wortman whenever and however I could; mostly with logging video of players, data entry and video taping games. While the Sonics were coached by George Karl, I would also go to every practice and shootaround that was possible for me to attend. Mostly, I just went to observe but eventually Coach Karl started giving me small jobs.

By the time Sonics President John Dresel had ultimately shown his true colors to me, I was ready to take a leap. When you are not happy in your job, everyone has advice on what they think you should do. Not surprisingly, no one's advice for me was to quit the Sonics and jump into coaching basketball full-time. However, almost everyone advised me to do something that I enjoyed and had a passion for.

This made the dilemma slightly more complicated. If that's true, I thought, then I should take a chance. I searched and thought and contemplated and consternated over what I should do. Once I had made the decision to leave the Sonics, every day that I spent going into the office made me more and more bitter about being there and what had happened in my meeting with Dresel.

Ego, stubbornness and impatience finally won out and I put in my two-week notice to leave the team on September 23rd, 1997. The question next was... what now?

Although my experience working with Coach Pepple at the high school level was as good as it gets from a learning and coaching standpoint, I had some interactions with the parents which soured me on going back to a high school coaching job. I had a mother of one player who wrote me letters every week telling me what a terrible coach Pepple was and asking how I could convince him that her son should be playing more. Other parents would pull me aside after games and question everything that Coach

Pepple did. I hated it. Here was a guy that had coached for 40 years, won over 900 games, multiple state championships and never had anything but the best interests of his players at heart, yet and he was being questioned at every turn. It wasn't just at Mercer Island High School however. All around the state, parents would complain to athletic directors who would never stick up for or back their coaches. It was (and still is) more about managing and massaging parents than it is about coaching kids. It was repugnant to me and I didn't want to be a part of high school athletics.

I tried to think about how I could be involved in coaching while at the same time do my best to avoid parents. I had stayed in touch with Ernie Woods, who was the head coach at Bellevue Community College. I figured that college kids would be more independent and their parents would be less involved. While there was some truth to that, I found that you can never fully escape the parents. I decided that I would call Coach Woods and see if I could volunteer to be an assistant for him while I looked for another job to pay the bills. I called Coach and told him that I had quit my job with the Sonics and was looking to see if he needed any help with his team.

Coach Woods had been at BCC for almost 30 years. He was one of the most respected coaches in the area and if you remember, he was the one who I had quit on (before I ever started) after I came out of high school. Luckily for me, that never affected our friendship.

Unfortunately, he told me that just two days prior to my phone call, he had decided to retire. He did however, get to select his replacement and he said that he would speak to the new coach about bringing me on to his staff.

I joined Pat Leonard's staff as a volunteer assistant coach at Bellevue Community College in mid-October of 1997; just days after he was named head coach and even fewer days before our first practice. Pat was head coach, his only paid assistant coach was Randy Hammack and he had another volunteer assistant coach named Russ Schoene. We were thrust into that season like the blind leading the blind. Because of the late retirement of Coach Woods, the short amount of time that we had to prepare and the fact that none of us had college coaching experience, we seemed to always be playing catch up in that first year.

I'll never forget our first game at Green River College in late November. In our attempt to do everything we could think of to get our team prepared and introduced to a new system on the court, we completely forgot some of the details involved in coaching basketball at the junior college level. One of which was uniforms.

On the afternoon of our very first game, we finally remembered that we needed to get the uniforms out of storage. Pat and I walked into the storage closet where all the athletic gear was kept. Our team had three of the dozen or so storage closets. Coach Woods left Pat with the combinations on two of the three locks but not the third. One combination was the numbers for Michael Jordan and Hakeem Olajawon (2334). We opened it up and found some old trophies in a cardboard box, covered in dust; some of which dated back to the early 1970's, but we found no uniforms. The next lock's combination was the numbers of Shawn Kemp and Sam Perkins (4014). We opened that one up. We found old camp tee shirts, team photographs, some stale concession stand candy… but still no uniforms.

We didn't have the combo for the third lock. We had to call campus security and ask them to come with bolt cutters to get us into the last storage closet. After waiting for another half hour, security finally showed up at around 4:30 p.m. with the cutters. Our team van was supposed to leave at 5 p.m. Bob, the security officer, cut off the lock for us. We opened up the locker and we found a box with old uniforms from previous seasons going back to the 1970s. We didn't find a whole set of any uniform and the ones that we did find seemed awfully small. We didn't have time to figure it out though, so we threw everything we could find in a bag, hopped in the vans and headed out to Green River College for our first game.

Once we arrived at Green River's gym, our team headed directly to the visitor's locker room to suit up for the game. Pat and I started handing out the uniforms. We had eight uniforms that matched and those went to our five starters and top three bench players. The others would have to wear mismatched uniforms, where the tops and bottoms didn't go together. We gave out the uniforms and at first our guys were griping about what number they had to wear. Then they held the uniforms up to look at them and completely forgot all about that concern.

These uniforms weren't just small, they were tiny; think Mini-Me in a scuba shorty. These uniforms would make John Stockton blush and our guys didn't want to have anything to do with them.

Pat, Randy and I were keyed up and super excited about our first game (Russ wasn't able to be there). We had been putting in a lot of work and wanted to get a look at our guys against another opponent. It was Pat's first game as a college head coach and we were totally focused on basketball. Our players on the other hand, didn't share in our single-minded focus. They were completely sidetracked by the uniforms and didn't even want to go onto the floor wearing these nut-huggers. To make matters worse, we didn't have any warm-up sweats that the players could put on to hide the mis-matches while they sat on the bench or before the game as they got loose.

The more upset they got about the uniforms, the more upset we got with them. We thought that it shouldn't matter what they wore; they should just be happy to be playing. That, right there, was my first lesson in minimizing distractions. There wasn't anything that we could have said to get our players minds off those uniforms. They did not have the mental make-up to be able to look beyond that and refocus on our real task at hand.

Looking back on it and knowing what I know now, I can understand their reaction a little better. Our parents told us to just "suck it up" when dealing with adversity, but that motto doesn't apply to many kids today; mostly because they've never had to deal with any adversity. So how can you really blame them? They've never had to "suck it up" before so it's hard to just expect them to have that ability. They are coddled from the time they shoot their first basket by parents who want everything be "fair". They don't keep score until junior high so there can be no winners; and more importantly, no losers. Everyone has to get a "participation trophy" at the end of the season whether they deserve it or not. Everyone has to play the same amount of time and if things aren't going your way? That's easy. Just quit and move to another team until you find the same problems there as well (and then quit again). If all else fails, then do everything in your power to have the coach fired.

Kids don't face adversity anymore.

We got smoked by Green River that night, not surprisingly. I learned that as a coach you better do one of two things. Either 1) coddle your players and do your best to not ever upset them or 2) coach them to overcome unexpected adversity.

I chose number two.

The other thing it taught me though was to not wait until a half hour before your first game to figure out if you have any uniforms.

***

Something exciting opened up for me in August of that year when I was approached by the Athletic Director at Bellevue Community College, Marilyn Anderson. She told me that she was taking a sabbatical from the school and asked if I'd be interested in applying for her job. She went on to say that she was on the hiring committee and that I would be her recommendation to replace her. This sounded like a great opportunity and was perfect for the skill set that I had acquired while with the Sonics.

The way that I had interpreted the conversation with Marilyn was that all I had to do was apply for the job and the rest would be a formality. This was a vast underestimate of the truth on my part. The interview process was rigorous and typically convoluted for a Washington State institution. I went through three interviews and was grilled by the hiring committee for an hour and a half before it was finally over. In all honesty, I was easily the best candidate for the job. I had a strong background in sports administration and management. I specialized in sales and marketing which at the collegiate level translates to fundraising. I had attended BCC so had an affinity for the school. I grew up in the area and knew the history of the program. I was currently working there as a basketball coach and had the support of many alumni and others within the community. I was being recommended by the outgoing director and had other allies within the office who were also on the committee.

Maybe I was over confident, maybe my inability to interview well caught up with me or maybe it was something more sinister within the politics of the school. Whatever the reason, I was not offered the job. It was offered to a guy from the East Coast who was moving to the Seattle area because his wife was being transferred to a new job. A day after accepting the position, his situation changed and his wife ended up not getting transferred. He called back the next day to "un-accept". I wasn't even the second choice as they then offered the job to another AD within the conference. He recognized what a cluster f*** it was at BCC and he took the advice of others that told him to stay put at his current job. He turned the offer down. That left me. Feeling somewhat jilted, I accepted the job at BCC as the new Director of Athletics and soon set out to show everyone there that I should have been the first choice all along.

We tripled the revenue of the department in my first year as BCC's AD. We increased it each subsequent year after that. I started the women's soccer program, built an on-campus softball field and initiated a massive facilities upgrade that thrust the program to elite status in the region. Our nine sports programs enjoyed tremendous and unprecedented success on the fields of play. Our student-athletes were working toward degrees or transfers to four-year schools because of the academic support programs that we put in place.

As I took the position, I pictured BCC as a beautiful house that had been neglected for years with the yard overgrown, the paint chipping away, a fence that needed mending and shutters that were broken. I knew that if we were able to clean it up, the home would be beautiful once again.

I technically had two jobs at this time. In addition to AD duties at BCC, I also had my own talk show for Talkspot.com. After three months of working both jobs, I decided that I needed to turn all my focus to one or the other. My show had been moved to evenings so I worked at BCC during the day then went into Talkspot each night for my show from 9 to midnight. However, layoffs were coming at Talkspot and the writing was on the wall that the ship there was sinking fast. I realized that my 30,000 stock options in the company were essentially worthless and I quit the show in January of 1999.

Another sinking ship was the men's basketball program at BCC. I was in a tough bind. In many ways, I was my boss's boss. I was Pat's assistant coach but as Athletic Director, I was also his boss. I had a responsibility as well a conviction to have the best basketball program in the conference. At the same time, my loyalty toward Pat was leaving me conflicted and torn about what to do. We had struggled to remain mediocre for the three seasons that we had been there, but that wasn't good enough for any of us. Head coaches at that level received stipends and not salaries. Pat was getting paid $5000 a YEAR to be the head coach at BCC; and to do the job right meant that you needed to be on campus fulltime. His "real job" was as an English teacher at a local high school and he had a young family. He was being pulled in too many directions to give the head coaching job the attention that it needed. I knew that we needed to make a change.

From an outsider's perspective, it may have looked unseemly. It probably looked as if I threw Pat under the proverbial bus. Parts of me were embarrassed by my decision to hire myself as head basketball coach but ultimately, I was the best choice. I worked at the school which was important to the success of any coach because of the time needed to do the things that were necessary things to turn the program around and maintain it. It was easy to compare what was happening at other schools in the conference and see that the teams who were having success were the ones whose coaches were on staff as full-time employees at the school. In fact, this was true for all the sports programs, not just basketball; and it subsequently became a top priority later, when there was an opening for a new coach within the department.

I provided continuity to the basketball program since I had been an assistant for the last three seasons and finally, I knew that I was a better choice than anyone else. My buddy Giles would later dub me the Greg Popovich of community college athletics because of the way I hired myself. But I knew it was something that I had to do.

I was nervous about my ability to actually run the basketball program myself. I wasn't really a credible choice to outsiders (at least in my own mind) and my insecurity about that made me wary about my chances for success. Even though all of the reasons that I mentioned for taking over as head coach were true, I have to admit that something still echoed in my mind as I contemplated the future of the team and my own as well. I thought of John Dresel telling me that he wasn't in the business of giving opportunities. I thought about being passed over twice before finally getting offered the job as athletic director at BCC. I started getting a "me against the world mentality" and feeling like I wouldn't be able to rely on someone else to make things happen for me. If I wanted it, I had to go get it for myself… and that's what I did.

* * *

I am getting bored of writing about myself probably almost as much as you are by having to read it. My intention has been to tell some fun basketball stories and I just caught myself taking this process (and myself) WAY too serious. So please allow me to get sidetracked for a moment…

This is not part of my nonexistent standup routine but as I was driving today I saw one of the dumbest bumper stickers I've ever seen. I have actually never understood why someone would want to put a bumper sticker on their car. To me it's like getting a tattoo. I don't get that either. All of a sudden, I'm feeling like Andy Rooney. I'm turning into a curmudgeon.

The bumper sticker read "I'm Only Speeding Because I Really Have To Poop"

To steal a line from Seth Meyers and Amy Poehler… Really?

This is the statement that you want to make to the world? Let me guess, you saw this at the counter at Nordstrom's and knew you HAD to have it. It was a tough choice between that and "My Other Car is… a Terrible Sense of Humor". These bumper stickers are like taking out an advertisement on what an idiot you are. Are people saying, "Read my sticker and know how funny I am"? Or "Look at me. I'm clever"? Or "Please like me better now"?

My Kid is an Honor Student at _____
Dog is My Co-Pilot
Vegetarians Taste Better
Dukakis/ Bentsen '88

Call me crazy but I'm not into broadcasting my poor choices for everyone to see. I can just imagine my life in bumper stickers...

I Did a Fat Chick
Hansen Bros. Rock
Computers Are Just a Fad
I Have a Hemorrhoid That Makes Me Poop Blood

I don't know. I just don't get it. It's like tattoos.

I can't help but thinking that this country is about 10-15 years away from a really bad tattoo hangover. Has anyone seen an old tattoo? Not attractive. These young kids get tattoos to express their individuality when all it does is emphasize their conformity. If you want to be an individual nowadays you do it by NOT getting a tattoo.

Saying these things just reinforces something that has recently occurred to me. Now in my early 40's, I am officially old. I realized the other day that there is nothing I can do that will ever "look cool" again. It's not like I didn't already know this but something clicked the other day that drove it home.

I imagined myself dancing.

I used to love to go out dancing with friends when I was younger. As I got older, I still enjoyed the occasional dance at a wedding reception or "grooving" to the music at a concert (the fact that I used the word "grooving" is more reinforcement to this fact that I am old). I was at a bar the other day and was watching some people dancing. I kind of wanted to get out there but knew that there was no way that I could avoid being the "old guy" on the dance floor. Instead of enjoying the show, I would BE the show. And the problem is... I don't know when it happened. Do this... picture yourself out on the dance floor with a bunch of twenty year olds. How does it look? I used to have rhythm. Now I dance like the gopher in the movie "**Caddyshack**" with the stereotypical white-man's overbite (damn that headgear).

When did I stop being "cool"?

As Lester Bangs told William in the movie **Almost Famous** "The only true currency in this bankrupt world is what you share with someone else when you're un-cool"

After three very successful years as head coach and athletic director at Bellevue CC, I got a phone call one day that would dramatically change my course. As I sat in my office one spring afternoon, my phone rang. It was a guy named Kevin Simon. He was being very cryptic with his questions but was asking me about the availability of the gymnasium at BCC for the next fall. I tried to get him to give me specifics but he was reluctant. He asked if he and his boss could meet with me to look at the gym and see if it would fit their needs. We set up an appointment within the next couple days.

Kevin showed up to my office the next Thursday afternoon. He introduced me to his boss, "Michael".

"Michael Blackmon" (we'll call him for purposes of this book) strutted in to the lobby outside the BCC gym like he owned the school. He carried himself with an arrogance and an heir of entitlement that was initially both off-putting and frankly, a little intimidating. At 5 feet 8 inches tall, his long, combed back- black hair was graying at the temples and he had a disheveled look to him like he lived his life 10 minutes behind everyone else. I gave him and Kevin a tour of the facility. They asked a few questions but I knew right away that they liked what they were seeing.

They eventually told me that it was their plan to build a mid-sized arena in downtown Bellevue, Washington. The building would have about 8,000 seats and be home to the Seattle Thunderbirds, a minor-league hockey team that was currently playing in Seattle's Key Arena as well as a minor league basketball team in the CBA (Continental Basketball Association). When I heard about the CBA team, my ears perked up.

At the time, the CBA was the gold standard for minor league professional basketball. It has had many incarnations, including being purchased by former NBA great, Isaiah Thomas in 1999. Zeke didn't do well with it and declared bankruptcy in 2001. In the fall of that year, some of the former owners re-purchased the league and returned it to its well-respected position among players and NBA talent seekers; as it also served as a proving ground for the NBA. The thing that excited me about the league was that, not only was it a place for over-looked players to be seen and hone their skills; it had become a great pipeline for coaches to advance their careers and get into the NBA. Phil Jackson, George Karl and Flip Saunders all coached in the CBA before moving on to the chartered jets and five-star hotels of "The League". I knew if I could somehow get my hands on one of those jobs, I would be able to either prove myself at nearly the highest level of basketball or find out that I wasn't as good as I thought I was. I would either sink or swim and at least I could get peace of mind from the results.

I asked Michael Blackmon while we stood outside my office, if he had a coach yet for his team. He told me right there on the spot, that he had offered the job to former Sonics great, Jack Sikma, but if he didn't accept it; the job could be mine if I wanted it.

That small little story right there, about offering me the coaching job in our first meeting, goes a long way in describing the type of personality you are dealing with in Michael Blackmon.

He was difficult to describe, he could be charming, funny and empathetic one minute and distant, aloof and obtuse the next. How could he offer me a head coaching job that I coveted so greatly without knowing anything about me? Was he serious? Is he an idiot or did I stumble into another lucky break?

I told my new boss, Tika Esler, at BCC about the meeting with Blackmon and his plans for renting out our facility to host CBA basketball games. She didn't know much about sports but anything that brought in new revenue to the department was generally good by her. I also threw out a question to Tika that I thought was pretty innocuous at the time. I asked if she thought it would be possible for me to coach Blackmon's CBA team and continue my role as Director of Athletics at the school. She told me that she would think about it and get back to me. Blackmon and I continued to talk over the next few weeks as we tried to work out the details of a lease. He was trying to get game dates from the league and I was trying to clear gym times with the demands from other programs like volleyball and women's basketball.

On July 9, 2003, Tika called me and asked me to come by her office. Her assistant, Vicki, had a funny look on her face as I walked in and asked to see Tika that sunny 85 degree afternoon. Vicki told me that Tika would be right back but to go on ahead in her office and sit down. I waited for just a few minutes when Tika walked in looking stressed. She sat down across the table from me.

"We've decided not to renew your contract" she said coolly and emotionless.

"Huh?" I muttered, not really "getting" what she was saying.

"Your contract ends on July 31st and the college has decided not to renew it"

Shocked, stunned, crippled, dazed, shaken, surprised, staggered, astounded, bemused… none of these words would adequately describe my emotion after the punch that she delivered.

"Why?" I managed to muster as I started to feel nauseous.

"This was a decision made at the highest level of the college and we've decided to go in another direction"

In other words, the president of the college made the call. I still didn't understand. I had a good relationship with Tika, I trusted her and I felt like she trusted me. The improvements that I had made within the athletic department in just over four years had been significant and dramatic. I was respected within the campus community as well as the league. It just didn't add up. In fact it still doesn't. Something funny happened that was out of my control. I could spend time here speculating on it and justifying with the rumors that I have heard as to why, but for the sake of this experience, it doesn't really matter. As I look back on what happened there, I am beyond confident that there is no amount of success that I could have had which would have made a difference in that decision. However, a small piece of me wonders if my question to Tika about coaching Blackmon's CBA team brought into question my commitment to the college. Over the few months that followed, I heard different rumors were going around as to the genesis of my demise there.

One rumor was that I was embezzling money from the school. Another, that I was having an affair with one of the women's volleyball players (I never heard which one, hopefully one of the hot ones). In hindsight, I wish that either one of these rumors had been true. That way, I would have either gotten paid or laid, both of which were better than the f*** job that I ultimately got from BCC.

A couple weeks later, I met with Blackmon outside a Starbucks on Mercer Island. He told me that he was going to speak with Jack Sikma later in the week and a decision would be made as to whether Jack would be coaching the new CBA team or not. He also asked if I would help him organize a golf tournament to benefit the Puget Sound Sports Hall of Fame which he had founded a year earlier. In late May, I had put on my own fundraising golf tournament for the BCC athletic department and had called in every favor I could to make that a great success. I didn't think that I could try and go back to the well with all of the people that had helped me so much just a few months earlier. So, my enthusiasm to work on Michael's tournament was extremely tempered. My problem, however, was that he had something I wanted; namely a head coaching job in the CBA. And even though I hadn't known him for very long, there was something about him that made me want to tread lightly. I did what I could to feign an eagerness to help with the golf tournament, while still trying to remain at arm's length from Blackmon.

Kevin Simon, Michael and I met at Cucina Cucina, a restaurant on Lake Union in Seattle to discuss the golf tournament and my role with it. I tried to explain my concerns about going back to the same people that had helped me just a few weeks prior. Blackmon wanted to hear none of it.

"Do you want a gold star Rick?" he asked me in the most condescending way possible.

He continued, "If you want to earn a gold star you can, but only if you want to work for it."

Earn a "gold star" I thought?

"Eat sh**" is what I wanted to say to him but then remembered that I also wanted to coach that CBA team. We agreed that I would reach out to some people I knew and try to get them involved with the tournament. I put out a couple of feelers but the response was lukewarm at best so I didn't press it very much. I was too embarrassed to let anyone know that I was working with Blackmon and I definitely didn't want anyone that I knew to meet him.

***

Lorenzo Romar was named head coach at the University of Washington on April 3, 2002. He had played at Washington for Marv Harshman before a career in the NBA. He won a national championship on Jim Harrick's staff at UCLA in 1995 and went on to be the head coach at Pepperdine University and Saint Louis University before coming to Washington. As I recall, a couple others had turned down the job before Coach Romar was officially introduced as the new head man but that didn't temper the enthusiasm about his return to Montlake.

I was lying in bed a of couple weeks after his hiring and had just turned off the television set around 11 p.m. to go to sleep when the phone rang. It was Coach Romar. My heart jumped into my throat. Coach Romar didn't know me, didn't know my home phone number and I couldn't figure out why he'd be calling. Was it possible that he had heard about my success at Bellevue CC from someone? For a moment I thought that he was calling to offer me a job on his staff. My excitement was quickly extinguished by disappointment. He was calling me to ask about my assistant coach Russ Schoene. He wanted to know what type of person Russ was as well as the kind of assistant coach he'd make at The U. I didn't want to lose Russ off my staff but clearly understood the type of opportunity that this was for him. Coach Romar hired Russ on April 24, 2002.

Fast forward to fall of 2003. I was out of a job and no longer at BCC. I was doing this CBA "dance" with Michael Blackmon but it wasn't going anywhere. I needed something to stay busy, improve my basketball knowledge and move my career forward. I called Russ to ask him to speak with Coach Romar about me volunteering at UW. I wasn't versed in all of the restrictions that the NCAA puts on a coaching staff and the number of people that can be involved with a team on a day-to-day basis. There was no spot for me to volunteer for, but Coach Romar said that I could attend practice and be an observer. I took that opportunity very seriously. I didn't want to just be there from time to time. I wanted to commit to being there everyday so I could get to know the players and the staff, which is what I did.

From the very first practice, I knew that this was a good idea for me. I treated it like a graduate program in basketball and I was studying to get my master's degree. I took notes at every practice. I wrote reports on players. I attended coaches meetings. I was in the team room for pre, half and post game meetings and sat behind the bench for all home games. In many ways, I felt like I was a part of that team. Throughout the season I met separately with assistant coaches Ken Bone and Cameron Dollar to discuss various philosophies and Coach Romar would often pull me aside after practice to ask me my opinion on different players and situations. It was a great experience. Washington also happened to be an excellent team.

That season, Washington started 0-5 in conference play before getting a miraculous win on the road in Corvallis against Oregon State. They won 12 of their next 13 games and finished second in the Pac10 tournament before losing to UAB 102-100 in the first round of the NCAA tournament. The roster included Brandon Roy, Nate Robinson, Bobby Jones and Will Conroy, all of whom have since gone on to play in the NBA. The next year, with the same nucleus of players, Washington went to the Sweet 16 before getting beat by UConn at the buzzer in a game that they really should have won.

That year at the University of Washington was one of the best coaching experiences that I've had in my career to this point. Even though I wasn't on the floor coaching the players, I was able to see from day one of the first practice, that the stuff that I was doing and the things that I was teaching my players, were not only sound but arguably better then what they were doing at UW. That is not a shot at Coach Romar. Everyone does things differently, but spending the season with them allowed me to realize that I was better than I gave myself credit for. On top of that, it gave me some very valuable experience at the Division 1 level of college basketball, which is difficult to break into.

In January of that season in 2004, I got a call from Michael Blackmon. He was driving to Yakima to attend the CBA owner's meeting and All-Star game. He asked if I would join him and told me that he wanted to name me head coach of the new expansion team, the Bellevue Nighthawks who were entering the Continental Basketball Association in the 2004-2005 season.

Michael and I drove separately to Yakima to attend the league meetings and the '04 All-Star Game. I wasn't allowed in the meetings themselves because they were restricted to team owners only, but everything that I heard seemed as if they went well.

Throughout the course of the next two days, Michael introduced me to the all the team owners, many of the CBA coaches as well as the commissioner, Gary Hunter. Truthfully, I was a bit intimidated because I felt like an imposter. I felt that way in part, because I (more than most) really coveted the job and appreciated what a great opportunity it was. Two of the basketball coaches that I respected the most, George Karl and Phil Jackson, each coached in the CBA before their NBA careers. Therefore, I could see a path of success if I was able to do well.

The other thing that made me feel like I was an imposter at those meetings was that I also felt like I had done nothing to really deserve the job. I was in the right place at the right time and Michael Blackmon didn't exactly conduct a rigorous interview or an extensive search for a head coach. Don't get me wrong, I thought I was the best choice; but I was a little insecure about what others would think about my background.

Regardless of how I got there, however, it was now (as they say)… on.

Any insecurity would have to be left behind. For the immediate future, I'd have to be able to talk the talk. In a few months however, I'd have to prove that I could walk the walk.

A meteoric rise from high school assistant coach to unpaid college assistant; then to college head coach, and on to a head coaching job in the CBA; this was easier than I thought it would be, after leaving the Sonics just seven years earlier. Everything that I had hoped for was right there in front of me. My plan was coming together perfectly and the only thing holding me back would be me. I wasn't riding someone else's coaching coattails. I had carved my own path and I had maintained a personal integrity that I was comfortable with. I didn't want my connection with Blackmon to jeopardize that integrity but for now, I was headed in the right direction.

5

Denver

To describe Michael Blackmon as strange is like saying the Grand Canyon is a hole. It certainly is a hole, a big hole in fact. But it is way more complicated than that. Was he bipolar? Manic-depressive? A compulsive liar? Or just a habitual one? Deceptive? Vicious? Extremely generous? Compassionate? I could never figure him out. I don't think anybody could, but being around him was like riding a bull. It was simultaneously exhilarating while also being a really stupid thing to do. He would say anything to anybody at anytime in order to get what he wanted. He was an equal opportunity offender and completely unpredictable.

I thought that we needed a salesman for this new CBA team in Bellevue and I had an idea of someone that could help. A friend of mine from the Sonics was available and I spoke with him about working with us. His name was Giles Dowden and he had been in sponsorship sales for the "Big Three" in Seattle sports: the Sonics, Seahawks and Mariners. He knew the right people to talk to around town and would be perfect for a new venture like this. There was one problem though. I was hesitant to get Giles involved with Blackmon.

I spoke to Giles and gave him all the appropriate warnings about Blackmon. He said he'd be willing to at least talk to him, so I set up a conference call for the two of them to speak later that night.

Blackmon called Giles that night and they spoke for about 45 minutes. Michael did what he does and blew enough smoke up Giles' pipes to have him declared a walking carcinogen. He told Giles that we had a meeting with the CBA commissioner and some other league officials the next day around 12:30 p.m. and asked if he wanted to come by and meet everybody. Giles told him that he would stop by around 1:15.

As Giles walked into the restaurant the next day to meet everyone, we caught eyes and shot each other a knowing smile. The whole thing was a little shady but neither of us had anything better going on so we just went with it. Giles walked up to the table and even though he and Blackmon had never actually met, Blackmon introduced Giles to the group as if they had been working together for years.

"Hi Giles, come on and sit down… Everyone, this is Giles Dowden, our Vice President of Marketing and Sponsorship."

Giles immediately looked at me. Without actually knowing, I knew that Blackmon and Giles never spoke about any official titles or whether or not he was actually going to go to work for the team; but that is typical of Blackmon. Nothing he said was ever completely true and for the sake of this meeting, it didn't really matter. It made Blackmon look like he was assembling a staff and appearances were always more important to him than reality.

***

Mike Blackmon created the Puget Sound Sports Hall of Fame and Museum out of nowhere but I never could figure out why. I did have my own theories. 1) He registered it as a nonprofit organization which I think provided some tax shelter benefits for him. 2) He used it as a way to enhance his plans for convincing various area municipalities to allow him to build an arena in their town. He told them that this non-existent museum needed a home and this "new arena" would be a great place for it. 3) He was a big time jock-sniffer and this was a way for him to meet local sports celebrities and rub shoulders with them.

All of these reasons seemed viable but none made much sense to me. He literally made this whole hall of fame and museum thing up and was able to convince people that it actually was something that existed. In the spring of 2004, he planned a luncheon at a very nice downtown Seattle restaurant. At the luncheon, he would induct the 2004 class into the Puget Sound Hall of Fame as well as introduce me as the head coach of this new CBA expansion team.

Even though I was treading lightly, the recent meeting with the league commissioner and a verbal agreement with a local gym to play games, allowed me to let my guard down a little and think that this team might actually happen. So, I embraced this Hall of Fame luncheon and invited many family and friends to attend. I called some local media people that I knew to get it some local news coverage and the event itself went off pretty well.

Blackmon had decided to "induct" five new members in to the invisible Puget Sound Sports Hall of Fame to join Gary Payton (2002 inductee), legendary high school basketball coach Ed Pepple, Seattle Rainier great Edo Vanni and the 2001 Mariners (2003 inductees). The new class would include MLB Hall of Fame sportscaster and Mariner play-by-play man Dave Niehaus, former Sonics All-Star Jack Sikma, Hydroplane driver Chip Hanauer, college football coach Frosty Westering and former Seahawk great Steve Largent. All but Largent attended the luncheon.

It was a Chamber of Commerce day at Daniel's Broiler on the shores of Lake Union as the luncheon got started. The sun shone off the deep blue water right outside the window of the large dining room and cast a dancing light show on the ceiling above the lectern where the speakers would accept their imaginary award. There was a room full of local sports celebrities graciously showing up to this event which was nothing but a mental folly of Blackmon's. They were driven there in part by their own egos but more so by the fear that this might actually BE something and it made their attendance fall just short of mandatory. They invited their families and their close friends to share in their Blackmon- fueled glory. They wrote and delivered heartfelt speeches and for an hour or so of the ceremony, it felt like a real event. Then Blackmon spoke.

His speech started out okay and came off as nearly professional until he began his rambling musings about his new prized possession... an acoustic guitar purportedly once owed by Bruce Springsteen that he recently bought on Ebay. Michael Blackmon was (is) a Springsteen FANATIC. He went on and on about how great The Boss was and how many times he had seen him in concert (supposedly hundreds). He talked about the best Springsteen songs, which ones were better live and which ones were better in studio. His ramblings had the potential to be endearing if given by somebody else, but there were no endearing qualities about Blackmon. In fact, I always thought that he saw himself as a sympathetic character, which was part of his problem. He wasn't and no one saw him as such. It was borderline pathetic to listen to, and at the very least, uncomfortably funny. The restless audience in front of him grew impatient with his incoherent ramblings and began to murmur.

He finally wrapped up his speech by presenting each of the inductees with a Tiffany's crystal dish that he had purchased at the last minute earlier that morning as an afterthought on his way to the event. The thing was however... none of the crystal pieces matched and none of them were engraved with anything that said what they were for. One guy got a dish; another got a vase while another got a bowl. He would have been just as well off grabbing some dishes out of his kitchen cabinet and giving them out as gifts.

The luncheon ended after he announced the formation of the new CBA basketball team and its admission to the league for the upcoming season. He introduced Gary Hunter, the commissioner of the CBA and Gary briefly spoke about the history and tradition of the league. He talked about how exciting it was to welcome a Seattle-area team into the league. Then Blackmon introduced me as the new head coach and I spoke briefly.

In spite of Blackmon as our host that day, this introduction was a proud moment for me. I invited people to come share in it with me and I looked out into the crowd as I took the podium. There I saw many of the people who were mentors to me and helped shape my path leading up to this moment. Mike Cashman, my high school basketball coach was there to support me. Ed Pepple, who had given me my first coaching job, was there as well. Lorenzo Romar came to the luncheon, mainly because of the induction of his former coach Marv Harshman, but it was great to have him there; and Rick Sund, the General Manager of the Sonics was also in attendance.

Afterward, the crowd lingered for a few minutes before finally heading back into the sun-filled afternoon. Blackmon, Kevin Simon, Giles and I stayed there to discuss how the luncheon went and what was next. As the restaurant staff cleaned up around us, the four of us talked about the luncheon. Giles had decided that he didn't want to "officially" work for the team but he would help when he could. He hadn't discussed this fully with Blackmon yet, but he was planning on doing so later that afternoon.

The manager of the restaurant dropped off the bill for the luncheon at the table where the four of us were talking. Blackmon gave her a credit card for the $3,500 tab. We continued to talk and she came back to the table with a distressed look on her face. She tried to whisper to Blackmon but he acted like he couldn't hear her and admonished her to just say what she wanted.

"I'm sorry but this credit card didn't go through" she said meekly

"What do you mean it didn't go through, I just paid the bill on it?"

"I tried it twice and it didn't work" she was now empathetic in her retort

"Give me your phone Kevin" Blackmon demanded

For whatever reason, Blackmon didn't own a cell phone. It seemed to be just another one of those stupid idiosyncrasies that he took pride in.

He looked at the credit card and dialed the customer service number listed on the back. He got up from the table and walked a few feet away, out of earshot from the rest of us. It didn't take long though, before the distance of earshot shrunk and conversation became heated.

Now, for the sake of cleanliness and out of respect for you, the reader; allow me to embellish his words.

For the purposes of recreating the phone conversation:

Jump will represent the "F" word
Pretzel will represent the "C" word (see you next Tuesday)
And *Hair Spray* will represent cottage cheese

Out of nowhere, the phone conversation exploded into this:

"You mother *jump*ing bitch. You're a *jump*ing *pretzel* you piece of sh** bitch. You've got *hair spray* coming out of your *pretzel* you *jump*ing whore. Go *jump* yourself you *hairspray pretzel*."

And with that, he turned and rifled Kevin's phone against the wall of the restaurant where it exploded into pieces.

Giles and I looked at each other, just like Cameron and Farris did after they sent the dad's Ferrari crashing through the window on Farris' day off.

"Holy s***" we silently said to ourselves, cringing like Al Czervik did after witnessing the Judge Smails meltdown on #9. Then Giles spoke

"I think we should go" he said while trying to keep a straight face.

"Uhhh, yeah" I agreed

And the two of us left.

***

In May of 2004, the CBA was trying to finalize the game schedule for the upcoming season. Every team is required to turn in dates when their facility is available. It is a complicated process and requires some flexibility and a willingness to work together to make the schedule as friendly as possible for all teams. However, flexibility and a willingness to work together are not high on the personality traits of Mr. Blackmon. As such, a difficult process like scheduling is only exasperated by his involvement.

Blackmon had decided to play our home games at Bellevue Community College; the same school that had unceremoniously let me go just a year earlier. It was still an open wound for me and I stayed out of the negotiation process as much as I could because of that. Blackmon and BCC worked out an agreement on fees and other details relating to the gym rental but what they hadn't agreed upon were dates. The deadline for turning in dates to the league was quickly approaching and Blackmon had nothing from BCC. BCC was waiting to finalize their own sports schedules and they didn't have any sense of urgency to provide Blackmon with firm dates. Actually, they acted as if they could take his business or leave it. It really didn't seem to matter to them. He pressed them for dates and they came back and gave him Sundays and some Mondays after 8 p.m. They were too stupid to know that this wouldn't work for a professional basketball team. Either that; or they just didn't care if Blackmon and the team walked away or not.

As the relationship between BCC and Blackmon quickly deteriorated, I saw my hope of coaching in the CBA disappearing with it. The league told Michael that he had to have firm dates and a signed contract from BCC by the owner's meetings in Denver on May 22nd.

It all came to a head a couple days before the league-imposed deadline when Blackmon went to the college to try and speak with someone about working out some dates. The person that he needed to talk to was on personal leave and she wasn't going to be back in time for the Denver meetings. He was such a pain in the neck to them by this point that no one else would agree to see him. He pleaded his case to the receptionist asking to see anybody that could help him. She kept stiff-arming him. Finally, he asked if she would make him a copy of the lease agreement that they had already worked out a few weeks earlier. She disappeared for a few minutes and came back with a copy of the signed document. He calmly thanked her and asked for a pen. She handed him a black Sharpie. He grabbed the pen and wrote VOID in big, bold letters on each page of it. Then he flung the contract back at her and said,

"Tell Bill O'Conner to go suck on this!" (O'Conner was the new Athletic Director)

He turned and walked out the door.

Blackmon and I got on a plane for Denver and the CBA owners' meetings the next day. We were in serious jeopardy of being denied admission into the league. The league owners' had put some conditions on Blackmon that he needed to satisfy in order to be let in for the '04-'05 season. He was going down there to make an appeal to them to allow us in for the upcoming season. He needed to show the league three things at that Denver meeting to satisfy their requirements. He needed a signed arena lease, confirmed and viable dates in order to complete a game schedule and a $100,000 letter of credit to ensure that if he couldn't meet his financial obligations, the league would take over the team and finish out the year using that credit line.

Remember, he had just "voided" the arena lease, he had no dates and I didn't know anything about his ability to secure the line of credit. So as we boarded the plane for Denver, we were batting .000.

As we sat down in our seats on the plane, Blackmon took out some documents. He had created a new contract for the gym lease which he signed himself and forged the signature of a BCC official. He handed me the CBA league document that outlined the procedures for providing them viable game dates and asked me to fill it out. It was a complicated formula which included a certain number of weeknights and another set of weekend dates. There was a priority process of ranking the dates from most desired to least desired as well, but in reality it didn't matter to us because we were faking it all anyway. I filled it out with dates that were totally meaningless. They were not ok'd by the school and we had no way of knowing which, if any of them, actually worked. Blackmon general philosophy in life was to ask for forgiveness rather than permission, so we went to the meeting with our forged documents and relied on his ability to b.s. our way into the league.

We landed in the late morning and headed straight to the hotel for the 1 p.m. meeting. We walked in and sat down at a large conference table set up in one of the hotel's banquet rooms. CBA commissioner Gary Hunter, was at the head of the table with his deputy commissioner, Wade Morehead, to his left and the league's lawyer, Russ Sauer, to his right. Around the table was Greg Heineman and his son Mike, owners of the Sioux Falls Skyforce, Bill Illet from the Idaho Stampede, Jeanie Scott from the expansion team the Michigan Mayhem, father and son John and Darren Uceny from the

Yakima SunKings, the owner of the Dakota Wizards, Bill Sorensen, who was an actual working magician, the Harris' – Sr. and Jr. from the Gary Steelheads and Greg Van Boxel from the Great Lakes Storm. The only one missing was the owner of the Rockford Lightning who was gravely ill at the time.

The first order of business was the Bellevue Nighthawks and Michael rose to speak.

He stood and addressed the group. I'm not quite sure why I was there. I guess to either give Blackmon moral support or provide him credibility; maybe both. I was secretly cringing as I waited to see how he would perform. As he spoke, he was as eloquent as I've ever heard him. He was humble, self-deprecating and passionate. He made a great presentation to the group. He handed them our forged documents and said that he was ready to meet all of the financial obligations the league required. He was detailed yet brief and I felt like he couldn't have done a better job selling us to the other owners. After hearing him take his best shot, whatever the owners decided now would be fair.

When Blackmon finished, they asked us to step outside so they could have a discussion and vote on what they wanted to do. We went down to the lobby of the Hyatt Regency and waited for them to call us (on my cell phone since he didn't have one) back to the room. That call came about 20 minutes later when they asked us to return to the meeting. We sat down and I didn't know how to feel. For some reason I was nervous about what they'd say even though I still knew that all of Blackmon's claims were built on a house of cards. Even if they let us in the league, we really didn't have an arena lease or dates. Whether we could actually ever get to the starting line was highly doubtful but nevertheless, I wasn't ready to give up on the idea of coaching in the CBA.

We awaited the verdict as my left leg bounced up and down under the table like a sixth grade boy waiting outside the principal's office. The commissioner thanked us and said that the league's lawyer would read the decision. I snuck a peek at Blackmon and he looked worn out and defeated. I turned back and stared down at the floor as the counselor spoke.

"By majority vote, the Continental Basketball Association owners have agreed to give the Bellevue Nighthawks, probationary admission to the league for the 2004-2005 season upon meeting the following conditions…"

Blackmon pulled it off. He fooled them again. Once the schedule was done, it wouldn't matter where we played. We could figure that out later. The CBA would give us more leash on that because they wouldn't want to redo the finalized game schedule. The lawyer continued outlining the conditions but from my perspective, the most important part of the decision had been made. He read the bullet points and then got to the final one.

"…and finally, provide the league with a $300,000 letter of credit."

Whoops.

I didn't know much about getting lines of credit but I did know that they just tripled what they initially told Blackmon that he needed to join the league.

Blackmon stood up. He looked at the other owners sitting around the table, paused while again, I cringed.

"Thank you, we're done" he simply stated to those gathered around the table

Then he turned and walked out of the room, leaving me there not knowing what to do next. Should I follow him? Should I stay and try to pick up the pieces? Was he pissed? Or was he just being dramatic? Everyone around the table looked at each other and didn't know what just happened. The commissioner turned to me.

"I'm sorry Rick but we're going to have to ask you to leave. This is a closed meeting and since you're not an owner we need to have you leave the room. I hope you understand" He was empathetic and polite but I was still a little embarrassed.

"Before I go, would it be okay to leave each of you my resume?" I joked while I gathered my things

They graciously laughed and asked if I knew what was going on with Blackmon. I said that I didn't and they tried to assure me that the letter of credit was a way to protect the league as well as the employees of the team. They added that if Blackmon had the kind of money that he represented to them, then a $300,000 line of credit should be no problem to get.

I said that I would try to get some answers and meekly left the conference room. I went back to my hotel room and waited to hear from Michael about what happened. I called his room multiple times but got no answer. I left messages but got no response. It was Friday afternoon and I was not supposed to leave until Sunday. I tried to get an earlier flight home but couldn't. I was stuck in Denver for two more days and Blackmon was no where to be found.

***

One thing that Blackmon and I did have in common was that neither of us gave up on things very easily. We got back to Seattle and tried to figure out how to salvage the situation. I suggested that we try to play in Vancouver, Canada and God bless him, Blackmon made a valiant effort to try and make that happen, but ultimately it was just too expensive. Especially for someone who didn't have any money.

We tried to put the team in the Tri-Cities area of Washington State (Richland, Kennewick and Pasco) but after some extremely intense negotiations with the City of Kennewick and new arena management; that plan fell through as well. He called me one night and asked if I had heard of the ABA, the American Basketball Association.

Of course I had heard of the old ABA with Marvin Barnes, Dr. J and the red, white and blue basketball but I didn't know of the new version.

The "new" ABA was launched in 2001 and by 2004 they had an aggressive expansion philosophy. They were getting some high-profile players and well-known coaches involved as they tried to gain credibility among basketball insiders. The ABA didn't have the respect that the CBA had yet and the overall talent wasn't quite there, but the gap was closing.

Blackmon told me that he had recently spoken with the ABA's commissioner, "Connie Joe Newman", and was considering joining their league instead. As it turned out, the commissioner's email address was conniejoenewman@whatever.com and so Blackmon thought that this was his name. Actually, his name was Joe and his wife's name was Connie. They had a joint email account that they shared but Blackmon called him Connie Joe for the first two months that they knew each other. It wasn't until I met Joe Newman at an owner's meeting in Las Vegas and he introduced himself to me as "Joe" that I figured all this out. I asked about his wife and he told me that Connie was doing fine and wished that she was there in Vegas with us. I pulled Blackmon aside to let him know that he should quit calling the commissioner Connie Joe.

Rather than me explaining how and why we joined the ABA, I'll let Blackmon give his version. From a June 23, 2005 article on Oursportscentral.com by Chris Rouhier...

Q and A with Michael Blackmon

By Chris Rouhier,
June 23, 2005 -

> Michael Blackmon is the owner and General Manager of the Bellevue Blackhawks and an unnamed Tacoma franchise in the American Basketball Association. He agreed recently to participate in this Q and A, and has supplied some of the most detailed answers I have ever seen from an owner.
>
> *- Why did you join the ABA?*
>
> A: I was President and General Manager of KONG-TV in Seattle from 1993 through March 2000 when we sold the station. We were an independent station, and I had acquired a lot of local sports programming, such as the Seattle SuperSonics and Seattle Thunderbirds hockey team. Out of those relationships came the knowledge that Bellevue, east of Seattle, would be the ideal site for a mid-sized sports arena. In June of 2001, I made a proposal to the Bellevue City Council for a $155 million sports and entertainment center. The heart of our proposal was vertical integration, where I would own, operate and finance the arena, and own and operate multiple sports franchises. We acquired the hockey team and needed a basketball team. I knew Gary Hunter with the CBA and negotiated a deal to buy a franchise we would call the Bellevue Nighthawks.
>
> I hadn't heard much about the ABA at the time. I paid my $125,000 franchise fee, and was accepted to play in the CBA for the 2004-05 season. But, the league

wasn't comfortable with my interim venue, Bellevue Community College--1,900 seats. At the CBA owners meeting in Denver in June 2004, the executive committee slapped a whopping $400,000 letter of credit requirement on me because they thought a community college venue, rather than a true sports arena, would result in huge losses. I basically told them to go to hell and demanded my money back. The league refused to return a dime, so I resigned myself to the fact that I owned a CBA franchise without a place to play.

I was visiting Vancouver, BC in July of last year trying to secure Pacific Coliseum as a venue for the CBA, when I went back to my hotel, went online and noticed that the ABA had announced four new franchises in the time it had taken me to drive from Seattle to Vancouver (3 hours). I called a sports marketing friend in Pittsburgh and asked, "What the hell is the ABA?" He put me in touch with Joe Newman, and after a couple of phone conversations, Joe agreed to sell me a market reservation for Bellevue.

The CBA had already investigated me and I passed their minimum financial requirements of a $3 million personal net worth, $125,000 franchise fee and $200,000 letter of credit, so the ABA gave me expedited approval to make it in for the 2004-05 season. Bellevue Community College was fine for the ABA (frankly, they didn't have the arrogance the CBA had), and on August 1st, I was approved as the Bellevue Blackhawks. I liked the fact that the ABA had hit on a great business strategy: Lower the bar for entrance, run teams on a parallel, but less expensive business model, maximize the number of franchises to get good geographic distribution to minimize travel costs. It made a lot more sense to me than being in the CBA with 8 teams in places like Bismarck, ND, Yakima, WA and Sioux Falls, SD.

There was already a team in the league called the Maryland Nighthawks so we had to come up with something different. We settled on the Bellevue Blackhawks and set forth putting a team together for the 2004-2005 American Basketball Association season.

There was still the matter of a schedule and even though the ABA was run much looser than the stricter and vastly more professional CBA, we needed to get "ConnieJoe" our dates. Blackmon approached this task the same way that he did with the CBA and the emails below shows what it was like to work with him

----- Original Message -----
From: Michael Blackmon
To: Rick Turner
Sent: Monday, July 19, 2004 1:23 AM
Subject: BCC available dates

We need to get available dates to the ABA by close of business Monday. I got no response from Bloom or Phflug, so I'm turning this over to you. You need to get me 30 <u>real</u> dates for 2004-05 from BCC/Don Bloom, or you need to get the fake ones you gave Wade Moorehead in Denver from the CBA office so we can submit something to the ABA to move to the next step. Obviously. real ones are better, but I know that probably won't happen. You need to persuade Bloom to cooperate ASA-fucking-P, or you need to recreate the list from memory. The dates do not have to be actual. I need to get something to the ABA so I can get them to officially admit us to the league.

I share the blame for not making a copy of the signed lease and available dates you picked up that Friday afternoon on our way to Denver, but it's now coming back to bite us in the ass. That was a stupid mistake that's more my fault than yours. The ball is in your court now. If you want to coach this year, this has to be done.

----- Original Message -----
From: Rick Turner
To: MichaelBlackmon
Sent: Monday, July 19, 2004 9:04 PM
Subject: Re: BCC available dates

I found the disc where I had the file. This is what we brought to Denver...

----- Original Message -----
From: MichaelBlackmon
To: Rick Turner
Sent: Tuesday, July 20, 2004 3:19 AM
Subject: Re: BCC available dates

Who the fuck made this list? What the fuck does "away game," "crossover" and "holiday" mean? I can't submit this.

You'll notice the times that these emails were sent by him. This guy operated in a completely different world than the rest of us. He was usually sleeping all morning and awake all night. But to his credit, for better or for worse, he found us a league to play in and ultimately we found a place to play.

Things fell apart at Bellevue CC and we then tried to play at nearby Interlake High School. Blackmon worked out a deal with the athletic director at Interlake only to later find out that the AD didn't have the authority to commit to a contract without district approval. The AD was fired, the lease was voided and we were left out in the cold again. Finally, he struck a deal with Renton High School which was a far cry from what we had hoped for but at least it was a place to hang our hats.

***

August 20, 2004 – **For Immediate Release:** American Basketball Association

Bellevue, WA. Puget Sound Sports and Entertainment, LLC, the parent company of the Puget Sound Sports Hall of Fame and Museum Foundation and the developer of sports arenas in Bellevue and Olympia, today announced that it's ABA professional basketball team has been named the BELLEVUE BLACKHAWKS. In addition, the team announced its coaching staff for the upcoming season that begins in November. They are:

Rick Turner, Head Coach/Director of Basketball Operations. Rick had a nine-year career in the Seattle Supersonics front office, was former Athletic Director and Head Basketball Coach of Bellevue Community College and NWAACC Region Coach of the Year in 2002.

Harold Wright, Associate Head Coach/Director of Player Personnel. Harold was a former point guard at Washington State University and has played professional basketball.

Russ Schoene, Assistant Coach. A nine-year NBA veteran, Russ was also an assistant coach at the University of Washington.

Eldridge Recasner, Assistant Coach. Eldridge was also an NBA player for 9 years after playing at the University of Washington.

I approached this job as I have everything else in my coaching career. As I mentioned before, I would heed the philosophy of Frosty Westering's book and try to **Make the Big Time Where You Are.** Right then, the "big time" was going to be the American Basketball Association and if I was going to get players to buy into winning games instead of playing just for themselves, then we had better treat our situation as such.

The difficulty at that level of basketball is that players are trying to get better jobs either overseas (which pay more) or they are still holding on to an NBA dream. It breeds selfish play, as players are usually more concerned about their own stats, than the success of the team. It was our job as coaches to convince them that team success would lead to individual success, promotions and ultimately more money... but it's not always an easy argument to make. You really have to have players with the right mental makeup while still balancing the absolute need to have tremendous talent.

I believe that talent trumps coaching almost every time. Not to say that coaching isn't important (I'd be marginalizing myself), but if you don't have good players, you can't win and I don't care WHO you are. I was at a Sonics training camp one season watching from the upstairs balcony. While I sat there, I was thinking about the impact of coaches and put together a little coach/player matrix to pass the time while the team was doing some shooting drills.

	Great Coach	**Good Coach**	**Bad Coach**
Great Players	Great team	Great team	Good team
Good Players	Good team	Good team	Bad team
Bad Players	Bad team	Bad team	Terrible team

I'm not sure how this would hold up to extreme scrutiny but on the surface it looks pretty accurate. As I've tried to apply this theory to real teams from the past, it seems to fall into place most of the time. Essentially, take the best coach of all time and make him coach the 2007 Sonics and they would still be bad. On the other hand, take someone like me, and give them the '87 Showtime Lakers and even I could nurse them to the playoffs (terrific talent). Worst case scenario, they would have just been a "good" team instead of the greatness that Pat Riley led them to.

Getting players was important but I would start building my "big time" program by putting together a coaching staff that would not only help me attract good players and develop them, but truthfully, also help provide me with credibility as I took on my first professional coaching job after making the jump from college.

I went out and unquestionably put together the best coaching staff in the league. First of all, we were one of the only teams that had three assistants and second, the quality of their background and character was beyond reproach. Not only were these coaches three excellent teachers of the game, they were three guys who had experienced minor league basketball as players before their NBA careers. They could help our players learn what it takes to move on and compete at the NBA level. Beyond those two important qualities, I trusted these guys immensely and felt like I could rely on them to support me when things with Blackmon got dicey… which it would invariably do.

Harold and I were the only "paid" coaches while Russ and Eldridge volunteered their time. Because they volunteered, they were able to view the situation from a totally different perspective. They could see things a little more objectively because money and a paycheck never clouded their vision. This was a valuable point of view which I greatly appreciated. We soon set out to put together a roster of players.

We sat down and made a profile of the type of players that we were looking for. We couldn't cast a very wide net because of our budget constraints, and even though Blackmon always said we could go get anyone we wanted, my experience with him, up to this point, told me that we would be inviting trouble if we took him at his word. We knew what we needed:

Players that didn't need housing: I knew we couldn't afford it and even if we tried (as Blackmon wanted to), it would quickly go sour with unpaid rents, damage deposits, furniture rentals, parties and problems and problems and problems. I thought we should find guys locally.

Players that had local name recognition: As we tried to get a new expansion team off the ground, we had hoped to draw fans. Getting guys that had a 'name' locally would help put butts in seats.

Players who loved to play: Sounds corny but I felt like we needed guys who would play even if they didn't get paid. Blackmon had already shorted me on some of my pay and I needed to find players that could play through that kind of distraction.

Players who liked to compete: Again, sounds obvious but one of the things that I learned while with the Sonics in the mid '90s was how important it was to have players who hate to lose more than they love to win. It was one of the things that impressed me the most when I went to practices back then. Everything that these players did was competitive even in the seemingly innocuous drills; guys like Gary Payton, Detlef Schrempf and Nate McMillan treated these drills with the importance of an NBA playoff game.

Immediately, I knew there were three guys that I wanted to try and get. **Brian Dennis**, or Yogi as he was called, was an undersized post player (in terms of height, 6'6") who had long arms, was a shot blocker and excellent defender. At 300 lbs, he didn't get up and down the floor like most but he was a load to handle and his teams always had a habit of winning. I always regarded him as a really underrated player in the area. The second guy was **Tim Ellis**, a local kid who played high school ball at Seattle's Rainier Beach High School, the same school which produced NBA players Jamaal Crawford and Nate Robinson. Tim played post in high school but by the time he finished at Kansas State University (by way of Southern Idaho CC; he had developed into an outstanding scorer from the wing in the Big 12 Conference. The third was a guard named **Alvin Snow** who had just finished at Eastern Washington University where he led them to the NCAA tournament for the first time in school history. Alvin was another Seattle product who attended Franklin High School. He wasn't super talented but he was a fierce competitor who hated losing and seemed to elevate the play of his teammates. He was the type of guy that made the big play when it was needed and always seemed to be in the mix.

As it turned out none of these three were available. Yogi just didn't want to play. He had a new "regular" job and told me his basketball days were behind him. Tim had signed to play for Yakima in the CBA which would be a better opportunity for him to possibly get an NBA call-up and Al was playing in Europe. Any of those three guys would have been perfect but now it was on to Plan B.

The word was out about the establishment of the team and my phone was blowing up from players looking for jobs. We planned on doing a tryout but I knew that we would have to sift through a lot of mediocrity to find any decent players, if we would find any at all. In the CBA, the NBA Development League (NBDL), the ABA and most other US minor basketball leagues, they do tryouts where the players have to pay a fee to participate, usually around $150. This was extremely off-putting to me. For whatever reason, I have always been hyper-sensitive to charging kids to play basketball. My sensitivity on this issue is borderline irrational because I do understand some of the reasons why you sometimes need to charge players money. There can be hard costs involved in staging these tryouts such as gym rental, referees and staffing. There is also an argument to be made that a fee will discourage some guys from trying out who have no business playing for a professional basketball team and wasting everyone's time.

I was reticent to make these tryouts a revenue generator but we were no position to lose money on something like this. I compromised my albeit weak stance on charging a fee for tryouts by charging only what we would need to cover expenses. This turned out to be about $50.

The first tryout was held at Juanita High School in late September. We had about 30 players show up, hoping for a chance to showcase their skills to someone who'd listen. Unfortunately, most were tone deaf. It has always amazed me how extremely overconfident some players can be. As a coach, it's important to watch in earnest because you never really know who will show up, but reality says we're just indulging dreamers with an extra hour of sleep.

The "a-hole" part of me actually allows myself to get offended at some of these guys who "dare" waste my time as most of them couldn't score a basket on Easter. We had players (and I use that term loosely) show up for a professional basketball tryout who had never played HIGH SCHOOL basketball let alone had any kind of college career. I would wonder out loud to our other coaches about what exactly these guys thought of our program to come here and tryout; given their tremendous lack of ability.

They must think that we're a joke…?

At the same time however, there is something to be said for a guy who is confident, persistent and passionate about something, which almost all of these guys were. Truth be told, I actually admire those qualities but like I said, the "a-hole" in me sometimes gets in the way.

Of the 30 or so players that showed up for that first tryout, about 25 of them were guards. We knew finding good guards would never be a problem but finding good big men presented a bit of a bigger challenge. From that first tryout, I think we invited four guys to report to our official training camp in mid-October. Most of them had size which we needed, at least for camp, but we needed to try and find some others. We decided to schedule a second "open" tryout a couple of weeks later at Highline CC and see who might show up. The results of that tryout were pretty nondescript, however, the events leading up to it turned out to be a seminal moment in my relationship with Mike Blackmon.

I hired local college referees to officiate our scrimmages during the tryouts. This helped maintain a professionalism for the camp, raised the competition level of the players and frankly, allowed me to get some extra work for the referees; many of whom I had become friends with. Besides, it never hurts to have a good relationship with the guys holding the whistles. You never know when that 50/50 call might go your way.

I huddled up with Harold, Russ and Eldridge for about 10 minutes before they tryouts would start. We were going over our roles for the day and the things that we were looking for when Blackmon strutted into the gym and poked his head into our huddle to hear what we were saying. I wrapped up the things that I needed to say to the coaches and turned to Blackmon. I told him that I would need some money to pay the referees for their work that day. The officials usually agree to help out on things like this with the stipulation that you pay them that day in cash. They don't want it later and they don't want to send a bill for it.

"F*** them" he told me

"Uhh… what?" I quizzed, having been knocked back on my heels by this statement.

He looked at me like I was five years old and spoke very slow as if he was addressing a kindergarten class

" IIII… saaaiiid…. F*******ck…. them. What part of that don't you understand?"

"They're here already. They're expecting to get paid today. I can't go back now and tell them something different." I tried to explain as I finessed our conversation off to the side and away from the other coaches.

"These mother-f***ers are asking for WAY too much money. Tell them I'll pay them half or they can go home."

"I can't do that. We already made an agreement on what we'd pay them and I already talked to you about this. We agreed"

"I don't give a sh** what you agreed to. If you don't like it, then you can pay them yourself."

For a guy like me who does a pretty good job of rolling with the punches, this situation took on an entirely different complexion.

A rage built up inside me that was both foreign and alarming. I felt the blood rush to my head and my face felt like it was on fire. My eyes literally burned and my ears gave off a glow that could light the stoop of any southern brothel. All that I could picture was me with my hands around this guy's neck, squeezing, as his legs thrashed and struggled in a battle for his final breath.

Blackmon stood in front of me defiantly as he watched me begin to lose composure for the first time in our short relationship. He wore a smirk on his face similar to that of umpire CB Bucknor, when he was confronted by Lou Piniella back in 2002.

I took a deep breath but to no avail. My voice still shook as I decided this would be where my professional coaching career would finish before it ever got started. I took a step forward, toward him, just to make sure my 6'4" frame would completely envelop his five foot nothingness. I took my index finger and pointed it directly at the area where I wanted to put the bullet. I quietly and purposefully spoke

"I've listened to you talk to everyone around you like they were children for way too long now. I don't care what you say to anyone else but that shit stops with me right here, right now. If you don't want to pay these guys, that's fine. You can tell them yourself, but I'm not going to be a part of it. You think you can do everything yourself? …Go for it. I'm done."

I turned around and took two steps toward the door. Then I paused. I took off the whistle that was hanging around my neck. I turned back toward him and threw it in his face.

"You might need this" I added for dramatic effect before walking out the gym doors.

The short walk to my car allowed me to gain control and collect myself before I drove away. I took a mental inventory. I had really wanted to coach this team and had sacrificed some of my own self-esteem to meet that end. Ultimately I knew though, that I would have never been able to last through the season with this guy. A confrontation like this was inevitable and it seemed to be a good thing that it happened now, before the season started, instead of a few weeks or months later when walking away would be more difficult.

I took a left out of the parking lot, drove about a ¼ mile up the road and jumped on Interstate 5 headed north toward my house. I got a little ways down the road when my cell phone rang. It was Russ. It was now 10 a. m. and the tryout was supposed to have started. He probably was wondering what was going on. I answered the phone.

"Did you see what happened with that jackass?" I asked as soon as I hit the green button on my phone.

"Rick, its Mike. You're right. I can't do this without you. Don't worry about the referees. I'll get them their money today. You're the coach of this team. Please get back here and start your practice."

I'm not sure whether Blackmon had an epiphany about me or if he was just stuck over a barrel. Either way it didn't matter to me. From that day forward our relationship changed. I no longer felt like I was held hostage by the job and I think he realized that I wouldn't put up with his endless crap. It wasn't all smooth sailing after that by any means but at least the power dynamic had been somewhat leveled and this I could live with.

6

Salt Lake City

By mid-October we were ready to start assembling a roster.

The first guy that we signed was a kid named Rashaad Powell. Rashaad was the perfect guy to have as our first signee in part because we had just agreed to play our games at Renton High School and he was a graduate of Renton. We thought that it would create some buzz within the community and attract a few more people to some games.

September 29, 2004 – **For Immediate Release**

Bellevue, WA. The ABA Bellevue Blackhawks professional basketball team has announced the signing of its first player in franchise history. Rashaad Powell, a 6'4" guard from the University of Idaho and Renton (WA) High School signed a one-year contract on Wednesday. Powell was named to the Big West All-Defensive Team in 2004.

Head Coach Rick Turner described Powell as: "An excellent player -- and an even better person -- who has a great passion for basketball, and will be a tremendous asset to this team." Turner continued, "Rashaad has great versatility. He plays very tough defense and can fill a multiple of positions on the court. He's exactly what this franchise is looking for: a talented athlete who can help us on and off the court."

Don't get me wrong, Rashaad was a good player and deserved a spot on the roster but there were also some ancillary benefits to the timing of his signing. The bad part was that he didn't quite understand that and thought that his signing was equivalent to him being a "first round" draft pick. Eventually his feelings of self-importance got in the way and compromised his ability to compete; ultimately costing him his job.

The next guy we signed was "the brother of NBA player Devean George". That may as well have been his name. Actually his name was Eddie, but he couldn't escape that label. Frankly he didn't do much to get out from under it. He wore it with pride and I can't say that I blame him. Again, we thought he was good enough to have a spot on the roster, but more importantly, it seemed to sound impressive in a press release. Unfortunately for Eddie, he got hurt before our first game and was just never really good enough once he came back to the active roster. He got cut about three weeks into the season.

Brian Bunche, or as the guys called him, "Bunchie" was the first 'big' that we signed. We found him in one of our tryouts.

We were concerned about the lack of big men in the area and we wanted to lock him up so we didn't get stuck, if no one else came along. He wasn't really skilled on the offensive end but he wasn't afraid to mix it up in the paint. He was about 6'8" and strong. He rebounded and defended pretty well and was just a terrific guy to be around. Bunchy was from the South by way of Little Rock, Arkansas and his southern demeanor was a great fit with everyone on the team. He allowed himself to be a verbal punching bag at times but not in a way that was weak. He was self-deprecating and pretty funny as shown when he tried to "free-style" from time to time on various road trips. He was the type of guy that brings a team together.

I got a call from a coach that I knew from my time at BCC. Eric Bridgeland was the head coach at a Division III school in Tacoma called the University of Puget Sound. He had great success there and he was a guy that I had a lot of respect for. So, when he called to recommend one of his players, I listened. Normally you wouldn't think that a Division III player would be able to compete at our level but, Coach Bridgeland explained to me that Matt Glynn was different.

Matt was an NCAA Division III All-American point guard while at UPS and had a great feel for the game. What he lacked in quickness, he made up for in decision making. He was a winner and although he was basically a rookie with no pro experience, he played like a vet. He was another who fit in well with the guys and was a great foil for much of their ribbing; which centered mostly on his 'whiteness'. Matt started out the season kind of slow and lacked confidence, but by the end of the year he might have been our most consistent, if not most valuable player … even if it didn't show in the stats.

One of my favorite stories is that of Justin Murray.

Justin played at Peninsula Junior College while I coached at Bellevue CC. I was never impressed with his game as he was an undersized and over-weight post player at Peninsula. He was fine for that league, but then he had "the audacity" to try and walk-on at Washington State University. Justin never really got off the bench while at WSU and when he showed up for one of our tryouts, I thought he was just another guy who didn't understand the level of talent in our league. After all, I thought, if he can't play at WSU, he can't play for us. I had to give him credit though; because when I saw him, he looked good. He had lost some weight and had really worked on his perimeter game. But there was still no way he'd be good enough to make our team.

Everyday Justin showed up and everyday I intended to cut him. The problem was however, each day he played better than the previous one. One of my assistant coaches, Harold Wright, was in my ear, praising him and we just could never get rid of Justin. Ultimately he became a starter and another guy we couldn't afford to keep off the floor. He made all the little plays and seemed to always be in the mix, whether it was getting a big rebound and put back or diving on the floor for a loose ball. He had worked and worked and worked to improve his game. He just needed someone to give him the opportunity and I was glad that I had the chance to provide him that.

Justin has gone on to play a number of years overseas and I would almost be sure that he has made more money playing basketball than all the guys that he played with at WSU put together.

One of the guys that I had targeted from day one was a local Seattle player who had gone on to play at Oregon State University named Jimmy Haywood. Haywood had some clout to his name in the Seattle basketball community and would help legitimize us a bit within those eyes. Plus he could really play.

I always really liked Jimmy, although he had a bit of a track record of being difficult with some of his coaches. I think we got along, in part, because he believed that I trusted him and gave him somewhat of a long leash. I allowed him to make mistakes without blowing up on him and my trust in him was reciprocated… at least on the court. At one point in the year, Jimmy disappeared for four days without any phone call or word of his whereabouts. He later showed up telling me that his sister was ill and he had to go to Minnesota to be with her. I took him at his word and moved on. I later had heard that he had spent the previous two days in jail because he didn't have the money to get himself out.

Haywood was a combo guard that could play either the 1 or the 2. He was more comfortable at the 2 but we mostly used him at the 1 because he had a little better handle than Matt Glynn and was quicker up the floor. Between the two of them, we were just fine in the backcourt and if one was getting pressure, the other would bring the ball up the floor. Jimmy had a big personality and stood out as a natural leader on the team. For me, he was a lot of fun to be around.

We were pretty solid in the backcourt with Haywood, Matt, Justin and Rashaad, but our only decent big at this point was 'Bunchie'. We needed a more skilled big man and when Seattle Pacific University head coach Jeff Hironaka called me, little did I know that he would have just what the doctor ordered.

Eric Sandrin was a 6'9" forward who could jump out of the gym but could also step out and shoot the 3-pointer.

"E" had been playing in Europe and wanted to come home to the Seattle area. He heard about our team starting up and he called his former college coach to see if there was any room on the roster. He was a perfect fit. He was extremely skilled for his size; he ran the floor, finished on the break and was an exciting player for our fans to watch because he played above the rim. He was a tough cover because he could take bigger, slower players outside as well as had the ability to post up smaller guys. In our first game of the season, Eric had 42 points against the Portland Reign in a one point win. After making the ABA All-Star team in Vegas mid-season, Eric left us for a more lucrative deal with the Harlem Globetrotters.

Another front court player who appeared out of the woodwork was 6'8" forward Dontay Harris from Tacoma.

Dontay played his college ball at Drake University in Iowa and was totally off my radar when he showed up to try out for the team. Harold knew about him and asked him to come and work out with us. Dontay's great strength was his approach and demeanor. He was as close to "thuggish" as we got and he brought an attitude to the floor that rubbed off on his teammates. He wasn't real smooth and was never very fluid in the way he moved. He didn't seem particularly skilled, but he always had a knack for making plays.

He took and made big shots when we needed them and he backed down from no one. He was absolutely not intimidated by anyone we played against, regardless of their exceptional talent or background. He came up huge for us after Sandrin left and he filled a scoring void that we didn't think he possessed. Again, he was another guy who just needed an opportunity to play in order to show what he could do.

We still didn't have a true point guard and were having a difficult time settling on one from a list of mediocre candidates. Harold really liked Greg Hendricks and although I didn't share his enthusiasm for Greg, we settled on him for our final roster.

Greg had a knack for scoring but I always felt that it was at the detriment of the other four guys on the floor. Beyond that, he just never fit in with everyone else. Not good for your supposed floor leader. When we went out to eat as a team Greg sat alone. On our first road trip to Utah he elected to not eat with us at all, deciding instead to have Top Ramen by himself in his room. This obviously isolated him from the other guys.

After our first five games of the season, Greg was our leading scorer. But we were 1-4. I just didn't have a good vibe about him and felt like if we were going to lose, I rather lose with guys who enjoyed being around each other. I cut Greg after five games and never felt any regret. He couldn't understand why, given his scoring numbers to start the season and he did a pretty good job of telling whoever would listen what an idiot that I was. It just never felt right with him.

A coaching friend of mine, Greg Sparling at Central Washington University made me laugh when he described one of his players as being on the "All-Airport Team". In other words, he couldn't play but looked great walking through the airport or during warm-ups in a lay-up line. For us, that was part-time firefighter Jajuan Winesberry.

I understood that we needed to have a guy or two on the team who would fill out the roster, work hard in practice; but in many ways we needed someone who was just happy to be there. The last thing you need as a coach is your 11th or 12th guy taking up your time and energy by complaining and being a cancer to the others. They have to understand their role. Jajuan was pretty good about this.

He was 6'9" and huge. He was the type of guy who Adonis would envy. An absolutely sculpted body with about four percent body fat but a game that left something to be desired. He was a walk-on at the University of Washington and as a guy who followed the Washington program closely, I had never heard of him. He was a definite project and someone who our Assistant Coach, Russ Schoene, took an active interest in.

Russ worked with him all year and Jajuan made the largest improvements out of anyone on our team. Jajuan worked hard but I give Russ a lot of credit for the attention that he gave the big man. As a matter of fact, Jajuan actually made some nice contributions at the end of the season when we were without Dontay for a stretch.

Early on, I considered Jajuan to be a practice player so we were still in need of another "big". Harold recommended a friend of his named Jackie Jones from the University of Oklahoma.

I knew that Harold and Jackie were "boys" so I was always hesitant about whether Harold wanted him just so he'd have someone to hang out with on the road or whether he could actually help. Jackie was 38 years old at the time, which was the same age as me, and he had been playing professionally for 16 years. He was a little broken down and seemed to me, at first, to be completely unreliable. I kept him around as a favor to Harold and he was also kind of like another coach.

Frankly, I was a little intimidated by Jackie, because he had been around for so long that I felt he could identify me as a coaching fraud. At that time, I still wasn't sure if I was any good at this coaching thing and I wasn't convinced that I could get professional players to listen to and respect me. With the younger guys, I felt like if I just acted like I knew what I was talking about and said things with confidence, it wouldn't really matter if I was right or not. With Jackie, I felt like he knew better.

Jackie hated practice and spent most of the preseason on the sideline with what he said was a pulled groin muscle. I had doubts about how bad it was, but I didn't mind having him around anyway. If it got better that was fine, but if it didn't… that was fine too.

By January, Jackie was finally healthy enough to play and he ended up being very instrumental in an eight-game winning streak that got us back into the playoff hunt. The more that I got to know him, the more I really got to like him and appreciate what he had to offer. He was the old man on the team and although soft-spoken, when he did talk, players listened.

We had most of the pieces in place. The last one that we needed was a shooter.

Lovell Brown used to come to BCC open gyms after his college career at the University of California, Bakersfield but I always thought he was a point guard. He graduated from Garfield High School in central Seattle but didn't have a spectacular career there. We tried him out at point guard and he just wasn't good enough. He never told me that he wasn't a point guard and I wasn't smart enough to try him somewhere different.

Shortly before I was about to cut Lovell, I put him on a team in practice with all the other guys that weren't good enough and had them scrimmage against our top eight. Since there were a couple of other point guards on that team, Lovell ended up having to play on the wing and he totally scorched our first teamers. I had no idea that he was that good of a shooter. As it turned out, he was a "catch and shoot guy" as opposed to someone who shot off the dribble like point guards often do.

Lovell became that shooter we were looking for and in fact had an ABA record 11 three-pointers in a game against Long Beach, midway though the season. Like Sandrin, he also left us for the Globetrotters after the All-Star break but later returned for the playoffs.

***

The 2004-2005 season opened in Portland against fellow expansion team, the Portland Reign. The Reign was owned by Mary Liss who along with filing for bankruptcy three times in the past 12 years, also had an outstanding arrest warrant for "failing to appear" in a hearing where she was charged for writing thousands of dollars in bad checks in a larger, area check-writing scheme.

Mary wasn't the only "questionable" character in this league.

Along with Mary Liss and our own Mike Blackmon, the league was littered with figures of ill repute; while at the same time, boasting quite a few legitimate basketball people with impressive credentials and spotless integrity. It was an entertaining minefield to try and negotiate for people like me, who seem to embrace chaotic surroundings. It was a non-stop adventure.

Dan Steinberg, from the Washington Post, captured some of the chaos in the ABA of 2004 in excerpts for an article he wrote on December 3rd of that year...

For ABA, It's Dribble and Drive
Fledgling League Serious About Expansion Plan Despite Struggles

By Dan Steinberg
Washington Post Staff Writer
Friday, December 3, 2004; Page D01

At the close of the Maryland NightHawks' training camp last month, Andrew G. Haines, the founder and co-owner of the area's newest professional sports franchise, gathered his team on a set of bleachers and began a lighthearted game of American Basketball Association trivia.

The prize? Vouchers for an all-you-can-eat pizza-and-pasta lunch worth $5.75, no small thing for players whose training camp salary consisted of a $20 per diem. Players earned coupons for identifying the city Haines lives in, his daughter's first name and the team's opening-night opponent.

When the group was asked a more pressing question about the league -- "How many teams are in the ABA?" -- even Haines didn't know the answer. The players' guesses ranged from 32 to 48, with starting forward Jason "The Birdman" Williams perhaps closest to the truth.

"No one knows," Williams said. "They could be folding as we speak."

The next day -- the ABA's opening day -- the league announced that its Calgary franchise would be replaced on the schedule by the Visalia (Calif.) Dawgs. A few days later, league chairman Joe Newman said the Calgary franchise had returned.

Four years ago, Newman and his partner Dick Tinkham -- who helped found the original ABA in 1967 -- brought back a league made famous by tri-colored balls and the flashy dunks of Dr. J. After ending last season with seven teams, the new ABA embarked on an offseason of prodigious expansion, in which a $10,000 "market reservation fee" and a promise to follow league guidelines were the primary starting requirements...

...When asked about the pace of expansion, the 67-year-old Newman replied: "Why not? Why so many newspapers -- because there's markets for newspapers. Why so many Wal-Marts, why so many McDonald's, why so many Lowe's and Home Depots? . . . Where there's a market for a product or service, it will be successful."

Some observers are slightly less bullish than Newman...

...Newman said he believed every team would make it through the year, "because I'm the eternal optimist, and because I see glasses as half-full instead of half-empty, and because I've got fingers crossed on both hands, and I've got my legs crossed."

Learning on the Fly

Haines, the 26-year-old Maryland NightHawks founder, has owned several professional and semi-pro football teams in addition to a variety of small businesses. He said he has made most of his money from starting and then selling a chain of window treatment businesses in his native Pennsylvania. Haines, who lives in Lancaster, Pa., was originally awarded his ABA expansion franchise in Hershey, Pa., but moved the team to Maryland in June when he had trouble finding an arena in Pennsylvania that could accommodate the team...

...Haines said the debts stem from his being "young and naive" and without legal counsel when he went into business at the age of 19. He said the dollar amounts on several of the judgments are inflated, and that several were the result of contractors taking advantage of his naiveté. He said he is being advised on the judgments by a family friend and plans to work out settlements with his creditors as soon as possible so he'll be able to buy a house in Pennsylvania...

...The Pottstown Police Department has an arrest warrant for Haines issued in 2001 for writing $717 worth of bad checks to a community television station; Haines said he thought the matter had been taken care of, but he would look into it. The Pennsylvania Department of Revenue also filed a tax lien for more than $2,000 against one of Haines's former companies in July, public records show. Haines said he hadn't known about the lien, but would also look into that situation.

Haines recently took on a local partner for the NightHawks: Montgomery County medical malpractice/personal injury lawyer and sports agent Tom Doyle. Haines and Doyle expect to have a budget of between $600,000 and $700,000 for the NightHawks, about half of which will be spent on marketing and arena rent...

...The NightHawks have a glossy pocket schedule, offices in Glen Burnie and several local sponsors. They have changed general managers and lost an assistant coach and assistant general manager since arriving in Maryland.

Such flux has surrounded several ABA teams. In August, the Gwinnett (Ga.) Gwizzlies -- so named because of a typo -- saw their head and assistant coach resign and be hired by a different ABA franchise; the league announced the moves on the same day. Later, a new Gwinnett head coach was hired and then resigned, the league office awarded the team to a different ownership group, the franchise changed its name to the Atlanta Mustangs and the second coach returned, according to a team spokeswoman.

Teams were awarded to a 29-year-old independent pop singer in Nashville; a group headed by a minister in Ontario, Calif.; a California distributor of the Western Outlaw Cowboy Hard Hat and devices that make it easier for women to urinate while standing up; and a community activist in Georgia who has run and lost races for five political offices. An all-Native American expansion franchise was launched and then scrapped; and a Vancouver franchise, which said it would use primarily Chinese players, named Jim Harrick head coach, although Harrick quickly told reporters that announcement was incorrect.

Prospective Little Rock owner Dwan Andre Brown was convicted on six counts of wire fraud in February, according to news reports. He was removed from ABA consideration when league officials learned of the legal troubles, Newman said. Mary Liss, the founder of the Portland Reign, has filed for bankruptcy twice in the last two and a half years, records show. A Pittsburgh franchise folded before it played a game, leaving employees who told the Pittsburgh Post-Gazette they were owed money; that franchise was immediately replaced by a different western Pennsylvania franchise.

Newman declined to discuss the league's background check procedure for prospective owners. Speaking generally, he said: "I judge it on the telephone. If *they sound like the kind of character I'd like to have in the league, we bring them in. And if they prove not to be, we get rid of them just as quick." He said he has taken franchises away from "half a dozen owners who haven't done what they're supposed to do."*

Newman said yesterday that the ABA has 35 teams, including one in Baton Rouge, La., that replaced an Oklahoma City franchise this week. The Colorado franchise isn't listed in the standings posted on the league's official Web site, and the Calgary team is not yet listed on the schedule, but Newman said yesterday that both teams were still in the league.

Some of the expansion teams have thrived at the box office; the Arkansas RimRockers, whose roster includes five former University of Arkansas players including Scotty Thurman and Todd Day, have averaged more than 4,400 fans in three games, a spokeswoman said.

Newman said he already has 40 franchise "reservations" for next year, including one in the District headed by an ownership group he declined to identify, one in Baltimore and one in Norfolk. More than 1,000 people have filled out the Web-based form requesting ownership information, he said...

Sparse Crowds

Six hours before the NightHawks' season began, General Manager Rick Matsko still didn't know what to call his opponents.

The New Jersey Jaguars, it seemed, were no longer the Jaguars, although Matsko, a 27-year-old former minor league pitcher in the Cleveland Indians organization, wasn't sure exactly why or when they had changed their name. The pre-printed tickets said the NightHawks would face the New Jersey Shorecats, but Haines said that wasn't right, either.

The scoreboard at the arena was changed from "Jaguars" to "Jersey," and soon after New Jersey's coach and owner, Ron Eford, arrived, he told Matsko, "We're the SkyCats." New Jersey's players said they hadn't known what they would be called until they got to the arena.

The NightHawks rallied for a 106-95 season-opening win. After the game, children -- including that night's official cheerleading squad, which hailed from Kettering Middle School -- mobbed the players, who stayed on the court for more than a half hour signing autographs, visiting with friends and celebrating before a postgame meal of pizza.

Another home game against New Jersey the following night drew 214 fans; the NightHawks are scheduled to play 20 of their 36 games against just three of the league's teams. The NightHawks played their third home game on Wednesday, and drew 203.

Players' contracts are not guaranteed, so next week could bring an entirely new Maryland roster.

"That's the business," Williams said. "Welcome to the minor leagues."

Staff researcher Julie Tate contributed to this report.

That, in part, describes the environment surrounding the league. While we tried to "Make the Big Time Where We Are", others were giving in to the small time. While some teams were stocked with NBA-level talent, others were stocked like the YMCA Rec. League. While some teams were drawing thousands, others were drawing ten's. But this is who we were, and as former University of Washington football coach Don James used to say, "Don't tell me about the pain, just show me the baby". We couldn't concern ourselves with what was happening anywhere else. We had to do our best to make our situation as good as it could be.

***

A friendly whistle, a buzzer beater to send the game into overtime and some clutch free throws in the extra period, made the Bellevue Blackhawks 1-0 at the start the 2004-2005 ABA season. Blackmon was beside himself after the game. The manic dial on his apparent disorder meter was set to "Goofy". I did my best to set his expectations low for our team going into the season and I guess I succeeded because he was immediately comparing me to Red Auerbach after the game. Don't get me wrong, I was pretty jacked up myself by the win. Portland was a much more talented team than we were on paper but my world was grounded a touch more in reality than Mr. Blackmon's. I knew we were pretty lucky to win, but at the same time, I knew that good teams needed their share of luck throughout a season and what better place to start than game one?

Blackmon never wanted to pay per diem to the players for meals. Instead he would give me a credit card and tell me to feed them. This was not how most professional teams operated. It did not "Make the Big Time...", but this was how it was going to be and we dealt with it. Although the players didn't like it, it may have turned out to be an unintended blessing with a very positive result. For a team that played 22 of their 30 games on the road that year, it meant that we ate a lot of meals together. I think in part, it contributed to our becoming extremely close by the end of the year. Just as you hear the so-called experts exhort the importance of nuclear families eating dinner together, this basketball family may have benefited from the by-products of this forgotten ritual.

I was pretty tight with the budget when it came to meals. Tight may not be the right word but I was at least prudent and firm. When Blackmon had the credit card though, the players recognized weakness and took full advantage of it. After that first win in Portland, Blackmon had everyone board his endorphin train and fly it over to the Red Robin restaurant on the outskirts of the Rose City heading back toward Seattle.

Russ, Harold and I sat together at one booth while the players got a large table to share. Of course, Blackmon sat with "his" players.

He fancied himself the Eddie DeBartolo of minor league basketball. Blackmon was a Bay Area guy who claims to have written a book about the 49ers and their benevolent owner Eddie DeBartolo. This was his first "DeBartolo" moment as owner of the Blackhawks and he was in jock-sniffer's heaven. He praised the players, fawned over their exploits of the night and cajoled about the various reasons why they should playing in the NBA.

"Order up boys!" he exalted

They obliged; first with drinks. I think they each looked for the most expensive drink they could find and ordered two. Long Island Ice Teas, Freckled Lemonades, Washington Apples and whatever other crazy drink they could think of.

Then the food... let me give you just one player's typical order:

Start out first with mozzarella sticks. Follow that up with wings and chicken quesadillas. Then, for dinner, a monster burger... and finally mud pie for dessert.

Oh yeah... and wash it all down with a shake.

I didn't even want to look at the bill when it was done. The place looked like a tornado had hit it. Just to add insult to injury, a couple of guys ordered more food "to go" for the three-hour ride back to Bellevue. Previous experience had made me leery of whether or not the credit card would work so I got out of there before I had to witness any Blackmon meltdowns during the bill paying ceremony. I waited in the van.

After a bit of a wait we were finally back on the road, headed home... tummies full, undefeated and in first place.

Three nights later we would play host to the Utah Snowbears for a two-game series at Renton High School. We had created a little bit of a local buzz about the team and we were expecting a decent crowd to witness our home opener, except for the fact that it fell on Thanksgiving night. I'm not sure whose bright idea this was, but I knew that our gate numbers would be low because of it. We would play Utah both Thursday and Friday nights before going back to Salt Lake City to play them again five more times.

I was concerned about our game presentation and operations.

Very concerned.

This was a large part of my background while I was at the Sonics and I understood 1) how important the presentation is to the fan's experience and 2) that it didn't just happen without a bunch of preparation. My focus however was on coaching; and I did my best to not stress myself out over this side of things because I couldn't do anything about it. I helped as much as I could and advised where I could, but ultimately it came down to Blackmon and a couple people that he had "hired" to help.

It is very labor intensive to put on and stage a professional basketball game. Maybe a better way of putting it is that it is very labor intensive to put on a basketball game professionally. I sat down with Blackmon and spelled out what he needed.

Ticket sellers
Ushers
Concession stand operators
Two stats people
One video camera operator
An official scorekeeper
Scoreboard operator
24-second clock operator
PA announcer

Not to mention the "stuff" that goes with that…

Printed tickets
Cash box for tickets and concessions
Food for concessions
Laptop for stats
Printer
A video camera
Tape for the camera
An official scorebook
A script for the PA announcer

These are just basic operational needs. This doesn't even include the hundreds of other tiny details that you need to have in place in order to put on a game.

Music (with the swear words bleeped out)
Timeout and halftime promotions
Towels for the teams
Ice
Water for the teams
Security
Trainers/Medical staff
Athletic tape
Referee's locker room
Etc., etc…

The weeks leading up to our home opener, I had continuously reminded Blackmon about lining these things up and being ready. I tried to stay out of it, but I felt like a bad game presentation would also reflect on me. If nothing else, I thought we should get there early on that first day to make sure we had everything in order, run through the script and test all equipment. We agreed that we'd arrive at the gym by 4 p.m. for the 7 p.m. start.

I got there at 3:30 p.m.

Blackmon showed up at 6 p.m.

Our entire game night staff for our home opener???

…Mike Blackmon.

***

By the time Blackmon showed up for Opening Night of the Bellevue Blackhawks inaugural season on Thanksgiving night, November 25, 2004, each team and the referees had already been there for a half hour. The referees, who had not yet dressed for the game, were huddled up on the south sideline opposite the team benches. Our team trainer was hurriedly taping ankles for both squads on a table set up in the northeast corner of the gym and a school's janitor was doing a last minute sweep of the court while dodging errant shots from a handful of players who were on the floor getting loose. I had just finished writing up our scouting report and game keys on the white board in our locker room and walked out to the floor to relax for a couple minutes before our pre-game talk.

I looked around and could tell that there was some snickering, pointing and disgruntled conversations going on in every corner of the gym. Ike Austin and the Utah coaches were not happy about the fact that we were playing on a high school-sized court. Pro and college courts are 50' x 94', high school courts are 50' x 84'; 10 feet shorter. Some players were concerned about the space between the basket and the wall underneath, worried that it was too close. Meanwhile, the referees were concerned about the lines.

Oh crap! The lines.

We were supposed to be playing with the NBA lines for three-pointers (23' 9" as opposed to 19' 9") and the extended lane. With this being the first game, the referees wanted to establish their authority from the get go. I can't say that I blame them. They told Blackmon that the game would not start until we got the court properly lined. Just like avoiding the bill paying at Red Robin a few nights earlier, I quietly disappeared for a while, while Blackmon, the school's Athletic Director and the referees tried to sort it out.

Shortly after 7 p.m. (scheduled tip-off time), with a decent amount of people in attendance waiting for the game to start, they finally finished lining the court… sort of. In order to put new lines on a basketball court, you need a specially made tape that won't do damage to the court once you decide to take it off. Thankfully for us, Renton

High School had some of this tape on hand when the problem came up. Otherwise we would have been screwed, because this kind of tape is not easy to find.

They lined one end of the court without much problem. It actually looked okay which surprised me because it is not easy to make straight tape, curve, to make a new three-point line. But they did a pretty good job. However on the other end of the floor, they ran out of the red tape after completing just about half of the new three-point circle. They had to finish it with blue tape; except that ran out with about six feet still to go. Blackmon tried to use white athletic tape to finish the job but the school's athletic director objected to this so, we played the game with a part red, part blue and part invisible three-point line.

Very professional.

By now it was 7:20 p.m. We were already 20 minutes late in starting the game and still needed to organize the scorer's table. Videotaping the game was out. Blackmon never found anyone to do it and besides, he didn't have a camera. Official stats were out. Blackmon never found anyone to do that and he didn't have a laptop nor printer. He decided that he would run the entire scorer's table himself. Scoreboard, clock, shot clock, official scorebook and PA; he would all do himself. The jobs of five relatively competent people would be done by just one completely disorganized, distracted and not-nearly-as-competent crazy man.

This was a bad idea.

Once again however, sanity was saved by the referees who informed Blackmon that as team owner, he could not do the official scorebook. I convinced him that he needed another person for the clock/shot clock and after soliciting volunteers from the audience, we finally had a three- person scorers table together. By 7:50 p.m. we were finally ready to start the 7 p.m. game.

The horn sounded to end warm-ups and introduce the starting lineups. Each team went to their bench under the rhythmic music of… nothing. Blackmon forgot to bring anything to play music as well as any music to play. So, to say that the atmosphere in the gym at that point was sterile and lifeless would be kind in description. Without the music, combined with a sparse crowd who had been waiting for almost an hour for the game to start, every little noise in the gym was heightened and hit your ears like a painful slap to the side of your head. Without any music to have to "yell over", people behaved like they were at a golf tournament and whispered to each other so the people around them weren't disturbed.

Our PA announcer, Michael Blackmon, grabbed the mic to get things started and in a normal everyday voice began…

"Hi everybody. Happy Thanksgiving. Welcome to Renton High School. Tonight the Utah Snowbears from Salt Lake City take on *(and now super-cheesy Mr. Announcer voice kicks in)* YOUR UNDEFEATED BEEELLLLLLEVUUUUE BLAAAACCKKHAAAWKS!!!!!!"

A smattering of forced and unenthusiastic applause fell well short of reverberating through the building.

In the quiet gym and with the microphone still on, you could hear the shuffling of papers over the speakers as Blackmon searched for the team roster. A big sigh and an "ahhhh f***" are audible as he scrambled to find the papers. It's an uncomfortable pause before he started back in...

"Now let's meet tonight's starting lineups. First for the visiting Utah Snowbears, coached by former NBA great Ike Austin... at guard #1 Jimmy Haywoo... oops wrong team. Sorry about that let me grab the right roster here... Now where is it?... No that's not it... Sorry, its opening night, we'll get better at this... oh, here it is... okay... at guard... but I don't know what number he is, Clay Tucker..."

He fumbled through the starting lineups for both teams but still wasn't finished.

"Now I'd like everyone to please rise and since we don't have anyone to sing the national anthem and no one wants to hear me try and sing it, we'll do the Pledge of Allegiance... I pledge allegiance to the flag of the United States of America..."

A pause... *(he forgot the words)*

"...uhh, indivisible?"

"... one nation... under God, with liberty and justice for all..."

Then he screams... "PLAY BALL!!!"

Laughing he says "... Sorry, I haven't done that since grade school."

I wanted to crawl out of the gym. You could hear the murmurs around the gym. I don't remember ever being that embarrassed before. I felt sorry for him, I was pissed at him and I was totally ashamed to be a part of this thing.

Finally the game started. Instead of doing regular PA announcing, like stating who scored the basket, Blackmon did a running play-by-play. It was irritating to listen to if you were a fan at the game and insulting if you were a player. At one point in the first half, Haywood took and missed an ill-advised shot.

"Ha... nice shot Jimmy!" Blackmon sarcastically lamented over the PA

Later on, Justin Murray missed a gimmie lay-up in the third quarter and Blackmon was there to publicly highlight it...

"Just another easy shot missed by Justin Murray…way to go Murray."

Needless to say, the players were not real happy about his running commentary. But, as we all know by now… Blackmon didn't really care.

***

After losing a couple of close games to Utah at home, we were on our way to Salt Lake City for two games. Then we had five days off before another game there in Utah. The way it worked in the ABA, each team would pay for their own transportation, but the home team (in this case Utah) would provide lodging. Blackmon didn't want to fly us back to Seattle for the five days that we had off and he talked Ike Austin into housing us during that stretch. So we spent almost two weeks in Salt Lake City, living in an extended stay hotel.

This was our first real road trip as a team because the game in Portland a week earlier was just a one-day trip with no overnight stay. I thought a lot about what my role was and what kind of expectations I should have for our players on the road. I had been coaching in college for the previous seven years so I had been used to strict schedules, hard and fast rules about curfews and drinking; as well as other conduct outside of basketball. With pros I felt the rules were different.

I felt that as adults, they had the right to do pretty much whatever they wanted to do outside of our team activities, but needed to understand that with that freedom came a responsibility to perform their job at a high level. If they couldn't perform, they'd lose their job. In other words, if they wanted to party until 5 a.m., I didn't care as long as they could perform their job when called upon. My expectations were that they would make good choices. If not, they'd be gone. Truthfully, it was a pretty easy philosophy to adapt because I didn't think any of them were indispensable. I felt like any one of them could be easily replaced at any time and actually, if I needed to do that… it would send a message to the others about how they should behave in order to keep their job. So in some way, I guess you could say I was almost looking for somebody to mess up.

Ignorance is bliss. As long as I didn't know about it, it didn't happen. Drink, smoke, hump, party… just don't tell me about it. I wasn't looking to be friends with these guys, that's the assistants' job. I didn't want any of their questionable decisions affecting the way I saw them. As their boss, they only needed to be able to do their job and I didn't want off the court stuff impacting our relationships. In hindsight, I'm not sure if that was the right approach and I'm not even sure that I still feel that way today, but I know at that time, it was precisely how I felt. I got the team together after our first practice down in Salt Lake City and tried to let them know where I stood.

As I tried to formulate the right words to say, I recalled what life on the road was like for the Sonics players when I traveled with them as well as the minor league baseball players when I was with the Bellingham Mariners. I felt like our experience would be a combination of the two. They would be easily recognizable as athletes, like NBA players are; but not have any money, like minor league baseball players. This dichotomy would make their decision-making abilities that much more important. The problem for them would mostly be… women.

There are women whose lives are spent chasing pro athletes strictly in order to hook up with them. Some are gold digging, some are looking for a husband and some are looking for another notch on their bed post. I could (sort of) understand why they would do this with NBA players, although I think it's pathetic. But I couldn't (and can't) understand why they would chase "minor-leaguers". You would think that if they were conniving enough to stalk these guys the way that they do, they would also be smart enough to realize that these guys are broke. Maybe they are betting on the "Come" (no pun intended) by getting in on the ground floor of any future earnings? I don't know, but if you thought that Susan Sarandon's "Baseball Annie" character in **Bull Durham** was a make-believe person, think again.

I remember countless road trips with the Sonics and no matter what city we were in or what time it was when we arrived; there were always women waiting for the team in the hotel lobby.

I specifically remember getting to the hotel in Milwaukee at 4 a.m. one time and being totally shocked that these gorgeous women were there; waiting for the players in the lobby and dressed to the nine's. They would pair off with a player and head upstairs… AT 4 A.M.!!!

The baseball equivalent to this was a bit different however. With the baseball team, all the "Baseball Annie's" would wait for the team at the bus after the game. Once the team got back on the bus, the girls would follow in their cars back to the hotel. They would keep more of a distance at the hotel (or in most cases… motel) and wait for the players in the parking lot so they could take them out to a bar or restaurant after they went up to their rooms and changed. There was a huge difference however between the NBA groupies and the baseball groupies.

The NBA women were major league, H-O-T… hot women.

The minor league baseball women were N-O-T… not.

I told the team that my position was, as adults, I expected them to make adult decisions. I told them that poor decisions would directly impact their employment but I trusted them to do the right things.

I don't like it when people say "It's not my job to… (fill-in-the-blank)", such as the case where I could say "It's not my job to baby-sit these guys" or "I'm paid to coach, not be a hall monitor". But isn't it the job of any employee, with any company, to do everything that they can; to ensure the success of their employer? Regardless of whether or not it falls within their "job description"? That's when you know you have a turd for an employee when you hear, "It's not MY job to…"

I addressed with the players, some of the female landmines that might be buried in the bars of Salt Lake City and suggested a few ulterior motives that some of the fine ladies of Utah might have. I reminded them that 'no', never meant yes and that professional athletes traveling to any town in the country, walk around with big bull's-eyes on their foreheads and bigger ones on their crotch.

Finally I added, "Don't do anything to embarrass me, don't do anything to embarrass Mr. Blackmon, don't do anything to embarrass the city of Bellevue and don't do anything to embarrass the ABA. Stay out of jail and out of the newspaper. Other than that, you're on your own."

***

I have the bad combination of being a bit of a control freak as well as a terrible delegator. This is, in part, why I always drive the team van. The nice thing about driving the van is that you sort of blend in to the background. You can hear most of the conversations going on around you but are kind of a fly on the wall. It is this scenario, the day after my big "talk" to the team in Salt Lake, that I experienced the drawbacks of being the fly on the wall.

At breakfast that morning, Harold told me that he got a 2 a.m. phone call from one of our guys the night (or morning in this case) before. This player had met a girl at the bar around the corner from our hotel and was asking Harold if he had a condom that he could use (he didn't). I laughed along with the story, but also felt kind of good that this player would actually be concerned about something like that, especially after our meeting earlier that day. Maybe he had taken some of my advice to heart a little bit. Even though I tried not to show it to Harold, I felt proud that maybe my wisdom had at least touched one guy.

We loaded into the van for a shootaround at about 9:30 a.m., on our way to Salt Lake CC where the Snowbears played their home games. I could hear this unnamed player, two seats behind me, recounting his story from the night before with the other guys as they all swapped accounts of their pursuits and triumphs from their second night in Salt Lake.

"Bitch was weird" I heard him say, "She was ca-ra-zy!"

Somebody asked, "Why, what happened?"

He spoke in a low voice, almost a whisper but not quite. Regardless, I could still hear him.

"So I got this bitch naked on the floor, with her feet on the bed and her head under the TV…"

"Yeah…?" the others on the team eagerly asked with baited breath, leaning forward and smiling with their mouths agape, waiting to hear what came next… I was silently cringing, continuing my position as a fly on the wall.

"She wanted me to choke her…" he said, sounding as surprised as I'm sure he was when it came out of the girl's mouth.

"Uh-oh" I thought, not liking the direction of this story.

"So whad'ja do?" one guy asked.

"Yeah, what happened?" asked another, as the anticipation was killing these guys.

He paused.

He looked around as I watched him through the rearview mirror. I looked away before he spotted me.

He paused some more.

"Fu** nigga, what happened?" Someone else begged.

Calmly, he shrugged his shoulders. He looked left, and then again, he looked right.

In a very simple and matter of fact way, he said it.

"So I choked the bitch out…"

The van exploded. Laughter, hollers, yells, high fives and knee slaps pulsed throughout the van.

I almost drove off the road.

All I could think about was a dead white girl lying in a hotel room in Salt Lake City as a result of some crazy sex fetish that went terribly wrong, involving a black pro basketball player from Seattle and his idiot coach who allowed it to happen. The gravity of my responsibilities became much clearer to me right then and the cavalier attitude that I walked off the plane with in Utah was quickly replaced by a fatherly concern for the charges in my trust.

As much as I wanted them to do their own thing and act appropriately, I knew that I had to continually preach to them about their own responsibilities.

When you hear stories from around the country about various athletes who have run into trouble, it's easy to blame the coach, the team or the school for creating an environment that lacks control. But when you are in it, you realize that it's sometimes just luck that allows for bad things to miss you. Here were two consensual adults, dangerously experimenting at three in the morning with things that I don't even comprehend; dodging the proverbial bullet and figuratively living to tell about it.

What if, for whatever reason, she got upset at this player and decided to claim that their liaison was not consensual? How tough of a time would he have had attempting to claim his innocence with his hand prints marking her bruised neck? I wouldn't like his chances.

Those are the sort of things that these guys don't think about and as a coach; it's your job to remind them… constantly.

7

Dallas

You see the world through your cynical eyes
You're a troubled young man I can tell
You've got it all in the palm of your hand
But your hand's wet with sweat and your head needs a rest

- Styx "Fooling **Yourself: Angry Young Man**"

Three things worked against us when we started the 2004-2005 ABA season. First, Utah was a very good team. Number two, they were a difficult match up for our team in particular because we had no size and c) we weren't that good of a team at the beginning of the season, as we were still trying to figure out who we were.

After barely winning our first game of the year in Portland, we lost seven straight games and five of them were to Utah. Our effort level was terrible, we doubted ourselves and our point guard situation was a disaster. The final loss in this seven-game stretch was the worst.

We were scheduled to play three games in Visalia, CA against the StrongDawgs. This Visalia team was a total joke. They were 180 degrees different from the Utah organization. Everything that Utah did to operate within a professional atmosphere, Visalia did the opposite. Their players weren't paid, there was no marketing of the team and the people involved in their management were a tad shady at best. The good news for us was that they were terrible. They were winless in the season and it was an opportunity to get us back on track.

From Salt Lake City we flew to San Francisco, rented a van and drove to Visalia which is just south of Fresno, about a four-hour drive.

One problem though; our flight into SFO (the San Francisco Airport) was delayed. We would really have to hustle to get to Visalia. Once we arrived in San Francisco, we realized that the van we had rented was just not big enough to fit all of us in it. We would need to rent a second van but the only credit card I had was Blackmon's. The rental car company wouldn't allow me to rent another van with someone else's card (go figure). So we had to wait even longer while Blackmon tried to work it out from his apartment in Seattle. Luckily, this time, when we called Blackmon, he actually answered his phone. As we drove toward Visalia, me driving one van and Harold driving the other, the fog got thick and our speed was decreased dramatically because of it.

We were tired.

Tired of traveling all day, tired of being scrunched up in these vans for the past four plus hours and tired of losing. The game was scheduled to start at 7 p.m. but we didn't even arrive at the Visalia High School gym until 7:30. We unfolded out of the vans, went straight to the locker room and immediately dressed for the game. The ABA refs gave us 20 minutes to warm up and then we tipped off.

I came out of the locker room just before the opening buzzer sounded. I looked up in the stands where I counted three people in attendance. Those three people were Matt Glynn's parents and sister who drove down from their home in Sacramento to watch their son play "professional" basketball. Yet again, I was embarrassed for us. Although I knew that there was nothing I could do to control the organization of other teams around the league, I still wanted the ABA to be a great experience for my guys and something that they could be proud of. I can only imagine what Matt's parents must have thought as they entered the gym to the rhythms of N.W.A. encouraging us to "F*** Da Police".

This was the game that smacked me in the face regarding the perils of travel while competing. I've often heard coaches and the media use travel as an excuse for a team's lethargy at various times. Up until that point, I felt it rang hollow and was a little overstated.

At that point though, as we lost to Visalia that night by two; giving them their first (and I think only) victory of the year I actually realized the effects of traveling and the correlation it can have with player performance (or lack thereof). We had no legs, no energy and ultimately lost to a team that had no business competing in this league. It was the lowest point of the season as we dropped our seventh game in a row.

We had driven straight to the game without checking in at our hotel beforehand because of time constraints. When we finally got to the hotel after the game, we found out that the home team, the StrongDawgs, was not paying for the rooms as they were supposed to. As you can imagine, this sent Blackmon through the roof. We had to put the rooms on his credit card before we could check-in. After getting that whole mess worked out, we all went to bed pretty unhappy that night, tired and questioning everything.

We still had two more games to play in Visalia and a good night's sleep went a long way to turn some frowns upside down. We met that morning to go to shootaround only to find out that the Visalia team had no gym for us to practice in. We took advantage of their disorganization by relaxing, catching up on sleep and having a good team talk before we left for the gym at 5 p.m. and our second game with the StrongDawgs in as many nights. This time we were back on our routine, Harold and I tried to keep everything as professional as possible and to a man, our attitudes from the previous night seemed to be completely turned around.

As we got to the gym, I found out that the Visalia "owner" didn't want to pay for ABA referees. The league arrangement was that the officiating crews would be paid for in advance of each game and in cash. It cost each team about $900 per game. If this didn't happen, then the game would be forfeited by the home team. The team's owner was on his cell phone pleading his case to the league by saying that he could get local high school officials for half the price of an ABA crew. He also didn't think that three referees were necessary and that we could get by with just two (I agreed with that). They tried to pull me into the middle of it by saying I should make the decision. The Visalia owner wanted me to side with him and accept the two high school officials. The league wanted me to side with them and force Visalia to use the three ABA referees. I was placed in a real awkward position. The fact was, I didn't really care who reffed the games as long as they were experienced and professional. The bottom line was, we just wanted to play. We didn't incur the cost to go there for forfeits. After a while, with each party going back and forth, and everyone involved making threats to the other; the league finally agreed to make up the difference in cost and pay for their own ABA referees to do the game.

Not only had we lost to the worst team in the league the previous night, we had lost to a depleted worst team in the league. Two of their best players were not there for the first game but they would be there tonight for game two.

Harold and I decided that we would just get our best five players on the floor to start and forget about positions. The rotating door of point guards would stop, and we wouldn't worry about who could do what, and just let them play. That was the first game that we started Jimmy Haywood and Matt Glynn together. Each of whom had played the 2 (or off guard position) previously, but tonight they would share the point guard duties. They started along with Justin Murray at the 3 and Dontay Harris and Eric Sandrin sharing the 4 and 5 spots.

We went into the locker room at halftime of that second game in Visalia leading the StrongDawgs by 50 points. 50 points… AT HALFTIME! From that point on, we never really looked back.

We went on to reel off seven straight wins to get back over the .500 mark including wins against the LA Stars led by former NBA scoring leader, Cedric Ceballos and the defending ABA champs the Long Beach Jam, who were coached by former NBA great Nate "Tiny" Archibald and had a slew of former NBA players on their roster like Olden Polynice, Jelani McCoy and Felipe Lopez. In fact, we were the first team to ever beat Long Beach on their home floor and in doing so; we were also the first team to ever score 100 points against them.

January 8, 2005 - Blackhawks win seventh straight game, 110-99, over defending champs

(Long Beach, CA)—The ABA Bellevue Blackhawks mounted a balanced attack Friday night, with five players scoring in double figures, to extend their winning streak to seven straight games. Bellevue never trailed in posting a 110-99 victory over defending ABA champions, the Long Beach Jam, at the Pyramid.

Justin Murray (Washington State) led Bellevue with 21 points and 10 rebounds. Franklin High School's Jimmie Haywood tallied 18 points and 3 steals, while new-signee Alvin Snow (Eastern Washington University) added 16 points, 5 rebounds and 4 assists. The Blackhawks--who have posted victories over Visalia, Portland, Los Angeles, Long Beach and Fresno during their seven-game run--have proven to be road warriors, winning four in a row as the visitors, and moving their season record into plus-territory for the first time in the 2004-05 season at 8-7.

Head coach, Rick Turner, said, "We've played well over the past couple of weeks, but we know we can get better. This team is excited to take the court every night."

Bellevue hosts the Long Beach Jam next Thursday and Saturday, January 13th and 15th at Renton High School. Great seats are available at: (206) 686-4636, ext. 11, or www.Blackhawkshoops.com, www.abalive.com, www.gettix.net.

Alvin Snow was one of the guys that I had targeted to get on the roster before the season started. I had followed his high school and college careers and he was a winner wherever he went. He had been playing in Europe and had recently come back to the States because of some payment problems with his European team. Coincidently, we had an open spot on the roster.

Rashaad Powell had been injured for the first 11 games of the season and when he came back we tried to work him in slowly. He wasn't in basketball shape after two months off and we needed to integrate him with what we were doing. However, there was a disconnect with Rashaad and me that I never really understood.

If you remember, Rashaad was the first player that we signed back in October and I think he looked at this like he was the equivalent of a first round draft pick. I liked him (and still do), liked what he brought to our team and thought that he would be a very valuable piece to our success but he acted as if we owed him something. He was mad that he wasn't starting and he was mad that his close friend Justin Murray, who had never been as good as Rashaad before this point, had passed by him and was eating up some of his minutes. He pouted around for his first few games back and I understood that he felt a little frustrated. I also felt like he'd figure it out and get over it. After we beat Long Beach, we were all feeling great; our team was coming together and we were riding a high… except Rashaad. Watching him grouse around, with his chin in his soup, and mad at the world while WE had won seven straight games pissed me off to no end.

So I cut him.

Our winning streak ran to eight games before the aforementioned Long Beach Jam beat us at home in mid-January. This was the game that Jimmy Haywood missed because he was "visiting his sister" and despite the game itself being somewhat nondescript, that didn't mean Blackmon didn't provide some fireworks.

The Jam had built a 30-point lead in the second quarter but after halftime we came out with some pressure and cut their lead to just 5, late in the third. The emotions of the comeback had gotten the better of Blackmon as he tried to balance his passions for the team and his self-appointed duties as the PA announcer. Any time a team mounts a massive comeback, as we did in a game like that, emotions will run high on both sides. It is hard to come from that far back without playing with some emotion, and if you're on the other side of it, negative emotion perpetuates the comeback. As the game heated up, so did Blackmon's mouth. After a hard foul by Long Beach's power forward Maurice Spillers, Blackmon said something over the PA saturated in sarcasm toward "Big Mo" as he came to the bench. Spillers took exception to Blackmon's comment and before you knew what had happened, the 6'7" Spillers was being held back by his coach, Tiny Archibald as he yelled and pointed at Blackmon. Blackmon just laughed in his face while Spillers ranted. The safety of Spillers being held back, and the public surrounding him, made Blackmon feel like he was Mike Tyson incarnate. I venture to say that his faux bravery would have been a little less on display had the two been in a room alone.

As the situation continued, our semi-new operations guy that Blackmon had recently "hired" to help out at home games, Darren Wilson, tried to step in and defuse the situation. Darren wanted to try and protect Blackmon and not let it get any more out of hand. He stepped in and calmly spoke to Spillers, walking him back toward his bench and then he turned and said something innocuous but direct to Blackmon. Something to the effect of "Okay Mike, that's enough. It's over". Blackmon didn't take kindly to anyone talking to him like that, especially someone who, in his eyes, wasn't another adult but rather, just another lackey who worked for him and should treat him with a respect that he never afforded anyone himself.

Blackmon looked at Darren with an incredulous snarl. How dare he "embarrass" him like that?

"Get off my court, you f***ing midget" Blackmon snapped at Darren.

Darren got off the court. In fact, he immediately got off the court and out the door, never looking back.

The winning streak was over, our point guard was MIA and we now found ourselves without the only other employee that the team had. Just in time for our longest home stand of the year.

***

I received a phone call from the coach of the Calgary Drillers on a Saturday afternoon, the day before our scheduled game with them at Renton High School. Their coach told me that they would be getting in late that night and wouldn't need the gym for a shootaround in the morning. That was good because we didn't have a gym for them to shootaround in anyway. He told me though, that they would like to have an extra half hour before the game starts to meet and go over things and asked if it would be all right if they came in at 5 p.m. instead of 5:30, before the 7 p.m. game.

Normally, I would have just turned this over to Darren and he would have taken care of it. But now, without Darren, I'd have to make it happen myself. I called Blackmon and told him about Calgary's request. With some slight guilt about the way he handled himself the night previously with Maurice Spillers and the Long Beach Jam, he told me that he would make sure he was there for the Calgary team at 5 p.m. on Sunday. I didn't trust that he would follow through so I went there early myself.

I got to the gym at about 4:30 so I could get things organized for Calgary's early arrival. To my surprise, Blackmon showed up shortly thereafter. It was the only time he had shown up on time for anything... ever.

For the first time all season, we arrived at the Renton HS gym and no one else was there. It was dark, empty and all locked up. Normally the high school teams used the gym before our games or the athletic director was there to open things up for us. This day, it was dark and locked. Neither one of us knew how to get ahold of the athletic director nor were we sure if there had been a mix up in scheduling. It was a Sunday afternoon and there was no one in sight. Without Darren there, we had no idea what to do.

Blackmon walked around to the front of the building and I stayed in the back looking in windows for a janitor and calling around on my cell phone to try and find someone who could help. I was on my phone with my face pressed up against a window, peering in, when I heard the squealing of car tires. I turned around to see three Renton police cars with lights on but no sirens come screaming into the parking lot behind me. I was immediately startled.

I remained with one hand holding the phone to my ear and my other hand in my front pocket trying to stay warm on the cold January night. Two of the cops shielded themselves behind their opened doors while the third, cautiously approached me with his hand on his gun.

"Drop your phone and let me see your hands immediately" the cop yelled to me.

"I'll call you back..." I quickly flipped my phone off and raised both my hands.

The officer continued with his hand on his weapon, "Are you Michael Blackmon?"

Senses of relief, coupled with excitement on how this would unfold, and a 'here we go again' frustration assaulted me simultaneously.

"Umm…no…" I nervously stuttered.

"Where's Michael Blackmon?" the cop urgently asked me

"I think he's around the front trying to find a janitor."

"Are you the one making calls to 911 threatening to blow up the building if someone doesn't come to let you in?"

"No, not me" I implored. "There's Michael Blackmon right there.." I pointed as he came around from the side of the building.

The Renton police officers converged on Blackmon and placed him in the back of one of the squad cars. Simultaneous to all of these events happening, a big beautiful bus with the words Calgary Drillers painted on the side of it came pulling into the Renton High School parking lot for their 5 p.m. shootaround. Right behind them was the Renton High School athletic director who was getting to the gym a half hour early because he thought he was supposed to be there to open the gym at 5:30.

I thought for sure we'd get a break from our nightmare PA announcer that night as Blackmon was being fingerprinted and photographed at the Renton Police Station, before his arraignment on attempted domestic terrorism, but we would have no such luck. Somehow, as Blackmon always seemed to do, he talked his way out of the back of the police car and was there, behind the microphone, to fully embarrass us one more time.

After introducing both teams he asked the fans to rise and help honor our Canadian guests and join him in signing the Canadian National anthem…

Everyone stood. It wasn't a great crowd but it wasn't our worst either.

"Oh Can-a-da…" he poorly busted out the first line of the well-known anthem of our friends to the north. He then predictably, forgot the rest of the words.

"…blah, blah, blah, blah, blah….let's just play basketball."

***

Being around Blackmon on a daily basis was essentially immersing yourself in complete chaos at every moment. Friends and family would ask me how I could stand it. They would tell me to get away from it and expressed their concern that his stink would end up on me. I have to admit though, the constant drama, while not comforting for most; it was strangely comfortable for me to operate in.

Very early on in our relationship, it was evident that Blackmon was full of crap and that you just couldn't trust the things he said to be true. Once I had lowered my expectations of him to the appropriate level, it was difficult for him to let me down, and soon his antics became somewhat entertaining.

He had a compulsion to lie. I'm not trying to make a diagnosis. I'm not saying he's a compulsive liar or a pathological liar in clinical terms but part of the entertainment value that he provided for me was the anticipation of what BS story would come out of his mouth next. He made various claims about his past. None of which I could ever confirm to be true nor did I really care to. It didn't matter to me. I just figured most of them were lies.

From Blackmon's own Wikipedia page:

> *Educated at the University of Oregon, Blackmon is an attorney who represented several San Francisco 49ers players in the 1980s. In 1989, he authored the national bestseller, The San Francisco 49ers: Team of the Decade. In 1992, Blackmon served as Chairman of the Facilities Committee on San Francisco Mayor Frank Jordan's Blue Ribbon Task Force on Sports, a panel that also included San Francisco 49ers Presidetn (sic) and CEO, Carmen Policy, and former San Francisco Warriors center Nate Thurmond. That year he was also named as Chairman of the Giants Stadium Committee, which was organized to build a new ballpark for the San Francisco Giants. In 1993, Blackmon was part of a private consortium led by Safeway Chairman Peter Magowan that bought the San Francisco Giants from MLB in 1993 and built the privately-owned AT&T Park*

There is probably a sliver of truth in much of this but I know that most of it is extremely and highly exaggerated.

What was funny to me though, was how he would lie to people about things that were totally inconsequential and completely random to what was happening at the time. They would just be flat out lies that had nothing to do with anything. Two of those moments jump to mind immediately.

One time we had a meeting at Entercom Radio in Seattle who had four or five AM and FM stations locally. The purpose of the meeting was to buy time on the stations to market our team. The only problem was that Blackmon didn't have any money for this. We walked into the conference room with Blackmon holding a red, white and blue ABA basketball and an autographed (by him) team jersey to give to the salesman. I asked myself why were we giving this guy gifts when he was trying to sell us something? If anything, he should be giving us gifts. That was how Blackmon was though. Kind of oblivious to protocol and roaming through life as an imposter, not really knowing how to conduct himself in various professional settings.

As we sat in the meeting, Blackmon and the salesman got to talking and realized that they knew someone in common. Normally I would just tune out at this point, but what made this strange, was that the person they were talking about was a woman who Blackmon had introduced to me once, the first time he and I got together to discuss the coaching position at a Mercer Island Starbucks. We were sitting outside Sturbucks on the sidewalk as she unexpectedly walked by. Blackmon introduced me to Jami as a longtime friend of his (and nothing more).

So as we sat in the conference room, and the two of them discovered that they both knew Jami, Blackmon blurted out something that made no sense. It was unimportant, unnecessary and unneeded in driving the conversation forward. Albeit innocuous, it was inconsequential at every level.

Blackmon told the salesman that Jami was his ex-wife!

WHY??? Blackmon had been a lifelong bachelor. Never married, never engaged, and at the time, no significant girlfriend.

So many other things he could've said about their relationship that would never be provable. But now the next time this guy saw Jami, he could say "Hey, I met your ex-husband…" (which he later went on to do). Blackmon continued on by launching into inappropriate details about their divorce, the fact that they remained friends and other pieces of just made up stuff. This was the first time that I started thinking that he might be legitimately a little crazy. It's one thing to lie in order to cover yourself. Like saying that it wasn't you who left the toilet seat up. But it's entirely another, to just make up a random lie that has no bearing on the conversation. It would be like you asking me what kind of pizza I ate last night and me telling you that it was pepperoni, even though it was cheese. Utterly unimportant.

This helped cement in my mind that I could never trust anything that he said. And when I say "anything" I literally mean "anything". It helped me to lower my expectations of him and let's face it; most bad relationships can be traced to two people having misplaced expectations. It also prepared me for another one of his bombshell doozies.

By February of the 2004/2005 season, Blackmon claimed to have a girlfriend named Betty. Even though I never met her, he spoke of her often, and I was pretty sure that she existed. However, I didn't really know the real extent of their relationship. Were they actually dating? Were they just friends? Was it serious or casual? Or was it completely made up (which still remained a possibility)?

This other "bombshell doozy" happened after Blackmon disappeared one week. Coincedently, it coressponded with all of us needing to get paid. When I say disappeared, I mean he was completely off the grid and no one was able to get a hold of him. The guys (including me) wanted their pay checks and Blackmon wasn't answering his phone, his email or even the doorbell of his apartment. Finally, after about four or five days of unsuccessful attempts to contact him… he called me back. I was expecting him to be pretty pissy when he called because he knew we wanted to be paid. Therefore, I was unusually upbeat when I answered.

"Hello…" I answered my cell, knowing who it was on the other end and bringing my voice up an octave to feign a friendly tone.

"Hey Rick, it's Mike."

"Hey, where you been? Is everything alright?" I asked, even though I knew he was avoiding us so he wouldn't have to write our checks.

"It's been a rough couple days. Betty's daughter committed suicide on Saturday" he told me, trying to land a sympathy rabbit punch to the side of the head. But I'd have none of it, and ducked before it could knock me silly.

For better or worse, I knew he was full of crap. In hindsight, I can't believe that my instincts were so callous. It's not normally the type of thing that someone would lie about. I mean, is that bad karma or what? Who would do that? But I knew who. However, I didn't want him to know that I knew, so I just responded like it was a little game that we were playing between ourselves.

"Oh my God! I am so sorry… Is there anything you need? Is there anything that I can do for you or Betty? That's terrible Mike. Take your time and just call me back when you get things settled."

I'm not at all good at expressing genuine emotion so just think how difficult it was for me to express fake, genuine emotion.

"No, I know I owe you guys money. I'll get down there with checks later today."

He showed up at our practice to hand out checks. He sure didn't look like a guy who was grieving but everyone is different I guess. Over the next few days I would ask him how Betty was coping with everything, feigning my concern, and knowing that the only thing she was coping with was dating him.

The next Monday, Blackmon came by practice…

"Hey Mike, how was your weekend?"

"It was pretty good. Sunday night I went to a movie with Betty and her daughter."

I never said a word…

***

None of us with the team knew from one day to the next what would happen. I did my best to insulate the players from any of the day-to-day drama but it was impossible to shield them from all of it. It was one thing after another with personnel, scheduling and getting paid on time or at all.

From a personnel stand point, it took a while for us to finally come up with the right group of guys to compete with. We were dealt a blow at the All-Star break when the Harlem Globetrotters poached the two leading scorers from our roster and signed Eric Sandrin and Lovell Brown. I cut Rashaad Powell, Greg Hendrix, Eddie George and Chris Baert from our opening day roster so there was a huge amount of turnover for us in a short amount of time. From day one, I wanted to have Alvin Snow on the team, but as soon as he joined us, midway through the season, it was easily apparent that he wasn't going to fit in. I cut him following the All-Star game in Vegas after only four games with us. We got lucky shortly after that when two other guys that I had targeted from day one, contacted us and expressed their interest in joining the team.

After losing Sandrin and Brown to the Globetrotters, as well as cutting Alvin Snow and an injury to Jackie Jones, we were down to six players and facing a monster road trip where we would play four games in five days against Texas, Arkansas, Kansas City and then back to Arkansas; all by bus. To make matters worse, we hadn't been paid.

We had gone through these payment lapses a number of times throughout the season, which included a complete player revolt at one point in December when the players got together and threatened to quit in unison unless they got paid immediately. Somehow Blackmon was able to turn the tables on them when he took the offensive and threatened to fire them all before they could quit. Amazingly and in disbelief, he had them apologizing to him for not getting paid. I came away scratching my head over that one, but it continued over the next couple months and even when we were getting paid, checks were bouncing.

Harold, Russ and I would plug one hole in the dike and another would spring open. The players felt used and disrespected. As coaches, we tried to have them look at the situation differently. We appealed to their professionalism and competitiveness. We started to develop a bunker mentality of 'us' against the world (or at least us against Blackmon) and this ongoing drama only pulled us closer together. We tried to make the players look at what a likely scenario would be if they quit. Most would have no where else to go. Not that late in the season. There were little, if any, opportunities to hook on with another team. They knew that if they ever held out any hope of getting the money that was owed them; they would never get it if they quit. None of them had contracts and we knew that Blackmon had no money anyway.

As for the coaches, Russ was a volunteer because he didn't want to feel tied to Blackmon in any way. Harold got his money upfront in October, and I just wanted to coach so I wasn't going to let money get in the way of the job. One of our players however, would get word from a higher authority.

We were to fly to Dallas, play the Texas Tycoons, and then go on to Little Rock before getting a bus for the rest of our Midwest road trip. We had the red-eye flight out of Seattle to DFW at 11 p.m. Blackmon decided to come on the trip, which took much of the pressure off of me for meals, transportation and many of the other little details that comes with moving a dozen people in the same direction, using only guile and someone else's credit card.

We were to meet at Sea-Tac airport at 9 p.m. At 10:30 Dontay Harris still wasn't there. Dontay was our most productive "big" now that Sandrin was gone, but more importantly, he was kind of the heartbeat of our team. He had an attitude and swagger that exceeded his ability which made him better than he really was. He backed down from nobody and made us a 'tougher' team. He never got in a fight during a game but he seemed to be in a lot of altercations and nose-to-nose discussions with opponents. But when it came to his life at home, Dontay was a pushover. I say that in the best way possible. He was a caring father but his wife absolutely held the hammer. When he came home from our last practice before the road trip without the check that he had been promised; Mrs. Dontay Harris put her foot down.

Dontay never called us to say he wasn't going to be at Sea-Tac airport for the trip that night. It was either because he didn't want to get talked into coming, or his wife wouldn't let him use the phone, regardless "Tay" was a total no show. This left us with five players from our original roster. Luckily, I was able to add some valuable ammo right before the trip.

Remember how I mentioned Brian "Yogi" Dennis earlier as a guy I really wanted to get? He was the 6'6", 300lb, long-armed, shot-blocker and excellent defender who was just a bit undersized to play at a higher level.

Well, we were finally able to "sign" Yogi the day before we left for Dallas.

I put "sign" in quotes because these guys never really signed anything, we just added him to the roster. As much as I loved Yogi as a player, he was out of shape (300+ pounds) and he didn't have a single practice with us before we played. He would have to play his way into shape. I also signed a little point guard named Ricky Frazier who I always liked when he was in high school at nearby Rainier Beach High School and Shoreline CC in Seattle. However, he was out of shape also.

We got lucky though when we were able to add the final player on my preseason wish list, two-guard Tim Ellis.

Tim was a teammate of Ricky Frazier's at Rainier Beach High School but he went on to play at Kansas State where he had a nice if un-spectacular career. Tim had been playing for the Yakima Sunkings in the CBA before he was released by them and thus he became available for us right before the trip. With the addition of these three players, we were able to go to Texas with eight guys, not knowing what to expect, but just trying to remain competitive without the bulk of our scoring punch and not knowing how to replace it.

We went 0-4 on the trip but during this time, we discovered a go-to scorer, a presence in the middle and a team identity that we had searched for most of the year. During the four-game trip, our new off-guard Tim Ellis went for 36 against Texas, 46 against Arkansas, 25 vs. KC and another 42 vs. Arkansas. We played three solid franchises who were also three of the best teams in the league. Yogi made an immediate impact defensively in limited minutes because of his conditioning, but we knew that would get better quickly. Although we lost all four games, we knew we had the ability to compete with any of those teams. I mentioned that a month earlier in Visalia we played in front of three people (Matt Glynn's parents and sister); well, in Little Rock we played in front of 11,000 and 8,500 spectators in two games. Texas and Kansas City drew nearly 2,000 fans per game. The highlights were on the local newscasts and there were articles about the games in the local papers. This attention had a way of energizing us and showing our players that they weren't just playing in a myopic vacuum.

In the ABA, it was hit-and-miss from one city to the next regarding what to expect. Some teams were very well run and some just were not. The level of play exceeded my expectations, but the organizations themselves fell far short of what I had experienced in the NBA or even in minor league baseball.

The recent resurrection of the ABA, at that time in 2005, was still so new that there were many great players who wanted to play in the league instead of trying their luck overseas. It was a chance to stay closer to home as well as a chance for that elusive NBA phone call. It wasn't until after that 2004-2005 season that quality players started to wise up as to what was really happening around the league.

There was no doubt that teams were stumbling to the finish line as the season wound down. Blackmon's strategy of just surviving to the end actually paid off, as the wheat slowly separated from the chaff coming down that home stretch. The high cost of travel meant many teams were only willing to play home games, and thus we became road warriors because teams wouldn't travel to Seattle for our home games. We played 26 games that season but only five were at home. Blackmon used our willingness to travel to the Midwest, California, Nevada and Utah as leverage when it came down to seeding teams for the playoffs. The ABA didn't use standings to determine playoff seeds; they used power rankings, which essentially meant it was a popularity contest.

Despite our 10-16 record, Blackmon lobbied "Connie" Joe Newman to include Bellevue in the 2005 ABA playoffs. His nagging persistence and steady stream of BS finally paid off and the commissioner awarded us a number 13 seed in the 16-team end of year tournament. We played 21 of our 26 games played on the road. Nine of our 16 losses came at the hands of a 29-1 Utah team (we were 0-9 against Utah!!!). Blackmon convinced the league officials that we were much better than our record. He was right, but I don't think he really even believed it himself as he tried to pitch it to Newman.

Whatever the case, we made the playoffs as the #13 seed and we would head back to Dallas for a rematch with the #4 seed, the Texas Tycoons.

The field was set for the 16-team playoffs.

(16) St. Louis Flight at (1) Utah Snowbears

(15) Ontario Warriors at (2) Arkansas Rimrockers

(14) Tijuana Dragons at (3) Mississippi Stingers

(13) BELLEVUE BLACKHAWKS at (4) Texas Tycoons

(12) New Jersey Skycats at (5) Maryland Nighthawks

(11) Orange County Buzz at (6) Kansas City Knights

(10) Kentucky Colonels at (7) Harlem Strong Dogs

(9) Las Vegas Rattlers at (8) Long Beach Jam

8

Maryland

Blackmon represented himself to all of us as a millionaire. I knew better but many of our players bought right into it. This was in part, I think, because they wanted for him to be that wealthy. It started to be more and more obvious that our team was being backed by other people. Blackmon would go days without being able to pay us then, he'd write us all checks. Some would cash, some would bounce. I figured that he had to continue to go back and get more money from someone to put in the bank account. He had a slew of credit cards that he would give me throughout the season to buy meals and various incidentals. After one card no longer worked, he would give me another. I told him that I didn't have my own credit card because I knew he would want me to use it with the promise of being reimbursed later; a promise that I knew he could not deliver.

He would often give me a handful of blank checks that he would sign and tell me to give out to players later. It was my guess that Blackmon found investors for the team by convincing them that an ABA sale, or merger with the NBA and its minor league equivalent called the NBDL or "D-League" was imminent and their "small" investment could be worth much, much more if that happened. The cold economics of minor league basketball coupled with the fact that the NBA had no interest in, nor did they need the ABA; made the promise of a merger nothing more than a pipe dream. But Blackmon was smart enough to know that successful venture capital people did not invest in pipe dreams, so he embellished his pitch enough to at least get us off the ground.

I don't know how much cash he started with, but I heard from somewhere that he got about $50,000 from a couple of "friends". I think he told them that he was putting in money of his own as well, but the problem was it seemed as if he didn't have any of his own money to put in. In fact, my theory was that the investment that Rob and Peter put into the team was Blackmon's only income, and therefore, the only money he had to his name. Not only did he use it to run the team as best he could, but he also used it for his own personal expenses.

I can't say for fact that this is true. I have extrapolated much of it from my own observations and conversations throughout that time period. It's just a theory based on what I saw and experienced. Actually, it doesn't matter to me how or where his money came from. It is probably a discussion more suited for the IRS, the State Attorney General or Dateline NBC, but I use it as background to help explain how things got so crazy.

By the time the playoffs came around, I think Blackmon was just about (if not completely) out of money. He asked me to call American Airlines and make flight reservations for us to go to Dallas. Blackmon told me that he couldn't make the trip, but he would come to the airport to see us off and pay for the tickets. Somehow he was able to talk Dontay's wife into letting him rejoin the team. I'm sure he made a promise about money that he later reneged on, but like another Don James-ism goes, "don't tell me how rough the water is, just show me the boat". I didn't really care how or why Dontay was there, I was just happy to have him back.

So for the trip to Dallas we had: Haywood, Glynn and Ellis in the backcourt. Justin Murray and Yogi were up front. We had Dontay coming off the bench (because he left us for a few days I didn't start him). Along with Bunchy, we had newly added local product Jimmie Rainwater and then Jajuan Winesberry rounded out the nine-man roster. Rickey Frazier's lack of basketball shape led to a severely sprained ankle during our long road trip, so he was left off the roster. Plus, he tried to hit on Harold's ex-wife at a club when we returned to town but that's another story altogether.

This time we had an early afternoon flight to Dallas. When we got to the airport, we checked in as a group. Blackmon called to let us know that he was on his way and decided that he wanted to go now as well. He asked me to book him a ticket. I asked the American Airlines agent if we could add a seat and she replied that our flight was booked, but Blackmon could get on another flight that would land only an hour later than ours in Dallas. I called him back to let him know about the flight. For whatever reason, he didn't like this scenario.

"I'M NOT GOING TO F***ING FLY SEPARETELY FROM MY F***ING BASKETBALL TEAM!!! GET THIS F***ING SH** FIXED OR NO ONE WILL BE GOING!!!" he politely explained before we somehow got disconnected.

"Uh-oh" I thought to myself. "I don't think he has the money for us to go and he's looking for an excuse."

At the airport Blackmon strutted slowly up to the ticket counter with his head cocked to one side and his nose turned slightly up. He was wearing his brown loafers with no socks, tight blue jeans and a navy blue v-neck sweater with a white t-shirt underneath. He carried a small travel bag in one hand with a garment bag flung over his shoulder in the other. When he saw me he had a big smile on his face and any thought of our previous conversation minutes earlier were nonexistent, as if it never happened. The team was all checked in pending payment and Blackmon reached into his back pocket for his wallet to pull out the card du jour.

Would it be a Visa today?

Or maybe AmEx?

Ahh... neither one. This time it was a MasterCard. The American Airlines agent swiped Blackmon's card and waited... and waited. There must be problems with that machine. She went to try another. A few minutes passed and she came back.

"I'm sorry Mr. Blackmon, do you have another card? For some reason this one's not working."

At this point, I walked away. In part because I was embarrassed for Blackmon and in part because I cringed about what might come next. Russ, Yogi, Matt Glynn and I watched from behind. Blackmon remained calm as the silent movie played out in front of us just a few feet away. He smiled, cajoled, laughed and pleaded his case to the agent. He reached into his front pocket, pulled out a checkbook and started writing. He carefully tore the check off its binding and handed it to the agent. I was quickly summoned to come and pick up the boarding passes. I grabbed the passes as the conversation turned now to Blackmon's own ticket. The agent was trying to be helpful as she explained there were no seats on our flight, but that another was leaving shortly thereafter and the two would land less then an hour apart.

"That's completely unacceptable..." I heard him say as I walked away to hand out the boarding passes to the players.

The guys were somewhat spread out around the departure area as I tried to keep one eye on Blackmon and another on my task at hand. I was flipping through boarding cards looking for "Haywood" when I heard it. Well actually, we all heard it. In fact, I think the entire airport heard it.

"GODDAMMIT YOU F***ING C(see you next Tuesday). PUT ME ON THAT GODDAMN PLANE!!!"

All heads turned as Blackmon stood there red faced with veins popping from his v-neck. Within seconds, two Port of Seattle police officers and two TSA agents converged on Blackmon. They immediately escorted him from the area with one cop on each arm, parading him in front of our players, and every other passenger trying to check in at the time. I'm so pissed at myself because Justin Murray had the wherewithal to snap a picture of Blackmon's police escort from the airport on his cell phone. He emailed me the picture but somehow over the years I've lost it. I would LOVE to able to share that with you.

At that point I guessed he wouldn't be coming to Dallas. Somehow, despite the histrionics, before he was forcibly removed from the premises... somehow, he convinced the American Airlines ticketing agent to take a personal check for 11 passengers to fly from Seattle to Dallas. I don't know how he did it. And I still can't believe it. Not only was it a check for at least I figured $3000 or maybe even $4000, but it was a check without an address on it like most checks you see. In the upper left hand corner it was blank, like the type of check the bank gives you before they mail you the real ones. I'm 99.9% certain that his check to American Airlines bounced but somehow he did it. We were on our way to Dallas and the 2005 ABA playoffs.

***

When we landed in Dallas, I turned my cell phone on and found a voicemail from Blackmon. It was good news. He told me that Lovell Brown had left the Globetrotters and wanted to come back for the playoffs. He was putting him on a flight so he would get there later that night. Lovell was our best outside threat. He was a little streaky, but when he got going, he could REALLY get hot. He could make a big impact for us off the bench.

The next day we had a late shootaround, so I let the guys sleep in if they wanted. We would go to the gym and then meet later for a pre-game meal, nap and then the game itself. Lovell arrived with no problems and the 12 of us (10 players plus Russ and me... Harold was stuck at home because of his 'real' job) stuffed ourselves into the van for the 40-minute drive to Fort Worth. It was an uncomfortable ride as the players were folded up and stuffed into this white van like pork in sausage casing. When they decided to call them "12-passenger" vans, they must have used fourth grade girls as their point of reference because 6' 8"-plus men would have dramatically reduced that number to something like "6-passenger". It was okay as long as there were good stories going around or music to keep their mind off of how uncomfortable they were; but as soon as it got silent in there, it was tough. This trip we were pumping Ludicris and the Red Light District CD. We (okay, they) were bouncing to "Pimpin' All Over the World" as we rolled into the parking lot.

Everyone unfolded out of the van and headed inside to get loose. I brought us all together and spoke briefly. I don't like to spend too much time talking. I got our first five out on the floor (Matt, Jimmie, Tim, Justin and Yogi) to walk through some things. I was focused on what we were doing on the floor and didn't notice Lovell walk over to the side and sit down. When I finally did see him sitting over there I didn't think much about it. I figured he needed tape, or a drink of water, or something else completely innocuous. I called over to him to sub in go over some of our game plan for later that night. He said no. I thought that maybe he was feeling sick so I just moved on. After a few minutes, I went over to see what was up.

"You okay?" I asked him

"I didn't come back here to sit." He muttered back to me

I was flabbergasted. I didn't know how to respond.

Incredulously, I pushed out a "Huh?"

"I didn't come back to this team to sit on the bench and not start" he came back at me with a petulance that I'd never seen or heard from him before.

Again, I was shocked. I didn't want to make a scene but my first instinct was to absolutely rip his ass right then and there in front of everyone. A bunch of feelings were coursing through me. Disappointment, anger, confusion, disappointment, disbelief and disappointment were fighting each other to win. I felt like I was being Punk'd and Ashton Kutcher would come walking out at any minute laughing his head off. We were just hours before our biggest game of the year and this dumb ass was putting it all in jeopardy because he wasn't in the starting line-up??? We hadn't seen him for a month, he had no idea of the new plays we were running, and it was his job to integrate himself with us… not our job to integrate ourselves to him. "Was he that stupid?" I asked myself. "This can't be real".

The mental psyche of a team can be very fragile at times. We didn't need a distraction like this to bring us down. Everyone liked Lovell and this seemed totally out of character to me and everyone else. I wondered what the heck happened to him while he was with the Globetrotters because this wasn't the Lovell Brown that I knew.

Just to clarify where much of my disbelief came from… if a coach hasn't already told you this somewhere along the line… It doesn't matter who starts a game, it matters who finishes. The only thing good about being in the starting lineup is that you get to be introduced in front of everyone and have your name called out on the microphone during the pre-game introductions. To me, if that is important to you, then you're just selfish. It's meaningless beyond that.

Rather than fight it out right there in front of everyone, and possibly create an awkwardness that we didn't need, I decided to just walk away from him. I remained on a slow steam for the next several hours, trying to figure out how to handle this in a way that wouldn't compromise our ability to compete and win tonight, or further down the road. I spoke to Russ about it. I called Harold, who couldn't make the trip because of his full-time job at home, and I called Blackmon. I had limited options.

I could bring Lovell off the bench and just hope that he turned his frown upside down. But I ran the risk of him not being able to do that, while at the same time, letting the other guys see that there are no repercussions for acting like a prick. At the same time, I wanted to send a message that it was important for me to stick up for team . I wanted them to know that I wouldn't allow Lovell to treat them (or me) like that.

I could more or less 'suspend' him for the game and have him not suit up. My fear with this was that he would just be a downer to everyone and create an unneeded distraction for a team whose season would be over if we lost this game.

I could also give in and let him start. This is what Blackmon wanted me to do. He couldn't understand either, why Lovell wasn't starting. This wasn't going to happen, so that option was out.

After considerable consternation, I settled on a fourth option.

I sent him home.

I put him on a hotel shuttle van, put him on the phone with Blackmon to figure out the details and sent him back to the airport. We had more important things to worry about than Lovell Brown's ego and I didn't want our team to have any distractions.

Blackhawks upset Tycoons, 101-94

March 11, 2005 - American Basketball Association (ABA)

Dallas, TX - The Bellevue Blackhawks professional basketball team mounted a balanced attack with five players scoring in double figures - led by guard Tim Ellis' 42 points - in upsetting the heavily-favored #4 seeded Texas Tycoons in the first round of the ABA playoffs on the Tycoons home court in Fort Worth. Bellevue, the 13th seeded team, led at halftime, 48-44, opened up a ten point lead in the third quarter, and held on for a 101-94 victory. Chris Davis led the Tycoons with 23 points.

The Blackhawks roster included all local players, Jimmie Haywood (Franklin High School/Oregon State), Justin Murray (Washington State Univ.), Matt Glynn (University of Puget Sound), and Dontay Harris of Tacoma, each chipped in eleven points; Brian Dennis (Western Washington University) grabbed eight rebounds, including two crucial offensive boards in the last two minutes of the game. Glynn led the victors with seven assists.

I called Blackmon after the game to give him the news on the win and he went wild with excitement; yelling and screaming on the phone, praising me and wanting all the details. He always wanted to be Eddie DeBartolo and this would be as close as he would come. It was actually fun to see how happy he was about our win despite all of the BS we had put up with over the past few months. I couldn't help but share in his enjoyment of the moment. There was also some funny irony; that if not for his airport meltdown of a couple days earlier, he would be there in Dallas to share in this fun with us. I couldn't help but think that maybe he would learn his lesson about acting like such a jerk toward people, but I quickly came to my senses and realized that it would have no impact at all. Our next game would be a week and a half later just outside of DC against the Maryland Nighthawks.

Blackmon, more or less, forced me to take back Lovell once we got back to Seattle but I wouldn't do it until he first apologized to the team. I didn't need his apology myself. I got one however, but to me he had already been exposed. An empty apology wouldn't repair the betrayal that I felt by him, but I figured if the other guys didn't care, I wouldn't stand in the way of his return. I put them in a room together and walked out leaving them to figure it out among themselves. I don't know what Lovell said in that meeting and I don't know what the team said. I never asked and didn't really care. They all seemed satisfied to move on and Lovell rejoined us for our trip to Maryland.

During the week leading up to the game, the #1 seeded Utah Snowbears had defeated the defending champions, the Long Beach Jam. In the aftermath of that win, there was a dispute between Joe Newman and Utah Owner/Coach Ike Austin. I think it had something to do with where the championship game would be played. The league wanted Arkansas to host it. The Arkansas RimRockers had already played their way into the championship and they were averaging nearly 10,000 fans per game for the playoffs. It was a better location for the league. Ike Austin however, thought the top seeded team (his) should be rewarded by hosting the game.

Whether it was that dispute, or the speculation that Ike ran out of money, or something entirely different; Utah quit the playoffs after playing just one game. That meant that the winner of the Bellevue/Maryland game would not have to play Utah and instead they would go straight to Little Rock to play the Arkansas RimRockers for the ABA title.

***

The Maryland Nighthawks were coached by former Harlem Globetrotter James "Twiggy" Sanders, who to me, was a basketball legend. He performed with the 'Trotters for 17 years. I remembered him vividly and fondly from when I was a kid who loved the team. We didn't have much information about the Nighthawks beyond some phone calls that I had made to other coaches who had played them. There was very limited scouting ability throughout the league, as teams were not required to share videotapes of games and none of the games were on TV. We were flying blind although I had heard that the Maryland coaches were in Dallas scouting our game a week earlier. So I think they knew a bit more about us than we did about them.

I've never wanted to be too dramatic in pre-game speeches. The problem is that you run the risk of constantly having to one-up yourself from one game to the next. I preferred to pick my spots. I have always tried to be economical with my words in hopes that they would be worth more when I did need to use them (if that makes any sense). A "less is more" approach, I guess. In this game, I wanted to lighten the mood in our pre-game talk because I could see that we were unusually tense, but at the same time, try to get a point across. I thought of something that I figured was just dumb enough to accomplish both.

There has been an ongoing rivalry in our area for quite some time between Seattle players in the 206 area code and the Tacoma players in the 253 area code. In fact, many think that it was so bad at the University of Washington in the early 2000s that it ultimately might have cost Head Coach Bob Bender his job. The Seattle guys and the Tacoma guys on his team just couldn't get along. We didn't have that problem even though we had Matt, Dontay, Justin and Jujuan from T-town and Haywood, Tim, Rainwater and Lovell from Seattle.

I wanted to emphasize to our players that we were doing what everyone said couldn't be done. We were winning with a bunch of local no-namers that no one else wanted. We were the rejects who finished under .500 and didn't belong here. We were the guys who everyone said weren't good enough. (Shh… I was exaggerating but they didn't have to know that). I was feeding our "us against the world" mentality. I wrote one thing on the white board for them when they came in for our pre-game talk. I wrote the number 884.

With about 15:00 left on the clock, the players came in to the locker room from their pre-game warm-ups. Glowing with sweat, they sat down in front of their lockers. They were ready. I could see it. I pointed at the number 884 and didn't say a word.

I grabbed the red marker, took the cap off and above the number 884 I wrote 206 and then I pointed at Tim and Haywood and Lovell and Rainwater.

Then I turned back to the white board and scribbled + 253 next to it and pointed at Matt, Jujuan, Justin and Dontay while still not uttering a word.

I then added +425 and pointed at Yogi and Coach Russ (this was Russ' and my area code, a Seattle suburb).

Then I added an = sign next to all three and silently circled 884…

I stuck my hand out and said "let's go". Everyone smiled. They knew what I was trying to say. They all jumped up and put their hands in the middle. I thought it was the dumbest thing I'd ever done but these guys totally ate it up.

Blackhawks advance with upset

March 23, 2005 - American Basketball Association (ABA)

Upper Marlboro, MD. The 13th-seeded Bellevue Blackhawks upset the 5th-seeded Maryland Nighthawks Tuesday night at Showplace Arena in suburban Maryland, 133-120, to win the second national semifinal game of the American Basketball Association (ABA) playoffs. Bellevue will play the Arkansas Rimrockers Saturday night in Little Rock to determine the 2004-2005 ABA champion. Arkansas defeated the Mississippi Stingers last Friday in the first national semifinal game.

Bellevue turned in another balanced performance, with four players scoring at least 20 points, and two players posting double-doubles. Former Franklin High School star point guard Jimmie Haywood scored 24 points and tallied 10 assists, while former Mt. Tahoma High School forward Dontay Harris had 26 and 11 rebounds. Former Rainier Beach High School shooting guard Tim Ellis tossed in a team-leading 27 points to go along with 9 rebounds and 7 assists, and guard Lovell Brown came off the bench to chip in with 20 points. Brown, an ABA All-Star in February, returned to the Blackhawks roster after a stint with the Harlem Globetrotters.

Former Syracuse University star Lawrence Moten paced Maryland with a spectacular 41 points, including six 3-pointers and 13 for 13 shooting from the charity stripe. Jason Williams tallied 23 points on 10 of 15 shooting and had 10 rebounds while Dennis Edwards chipped in 21 points.

Thirty-six teams played in three divisions in the ABA during the 2004-2005 regular season. Sixteen teams qualified for the post-season playoff tournament, and now two are left: Bellevue and Arkansas. Coach Rick Turner stated, "Our travel the last month has been amazing going from the Northwest to Texas, Arkansas, Maryland - and back. We're travel weary, but we're well seasoned and are ready to give the Arkansas Rimrockers a very competitive game. And as they say, it's not over till the fat lady sings."

Let me say just one thing about that press release. It was written by Blackmon (poorly I might add) and I never uttered that quote. It isn't uncommon for someone who writes a press release to attribute a quote to someone that isn't actually their own, but usually they don't make the person look like a dumb ass by saying something like 'It's not over until the fat lady sings'...

Other than the quote, winning that game was a lot of fun and it was even a little more special because of how Lovell responded. He had 20 points off the bench and was a huge, huge spark for us. I was really proud of him and (obviously) happy that he was able to rejoin the team. Without him, we would not have won that game.

***

The ABA Championship game would be played four days later in Little Rock, Arkansas at the Alltel Arena, against the league's number two seed, the Arkansas RimRockers. The RimRockers had found a formula that worked and they were the model franchise in the league. Their roster was laden with former University of Arkansas Razorback greats like Todd Day, Scotty Thurmond, Oliver Miller, Kareem

Reid and others sprinkled in with some other very good players like Brian Jackson from Oregon State University.

The players on their team had a total of 1,034 games played in the NBA. Our roster had 0 games played in the NBA. Because of the passionate Razorback fans in the Little Rock area, they came out to support the team, and averaged about 8,000 fans per game during the regular season. We averaged about 32 fans per game. It was run like an NBA team, played in an NBA-style arena, with a support staff that was very professional. The difference between playing there and playing at a place like Visalia High School was like going from playing Guitar Hero on your couch one night to playing lead for Van Halen at the Hollywood Bowl the next. All of a sudden, our players who had been playing in complete anonymity all season, were getting interview requests, press conference times and profiles on local TV sports reports. Over the course of a long season, that type of attention can become burdensome for some, but when you don't experience it day-to-day, it can be fun for a short time, like it was for us.

We played on a Tuesday in Maryland, then traveled all day Wednesday to get to Little Rock with only two days to prepare for our game on Saturday with the RimRockers. It wasn't the optimal scenario for many teams but we were healthy and riding high. In fact, it was probably a pretty good scenario for us.

Somehow, Blackmon got us to Little Rock. I don't know how, but we had one-way tickets on Southwest Airlines from Baltimore to Dallas and then Dallas to Little Rock. He was on top of the world and couldn't be more proud of "his" team. He told all of us that if we won the championship, he would take us all to Hawaii. We knew he was full of crap but everyone just went with it. The Rimrockers put us up at the Comfort Inn & Suites at the Clinton Library within walking distance of downtown Little Rock. This was the same place we stayed just a few weeks earlier when we played two games in Arkansas at the beginning of March.

On Thursday, we practiced at a small Catholic school near the hotel. The Arkansas team preceded us on the floor and the first thing I did when we got there was to seek out the Rimrockers head coach, Joe Harge.

A few weeks earlier, I was upset after our second game with them, when in my eyes, they had run up the score and were goofing on us near the end of the game. With less than two minutes left and a 20+ point lead, they were full-court pressing and running set plays for lob dunks that I thought, at the time, was unnecessary and rubbing our faces in it. In hindsight, I think I was more pissed about our own performance than I was with Coach Harge and after four games in five days in three states; I was probably just generally pissy anyway. When the game ended, I refused to shake his hand and gave him a little piece of what I thought about his team's conduct. It was immature on my part, and when we got to the gym that Thursday for practice, I made sure to go talk to him and apologize. After apologizing, I expected him to be gracious. Instead what I got would be described as aloof at its best. Suddenly, I didn't feel all that sorry anymore and it further fueled my desire to kick their ass two days later.

Emily Wade was a young go-getter for the RimRockers organization working in their front office as a Community Relations Manager. She also served as basically a host for us while we were in town. If we needed anything, Emily would do her best to take care of it for us. Whether it was transportation, practice and shootaround times, hotel issues, places to eat; she was like our concierge. Since we had been there three weeks earlier for two games, we already knew Emily pretty well when we arrived for the Championship weekend.

She was extremely diligent in making us feel welcome and taken care of, even though she (along with the rest of the staff), was also very busy with preparations for the big event. Emily was a young and attractive southern girl and I'm quite sure each of our guys probably took a swing at her at one point or another. To the best of my knowledge, she handled their advances with great aplomb and remained very professional. But then again, as I said earlier, ignorance is bliss sometimes and if I didn't see it, it didn't happen. Nevertheless, I thought she did a great job of exhibiting discretion with the players while they surrounded and hounded her constantly. Her discretion with the media, however, could have used some attention.

The Thursday before our game was the second round of the NCAA tournament, and Russ and I took the guys out for beer and pizza and to watch games. We went to a pizza place in downtown Little Rock called Gusano's. We spread out over three or four tables near the TVs so we could eat and watch the games. In the back of the restaurant, Emily was there as well with some friends. We ordered a bunch of pizzas of various toppings as well as their beer special of $9 buckets of Coronas. The pizzas came and we hunkered down at Gusano's for a while eating, having beers and watching the University of Washington lose to Louisville in the NCAA round of 16.

I had hurt my hand at some point in practice over the previous couple of weeks and for some reason it was really bothering me that night. I had the idea to just soak it in the bucket of ice, left over from the beer we ordered. As I sat there, belly stuffed full of pepperoni and sausage deep pan pizza and a couple of Coronas, Emily walked by us as she left the restaurant with her friends. On the way out, she spotted my hand in the bucket of ice.

"Oh, hiii coach…" she sung, with her thick southern drawl as she spotted my hand in the Corona ice bath.

"… what happened to your hand?" She asked

"I beat the crap out of some guy who popped off to me earlier. You should see him" I responded with the driest wit I could muster.

"Oh my gosh, hope you're okay"

"Yeah, I'm fine. Thanks though… we'll see you tomorrow."

I never thought anything more about that conversation with Emily. The NCAA games on TV ended and we walked back to the hotel to plan for our Friday morning practice at Alltel Arena. I laid in bed and watched a Letterman repeat, with special guest "The Rock" and music by Solomon Burke, before finally turning off the light around 1 a.m. I woke up the next morning to a headline in the Arkansas Democrat- Gazette:

TURNER'S TEMPER

In amazement I read the accompanying story:

> *Bellevue Coach Rick Turner has been to Arkansas three times this season, and three times has shown a temper.*
> *In the Blackhawk's first game on Feb 25, Turner got into a heated verbal confrontation with Arkansas guard Kareem Reid. On March 1 Turner, believing Arkansas was running up the score, refused to shake Rimrockers Coach Joe Harge's hand after a 142-108 blowout victory by Arkansas. "I told Joe I was wrong, I apologized to him" Turner said "... I had a chance to reflect and I went to him, shook his hand and told him I was out of line."*
> *Finally, Thursday night Turner was seen walking out of Gusano's restaurant on President Clinton Avenue in Little Rock holding his hand after punching someone in the restaurant over an undisclosed altercation.*

Thanks Emily.

My three days in Arkansas in late March of 2005 are probably as close to "famous" as I'll ever get, and while it's a long, long way from what real fame is, it did give me a teensy, tiny glimpse of what actual "famous" people have to deal with almost daily. The narcissism in me totally ate that story up though. I loved it. I laughed when I read it, but at the same time, I was a little embarrassed because it was so far off the mark. The handshake part was true, but the "verbal confrontation" with Kareem Reid was completely blown out of proportion, and the "fight" was just flat out false. How could a guy report that I punched someone in a restaurant without trying to check out the validity? That seemed to be sloppy journalism at its best and borderline slander at its worst. When I read things now about actual, famous people, I usually take it with a grain of salt because I now know how some of these stories come to be "fact". For the record, I haven't punched anybody since the fifth grade when I picked a fight with a third grader who beat the pee out of me in the sandbox at Ben Franklin Elementary School. The embarrassment of that beat down lasts to this day, so I have avoided any physical confrontations since.

***

The good guys took a 51-49 lead into halftime of the 2005 ABA Championship game against the Arkansas RimRockers. Tim Ellis led the way, with 17 points on 7 of 13 shooting in the half, while Lovell Brown provided a spark off the bench hitting 2 of 3 three-pointers and pouring in 12 points. However, a disturbing trend was developing. Arkansas trailed by 2 points but had already shot 22 free throws in the half going 14 for 22 compared to Bellevue's 4 of 5.

The second half was a bit of a blur, but I do know that Arkansas took back the lead with 10:15 left in the third quarter, and we played from behind the rest of the way. "Turner's Temper" made an appearance during Arkansas' continuous parade to the free-throw line and I finally got slapped with a technical foul late in the third quarter.

Here it was, the Championship game for the ABA, the pinnacle of the season and a showcase for the league; and the game was getting hijacked by the referees. Don't get me wrong, Arkansas was better than us, they played better than us and deserved to win, but when you get out shot from the free throw line by a margin of 50-20, you feel like you are playing five against eight. Arkansas MADE 15 more free throws than we even attempted and we still stayed in the game most of the way. Ultimately, Todd Day's 32 points and game MVP Kareem Reid's 36, were too much for us to over come and Bellevue lost 118-103.

It's always a very strange feeling when the season ends especially when you are in the playoffs. The suddenness of its finality is difficult to prepare for. My driver's education instructor, Ron Lince, warned the class of getting "velocitized" when exiting the freeway. He talked about how slow 35 mph seemed after driving 60 mph for a while and how it takes some time for your eyes and mind to adjust. We all know that feeling. You've just come off the freeway and now are on a side street. Your first inclination is to get back up to 60mph but you catch yourself and keep it at 35 mph. That 35 feels like 15 until you adjust. It takes a couple of minutes but then you are back to normal. That is kind of what it's like for a coach when their season ends. You are working, working, working everyday; 18-20 hours per day. You are consumed by trying to keep the season alive as games become increasingly meaningful. You are in survival mode, swimming in chaos soup. Taking each day as it comes, without a realistic ability to plan too far in advance because tomorrow is never guaranteed nor is your next opponent.

Then… all of a sudden… it stops.

"Now what?" you think to yourself.

I specifically remember thinking, as I sat in the locker room after that final game, that this group of men had really caught lightning in a bottle. I became borderline maudlin as I reflected on where we came from, and even more so, how we'd never be able to recreate this moment or this season ever again.

Partly because Blackmon couldn't possibly pull this off again. Not with the lies, the money (or lack thereof) and his overall inability to interact civilly with people. The players wouldn't put up with his crap anymore, and thus they would go off in different directions, to teams with a different set of problems; or possibly they just might be out of basketball altogether. Plus, who really knew what would happen with the league next year. Not to be overly dramatic about it, but I couldn't help thinking that this group of guys would probably never be together again after this night. I suppose that is true for just about every coach, in every season; particularly at the college and professional levels, but it gave me pause as I sat there in the quiet locker room at Alltel Arena…velocitized.

Even if we were able to somehow keep this team together for another season, it would never be the same. The expectations would be completely different and there would be no sneaking up on teams who took us lightly. That "us against the world" mentality is difficult to recreate with the same group of players because it just gets tired and worn out. And of course now, the "bloom is off the rose", meaning our "time" was over. This group's carpe diem moment had passed but at least we did a pretty good job of grabbing on and seizing it while it was there.

It's funny as I look back on that team, and those players, because I'd really like to know how each of them recalled that season. As George Bernard Shaw told us, "Youth is wasted on the young.", and my inclination is that they don't share the same nostalgic sentiments that I do, nor would they tell me if they did (which is why I just don't ask).

I wonder if they enjoyed that season as they look back or if they view it as just another year of basketball, with another group of guys, on another fill-in-the-blank team.

I wonder if they look at what we did as an accomplishment or as an afterthought.

I wonder if it is a highlight of their career or something they'd just as soon forget.

I mentioned at the opening of this book that what we did that season would barely jiggle Jell-O on the basketball Richter scale. I've spoken to a number of "basketball people" including NBA general managers, other coaches and college athletic directors about it. They seem to be thoroughly unimpressed by our accomplishments that season because they have no point of reference for what the league was at that time.

It was as if, because the games weren't on ESPN every night, they were illegitimate and less important. Even though most of the players in the league were the best players on their college teams, and many had extensive backgrounds playing professionally (including the NBA), somehow in the eyes of those "basketball experts" it seemed to be nothing more than a YMCA men's league. The kind of thing you roll your eyes and scoff at when you hear stories of success. Obviously I saw it much differently, but I also realize that there isn't much I can do to change their opinions. While going after various coaching jobs, I've continually pointed to this season as a relevant ingredient as part of the support for the overall body of work I have compiled as a coach. However, I find more often than not, during the course of my conversations and interviews, that this work is dismissed as virtually meaningless to anyone other than those of us involved.

For myself, I am proud of what I accomplished with that team in 2005 and when I say "I", I mean we… Russ, Harold and me. When you try to translate or transfer the skills needed to succeed at another level, with the resources we were given; I think we have the skills and ability to coach any team in the country (and when I say "we", I mean me). And I really do mean any team in the country.

We were able to recruit, evaluate, motivate, teach, lead, discipline, cajole, persuade and direct a random group of young men to pull in the same direction, despite disparate goals and wavering beliefs, to compete and win games; even though 80% of those games were played on the road. The team had never played together before and they rarely, if ever, got paid in full or on time.

We had no ability to scout our opponents, we practiced in a mini-gym at a local athletic club that wasn't even the size of a high school floor, and we couldn't sign any player that didn't live within driving distance.

Can you imagine what we might have accomplished with an actual budget? Or with a real organization?

Speaking of budgets, our trip to Little Rock wasn't quite over yet. The plan was for Harold and Russ to take a group of guys to the airport with them on Sunday morning (Easter Sunday), and I would take another group Sunday afternoon for the trip back to Seattle. The early morning group had to leave the hotel at 5 a.m. and I'm pretty sure most of them didn't sleep at all prior to their departure from the hotel, including Blackmon. He was going to accompany the first group to the airport so he could purchase tickets for them, and then come back, and leave with the second group.

We should have been suspicious when he didn't just take care of this over the phone, but as with everything else, he marched to the beat of his own drum.

At about 7 a.m. my phone rang. It was Harold. It seemed as if Blackmon's credit card wouldn't work and he couldn't buy the tickets. Apparently Blackmon made quite a scene at the airport before storming out, and everyone was heading back to the hotel. Both Harold and Russ needed to be back by Monday, so they had to buy their own plane tickets home which they did, and soon after, they were on a flight back to Seattle.

Here it was Sunday and no banks were open. Not only that, but it was Easter Sunday, so nothing in Little Rock was open AND it was spring break, so almost all the flights were full. I knew there was nothing that I could do about it at 7 a.m. so I went back to sleep for a while wondering what would happen next. Around 11 a.m. my phone started blowing up with guys calling me because they were hungry. I told them to call Blackmon, but I guess he had taken his room phone off the hook and remember, he was the only man left in America without a cell phone. There wasn't much we could do.

Checkout time came and went. The front desk called to ask me when would we be leaving. I explained our situation and they explained to me, that if we wanted to stay an additional night we would have to pay for it ourselves because the RimRockers team was only paying for us to stay until Sunday. "Good luck with that" I thought. Blackmon's phone was still off the hook so the hotel manager agreed to call Otis Birdsong, the GM of the RimRockers. After some arm-twisting, Otis agreed to have his team pay for one more additional night so Blackmon could try and get it figured out on Monday.

Easter dinner 2005 ended up being Funyans, Slim Jims and 64 oz Mountain Dews from the AM/PM store across the street. The players didn't carry much "walking around" money so their options were pretty limited. We all just hunkered down for the night and hoped to get out of there as soon as we could on Monday.

By noon on Monday, Blackmon still hadn't emerged from his room. In fact, he had locked himself in there and unplugged the phone. Hotel staff tried to get in to his room but he had latched the door from the inside. I'm pretty sure that along with the lack of money to get us home, Blackmon had also crashed pretty hard emotionally after that final game. It all probably caught up with him as it did me and the others, but either he wasn't prepared for it or didn't have the mental tools to deal with it. I just had this picture of him curled up in a ball in a curtain-drawn and darkened hotel room; holding his knees and rocking back and forth on the floor in a corner. Actually what I'm almost certain he did was pound some Ambien and crash out for a while; remaining in his seemingly perpetual state of oblivion.

We all decided to meet in the lobby and figure out a plan while we waited for Blackmon to emerge from his self-imposed exile. The players were hungry. I had some cash on me (not much), so we borrowed the hotel van, and I took them all to Chick-fil-A for lunch. We talked about our options which were basically two. We either wait for Blackmon or we pay our own way home. A couple of guys got on the phone to their parents and had them go online and buy them a ticket. A couple of guys had nothing better to do than wait around, enjoy the chaos and see what crazy story this adventure would bring next. As for me, I couldn't get away from Blackmon fast enough. The season was over and I needed separation from him ASAP. But at the same time, I didn't want to abandon the players. I wasn't sure what to do and I couldn't figure out what my role was here. A part of me said that I should stick it out with them, but another part said these guys are grown men capable of taking care of themselves. I went back and forth on what to do.

We got back to the hotel and the manager was waiting there telling me we had to get out of the rooms. I did my best to remain polite and diplomatic but my hands were tied. Even though it wasn't true, I told him that I didn't have a credit card to put the room charges on and I said we would try and roust Blackmon out of the room to get it all figured out. So Tim, Haywood and Bunche went upstairs to knock on Blackmon's door. Bunchy did the knocking… no answer.

They knocked again.

"Yo Mike, what's up? We're looking to get up out of here." Haywood pleaded through the door.

"Yo Mike, you there?" Bunchy yelled after another three knocks.

They put their ears to the door in silence trying to hear anything stirring in the room.

One more time they knocked.

Finally, a voice came from inside the room.

"GET THE F*** OUT OF HERE AND LEAVE ME ALONE!!!" the voice reverberated through the door and out into the hallway.

"C'mon Mike, open the door. We tryin' to go home." Jimmy beseeched.

"F*** off!" Blackmon said again, reiterating his position

The three of them acquiesced to Blackmon's request and f***ed off. They went back downstairs to report to the rest of us what had just happened. This was the cherry on top to the insanity that we had witnessed the previous six months. No one doubted that this was exactly what happened when Jimmy, Tim and Brian went upstairs, and in fact, we probably didn't expect to hear anything less. I didn't know what the hotel could do but I was pretty sure that they couldn't physically remove us from the rooms. I was fairly certain that by staying we weren't doing anything illegal, so I felt confident when I made the decision to leave later that afternoon, the players would be okay riding out the storm.

And ride out the storm is exactly what they did. Monday turned into Tuesday and Tuesday became Wednesday before Blackmon finally surfaced from his room. In the meantime, Otis Birdsong and the RimRockers sent pizzas over to the hotel so the players could eat on Monday and Tuesday night. Blackmon emerged on Wednesday afternoon as if nothing ever happened. He made a quick explanation to the seven guys left in Little Rock and then took them all out to a nice meal downtown to celebrate the great season. My best guess is that he needed a few days to get some money together. He was probably on the phone with anyone and everyone he could think of, angling for an infusion of cash. It just took a few days to make it happen.

Everywhere he went for the next six months (and this is not an exaggeration, I mean EVERYWHERE) he carried with him the ABA second place consolation trophy. Meeting for coffee? He brought the trophy. Having a lunch appointment? He brought the trophy. Getting drinks at happy hour? He brought the trophy. He was so proud of that thing that it never left his side. I was frankly embarrassed by it. Isn't second place just first place for losers? You don't see foam fingers in stadiums around the country holding up the number two, do you? And nobody knows who holds the record for the most silver medals in the Olympics.

Nonetheless, the diminutive trophy followed him around like it was the Stanley Cup. And on that final Wednesday night in Little Rock, Arkansas, after being stranded at the Comfort Inn for four days, living on a steady diet of pizza, Pringles and Ding Dongs; seven players and team owner Michael Blackmon sat around a big table, eating steak and swapping stories. Reveling in their success and briefly forgetting the baggage. In the middle of that big table sat the one thing they would take away from this shared experience. Because you see, there would be no bonuses or million-dollar endorsement deals after this. Some would go on to play for a different team in another struggling league, but for others, this would be the end of their pro basketball careers. There would be no parades, no ESPN highlights and no autographs to be signed. The one thing they had to take away sat in the middle of that table… the tiny little ABA consolation trophy… that's right,

…we're number two.

PART III:

THE BUD

9

Tacoma

If I gave you everything that I own
and asked for nothing in return
Would you do the same for me, as I would for you?
Or take me for a ride
and strip me of everything, including my pride?
But spirit is something that no one destroys

- Traffic **"Low Spark of High-Heeled Boys"**

The thought of returning to the ABA and another year of Michael Blackmon was motivation enough for me to pursue new opportunities for the 2005-2006 basketball season. Armed with a boatload of confidence and a newly awarded 2005 Coach of the Year title from the ABA, I set out to find a "real" basketball coaching job.

Not that what I had been doing wasn't "real". Actually, I would defy you to find anyone who could've done what I had done leading up to that point. Not because I am anything special but more so because I don't think too many others would have put up with the crap that I put up with for as little or nothing that I got in return.

My first three seasons at Bellevue CC, I worked as a volunteer assistant. The next three seasons as head coach, I gave my small stipend of $5,000 per year to my assistant coaches and was paid only as the school's Athletic Director. The next year I spent at the University of Washington as an unpaid volunteer and then came the year with Blackmon in the ABA. He agreed to pay me $1,500 per month. That was when the checks actually cashed or he actually decided to pay me. One month he gave me $500 and said it was because that was all I was worth. Two other months the checks had bounced and I knew in the end he would never pay me at all. He told me he'd make good on everything that he owed me once he got his share of the gate receipts from Arkansas and the Championship game which he figured to be about $30,000.

I didn't hold my breath.

The following is a chain of emails that I was copied on or blind copied on between Blackmon, ABA Commissioner Joe Newman and Arkansas RimRockers owner Larry Crain, in regard to the $30,000 or so that Blackmon was expecting to receive from Arkansas. When Blackmon emailed people he liked to copy others usually blindly or in the case here, people who he felt had an active interest. Others copied on these emails are his "partners" Peter and Rob, his contact at Commerce Bank in Seattle, who he either got a loan from or was trying to get a loan from, a man named Marty Steele and a couple other guys; ABA Executive VP, Ricardo Richardson and Kansas City owner Jim Clark. These are the guys that I know of. There is no telling how many people, like me, were blind copied on some of this stuff. I think you'll realize why it was a good idea not to hold my breath on getting paid. In addition, I have left these emails exactly as they were written including all spelling, punctuation and grammar errors.

> ----- Original Message -----
> From: "Michael Blackmon"
> To: <conniejoenewman@>; larryc@
> Sent: Monday, April 04, 2005 8:02 PM
> Subject: Re: ABA Revenue Sharing
>
> Joe,
> Before we hit the road for Texas in the first round, you told me the split for the visitors would be 20% of gate receipts. I haven't received anything yet from Texas, Maryland or Arkansas; although Charles Key has indicated he was sending my share. Based on the gate receipts at Arkansas ($160,000), I'm expecting $32,000 from Larry Crain.
>
> Thanks for following up on this.
>
> Michael Blackmon
> President and General Manager
> ABA Bellevue Blackhawks

ABA Commissioner Joe Newman responds to Blackmon in an email sent to Arkansas owner Larry Crain at 2:40 p.m. April 4th

> *The following message was sent by conniejoenewman@*
> *on Mon, 04 Apr 2005 2:40pm.* (To Larry Crain)
>
> Larry,
>
> The Revenue sharing for the ABA playoff games was supposed to be a minimum of 15% of the ticket revenue (all ticket revenue), and a recommended 20%. I have received inquiries from the three teams you played at home - Kentucky, Mississippi and Bellevue - requesting information on the basis you determined revenue sharing. The amounts did not seem consistant with the crowds or revenue generated for the games.
>
> The home team had the advantage of keeping all sponsorship money, all merchandising money and all concessions. Your crowds were substantial. Please respond so that I can advise the teams. Thank you. Hope all is well with you.
>
> Joe Newman
> ABA CEO

Larry Crain responds to Blackmon's email at 11:45 p.m. the same day

> *The following message was sent by "Larry Crain, Sr"* (Owner of Arkansas RimRockers to Michael Blackmon) *on Mon, 4 Apr 2005 11:45pm*

Mike----I do not understand this email. I talked to you about the revenue sharing before the game. I explained to you there never was requirement to share revenue. The league orginally said that whomever had won the highest seed had earned the right to all the revenue as in a regular scheduled game. In Joe's email on February 16 it was suggested that the visiting team be given 15%.

On March 1, Joe emailed asking for a voluntary percentage of 20%. I explained to you how I would make the calculation for the final game. You said that you felt that was fair. I explained to you that Alltel normally settles up us with four to five days after the game. I got the settlement statement on March 31 and on April 1, I made the revenue sharing calculation.

I gave my assistance in my office the instructions to get all the documentations ready for your review as well as to go ahead with cutting the check. I am out of town and will not be back until Friday. I received an email today from Joe about questions that Kentucky, Mississippi, and Bellevue had about how the sharing was being made. I immediately called Joe to explain and discuss but he wasn't in and hasn't returned my call. I attempted to call you at your office (voicemail box full) and on your cell(no voicemail).

With all being said above, I want to set forth a list of we have done to be fair about the distribution.

(1) I visited with Joe before making any payments and explained to him that I would do the 15% but not the 20%.

(2) When I visited with Joe I asked about how to handle a number of issues including promotion, advertising, etc. Joe suggested to me that just to be fair since he realized that our facility cost and other costs were much greater than the other teams. I have made all the distributions to the other teams using a 15% payout.

(3) We have paid three of the four teams who we hosted for playoffs. We have paid out the following:

(1)Ontario---3/8 check #1850 $2,500--3/17 check # 1892
        $2,230.00=total $4,730.09
(2) Kentucky 3/17 check #1893 $2,882.68
(3) Mississippi 3/25 check #1922 $8012.14

(4) We have and will pay all teams a substantial amount by comparison to any other team in the playoffs. We will probably be the only team to make a distribution in all the playoffs. It is my understanding from all the teams I have talked with including Kentucky, St Louis, Bellevue, Long Beach, etc no one has gotten any payouts from their opponents. We have honored the league and teams we played by making distributions when no one else has.

(5) We average spending over $10,000 per game in advertising. We have spent additionally for all kinds of events to come in to pull more attendence. We spent over $3,000 to have Matt Jones former Arkansas Razorback Quarterback to come in for the Ontario game which was held on a Tuesday Night. We have drawn more attendence than any team but our attendence has been hampered when we do not play on a Friday or Saturday. Our attendence announcements are based on drop counts

furnished by the   arena. We have a large amount of compementary tickets issued each game usually more than 1,000. We announce based on drop count and add to the count from 1,000 to 2,500 for all those fans that get in without a ticket including dance teams, media, arena slips,etc. The paid attendence was considerably less than announced at all the the playoff games. We also sell a number of discounted group tickets. We do not get all the   revenue from suite sales, etc. We average less than 15.00 per ticket and have to pay out of that facility fees, taxes, etc.

(6) We visited with Ontario before they came to Little Rock and explained to them that they would only get 15%. We have not heard anything from them as to having any problem with their distribution. I would bet it was the biggest gate receipts they had all year and quite likely was more than their ticket sales for the entire season.

(7) We have not heard any questions from Kentucky as to a concern about their payout.

(8) We discussed with Andy Stoglin about what he understood about the distribution and we expressed some concern with him and frustations that we had experienced during the season with how much we spent to get teams to fill dates that the league assured us would play.

(9) We have computed the amount due Bellevue in accordance with what we discussed with you (Michael) and the amount is over $17,000. We are in process of trying to contact you to send you the documents to see if you have any questions. In light of this, I am at loss as to why you would raise any question about the payout before you even allowed us to forward the results to you. You must know something that we don't know since the total gross was considerably less than $160,000. You also are aware of the fact that I have explained to you that we have amounts due from the league that need to paid to us before we settle up with you. You have told me that you have only paid $1,000 toward your reservation fee. We have paid $10,000 as you know.

(10) We have paid out to the following teams amounts necessary to get someone to cover for no show teams that the league scheduled to be here and who the league assured us would play: Utah (Feb 12 for Hermosillo)(Feb 10 for Detroit) $5,200, Carolina (Feb 19 for St Louis) $5,995 Bellevue (Feb 25 for Baton Rouge and March 1 for Cincinnati) $2,950 a total of over $15,000 to do make ups. The league had terminated Hermosillo, Detroit didn't play away games except on weekends, St Louis stiffed us on the Feb 19, Baton Rouge Feb 25, Cincinnati on March1.

(11) We will pay out for the playoffs over $33,000 to visiting teams. We are short on paying out to visiting teams over $15,000.

(12) In spite of having a great year by winning the ABA Championship and drawing over 100,000 in attendence, we sill lose somewhere over $200,000. We believe that we have done everything possible to uphold our end of the bargain. We are proud of the fact that   we have acted in what we believe to be a professional manner and taking care of obligations that were not our responsibility.

We have offered this explanation so that everyone will have the facts as we know them. We welcome calls from anyone who has questions as to the facts.

Thanks,
Larry Crain

Blackmon receives Crain's email and sends a response back the next morning trying to remain as diplomatic as possible, so as to not jeopardize the check he is expecting.

-----Original Message-----
From: Michael Blackmon
To: Larry Crain, Sr
Cc: conniejoenewman
Sent: Tue, 05 Apr 2005 8:20a
Subject: Re: ABA Revenue Sharing

Jeez, Larry, we're really watching two different movies. First of all, I was just responding to Joe's email, I wasn't making ANY accusations. You're free to do whatever you want... as always.

Our discussion in your car on the day of the game was that you expected 10,000 tickets sold and $100,000 in gate receipts, and that I could expect $15,000 under those conditions. The announced attendance was 14,989... considerably larger. After the game, Ricardo Richardson estimated my share should be around $30,000. On Monday when I met with Ricardo and Otis Birdsong in the hotel lobby, they both indicated my share should be $30,000. The number of $160,000 in gate receipts was mentioned at that meeting.

Look, Larry, you're a god to me. I'm proud to have you as my friend. You and Janet have always been extremely good to me, whether it was lunch in Las Vegas or dinner in Little Rock. I'm sure we'll continue to be good friends. You don't have to give me a rundown of your costs. Send me what you think is fair.

I just hope you factor in a couple of things...

You got the game you wanted... on the day you wanted... at the venue you wanted... and you got the outcome you wanted. Bellevue was like the Washington Generals to you... we gave you three good home games, all of which you won, and we responded to your need for an opponent twice during the regular season.

We travelled 3,000 miles to Maryland, then 1,500 to Little Rock and 2,000 back to Seattle, and that's after traveling 4,000 miles roundtrip to Dallas the week before. You want to talk about each other's costs? I spent $35,000 on playoff travel alone. I haven't had a single home game (read: revenue), since January 29th. The Bellevue Blackhawks travelled over 20,000 miles this season by van, bus, sleeper coach, and mostly... airplane. By far the most in the league... probably the most in ANY minor league basketball season.

All I'm asking is for the league's most powerful team to share a little bit of its good fortune with the visiting team that was most involved in that success. (I'm not taking credit for work you did! Just pointing out that I delivered my team as your opponent for three big games. At least I didn't implode like Ike Austin.)

We have no legal contract. Just do what you think is fair given all those circumstances. I trust you'll do the right thing.

Thank you very much.

Michael Blackmon
President and General Manager
ABA Bellevue Blackhawks

ABA Commissioner Joe Newman, who is as slippery as they come, just wants to play peacemaker here and avoid any contracted dispute. He had a reputation for never taking sides and never making a tough or difficult decision. The results of this lack of leadership usually produced the exact opposite outcome that Joe had hoped to cultivate. Instead of placating both sides, he more often pissed off both sides. Essentially when it came time to lead, Newman usually pulled an Obama and voted 'Present'.

Newman responded to Blackmon's ass-kiss of Larry Crain…

> *The following message was sent by conniejoenewman@ on Tue, 05 Apr 2005 11:30a.*
>
> Mike. Thanks for the email. An eloquent response to Larry. We do not have the actual attendance figures or revenue figures available so we do not know for sure what the final ticket revenue was. It was not necessary for Larry to justify his actions in the form he did. As usual, he is the victim. I cannot imagine his losing $200,000 this season with the venue lease he had, the salary cap, and his limited travel. And the huge attendance figures. But who knows? You're right. He should do what is fair. Meantime, we will make it up to you as you had the most difficult time this season. Hopefully you'll be in Indy for the meeting on the 19th and 20th.
>
> Any progress on Olympia? I had a verbal commitment today from Vancouver BC and Vancouver WA - and expect the same from Calgary and Edmonton in the next 24 hours (I hope), completing the NW division). Again, thanks for everything.
>
> Joe Newman

Believe it or not, within a couple weeks, Blackmon actually got a check from Larry Crain and the Arkansas RimRockers. Granted, it was only half of what he expected but it was 100% more than I ever expected him to receive which was exactly $zip. But of course with Blackmon, nothing ever comes easy. Before he could get to the bank and get that sucker cashed, he received an email from Larry Crain's assistant, Tonia Hoffman.

> *The following message was sent by <toniahoffman@ (Larry Crain's Assistant) on Wed, 20 Apr 2005 10:35a*
>
> Michael,
>
> Mr. Crain asked me to send you an email and let you know that we have issued a stop payment on the check that we sent you. We received a telephone call yesterday from the bus company that took you from Ar. to Kansas, and the bill has not been paid. We made the arrangements for that bus and now they are asking us for the

payment.

Mr. Crain will give you a call to discuss this.

Thank you
Tonia Hoffman

As you can imagine, Blackmon goes ballistic over this email. You'll see this is where he starts copying other people on the emails (I had been blind copied on the others). My guess is that he had promised money to many of us who were copied and he included us on the emails to provide some credibility and cover as to why we were not getting our money. You will also see that the "Godlike" quality of Larry Crain has quickly worn off for Blackmon.

----- Original Message -----
From: Michael Blackmon
To: conniejoenewman@
Cc: Peter; Marty; rickturner ; jamesdclark@ ; rrichardson@ ; rspit@
Sent: Monday, April 25, 2005 11:44 PM
Subject: Fwd: Check from Ar. RimRockers

Joe,

The forwarded message below is from Larry Crain's secretary regarding a stop payment Crain placed on my revenue sharing check.

On Monday, April 18th, I received a settlement statement from Crain for the championship game, which included a statement from Alltel Arena itemizing the revenues and deductions that were made. My net check was for $16,445, which was included in Crain's letter. I believe that was roughly half of what I should have gotten, but under the circumstances (gross disorganization of the playoff format), I felt lucky to get anything. I got $400 from Texas and nothing from Maryland. Tom Doyle told me last week in Indy that Ticketmaster had not settled with them. That is, of course, bullshit, but I didn't want to embarrass him.

On Monday, April 25th my bank informed me that Crain had issued a stop payment on the check. I spoke with Crain Monday night at 8:30 PM Pacific time, 10:30 Central. Needless to say, he's a difficult man to like. He was obviously drunk. He slurred his words and was all over the place in his logic. He claimed that he stopped payment on my check because the ABA owes him money, and because Kansas City never paid for the bus that transported my team to our game in KC on February 26th. The amount due to the bus company is $2,400. I asked him what that had to do with my settlement check from the ABA championship game, and he replied: "Were you on the bus?" That should give you an idea of how the conversation went.

I'm SICK of this bullshit. I know that Crain and Jim Clark have had their fill of each other, but I'm the innocent bystander dragged into this dispute. I flew my team cross-country to step in as an opponent for Texas on 2/24, Arkansas on 2/25, Kansas City on 2/26, and Arkansas again on 3/1. I received $1,000 per pre-agreement with Texas and $2,900 from Arkansas. I was never asked to pay for the bus to KC, and I would never have put my team (or myself) through a grueling ordeal like a 7-hour bus trip just to play one game with KC, then drive 7 more hours back to Little Rock the next day. I certainly never would have done it if I was expected to pay $2,400 for the bus.

As much as I hate Larry Crain right now, I believe he's right in saying that he shouldn't have to pay for the bus. He dealt with it in an unacceptable way, but hey... once a used car salesman, always a used car salesman. I was only peripherally involved in the travel arrangements, but my recollection is that KC agreed to pay for the bus. Based on my receipt of the $16,445, I issued checks to pay outstanding bills related to the Blackhawks season. Those checks will all bounce and the reputation of the ABA will be besmirched yet again.

This needs to be resolved immediately. I told Crain to deduct the $2,400 and reissue my check for $14,000. Incredibly, he said he'd think about it and get back to me on Wednesday.

I didn't do anything wrong here. I was by far the most "stand-up guy" in the whole goddamned ABA this past season. I expect Kansas City or the league to reimburse me immediately.

Michael Blackmon
President and General Manager
ABA Bellevue Blackhawks

It didn't just end there. Like Col. Nathan R. Jessep did to an innocently by-standing Lt. Weinberg while being cross-examined in **A Few Good Men**, Blackmon took an unwarranted swipe at Maryland Nighthawks owner Tom Doyle in the previous email when he wrote:

"Tom Doyle told me last week in Indy that Ticketmaster had not settled with them. That is, of course, bullshit, but I didn't want to embarrass him."

Well, that little comment sent off another email storm, this time from Tom Doyle, owner of the Maryland Nighthawks... I love the subject line.

----- Original Message -----
From: Doylete@
To: Conniejoenewman@ ; michael.Blackmon@ ; RPTINKHAM@ ; Jadvocat@
Cc: pret@ ; Martys@ ; rickturner ; jamesdclark@ ; rrichardson@ ; rspit@ ;
rmatsko@ ; Jmcc1713@ brad@
Sent: Tuesday, April 26, 2005 5:40 AM
Subject: you do not want to embarrass youself

Mr. Blackmon,

While you may think your obnoxious attitude and running off at the mouth with insults and falsehoods is something you can do without recourse, in my case it is not. Your statement that I have not settled with my arena is "bullshit" could not be further from the truth. I will be copying you the last letter I wrote to the arena as well as the dates of my follow up calls. The only thing that is embarrassing candidly, is you. Have the guts to call me. I told you face to face, Rick Matsko was present, the status of my dealings with the arena. For you to make this comment in a letter directed to others really displays the coward you are. I pay my bills and honor my obligations. I have received nothing from the ShowPlace arena, if you think otherwise or did not believe me when I told you the status while looking each other in the eye, why did you not have the strength of character to say so. Embarrass me? I think you are now the embarrassment. You want a fight? you took on the wrong person. Stop hiding like a coward, if you have an issue, call me about it. You will be receiving the information I mentioned above.

Tom Doyle

Blackmon never responded and Doyle took another swing a few hours later. He added some names to the email that I don't know, the exception being Rick Matsko who was the GM of the Maryland team.

----- Original Message -----
From: Doylete@
To: Conniejoenewman@ ; RPTINKHAM@ ; Jadvocat@
Cc: pret@; Martys@; rickturner@ ; jamesdclark@ ; rrichardson@ ; rspit@ ; rmatsko@ ; brad@ ; Jmcc1713@
Sent: Wednesday, April 27, 2005 3:54 AM
Subject: Re: Check from Ar. RimRockers

Mr. Blackmon,

Perhaps you are unable to respond to your false accusations about me because you know the truth. After my e-mail to you this morning, as I stated I would, I faxed you all of the documents of my dealings with the ShowPlace Arena. As I told you in person, and reiterated in my e-mail, I have not received any funds from the arena for the playoff game. After my e-mail and fax I attempted to call you at every number I had for you leaving messages requesting you call me. You have not, I can only surmise, because you simply lack the character to apologize for your false statement. You, as I stated, are the embarrassment.

SIEGEL & DOYLE, L.L.C.
Attorneys at Law
Thomas E. Doyle

The email wars go silent for about three weeks before Tom Doyle can no longer take it. He lobs this volley across Blackmon's bow on May 24…

----- Original Message -----
From: Doylete@
To: michael.Blackmon@ ; RPTINKHAM@ ; Jadvocat@; Conniejoenewman@
Cc: prett@ ; Martys@; rickturner@ ; jamesdclark@ ; rrichardson@ ; rspit@ ; rmatsko@ ; bradm@
Sent: Tuesday, May 24, 2005 5:07 PM
Subject: Re: Check

Mr. Blackmon,

Perhaps you are simply to embarrassed to have the courtesy to return at least one of my messages or e-mails, I really am not accustomed to dealing with cowards that make false statements and when called out on it do not even respond and admit to the mistake. I have probably dignified your unprofessional behavior more than I should but alas, I cannot help myself. To the point of my e-mail; I recently received the final accounting of the game from the arena and want to ensure I send your check to the correct address. To that end kindly contact me to provide me with this information, my numbers are listed below. If I do not receive a response from you within seven days from this e-mail I will donate the funds to one of the local charities my office supports.

Tom Doyle
SIEGEL & DOYLE, LLC
Attorneys at Law

I love this one. I have the check that I owe you but will only send it if you call me back because I don't know if the address that I have for you is correct...??? What a dipshit. Just send the check and be done with it. Or for that matter, don't send the check because you're mad, but don't then say that you're going to donate it to your favorite charity if you don't get a phone call back.

I am just imagining the so-called 'charity' that his office supposedly supports, sitting there with their fingers crossed hoping that Doyle never gets a call back from Blackmon so they can feed more hungry people. Then Blackmon calls, verifies the address and five homeless people die of starvation.

I have an idea Doyle... send the money you owe to Blackmon AND donate the money jackass.

It gets better.

You know that faced with getting his money or having it go to some unknown charity in the greater DC area, Blackmon was going to make that phone call right? Again, check out the subject line and the email from Tom Doyle...

----- Original Message -----
From: Doylete@
To: michael.Blackmon@ ; RPTINKHAM@ ; Jadvocat@ ; Conniejoenewman@
Cc: prett@ ; Martys@ ; rickturner@ ; jamesdclark@ ; rrichardson@ ; rspit@
Sent: Thursday, May 26, 2005 5:39 PM
Subject: mending fences

To all who have received e-mails between Mike Blackmon and myself recently, please bear with this one, it is the last. I received a call from Mike today and my first impression of Mike that he is a stand up guy, was reaffirmed. It took very little time for us both to realize things had gotten too far off track. I appreciate Mike calling and offering his apology to me and I gladly offered mine to him. As I once was told, and have learned in life, a friend is someone who you can fight with, differ with but in the end will understand you and respect you. I am pleased that Mike and I remain friends and harbor no ill will, he is indeed a gentlemen.
Thank you all for your patience.
Tom Doyle

Good grief... and now, here comes Joe Newman again, just in the nick of time. Where had he been while all of this was going on? Probably playing both sides of the fence...

----- Original Message -----
From: conniejoenewman@
To: Doylete@ ; michael.Blackmon@ ; RPTINKHAM@; Jadvocat@
Cc: prett@ ; Martys@; rickturner@ ; jamesdclark@ ; rrichardson@ ; rspit@
Sent: Monday, May 30, 2005 6:47 AM
Subject: Re: mending fences

Tom. Thanks for this email. It really was hard to understand the problems that developed between Mike and you. You are two of the best people we've had in the ABA; both smart, energetic, creative, committed, talented and intelligent. For one, I am glad you resolved your differences. You're both great - and it concerned me. Congratulations.
What a very nice email. Have a good Memorial Day.

Joe Newman
ABA CEO

Larry Crain decided to take the Arkansas RimRockers to a different league, the NBA Development League (or NBDL), for the 2005-2006 season, leaving the ABA in his rearview mirror. There was no written agreement for him to share any of their playoff revenue with any other teams, and I think ultimately, Larry just decided to ignore it all together. Blackmon tried to take one more desperate shot at getting his money…

-----Original Message-----
From: Michael Blackmon
To: conniejoenewman@; larryc@; rrichardson@
Cc: rspit@; prett@
Sent: Sun, 29 May 2005 17:58:40 -0700
Subject: Re: Bellevue Revenue Sharing

Gentlemen,

Enough is enough. Two months have now passed since the ABA championship game. I certainly wish Larry well in all his future endeavors, but I'm not interested in talking with him about anything, it serves no good purpose. I'm done

The league directive on playoff revenue sharing was distributed to all playoff teams following the regular season. It supersedes any previous agreements, and has nothing to do with the ABA Operating Agreement or whether a team owner has signed it. You'd have a hard time convincing a judge that you didn't give implied consent to the league rules after playing 37 ABA games--more than any other team. The power to issue league directives wrests with ABA CEO Joe Newman, and Larry, you acceded to that directive the moment your team took the court for your first playoff game. You never voiced any disagreement with the 85-15% split of gate receipts until after the playoffs were concluded and the championship awarded. I shudder to think what you would have done if you'd lost the game. No team would have traveled to play you without the hope of some revenue sharing.

The books are closed on everything between Bellevue and Arkansas, with the exception of the championship game. We all know I'm not responsible for

Ricardo's computer, the bus ride to Kansas City, or anything else prior to the final game. I'm not interested in suing Larry, and I'm not interested in being a plaintiff in any ABA lawsuit against Larry. Arkansas has left the ABA, and I agree with Joe that Larry Crain is part of the ABA's past, not our future

Therefore, as far as I'm concerned, unless I'm paid the $12,900 due me without further delay, I will exercise my rightful option: I hereby officially request the league to strip Arkansas of the title and award the 2004-05 ABA Championship to the Bellevue Blackhawks.

A horse race isn't always won by the first to cross the finish line. The race has to be sanctioned by the governing body before it becomes official. The ABA will withstand any consequences of such action because this is an open and shut case. I'm not trying to take anything away from what was earned "on the court," but Larry, you've given new meaning to the term "sore winner."

It's usually impossible to put a price on a championship. But, in this case its $12,900. Pay it and keep what you rightfully won on the court, or continue to defy the league's authority and lose the title.

Larry, I hope someday we can speak again under more pleasant circumstances, but until I get my money, I'm done talking with you at all

Michael Blackmon
President and General Manager
ABA Bellevue Blackhawks

Newman's response…

----- Original Message -----
From: conniejoenewman@
To: michael.Blackmon@ ; larryc@ ; rrichardson@
Cc: rspit@; prett@
Sent: Monday, May 30, 2005 5:48 AM
Subject: Re: Bellevue Revenue Sharing

Mike. Thank you for the email. Sorry for not responding sooner. Was in Florida at my granddaughter's high school graduation. Everything you said in your email is correct. The league playoff revenue sharing was clear to all, including Larry Crain. There is no justification for set-offs; there are no excuses for not paying Bellevue its full share. And there is no reason for any conversation between Larry Crain and you.

Larry. Please be advised that if you do not send a check to Mike Blackmon for the full amount due him - $12,900 - by Thursday, June 2nd, your league championship will be voided and will be awarded to Bellevue.

Joe Newman
ABA CEO

Frankly, I don't know if Blackmon ever got paid by Larry Crain. I can't remember what he told me about that. I do know that I wasn't copied on anymore emails about the subject, Arkansas never did have to vacate their title, and even though Blackmon promised me half of that money as back payment for what he owed me, plus a bonus for a good season…

I never saw a dime.

If nothing else though, I did get two good months of entertaining emails between grown men who acted like children. And as the credit card commercial says, things like that are… priceless.

***

Despite my better judgment and IN spite of tireless efforts, I found myself with no options to coach in the 2005-2006 season except with Mike Blackmon and the Bellevue Blackhawks. Whether that was a poor reflection on me or bad luck/timing still remains to be seen; but regardless of the reasons why, there I reluctantly was for one more season.

Blackmon was emboldened by our playoff run the season before and decided that if one team could be so much fun, then two must better. This guy with no money, no business sense and no ability to generate revenue would up the ante for himself. He decided that he would have one team again in Bellevue but also added another in Tacoma. As I tried to distance myself from him a bit, we spoke much less over that summer leading up to the preseason in October. He also was focusing more on getting Tacoma off the ground, and thus, totally neglecting Bellevue. He did this in part I think, because in his mind he could just repeat the previous season's formula in Bellevue. What he didn't count on was all the people that he had alienated that previous season, with his sarcasm and tantrums, or simply by just not paying them what he owed. The list of outstanding bills and broken promises included Renton High School where we played our games, the Redmond Athletic Club where we practiced and a couple of local businesses who supplied equipment and apparel for us. He had burned those relationships beyond repair which made us have to look elsewhere for these services and more. His reputation for bounced checks and overall lack of payment got around quickly and soon anyone that we wanted to do business with asked for payment up front. I couldn't blame them but it made it very difficult to get anything done. By the time we were ready to open up training camp, we had no where to practice because he refused to pay rent on a facility.

I knew that adding another team within a 45-minute drive to Bellevue would dilute our talent base to draw from. Blackmon let me know that I would have the ability to bring guys in from out of town and he would house them. I got on the phone with some agents and started recruiting the best players that I could to come play for Bellevue. I wanted to keep Haywood, Ellis, Matt Glynn and Jimmie Rainwater (all guards). Yogi decided to play somewhere else, Bunche moved back to Arkansas, Lovell blew out his knee in the off season and Donta would only play in Tacoma since that was where he lived. I set out to find some "bigs" as well as a place for us to practice.

I couldn't get any straight answers from Blackmon about anything but I continued to recruit, and if not sign, at least come to verbal agreements with players about contracts. I sent Blackmon an email a couple of days before we wanted to start camp, which was about a month later than the previous season, and a month later than I wanted to.

> From: "Rick Turner"
> To: MichaelBlackmon
> Subject: meet
> Date: Thu, 03 Nov 2005 10:08a
>
> Do you have some time when we can get together tonight and figure out everything? I have some gym options but need to know if there is budget and come up w/ a plan for practicing and getting guys here from Fresno, Portland, Maryland...I want to start on Saturday.
> btw do we have a game schedule yet?

He responded in typical fashion.

> ----- Original Message -----
> **From:** Michael Blackmon
> **To:** rick turner
> **Sent:** Thursday, November 03, 2005 10:40 AM
> **Subject:** RE: meet
>
> There's no budget for practice. There's no housing budget and there's no transportation budget. Other than that you can have anything you want.

I don't know if I made this clear in my description of Blackmon earlier, but he was what I would consider an epically helpless jock-sniffer. In combining two definitions from UrbanDictionary.com, Blackmon's type of jock-sniffer is:

(n) one who seeks a homoerotic friendship with professional athletes or jocks in general, thinking this will make them higher on the social food chain.

If you were a former or current pro athlete, Blackmon wanted to be your friend, kiss your ass and pretty much, threw himself all over you. He's not the only guy like this (see Howard Shultz); in fact one of my good friends almost wet himself one time when we saw Seahawk running back, Curt Warner, at a Burger King in high school. So it's not just Blackmon, but it is no less irritating or embarrassing to be around.

When Blackmon decided to hire former Sonics player, Vincent Askew, to coach the newly formed Tacoma Navigators, I thought, "let the slobbering begin".

Quite frankly, Vince Askew was a bit of a shady guy. He played nine seasons in the NBA with eight different teams after a nice career at the University of Memphis. His best success in the league came under Coach George Karl while he was with the Sonics from '92-'96, playing a key role on a team that went to the NBA Finals. I knew Vince a little since I had been working for the Sonics during that same time. I spoke with people in the NBA that knew him better than I did, because I figured he and I would be working a lot together with our now shared connection to Blackmon.

Since misery loves company, I thought Askew and I would be kindred spirits that season, arm-in-arm, walking in lock step to the unfailing beat of our distain for Blackmon. However, most of those I spoke to said to be very wary of "Vinny" because he was a slippery one. One former GM even told me to keep a hand on my wallet when around him. He went on to say that although Askew was good teammate on the floor, his off the floor character left quite a bit to be desired. He was maybe a few quarts low on integrity.

I guess you could say that unfortunately, this would later play out publicly in 2008 when he was arrested on allegations of having sex with a 16-year-old girl he tried to recruit to a high school girl's team that he was coaching in Florida.

At the risk of sounding like a jilted lover, Askew got pretty much whatever he wanted from Blackmon that season in Tacoma, while I continued to eat poop. Now, that is a somewhat qualified statement in that Blackmon didn't have the ability or resources to give anyone too much of anything, but at least in Askew's eyes, whatever he asked for, Blackmon said yes.

Not only did Blackmon figure out a way to rent a place for Askew to live while he was in Tacoma, he (somehow) leased him a car and paid for all his meals. Blackmon also hired a General Manager to run the day-to-day operations of the Navigators and moved this guy to Tacoma from Michigan. Meanwhile, Bellevue's entire operation was one reluctant employee...

...me.

The GM Blackmon hired for Tacoma was a young guy named Peter Jackson, whom he had met during CBA meetings when Jackson worked for the Michigan Mayhem of the Continental Basketball Association. Blackmon brought him in and totally abused him from day one like he did with most of the people around him. He treated Peter with a lack of respect that was indignant to the point of complete contempt. Blackmon's utter disregard toward Peter quickly rubbed off on Askew and soon the two made Peter the meat in a Blackmon/Askew shit sandwich on a daily basis. Peter had finally had enough after Coach Askew threatened to (literally) kill him one night after a practice. He was genuinely afraid of Askew after that. The threat, coupled with the fact he had never gotten paid by Blackmon in the first three (going on four) weeks that he had been in Tacoma, forced his hand on an easy decision and Peter Jackson quit before the ink on his business cards could dry.

As I stared down the barrel of another long "effing" season with Blackmon, there was one small beam of light.

The first road trip of the 2005-2006 season for the Bellevue Blackhawks was supposed to be against a new expansion team in Honolulu, Hawaii. That meant three games, spread over the course of nearly a week. This gave me some incentive to want to hang in there with this disaster a little longer, in hopes of getting a free trip to Hawaii and out of the Seattle grayness for a least a few days. But as I suspected would happen, the Hawaii team never played a game that season. Our first two home games that year were supposed to be against the Fresno Heatwave, but the financial realities of the ABA slapped them across the face and the Heatwave never showed up to play.

BTW, I didn't say they cancelled the games with us. Just to reiterate, the Fresno Heatwave didn't show up. With no Hawaii and no Heatwave, I knew it was going to be a cold winter. Instead, we played our first game of the season on the road at Tacoma (go figure).

A week or so later we would finally play our first home game against who else...? Tacoma.

But game three? Well with that game we got a chance to play... Tacoma.

I rapidly got the sinking suspicion that Tacoma might be the only team we would play all season.

Believe it or not, Blackmon actually found a place for us to play our games. We couldn't practice there but at least we could host games. It was the Meydenbauer Center in downtown Bellevue.

It is a beautiful convention center that was a perfect location for a venture like this. However, there would be a major challenge. Even though the building and location were almost perfect, it was really just a big open space. Blackmon would need to essentially 'furnish' it with a court, hoops, scoreboards, shot clocks and bleachers; all the amenities necessary to stage a professional basketball game. I was simultaneously confused and impressed that he was able to get a lease done with the Meydenbauer Center and further impressed and more befuddled when he told me that he located a floor. I was still, however, holding my breath on his ability to execute this plan.

The floor Blackmon located was an actual regulation NBA court. In fact, it was the former floor for the Golden State Warriors and was still painted to reflect that. It had been purchased from the Warriors by the Tri-Cities Coliseum in Kennewick, WA. Blackmon talked the Tri-Cities Coliseum people into renting it to him and trucking it over the Cascade Mountains, about 220 miles west, in time for our home opener on November 30th.

As game time approached for our first home contest of the year with Tacoma, it turned into a typical Blackmon production. It was Keystone Cops redux (cue the circus music). The court arrived in 6x6 pieces that needed to be assembled and the Meydenbauer

Center had no one staffed that night to do it; mostly because Blackmon neglected to tell them.

It was like going to IKEA and buying an NBA floor. There were no instructions on how to assemble it and no tools with which to do it. And believe me, these things are not easy to put together. It's like a 100 ft by 60 ft Rubik's Cube. Each piece has its own place to go and you can't just mish mash them together. So up to and beyond game time, the floor was being assembled by anyone and everyone that Blackmon could find to help. Each piece needed to be fastened together securely and they had one drill to work with. By 9:30 p.m., the floor was ready for the 7:00 p.m. game.

As it finally turned out, the floor and hoops were actually perfect. Everything else however, was completely forgotten about. There would be no scoreboard and no shot clock. The few friends and family that were there to watch (and who actually stuck around through the two-and-a-half hour delay) sat in fold-up chairs, stood up to watch or sat on the cement ground to the side of the court. There were no locker rooms to change in, to meet in for pre-game, half or post, and no showers. There were no concessions and no audio system for music so the atmosphere in there was d-e-a-d... dead. Especially by 9:30. But if you are thinking at all like Russ and I did at the time, you know that the good part of no audio system was the blessing that Blackmon would NOT be on the PA that night.

Remember Rashaad Powell? He was the first guy we signed for Bellevue the previous season. The guy that I cut when he came back from injury because he was moping around about playing time during our winning streak... Remember Rashaad? Well, he was playing for Askew in Tacoma now and I think he may have had this game circled on his calendar for a while because he AB-SO-LUTE-LY shoved it up our stuff in that opening game.

Inside, outside, defensively, to the basket, three's, rebounds, you name it... Rashaad did it in that game. The only thing that wasn't working for him that night was his normally even-tempered disposition. Every basket or big play that he made (and there were quite a few), he ran by our bench with his jaw flapping just to make sure I knew who was doing it.

I did.

How could I miss it with him reminding me all the time? 35 points, 12 rebounds, 4 assists and 4 steals, were the final numbers for Rashaad that night, but it felt like it was even worse than that.

Poor planning and lack of forethought were trademark qualities for the owner of the Bellevue Blackhawks and Tacoma Navigators. We were scheduled to play each other again two nights later at the Meydenbauer Center. What Blackmon didn't know, or bother to check on was if the Center had another event on the night in between games; which of course, they did. This meant that the court would need to be disassembled that night, stored and then reassembled two days later. Blackmon couldn't get a sympathetic ear from the Meydenbauer people, and the daunting task of putting that floor back together himself for game two at the Center was out of the question. Instead of diplomacy to arrive at a solution, he relied on what he knew best and that meant… temper tantrum. A scathing array of F-bombs and vulgar insults were peppered mercilessly at the Meydenbauer staff and management.

Somehow they remained unmoved by Blackmon's colorful display and our second "home" game (the third game of the season) would be played in Tacoma instead of Bellevue. In fact, Bellevue had already played its one and only home game for the 2005-2006 season.

We would get a reprieve from Tacoma briefly for game four. Actually, there was another expansion team in the Northwest that season. The Bellingham Slam joined the league, and thank goodness for everyone involved, they had no affiliation to Michael Blackmon. Yogi had gone to college up in Bellingham and he decided to play that season for the Slam. As I figured would be the case, three of our first four games would be played against Tacoma. The fourth was against Bellingham.

We still had no place to practice and Blackmon expected me to find someone to donate practice space to us free of charge. I had no luck down that path. I barely had five players on the roster as Matt Glynn decided to "retire" from basketball altogether to start his own business. I filled the gaps with some temporary guys, but I knew that ultimately we wouldn't be able to compete without a real talent upgrade. Meanwhile, without us practicing, Vince Askew seized on the opportunity by inviting Haywood, Ellis and Rainwater to come practice with them. Before I knew it, Askew had talked Blackmon into having those guys play for Tacoma instead of Bellevue.

In defense of those players, all they wanted to do was play ball, and at least with Tacoma they practiced everyday and played games. I couldn't blame them for bolting on me, but I remember distinctively the feeling of being betrayed by them at the time. And excuse my expression, but I thought it was a real chicken-sh** thing to do by Askew. I suppose if I had actually felt vested in Blackmon's success, I would have put up more of a fight to keep my players, but in truth, I was worn out with Blackmon to the point of indifference by then and I felt more defeated than resolved. Everything about this was a total circus, and without good solid teams like Utah and Arkansas, the league was turning in to a joke.

I think the Blackhawks played five games (maybe six???), all against Tacoma and Bellingham before Blackmon realized that he was in over his head and couldn't keep two teams alive. He turned his focus toward Tacoma while Bellevue stopped playing games and just faded away. There were no declarations or formal announcements. My best players were in Tacoma now anyway, and I just walked away from it all hoping that my "sentence" with Michael Blackmon had finally led to my parole.

10

Vancouver

If you think that a kiss is all in the lips
C'mon, you got it all wrong, man
And if you think that a dance was all in the hips
Oh well, then do the twist
If you think holding hands is all in the fingers
Grab hold of the soul where the memory lingers and
Make sure to never do it with the singer
'Cause he'll tell everyone in the world

- White Stripes "**Denial Twist**"

2006 was a year of reshaping and redefining the landscape of professional basketball throughout the United States. Truth be told, it had been going through a transition phase for a few years leading up to the '06-'07 season but now it was beginning to shake out. Throughout the '80s and 90s, the second best professional league in the country, behind the NBA of course, was the Continental Basketball Association. The league had produced many players who went on to have prosperous careers in the NBA, but more importantly to me, it had also produced a number of excellent NBA coaches. Among those coaches who had CBA jobs and went on to coach NBA teams were Phil Jackson, George Karl and Flip Saunders. It seemed to me that if I could somehow get to the CBA, I would be able to write my own ticket for my coaching future. In other words, I felt like I would either have success in the CBA, which would give me the ability to move up to bigger and better things… or I would fail miserably and come away with the piece of mind that I did my best at that level but I just wasn't good enough. Frankly, I would have wagered on the former but I just needed to get there.

There was a shake-up though in the CBA that year. The backbone of the league, the three most solid franchises (Idaho, Sioux Falls and Dakota) along with its commissioner, Gary Hunter, bolted for the NBA's Developmental League or "D-League" as it is known. This dramatically strengthened the D-League while simultaneously weakening the CBA. The CBA would welcome in a completely new League Office and a number of new teams; which meant a total face-lift for the league. They moved their operations across the country from Boise, Idaho to Albany, New York and hired a new commissioner and executive board. I knew that, at least for the time being, the CBA and D-League would slug it out to remain the best, most viable minor-league basketball option in the States. It was obvious that the D-League's stock was rising while the CBA's was falling, but during this period of volatility, their opposing paths were still very much equal. Maybe a more clear way of stating it is that if two teams from each league played each other, their talent level would be very close, with a slight edge still going to the CBA, who had more experienced professional players; while the NBDL model focused on younger guys recently out of college.

Both of the league's salary structures were similar, so the players were making virtually the same amount in each ($1,500-$2,500 per month) and each league had safeguards in place to ensure that all of their franchises met their financial commitments. When I referred earlier to wanting a "real" coaching job, I looked at both of these leagues as "real" jobs. Not to say there weren't inherent headaches within them as well, but at least you knew you'd get paid and have at minimum, a modicum of more resources at your disposal to help you succeed; like facilities, staff, and a budget for housing, travel and per diem. There would be someone else to drive the van, someone else to wash the uniforms after every game, and someone else to do all the marketing for the team (or at least help). I was pushing to find an opportunity in either league. I spent most of the spring and early summer of '06 talking with various team owners and GMs about openings in each. I was very close on some and not even on the radar with others, but I felt like I was at least making some headway on breaking through.

Michael Corleone said it best in **The Godfather Part III**, "*Just when I thought I was out, they PULL ME BACK IN*"…

After about five months away from Blackmon, I received an email from him about his impending new franchise in the CBA located in Vancouver, Canada. Things with him and Askew had finally unraveled as was inevitable and Askew was long gone.

His relationship with the ABA had deteriorated to the point of being irreparable. He had a major problem with his payment of the ABA's referees and that, along with other conflicts, had damaged any credibility that he had built with Joe Newman. Some random guy named Alex Lipkowski, sent out a mass email that busted Blackmon's chops about all the money he owed to officials. I didn't know who the guy was and neither did Blackmon. He had no affiliation to the league but for whatever reason he had spoken to someone that had this information on the money he owed. I think he sent it to embarrass Blackmon. It listed all of the referees who were owed money by Blackmon and a breakdown of each. Thankfully, for my own entertainment, Blackmon copied me on his response to the guy.

> From: Alex Lipkowski
> To: ababasketball@
> Subject: List of Game Fees for Michael Blackmon
> Date: Thu, 2 Mar 2006 17:39:23 (PST)
>
> These were sent to me from a member of the league
> office on the condition of anonymity.
>
> -Alex Lipkowski

Game Fees

Name	Date	Fee	Total
Stu Gorski	Nov 26	$200	**not paid $200.00**
Monte Page	Nov 26	$225	**not paid $457**
	Jan 28	$220 bad check	
		$12.50 fee	
Morgan Witt	Nov 19	$200	**not paid $570**
	Nov 30	$200	
	Dec 27	$170 bad check	
Todd Pelham	Nov 26	$225	**not paid $728**
	Nov 30	$250	
	Jan 28	$220 bad check	
		$33 fee	
LeMont Lucas	Dec 1	$225	**not paid $225**
Mike Manning	Dec 4	$400 bad chk	**not paid $720**
	Dec 10	$120 owed	
		paid $100 cash	
	Dec 29	$220 not paid	
Harvey Marshall	Dec 27	$220 bad chk	**not paid $685**
	Jan 18	$215 game was canceled last minute, officials were on our way to game and he said that he would pay us still.	
	Jan 28	$250 bad check	

ADDITIONS:

Name	Date	Fee	Total
Jerry Meneese	Dec 1	$200 bad check	**not paid $1,160**
	Dec 4	$200 bad check	
	Dec 8	$215 not paid	
	Dec 10	$115 owed (paid $100 cash)	
	Dec 29	$215 not paid	
	Jan 18	$215	

The classic and quintessential Blackmon response was sent to Mr. Lipkowski…:

----- Original Message -----
From: Michael Blackmon
To: ABABasketball@
Sent: Sunday, March 05, 2006 6:32 AM
Subject: RE: List of Game Fees for Michael Blackmon

This is sent to you on the condition of anonymity:

"Go fuck yourself asswipe."

Hope that clears it up. Have a nice day.

Michael Blackmon
President and General Manager
Puget Sound Sports and Entertainment, LLC
Phone (206) xxx-xxxx

I kept thinking to myself that once I got into the CBA or D-League, I'd be "in". In other words, I could navigate around much better from inside the league rather than as an outsider trying to "break in". This is why I considered reattaching to Blackmon. For a shot in the CBA regardless of the crap and heartache that I knew would be inevitable. The thing about the CBA was that you actually had to have money to participate as an owner of a franchise. You had to be able to prove it on paper, and pay a fee to the league, which ran much of the game-to-game operations such as travel, referee's fees and administration.

You couldn't just say that you had money; you had to show it up front. This is what would be difficult for Blackmon. But I felt if he could pull it off, and prove it to the league there would actually have to be money there. If he didn't pay me, the league would step up and use his credit line that he had to provide them to get me paid.

So how did he get this far with them? Especially with what he had been through with the CBA two years prior? Again, I'll let his words try and explain in an email that he sent to a potential partner in May of '06. Suffice it to say it was somewhat of a perfect storm that had set up for him in his attempt to slide into the league. An influential group of owners that knew him from before had left to go to the NBDL, an ex-ABA executive that Blackmon knew was hired in the CBA League Office, and the former CBA commissioner hadn't yet caught up to Blackmon's fraudulent ways.

This email was sent to a guy named Richard Kipping, who was trying to set up investors for Blackmon in Canada.

> ----- Original Message -----
> **From:** Michael Blackmon
> **To:** Richard Kipping
> **Cc:** jtm@ ; prett@ ; rspit@
> **Sent:** Wednesday, May 17, 2006 10:49 PM
> **Subject:** CBA VANCOUVER
>
> Rich,
>
> As I mentioned on the phone... we caught a major break today with regard to CBA Vancouver.
>
> A little background...
>
> Last month, four CBA teams joined the NBDL: Bismarck, ND, Sioux Falls, SD, Boise, ID and Broomfield, CO. CBA Commissioner Gary Hunter, one of the most respected pro sports executives in the business, accepted an offer to become

president of Broomfield Sports, the company building a sports arena in Broomfield (Denver) Colorado. Part of his retirement package from the CBA is that he was granted a free franchise for the market of his choosing. He selected Bend, Oregon. Since I went to college at the University of Oregon, I know some heavyweights in Bend who were fraternity brothers, including Randy Pape' who owns the Mt. Bachelor ski resort. I called Gary yesterday to see if he wanted me to bring Randy in on the Bend ownership group. In the course of our conversation, I asked him if he would consider using his free franchise card for Vancouver instead of Bend. He expressed serious interest in doing that. He told me to send him a proposal.

What this means is that we would be able to trump Brave Lion Capital and secure the Vancouver franchise... with the former league commissioner as our partner. THIS IS HUGE!!!

The CBA board of directors meeting will be held on Friday. They're expected to approve the new operating agreement and announce that Ricardo Richardson, the former ABA EVP, will be retained to review applications from parties interested in joining the league. When the announcement is made, there is going to be a deluge of applications to join the CBA. Ricardo told me yesterday that he's already received calls from 20 ABA teams who want in. We would have the ultimate insider in Gary Hunter.

I get along VERY well with Hunter. He wants me to put a proposal on the table in which he would contribute the franchise fee for the Vancouver Dragons and have some kind of consulting role. We have to put together the financial team, but all of the franchise's equity would be available to investors. We need to get a small group together ASAP who are willing to step up as members of the ownership group. That means that they'll have to agree to be included in the official application, but won't have to put up any money until the franchise is granted.

For simplification, Puget Sound Sports will be the official applicant. We've already been approved for Bellevue, so we'll have a huge advantage. CBA requirements include a $5 million net worth (of the entire group), so I need a small group of 3-4 guys who are willing to submit financial information as part of the group. We will ultimately need to raise $500,000 of operating capital, but that can be done after the franchise is granted. After Friday's board meeting the next deadline will be June 1st to have applications completed, then all the financial requirements, including venue dates, must be completed by July 1st so a final schedule can be done by July 15th.

To sum up, I need your best 3 or 4 guys in terms of balance sheet to be submitted BY FRIDAY. I'll be the managing partner for CBA Vancouver and guide us through the application process. We have to demonstrate significant local financial backing, business acumen and a group of people Gary Hunter feels comfortable in.

This deal fell right into my lap today, and we have a golden opportunity to own the ONLY pro basketball team in Vancouver. Hunter confirmed what I already knew... the NBA will never go back to a city that lost a franchise.

Let's make this happen, Rich.

I put the likelihood that Blackmon would actually have a CBA team in Vancouver for the 2006-2007 season at about 20%. It was only that high because Gary Hunter was involved and I had the utmost respect for the ex-commissioner of the CBA, who seemed to have a great amount of integrity in all my dealings with him. Frankly, I couldn't see why he would get involved with Blackmon because I knew Gary was a sharp guy. I figured he was working another angle that I wasn't aware of and I didn't really feel it was appropriate to ask him about it. Hunter and I both gave Blackmon some legitimacy by our involvement, but I was concerned that if I wasn't careful, my veracity could be called into question. I suspect that Hunter was concerned with that as well. Nevertheless, I allowed Blackmon to name me the Head Coach of the new Vancouver Dragons in the CBA even though I wasn't sure they would ever play a game. I did this, in part, because I thought having this title on my resume while I continued to look for a job might provide a bit more gravity in my search throughout the summer.

By mid-September, I did not have another gig and Blackmon hadn't found any investors for the Vancouver Dragons. He and his buddy Richard Kipping were still turning over rocks up in Canada trying to find some money to operate this team. They thought they had some fish on when they decided to host a luncheon in downtown Vancouver to pitch potential investors. Blackmon invited Gary Hunter to come up from Denver to attend and asked me to drive up from Seattle. This, it seemed, would be make or break.

We each arrived quite early at a very nice steak house in Vancouver's downtown area to strategize the "pitch". It was the first time that I had seen Gary Hunter since Blackmon had stormed out of the owner's meeting in Denver a couple of years prior. It was great to see him, but internally I still couldn't understand why he would involve himself with Blackmon. Hunter was probably thinking the same thing about me.

There we were, two reluctant pawns in Blackmon's folly, working to serve our own interests, while attempting to maintain an arm's-length from this crazy man. For one of the very few times that I had ever seen, Blackmon was noticeably nervous about this meeting. He was really trying hard to be organized but that just wasn't a part of his DNA. He tried to pre-choreograph the luncheon but we all knew that this new found discipline would be short-lived. And in fact, once people started to trickle in around noon, the goofy and socially awkward Mike Blackmon was back in full effect.

The first three people to show up were from a PR/Marketing firm that hoped to get our business. They had no investing interest in the team but Blackmon had invited them to come anyway. Two of them ordered the filet while the third got the alder-planked salmon. Two more guys came in shortly after. They were friends of Richard Kipping. Neither one of these guys had interest (or funds) to invest in a pro basketball team, but they wanted to be there to see what it was all about... plus they were hungry. One had the New York strip while the other ordered the filet, but not before they ordered the entire table, drinks and appetizers. It was quite thoughtful of them. Two more guys came in after that. They were there to meet their friend, who actually was interested in becoming a partner in the team. As it turned out, that guy who they were meeting got tied up and wasn't able to make it; but his buddies had a great lunch. Coming in at about the same time was a reporter for the business section of the Vancouver Sun that Blackmon invited. She also had the salmon and a small side salad. Finally, two more guys came in who were not connected to anyone there, but had heard about the luncheon from someone who was invited and couldn't make it. My recollection is that one of them was involved in exotic cars and actually had a small interest in finding out more about partnership in the team. So there we sat, all 14 of us, and maybe… just maybe, one guy who actually had any ability to invest in this basketball team. I will say this though, the lunch was fantastic (I had the filet as well).

As you might expect, Blackmon completely tore Richard Kipping a new one right there in the restaurant after the last guest left. He blamed Kipping for not delivering any potential partners to the luncheon. Feeling embarrassed and empathetic for Gary Hunter, who had to witness all this, I tried to distract him with conversation while Blackmon rained his verbal assault on top of Kipping. My effort was valiant but it was obvious that both Hunter and I were listening to Blackmon's ranting ass-chew while trying to seem as if we were engaged with each other. Neither one of us had any idea of what the other was saying but we kept the conversation going long enough to ease the awkwardness. The lunch was an expensive disaster and guess whose credit card didn't work after it was over…

I guess Blackmon had a different sense of the luncheon or at least that is what he reported to "friends" Rob and Peter the next day in this email account of the event.

> ----- Original Message -----
> **From:** Michael Blackmon
> **To:** Peter; Richard Kipping ; Rob
> **Cc:** Gary Hunter ; Rick Turner
> **Sent:** Monday, September 18, 2006 5:34 AM
> **Subject:** Vancouver Dragons lunch
>
> Well, it could have been better-attended, but, all-in-all, I thought it went very well. I sensed real enthusiasm from the 6 or 7 who showed up. We had Gary Hunter and Rick Turner there, and they're always good. I checked the Evite, and about a dozen of Rich's invitees either never opened the Evite in the first place or never responded. That was probably due to my lateness in getting the Evite put together. We collected no checks, but I think we got some real interest. Richard did an outstanding job in a very short time.
>
> If this were June, I'd say we were off to a great start. Unfortunately, we're in September and our bacon is hanging too low out of the truck. The league has mandated teams have a minimum of $150,000 in cash before they're officially admitted… but that ship has sure sailed.
>
> Rich, you gotta follow up these guys ASAP. Don't beat 'em up for the order, but call them all and ask if they have any more questions, of it they'd like to speak with me, Gary or Rick. Tell them time is running out and we'd appreciate a commitment straight away. I'd tell those managers that the first one of their clients that writes a

$25,000 check, gets a bonus Unit. We gotta make something happen this week. If we don't have the $150,000 in the bank by Friday, we're really screwed for this season.

I've available all week. I'd like to come up there midweek and try and get face-to-face, one-on-ones with the biggest hitters: David Eisenstat, Bruce McDonald, Nick DeCotiis, Nick Louie, Jessel,Troll, etc.

Gotta get it done, boys. It's a multi-million dollar deal.

Michael Blackmon
President and CEO
Puget Sound Sports and Entertainment, LLC

While Blackmon continued to swim against the current in an effort to find money in Canada, the CBA College Draft was quickly approaching and the new, Vancouver Dragons expansion team had the seventh overall pick.

I was still highly skeptical whether the team would ever play a game, but at this point, I had to at least protect what professional integrity that I had and approach the draft as if we were a go for launch. I was in a tough spot because I felt like I was perpetrating a fraud. Going through with the draft made me an accessory to this racket but I felt that quitting would compromise me even worse. I decided to not worry about the things that I couldn't control. I followed the Frosty Westering creed of "Making the Big Time Where You Are" and I dove into the draft as if I were doing it for the LA Lakers or any other team in the NBA. I felt like this would be the only way to get something positive out of the experience. I knew that if I wanted another job in the CBA, or D-League, or even the NBA, this draft scenario would come up and the experience I gleaned from it would only help me. So I worked the phones and spoke with all the NBA scouts, college coaches and various agents that I knew who were scattered around the country. I made profiles on a variety of players who were eligible for the draft and tried to mock up as best I could, a potential draft day scenario. Blackmon secured a conference room at Rob Spitzer's law office in downtown Seattle that became our "War Room" and I had everything mapped out on the white board and spread out over the conference room table as the draft was conducted by conference call in Albany, New York.

When preparing for the CBA Draft there are some inherent challenges. The first of which is, identifying players who are good enough to play for you (as well as a possible NBA call-up) and who will not look to go overseas for bigger money. You try and look for guys who are very talented but might not have the NBA measurables. These are guys who might slip through the cracks because they are undersized, lacking NBA quickness or still developing offensively. Another challenge is because of budget limitations, you rarely get to meet the various players in person before you draft them. There is no budget to hold workouts or personal interviews; so you have to rely on your network of others who do have personal knowledge of the players. This leads to leaning toward players for who you do have some familiarity with and players with region appeal. Guys who might have played college ball in the area, which you've seen, and your fan base can immediately identify with.

The make up of the 2006 CBA was much different from that of the previous season. Idaho, Sioux Falls and Dakota bolted for the NBDL. Michigan folded, as did Rockford and Gary, leaving only Albany and Yakima as the lone holdovers. The new look of the CBA had 10 teams. They were (in draft order):

Minot Skyrockets
Butte Daredevils
Great Falls Explorers
Indiana Alley Cats
Atlanta Krunk
Pittsburgh Xplosion
Vancouver Dragon
Utah Eagles
Albany Patroons
Yakima SunKings

No, that's not a typo. The Atlanta team was called the Krunk. As far as I can tell, Krunk means "crazy drunk" in Ebonics, but I'm as unhip as they come, so I don't really know. Regardless, I wasn't sure how appropriate it was for a team name but maybe their mascot would be Dennis Hopper as "Shooter" from the movie **Hoosiers**? Get it? Crazy-drunk???

As the first pick of the 2006 Continental Basketball Association draft approached on September 26th at 5 p.m. Pacific Time, I had two goals.

1) I didn't want to embarrass myself

2) I wanted to make some good selections just in case we actually ended up fielding a team.

In that order.

Our first selection was JP Bautista, a 6'9" power forward from Gonzaga University who fit as a guy not quite good enough for the NBA and who also had a regional appeal. I knew that in all likelihood he would play overseas but I also didn't want Yakima (located in Eastern Washington) to get him. I felt like if we did have a team, I could pitch JP to stay in the States in the hopes of an NBA call-up. Our next pick was Justin Williams, a 6'10" defensive specialist from Wyoming who was one of the top shot blockers in college basketball in '05. Third pick was Brendan Winters from Davidson College whose dad is longtime NBA vet Brian Winters. Brendan was skilled and smart. The forth pick was PJ Tucker, an undersized forward from Texas who had been drafted by the Toronto Raptors in the second round of the NBA Draft. He was a b-i-t-c-h (in a good way) who was physical, could score, rebound, and wouldn't shy away from contact. My hope was that he wouldn't stick with Toronto and would want to stay in the States for a potential call-up. Our fifth pick was another undersized low post scorer named Jamaal Williams from the University of Washington. I took Jamaal first because he was good, second because he had the obvious local connection, third because it meant Yakima wouldn't get him, but also because I thought it would be good for Coach Romar at UW to have another one of his guys drafted. It was a bit of an ass-kissing ploy on my part (as small as it might have seemed). Our final pick was a point guard named Squeeky Johnson from the Univeristy of Alabama-Birmingham, who came highly recommended by the new staff at Mizzou where one of my former players, Brian Dailey, was now working. In case you're interested in seeing some of the other names, the entire draft board looked like this:

2006 CBA DRAFT
Round-by-Round

FIRST ROUND
1. Minot – Dayshawn Williams (Forward, 6'6", 232) Syracuse
2. Butte – Kenny Adeleke (Forward, 6'9", 240) Hartford
3. Great Falls – Pooh Jeter (Guard, 6'1", 175) Portland
4. Indiana – J.J Sullinger (Forward, 6'1", 210) Ohio State
5. Atlanta– Nik Caner-Medley (Forward, 6'8", 240) Maryland
6. Pittsburgh – Kevin Pittsnogle (Forward, 6'11", 250) West Virginia
7. Vancouver – J.P Bautista (Forward, 6'9", 269) Gonzaga
8. Utah Eagles - Steven Smith (Forward, 6-8, 235) LaSalle
9. Albany – Brad Buckman (Forward, 6-8, 235) Texas
10. Yakama - Michael Hall (Forward, 6'8", 230) George Washington

SECOND ROUND
11. Minot - Dee Brown (Guard, 6'0", 185) Illinois
12. Butte - Chris Quinn (Guard, 6'2", 185) Notre Dame
13. Great Falls - Paul Miller (Forward, 6'10", 235) Wichita State
14. Indiana - Kevin Bookout (Forward, 6'8", 270) Oklahoma
15. Atlanta - Marcus Somerville (Forward, 6'7", 225) Bradley
16. Pittsburgh - Kelly Whitney (Forward, 6'8", 240) Seton Hall
17. Vancouver - Justin Williams (Forward, 6'10", 225) Wyoming
18. Utah - Jose Juan Barea (Guard, 6'0", 175) Northeastern
19. Albany - Wesley Wilkerson (Forward, 6'10", 270) Nebraska
20. Yakama - Dwayne Mitchell (Forward, 6'5", 210) Louisiana-Lafayette

THIRD ROUND
21. Minot - Marco Killingsworth (Forward, 6'7", 235) Indiana
22. Butte - Akin Akingbala (Forward, 6'9", 234) Clemson
23. Great Falls - Louis Amundson (Forward, 6'9", 230), UNLV
24. Indiana - Airmen Kirkland (Forward, 6'10", 240) Cincinnati
25. Atlanta - Travis Garrison (Forward, 6'8", 240) Maryland
26. Pittsburgh - Tedric Hill (Center, 6'10", 240) Gulf Coast Community College
27. Vancouver - Brendan Winters (Guard, 6'5", 205) Davidson
28. Utah - Bryant Markson (Forward, 6'7", 220) Utah
29. Albany - Taj Gray (Forward, 6'9", 238) Oklahoma
30. Yakama - Brandon Bowman (Forward, 6'9", 223) Georgetown
31. Yakama - Allan Ray (Guard, 6'2", 190) Villanova

FOURTH ROUND
32. Minot - Ryan Hollins (Center, 7'0", 230) UCLA
33. Butte - Andre Patterson (Forward, 6'7", 240) Tennessee
34. Great Falls - Cedric Bozeman (Guard, 6'6", 207) UCLA
35. Indiana - Patrick Sparks (Guard, 6'0", 180) Kentucky
36. Atlanta - Curtis Withers (Forward, 6'8", 245) Charlotte
37. Pittsburgh - Hassan Adams (Guard, 6'4", 220) Arizona

38. Vancouver - P.J. Tucker (Forward, 6'5", 225) Texas
39. Utah - Denham Brown (Guard, 6'6", 220) Connecticut
40. Albany – INELIGIBLE SELECTION
41. Yakama - Marcus Slaughter (Forward, 6'9", 220) San Diego State

FIFTH ROUND
42. Minot - Pele Paelay (Guard, 6'3", 195) Coastal Carolina
43. Butte - DeShawn Freeman (Guard, 5'11", 175) Sacramento State
44. Great Falls - Yemi Nicholson (Center, 6'11", 260) Denver
45. Indiana - Daniel Horton (Guard, 6'3", 205) Michigan
46. Atlanta - Tony Skinn (Guard, 6'2", 175) George Mason
47. Pittsburgh - Jai Lewis (Forward, 6'7", 275) George Mason
48. Vancouver - Jamaal Williams (Forward, 6'6", 240) Washington
49. Utah - Paul Davis (Center, 6'11", 270) Michigan State
50. Albany - Jimmy McKinney (Guard, 6'3", 212) Missouri
51. Yakama - Leon Powe (Foward, 6'8", 240) California

SIXTH ROUND
52. Minot - Ed Nelson (Forward, 6'8", 260) Connecticut
53. Butte - Ben Jacobson (Forward, 6'3", 205) Northern Iowa
54. Great Falls - Johnny Gray (Guard, 6'2", 190) Pacific
55. Indiana - Ravi Moss (Guard, 6'2", 190) Kentucky
56. Atlanta - Chris Hunter (Center, 6'11", 225) Michigan
57. Pittsburgh - Carl Krauser (Guard, 6'2", 200) Pittsburgh
58. Vancouver - Carldell Johnson (Guard, 5'10", 185) Alabama-Birmingham
59. Utah - Antywane Robinson (Forward, 6'8", 220) Temple
60. Albany - Gerry McNamara (Guard, 6'2", 180) Syracuse
61. Yakama - Eric Williams (Forward, 6'9", 265) Wake Forest
62. Albany – Chris Copeland (Forward, 6'8" 235) Colorado

As I suspected, within the next couple of days following the draft, someone decided that the Vancouver Dragons would not play the '06-'07 season. The team didn't fold, just suspended its operation. It was said that we would come into the league the following season instead. The bad news was that I didn't have a team to coach, the good news was that if nothing else, I still had a title as the team's Head Coach and Director of Basketball Operations for '07-'08.

I had a fear of going through a basketball season without a job. I saw my career as a continual struggle against the forces of the traditional basketball coaching tract. I saw myself as somewhat of an outsider who was trying to blaze his own trail; not borne from any romantic ideology about how things should be done, but more out of necessity because I started this journey so late in life. I always felt that in my constant struggle to swim upstream in the basketball coaching fish ladder; to go a season without a job would quickly sweep me back down river to where I began. This was just one of the numerous times that minor twinges of panic set in about my chosen career path. The questions filled my head. What was I doing? Who am I fooling? When is enough enough? I would change my mind hour by hour about whether I should keep pushing forward or give in and punt.

Two main thoughts have kept me going in pursuit of my personal grail. The first is that I'm good at this. There is something to be said for finding job that you enjoy which you also happen to be good at. I didn't know if I would be any good when I embarked on this journey in 1997, but as it turned out… I am. The second thing that has kept me going was the fear of pulling the plug too early like I did with my broadcasting career. When I was 23 years old, my goal was to be a Major League Baseball play-by-play announcer. I knew the path that I needed to take to get there but I wasn't willing to follow it at that time. I moved on to the next challenge instead. I felt that if I would have stuck with that plan, I would have reached that goal by now. So, in turn, I haven't wanted to bail on the coaching thing until I knew I had squeezed every last drop from it.

Panic had pretty much turned to resignation in October of 2006 when I got a call from the owner of the Bellingham Slam of the ABA. Without Bellevue and Tacoma in the league, the Slam was looking at much higher travel costs. They ran the numbers and figured that it would be less expensive to operate an additional team locally (within driving distance) on a small budget than incur the increased travel costs of playing more games further away. They asked me if I thought I could put a team together on short notice. I told them that I thought I could and they offered me a chance to coach and run my own team in Seattle.

ABA's King County Royals Name Head Coach and Venues
Veteran coach Rick Turner to lead Royals in first season

SEATTLE - The King County Royals, an expansion team in the American Basketball Association, have announced the signing of the team's first head coach and have also named the team's home venues for their inaugural season. ABA veteran Rick Turner will serve as head coach and also as the team's general manager. In addition, the team has announced it will be playing its home games at North Seattle Community College in the Northgate area of Seattle.

A veteran head coach, Turner has strong ties to basketball in the Puget Sound area. From 1989 to 1997, he served as director of broadcasting for the NBA's Seattle Sonics, before moving on to coach the Bellevue Community College men's basketball team for six years, including four years when he also served as the school's athletic director. In his first year as Bellevue's head coach in 2001, Turner guided the team to a fifth- place finish in the 36-team Northwest Athletic Association of Community Colleges (NWAACC), after a nine-year playoff absence for the school.

After leading his team to the conference championship semifinals and being named the NWAACC's coach of the year in 2003, Turner left Bellevue Community College to volunteer with the University of Washington men's basketball program under coach Lorenzo Romar for one season. In 2004, Turner joined the professional coaching ranks when he joined the Bellevue Blackhawks for their inaugural season in the ABA. Turner led the Blackhawks to the 2005 ABA Championship game, in which the team narrowly lost to the Arkansas Rimrockers. Most recently, Turner was named head coach this summer of the now-defunct Vancouver Dragons of the CBA.

Turner and the King County Royals will kick off the team's first season in the ABA at North Seattle Community College on Sunday, November 12 against their I-5 rival, the Bellingham Slam. For more information, e-mail the team at info@kingcountyroyals.com or visit their website at www.kingcountyroyals.com.

11

King County

Baby, life's what you make it
Celebrate it
Anticipate it
Yesterday's faded
Nothing can change it
Baby, life's what you make it

- Talk Talk "Life's What You Make It"

It wasn't the CBA and it wasn't the D-League, but it was a chance to continue coaching and keep my upstream swim alive and kicking. More importantly, it had absolutely zero connection to Blackmon. I knew what it would take to win in that league, now it was just a matter of finding players at such a late date. There were less than two weeks before our first game with Bellingham and we had no time to waste.

The budget was tiny. I would get $200 per game and could have seven players who would be paid $100 per game each. I took $100 from my stipend so I could get an eighth player and split the other $100 with Harold who agreed to work again as my assistant coach. Confronted with the same challenges to find practice space without a budget for it, I traded my own personal services with a local private high school to secure gym time. I put on various clinics for students at the school, and in return, they let the Royals practice in their gym.

Finding players was another difficult challenge. I was operating on the same model as I did with the Bellevue Blackhawks where all players had to be local, but many of the usual suspects in the area had moved on to other things. In fact, there was no one from that '05 Blackhawks team who was available to play for the Royals that season. We would have to start completely from scratch and it turned out to be much more difficult than I anticipated.

By our first game on November 12th, I had only "signed" four players that I knew I wanted. The top guy was Randy Green, a 2 guard from Washington State University who played high school ball at Seattle's Rainier Beach. The other three were Jamaal Miller, another guard who was a prolific scorer; Darnell Taylor, a small point guard from Western Washington University; and Wale Adeyemi, a raw 6'9" forward who went to high school at Seattle's Garfield High.

In case you weren't aware, you need five guys to play a game. I only had four.

With the help of some local coaches, we scrapped around and found some others to fill out a roster for that first game. One was a 7'0" bank teller named Sunri Nichols, who was grossly out of shape, but had some skill for his size. Sunri let me know immediately following the first game that he was going to focus on his banking skills and that basketball was out. Another was a guy from Seattle Pacific University named Chad Williams, a lefty who was pretty good, but didn't want to make the commitment to playing all season. We found a local firefighter named Paul Richards who was all hustle, but couldn't play on days that he worked. He worked one week on and one week off, so that made things pretty difficult.

That gave us seven players for the first game, three of whom I had never met until the day of the game, and one player, Jamaal Miller, never even showed up at all. So actually we only had six players. Needless to say, we lost our first game to Bellingham that night, 108-96. More bad news was that we lost Darnell Taylor to a knee injury in that game and finished with five guys. The good news was that Randy Green had 36 points and played much better than I thought he would. I knew he was going to be a good player for us. Now I just needed to find some others to join him.

On a little side note, Bellingham loaned us one of their front office people, Kip Leonetti, to serve as our basketball operations guy. It was so nice to have help and to work with someone who was professional, organized and good at their job. Kip took a huge load off of my shoulders in terms of promotions and especially game day management. Plus, he was a good guy to be around. I'll never forget the feeling that I had sitting on the sidelines in the 15 minutes leading up to our first home game. I'm at somewhat of a loss to describe the sense of peace and/or relief that I felt knowing that all the tiny details of putting on a professional event were taken care of. There was music playing in the gym, we had a scorekeeper, we had a real PA announcer, we had a shot clock operator, we had a stats keeper, and we had someone videotaping the game. The referees were there and already paid in full. I had no fear of embarrassment. I was proud of what I was doing and it was just an indescribable "moment" that I had there; sitting by myself courtside; watching our team warm up. The team itself wasn't where I wanted it to be, but I knew that it would get better.

We played the Beijing Olympians a week later. They were a Chinese team that was based in Los Angeles and had some very good players like Sun Yue, a 6'9" point guard who was drafted by the Lakers in '07. We were still trying out potential players as we went along, and we lost 107-92 in a pretty one-sided affair. We wouldn't play again for two weeks and this would give me some time to find more guys.

It was tough to find guys to commit to playing and practicing for just $100 per game. The good part was that I literally paid them right after the game in the locker room, and there was never a payment missed. That certainly helps your credibility as you continue to recruit players. The hard part wasn't so much finding enough guys to play each game. The tough part was trying to build a team. It was getting the guys to commit to practicing when many had outside jobs. They didn't want to jeopardize their "day job" by missing work for games and road trips, especially for $100 per game. By about the fifth game of the season, the shape and face of the team started taking place.

Our guards were good: Randy Green, Kyle Keyes, Jamie Booker and Vershan Cottrell were a solid group. We had problems finding "bigs". We had JD Huleen, a 6'8" forward from Boise State, but he sold medical supplies as his "real" job and his wife kept his balls in her nightstand. She wouldn't let him go on any road trips. Wale Adeyemi had good size and was fairly athletic but was still trying to find his way in pro basketball. I added 6'9" Jackie Jones from Oklahoma who played for me with the Blackhawks, but by then he was 39 years old. Our hole card was Jeffery Day.

Jeff was a 6'9" forward from Creighton by way of the University of Washington, who was highly skilled, explosive, athletic, completely unreliable and immature. Don't get me wrong, he was a great, great kid to be around. He could dominate games at times but just didn't have the drive to be great consistently. He didn't have the ability to push himself like great players do. He needed someone else to push him. Unfortunately, he also needed someone to push him out of bed in the morning (or most cases afternoon). I had the ability and means to push him on the basketball floor, but I couldn't be with him 24/7. As much as I loved the guy, he turned out to be probably the most unreliable player that I ever coached. It was disappointing because he was really, really talented. Jeff would show up for a stretch of games and then disappear for awhile, never telling me where he was or why he left. He always claimed to be having cell phone problems.

"Uh, yeah coach... my cell phone wasn't working for a few days" was the typical excuse.

The Royals limped along for a while hovering near .500 as we continued to search for the right combination. In January, we had a three-game road trip to Modesto and Sacramento. The owner of the team said that we could fly down for it, but I was still trying to juggle the roster, and couldn't provide him with names for airline tickets in time to get a decent airfare. I told him that we (actually I) would drive a van from Seattle for the trip, so I could try and nail down some new players before we left. We decided to leave at 6 a.m. for the 12-hour drive to Sacramento. Jackie couldn't go because he had no one to watch his kids while his wife worked. JD couldn't go because he had to work (plus his wife wouldn't let him), so we were down to just seven guys. When we all got to our meeting spot at 6 a.m., there was no sign of Jeff Day. Normally, I would have just left without him but then we'd have just five guards and Wale. It would be difficult to compete with that group. I got on the phone and called his cell number. It went directly to voicemail. I called his home phone (he lived with his mother), but there was no answer. We waited a bit longer, still no Jeffrey. Finally at almost 7 a.m., we took off for Sacramento, sans Jeff Day and with only six players.

All in all, the trip was a disaster. Jeffery finally called me once we were down there to apologize for missing the van. I told him that I would fly him down to meet us for the final two games. He said okay and would make arrangements with our team's operations guy, Kip. He never followed through with Kip, and thus, never showed up for any of the games. We went 0-3 on the trip, but I think we would have been 2-1 if Day would've shown up. It really put a dent in our playoff hopes.

During the trip, I did everything for those guys. I drove the van the entire trip (that's lots of driving), I washed uniforms after games (which may not sound like much, but it means sitting in a laundromat for two hours), I drove them to get food, I hustled around to find practice space since neither of the teams we played provided us with any. I was working hard for these guys, but at the same time, I really enjoyed it. That is, until the afternoon before our final game of the trip.

I was in my hotel room watching the AFC Divisional Playoff between the Patriots and the Jets, surrounded by wet uniforms that were now drying from the previous night's visit to the local laundromat. I had jerseys, shorts and warm-up tops hanging everywhere throughout the room because I didn't trust my ability to dry them with a machine. I was afraid to ruin them. Then my phone rang.

It was Kyle Keyes. He had rented a car and needed his game money so he could pay for it that afternoon. It was some sort of shady deal because he didn't have to put down a credit card for the rental. I think he rented it through a guy he knew and was supposed to pay that guy cash. I actually don't really know the whole story other than he needed his game money and I didn't have it. I didn't feel comfortable carrying around over $2,000 dollars in cash for the whole trip, so I told our owner that I would get the money from him and pay these guys when we got back to Seattle. I didn't think anything more about it. I explained to Kyle the situation, told him that I'd pay him and everyone else when we got back to Seattle, and reminded him that we would leave for the game around 3 p.m. We hung up and I went back to watching football.

I was sitting there on the edge of my bed in a t-shirt and boxers, remote control in my hand, when I got a knock on my door. When I opened it, I had all six guys standing there in the hall wanting to have a "talk". I invited them in and muted the TV. I sat back on the bed and asked what was up. As the oldest and most experienced of the group, Jamie Booker stepped forward to talk.

"Uh, coach… we want to know where our money is" he kind of mumbled.

"I don't have it here with me. You'll all get it when we get back" I told them as matter-of-factly as I could.

I could see in their faces that something wasn't right. There was a disconnect with my ability to understand why they were upset and their ability to understand that there was nothing to worry about. Booker continued…

"I just think this is bullshit, I didn't come here to play for free."

"You're making something out of nothing, have you ever not been paid before?" I asked, knowing the answer was no.

"Yeah…Tijuana, Hollywood, Hermasillo…"

"No, no, no… by this team. Have we ever missed a payment?" I asked again.

"Not yet, because we haven't let you and we're not gonna let you miss this one." Booker began to get bolder in his argument.

The back and forth went on for about 15 minutes with the guys making demands and threats about not playing that night unless they got paid. I couldn't understand where it was coming from. Finally, I had to put an end to it.

"I don't know what to tell you guys. I don't have money for you right now. I will have it when we get back to Seattle. Do what you have to do. Do what you feel is right for you, but I'm leaving for the gym at 3:00 with or without you."

The players left my room and I sat there dumbfounded. I felt totally betrayed by these guys who I was busting my ass for all season. I was pissed beyond pissed and marinating in my anger as I tried to rationalize what just happened. A piece of me was kind of happy that they stuck together as a group, but as I thought about each guy individually, it became clear how this came about. I knew Green, Vershan, Wale and Shamon Antrum didn't need the money right now. They were just happy to be there and playing pro basketball. Booker was a loose cannon and someone who I feared might be a headache even before we signed him. However, to my pleasant surprise he had been very professional and respectful from the first day on. In fact, I leaned on him quite a bit as a veteran presence for our young guys. That left one guy…

… F***ing Keyes.

Here was a guy that I totally rescued, gave a second chance to revitalize his career after long bouts with injuries. I placed more confidence in him than any coach he'd ever had, gave him a long leash to perform, and as Kenneth said to Ronnie in **Can't Buy Me Love**, he "shit on my house, man".

I may not be adequately explaining the situation or the feelings that coursed through me at the time. It was easily one of the lower points in my career as a coach. It was fueled somewhat, I'm sure, by the circumstances of the moment. The long trip, losing games, my own self-doubt, and a frustration about our roster all fed into it, but up to that point I was able to kind of power through all of that. The mini-mutiny by the players had totally taken the wind from my sails, and left me really questioning myself, and the decisions that I had made to take this team on.

Still steaming, but holding it all inside like I'm so good at, I packed up everything, checked out of the hotel, and went downstairs to meet everyone at the van for the half hour drive to the gym and our 6 p.m. game. I knew we'd be a little early, but we had to out of the hotel by 3 p.m. or they would charge us for an additional night. I also knew that we wouldn't all be ready to leave by 3:00 so there was some padding left in there. Guys were emerging from the hotel and piling their bags in the van when Keyes approached me.

"Uh, hey coach. Can you take me to drop off my rental car? It's about five minutes from the gym." He asked me, completely oblivious to my mood or the ambush that he orchestrated a couple hours earlier.

"Couldn't we have taken care of this earlier, instead of an hour before the game?" I answered in a disdainful tone.

"Oh yeah… uh, I forgot… but it's close to the gym so it won't take long."

My internal conversation was imploring me to try and act like an adult. All my instincts said to pout and be a martyr. But I fought them and acquiesced. Maturity won out for once and I swallowed every bit of my pissed offedness that I had for Keyes at that moment. I said okay to taking him back to return his rental car even though it took every ounce of composure that I could muster. Besides, we had a game in a couple of hours and I didn't want to have any distractions.

From a timing aspect, we were caught in no man's land before the game. I didn't think we had enough time to return his car with the whole team, but if I dropped them at the gym first, before returning the car, they would be there unusually early. Pro athletes like to have a routine and when that routine gets interrupted, they don't always react well. I chose to drop them off at the gym, two and a half hours before tip-off, which was one hour longer than normal. I followed Keyes back to the rental car place which was supposedly "five minutes away".

A half hour later, he was still driving his rental car and I was still following behind in the team van. Fifteen minutes after that he was officially lost. Over an hour later, after we dropped the rest of the team off at the gym, we had finally returned his car to some random parking lot that wasn't even a rental car lot nearly 40 miles from the gym. We finally arrived back at the gym at 5:50 p.m., just ten minutes before the game was to start. I was so pissed at Keyes that I couldn't see straight. I had no built-in mechanism to express my anger, so I just stewed in it for the entire drive back to the arena.

We got the pee beat out of us that night by a Sacramento team that wasn't all that good. We were tired, lethargic and ready to go home. I was facing an overnight 12-hour drive back to Seattle with a group of guys who I was pissed at and completely sick of being around.

It was a pretty quiet ride back home. By midnight, everyone in the van was asleep. I was left there sitting in silence. Driving up I-5 and contemplating life as I struggled to keep my eyes open as we winded through the Siskiyou Mountains in Northern

California, up through Oregon and finally into Seattle. We pulled back into town at 8:30 a.m. the next day. We were road weary and I was sick of losing. Something had to be done to fix it.

I tinkered around with the roster for the next couple games and with the re-additions of JD and Jackie once we got home, it seemed to breathe some life into us again. On January 17th, we hosted the Maywood Buzz from Southern California. They were not a good "team" but had a lot of extremely talented players. Dangerous. The Buzz connected on 13 of 23 three-point attempts, including a deep, deep 3 by Will Burr, with under a minute to play, to steal a 117-114 win on the road against us. We were all in the locker room afterward decompressing from the game when out of nowhere Tim Ellis walked in to talk with me and Harold. Tim was back from Iceland where he had been playing ball and wanted to know if we had a spot for him on our team. Harold and I looked at each other and smiled.

"Yeah, absolutely we do" I told him. If we could add Tim and just one more "big", we could win the whole thing.

Tim had 42, 38 and 45 points in his first three games with the King County Royals. He and Green were a potent one-two punch. Booker had a complete all-around solid game and was an excellent defender as well as being a stabilizing force for us. Keyes was making better decisions at the point and not trying to do too much while JD and Jackie were solid, if not spectacular, upfront.

If we could just find one more good "big"…

In late January, both the local Seattle newspapers (the Times and Post-Intelligencer) did long feature stories on our team. Call it coincidence, or something different, but Jeffery Day called soon after the articles came out with a mea culpa and asked to get back on the team. He was just what we needed if he could get right.

We finally had a group together that we could win with. I felt strongly we could win the entire ABA Championship, but we had dug ourselves such a hole, and I knew getting in to the playoffs would be tough. One thing that I did know through my experiences with Blackmon though; was that if our owner advocated strongly enough for us, Joe Newman would capitulate and put us into the playoffs regardless of our record. I would just need to convince our owner to do that if need be.

Running against my wishes however, was the fact that Bellingham was going to be in the playoffs for sure. This meant that our owner would have double the expenses with two teams in the playoffs and I don't think that he was counting on that. We had been put together to save them money, not cost them more. Besides, we generated no revenue and provided no way for the owner to recoup any losses. We were really just a Washington Generals for the Bellingham Slam to use and abuse, but what they didn't see coming was that… we got good. I pressed and pressed to get our ownership to convince the league to put us in the playoffs. I couldn't believe that, at that moment; I actually missed Blackmon's unabashed self promotion. The owner finally agreed that if the team had a strong showing in our final three games in LA, he'd do his best to get us in. That was all I needed to hear. With the additions of Tim Ellis and Jeff Day, I knew we'd play well in Los Angeles.

We had two games against the Beijing Olympians and one game against the Maywood Buzz to complete the regular season. We would stay in Pasadena, which was close to the campus of Asuza Pacific University, where the Beijing team played its home games. It would be a quick trip with back-to-back-to-back games on Saturday, Sunday and Monday. We had an early flight Friday morning out of Sea-Tac Airport to Burbank on Alaska Airlines. On Thursday, I called everyone just to confirm what time to meet at the airport and remind them to set their alarms (at little extra hand-holding never hurts). I spoke to Keyes and Green, Wale and Vershan. I left a message for Jackie, Booker and Day. Then I called Tim Ellis.

"Hello?" Tim answered on the third ring.

"Tim, it's coach. Just want to remind you that we need to be at the airport tomorrow at 5 a.m. and no later, okay? Make sure you have your alarm set."

"Uh, I don't think I can go."

"Huh?" I responded brilliantly with mouth agape.

"Yeah, I gotta work."

Work? I thought to myself. You're a basketball player, this IS your job. Especially for Tim. He was the one guy (and maybe Randy Green) who actually had a chance to make some money at this game. I didn't even know he had another job.

"What do you mean, you gotta work?" I asked.

"My boss told me that if I'm not there tomorrow, I'll be fired."

"What do you do? Where do you work?" I asked as the tone in my voice rose up in disgust.

"I move furniture" he explained.

By now I was incredulous.

"Tim…" I paused for effect. "You can get a f***ing moving job anywhere. Those places don't fire people; they can't find ENOUGH people to work. You're not going to blow this so you can move some woman's couch that smells like cat piss up three flights of stairs only to move it back down because she decides it doesn't look good in that room… c'mon man."

"Sorry, I can't do it" He repeated.

"Can you come for a part of the trip? Even if you had to miss Saturday, could you play Sunday and Monday?" I was scrambling to save our season.

"I don't know, I'll check. I'll call you back."

I never heard from Tim again.

The next morning, the morning of the trip, I was in my car driving toward Sea-Tac airport at around 4:30 a.m. when my cell phone unexpectedly rang. You always think the worst when you get a late night or early morning phone call, but when I looked down at the display I could see that it was from Jeffrey Day. This was good. At least he was up and out of bed.

"Good morning Jeff, what's up?" I answered brightly.

"Uh, hey coach… I don't think that I can be there this morning" Jeff told me in a surprisingly lucid tone for this hour.

"What do you mean? Why?"

"I can't find anyone to do my paper route and I can't get a hold of my boy who said he'd do it for me." Jeff went on. "I've been calling him but he's not answering his phone."

(Thought bubble pops up over my head) "Paper route? This has to be a joke. You're blowing this off because of an effing paper route? Are you serious Jeff?"

I was left speechless.

Like Tim, I didn't even know Jeff had another job. We had never talked about it and I just thought he spent his days sleeping. I have to tell you, however… as upset as I was that this was happening, I couldn't help but feel a little impressed that each of these guys were showing more responsibility then I had ever given them credit for having. I really would have expected both of them to choose basketball over their jobs (especially those two jobs). I would have paid them $300 cash (which I did bring with me this time) for the three days and figured it was more than they would make moving furniture or delivering newspapers in the same amount of time. It didn't make a lot of sense to me, but I couldn't really argue with Tim and Jeff both choosing responsibility over a short-term indulgence. I just didn't expect it from either of those two guys.

I made the same offer to Jeff as I did with Tim. Take some more time to figure it out, find a fill-in for work and come down on a later flight.

And as with Tim, I never heard form Jeff again.

Without Tim Ellis and Jeff Day we had six players. This left us in somewhat of a bind. I was forced to get one of my buddies, who I grew up with and who lived down in Southern California, to suit up for us and be an extra body off the bench in case something strange happened.

Omar Parker was (is) one of my closest friends and one of the few guys that I knew who could still pass for a basketball player at the advanced age of 40. Unfortunately for us, his emergency addition to the squad wouldn't even make him the oldest guy on our team. That went to Jackie Jones who had outlived Omar by a couple months. The difference however, between a 40-year-old Jackie and a 40-year-old Omar was about 10 inches, 80 pounds and 15 years of pro basketball experience. Omar was in really good "old man" shape but he wasn't even close to professional basketball player shape. In fairness to him, Omar was a good basketball player in his younger years and asking him to fill in for us wasn't that much of a stretch. He played college ball at the University of San Diego and later transferred to BYU-Hawaii where he helped lead the Seasiders to the national tournament. He also happens to be one of the best coaches that I have ever known and he played a large part in inspiring me to pursue a coaching career. Frankly, I'm not sure whether to thank him or blame him for that. But with only six players and three games in three nights, I talked Omar into suiting up.

Reluctantly, Omar agreed to help me out. It took some light arm-twisting but I ultimately talked him into "signing a three-day contract". Of Omar's many good qualities, the one that I get the biggest kick out of is his ability to totally own every situation that he's in. There is not a shy bone in his body. When he showed up to play for the King County Royals it was no different. When he walked into the locker room he looked great. I felt comfortable that everything would be okay with him as our theoretical "12th man". Besides, I probably wouldn't need to use him anyway. He would be a safety net for us, and someone on the bench that I could talk to about various game situations, as we somehow try and make a late push into the ABA playoffs. He would be my assistant coach, but instead of wearing a suit, he would be wearing a uniform. Beyond all that, it was great to see him and hang out with him since we hadn't been able to do that much after he left Seattle a few years earlier. If nothing else, we'd have a great story.

But by the time he dressed down and walked onto the court for warm-ups, I was having second thoughts. I never realized how tiny he was until he was out there standing next to actual basketball-sized men. His uniform was too big, he seemed to be swimming in the smallest one that we had; he looked every bit of his age and he was wearing a gay little headband that did nothing to promote his image as a serious hooper. He looked like a guy that we pulled out of the master's division of the local rec league

But like I said... he OWNED it.

Omar happens to be one of the most competitive guys that I know, and I knew that if he did have to play for some reason (god forbid) he would back down from nobody…

And that is exactly what happened.

Some early foul trouble and a minor ankle tweak forced me to call Omar's number late in the first quarter against the Beijing Olympians, in a game that was being broadcasted back across the Pacific to one billion Chinese citizens and rabid basketball fans; something that Omar and I found to be hilarious. I can only imagine what they must have thought of American basketball and the ABA; when they saw this diminutive, over-aged white guy check into the game, wearing a uniform that was four sizes too big, playing against Chinese heroes like Sun Yue and Yi Jianlian.

As any of us who knew Omar would expect, the first thing that he did upon checking in to the game was shoot a deep three on his first touch of the basketball. Not only did he look old out there; which I honestly underestimated that he would, he played an old man's brand of basketball. It was very Bob Cousy-esque.

Since he was the smallest player out there for us, we put him on Beijing's smallest player, 6' 6" Toby Bailey.

Toby played at UCLA, where he won an NCAA National Championship as a freshman in 1995, and went on to become the Bruin's fourth leading scorer in school history behind Don MacLean, Kareem Abdul-Jabbar and Reggie Miller. He was drafted by the Lakers in '98 and played for the Phoenix Suns for a couple of years before getting hurt. He had hooked on with this Chinese team as a way to try and possibly make a comeback after a bad knee injury. I yelled out to Omar from the sideline as he checked in.

"Hey Omar, you've got Toby!"

Priceless.

Thankfully, Toby took it easy on Omar. I can't say the reverse was true however. It was kind of like watching an adult put his outstretched hand on the little kid's forehead while the kid is swinging wildly at the guy but can't reach him. (Toby as the adult here and Omar as the kid). Omar threw his entire repertoire at Toby including a running left-handed, sky hook from about 12 feet away that started from his socks and banked in off the glass as the crowd went crazy. As Omar Cadillac'd back down the court to play defense, after scoring the first ABA points of his career, I looked up into the stands and saw spectators laughing and imitating his hook shot from their seats as they cheered for the Royals' version of "David".

Omar filled in admirably for us, given the bind that we were in, but even his inspirational play wasn't enough to overcome our shortcomings.

Our guys fought hard, but three games in three nights, against two pretty good teams, was too high of a mountain to climb. We went 0-3 on the trip and there would be no playoffs for the King County Royals in 2007.

The Bellingham Slam changed leagues and moved into the International Basketball League the next season. The IBL was a spring league with more regional teams which cut down on travel. There was no need for a travel partner, and thus, there would be no more King County Royals. From my perspective, I had mentally moved on anyway; I was burned out on the ABA and wanted to take on some new challenges.

12

Hawaii

I never had a day where money didn't get in my way
I never listened to much Elvis
I can't remember a warm December
Am I the son I think I am
Am I the friend I think I am
Am I the man I think I wanna be

- Train "**I Am**"

"The apple doesn't fall far from the tree". You hear it quite often about kids and parents, but as I started thinking more about that thought, it occurred to me that it is basically the same as saying that a team "takes on the personality of its coach".

That is something that we hear all the time and I 100% believe it to be true. You expect it from your kids, but for whatever reason, when I first started coaching I thought it was just something that TV announcers said to sound smart. If coaches are trees, then our players are the falling apples. If you believe that a team does take on the personality of their coach then you might ask; what kind of apples does my tree produce? Like other coaches, I think that my personality contributes to a number of traits that my teams exhibit. Some are good and others, not so much. Like with your children, these traits of your players are not chosen but just happen. They happen because our players are an extension of us coaches.

If I had to narrow it down to one trait (or quality) however, that best describes both me and my teams… one word stands out above the rest.

Resolve.

I'm not sure if that answer wins any job interviews or inspires athletic directors. I don't know that it makes headlines or wins over NBA GM's. Actually, I shouldn't say that. The fact is that I do know whether it does those things, and at least so far… it doesn't.

What I do know though is that resolve wins basketball games. I do know that it helps make "underdogs" into "overachievers". It makes you believe you *can* when everyone else says you *can't*.

Where did it come from?

In 1961, my dad graduated from Lake Washington High School and went off to Washington State University in an attempt to walk-on the WSU football team. He was a wiry ankle-biter with more hustle than muscle and more heart than smart. An undersized scrapper who wouldn't (and couldn't) "back down from no one". He was a self-described country kid just trying to escape life on my grandparents' farm.

Shortly after starting fall practices with the Cougars, my dad suffered a pretty serious head injury that would immediately end any hopes of playing Pac-8 football. He suffered a significant skull fracture (as if there's any insignificant ones) playing football. He was lucky to even survive. Not only did he have to quit the game altogether, but he had to leave school as well, as he tried to recover.

After he started to get back on his feet and now back home, he took a job working for his girlfriend's dad in a used car lot in downtown Redmond, Washington, where he grew up. It was at the used car lot where he and one of his buddies got the idea that they would pack a suitcase and move to Hawaii. My dad had never been out of Washington state and had barely ever left Redmond. Nonetheless, he started saving up his money to go seek the sun.

My grandma wouldn't let him go unless he had a plane ticket home, so he had to save up twice the amount of money he needed to fly there. He also needed to buy a coat and tie so he would have the appropriate clothes to get on an airplane. In 1962, getting on a plane in a t-shirt, shorts and flip-flops would have been totally unheard of. People got dressed up to fly and my dad didn't have anything close to resembling a suit and tie.

As my dad finally saved up enough money to make the trip, his friend told him that he changed his mind and wasn't going. Actually, the guy's mom wouldn't let him go, but by now, my dad had his mind set. He decided he would go to Hawaii alone and totally on his own.

Eighteen years old, green and just enough money to get by, my dad got out of Redmond, Washington and ventured across the Pacific Ocean to the island of Oahu.

His first night on the island he got a room at a beautiful hotel on Waikiki Beach. Simple economics dictated that these accommodations would be short lived, so he got up the next morning, grabbed a newspaper and found a furnished one-bedroom apartment that he could rent month-to-month. He walked up the beach, found a bicycle for sale and along with the bike, he bought enough groceries to last him a month. This left my dad with $10 in his pocket. He figured that if he couldn't make anything work in a month, he would ride the bike back to the airport and fly home.

With all the necessities taken care of (at least for the time being), my dad did what any 18-year old, freckle-faced country kid would do in his first free moment in Hawaii. He went to the beach. "Young, dumb and full of cum" he walked on to the fine, white sand beach of Waikiki, found a great spot to lie down, closed his eyes and fell asleep in the warm embrace of the Hawaiian sun.

As el sol dropped behind Diamond Head for another day, my dad awoke from his sandy cat nap and grabbed his bike to head back to his wicker wonderland apartment. Upon arriving, his new neighbors, a retired army colonel and his wife, immediately saw that the Hawaiian sun's warm embrace had turned into more of a violent strangulation on the fair skin of my dad.

He was scorched.

He had no previous relationship with the sun, growing up in the outskirts of Seattle, and he had no idea what the tropical rays could do to a pasty white kid's skin. The colonel's wife stripped him down to his underwear, put a rubber sheet on his bed and poured vinegar all over his body in an attempt to alleviate the pain caused by his ill-timed slumber. She convalesced my dad for three days by swabbing and dressing his blisters before he was finally able to get out of bed and attempt to take on the Hawaiian sun once again. Before he did, however, she introduced him to sunscreen, which he amply applied for the first time ever, and she advised him on the 411 of sun survival in the tropics.

Shortly after my dad's 1962 foreshadowing of Fire Marshall Bill, he set out on his bike to find a job.

He had two things working against him at that time. Number one, he was under the legal drinking age in Hawaii, which meant that he couldn't work anywhere that served alcohol (which in a tourism hot spot like Hawaii, that meant everywhere) and number two, he was a haole. He knocked on door after door trying to remain upbeat and positive when speaking with various people along the way. But, door after door kept getting slammed in his face. Near the end of his rope and desperate not to have to go back to Redmond with his tail between his legs, my dad's diplomacy waned.

After exhausting every option he could think of, he rode his bike up to a pineapple factory a few miles up the road. He walked in the office and spoke to the woman at the front desk about a job. The woman quickly and coldly told him that there were no jobs and that they were not hiring at the moment. Hot, from his long bike ride and even more so under the collar, my dad went storming out of the office. He angrily pushed open the office door and it nearly came off its hinges. As the door flew open, it unexpectedly hit a man on the other side who was about to walk in. The man was the owner of the pineapple factory.

"Whoa, whoa son... what's the problem here?" he asked rather empathetically for someone who just got hit by an out of control door.

"Look at me!" my dad snapped back the guy, not knowing who he was.

The guy looked at him up and down.

"Here I am a strong, hard-working 18-year old man who doesn't drink, doesn't smoke and will bust his ass for anyone willing to give him an opportunity and I can't get anyone to hire me!!!" my dad said, wearing his heart on his sleeve.

"I like your spunk son, let's go back inside and talk."

The two went back into his office where my dad explained his situation and told the man that he was willing to do anything that the guy needed just for a job. The man pointed out the window, up to his house. It was way up on the hill, above the pineapple plantation.

"Be at my house tomorrow morning at 6 a.m." he said

My dad arrived the next morning a half hour early at 5:30. After riding his bike up the big hill to the plantation owner's darkened house, my dad knocked on his door and waited. He knocked again. Obviously, the man was still asleep. He knocked one more time. Finally, he heard footsteps coming from inside the house and the door opened. The man stood there in his bath robe, clutching the door handle in one hand, and wiping the sleep from his eyes with the other. He looked at my dad standing there. Then he looked at his watch and smiled.

My dad had a job. Redmond would have to wait a little longer.

The lesson of this story, as my dad would repeatedly retell it to me in my youth, was to never take no for an answer.

"Beat his goddamned door down if you have to" was the advice I received many, many times as I went after various opportunities during my life.

I always hated how simple he made it seem. Like all I had to do was tell someone how much I REALLY wanted the job and they'd give it to me. However, right or wrong, this is exactly what I've done.

My inherited stubbornness, and probably naive idealism, have driven me to hold onto the thought that a proven track record of success (along with hard-work, strong-will and passion) should win out for a job over cronyism, nepotism and the guy who has the most impressive coach make a phone call on his behalf.

Armed with this aggressive approach chiseled into my DNA, I set out to find a variety of coaching gigs throughout the off seasons of '06, '07 and '08. My aggressive approach worked with Delta Airlines and Larry Bauer back in 1990, and I fully expected that it would again.

When I worked at KJR and the Sonics back in the early '90s, I worked with a guy at KUBE (sister station to KJR) named Mike Tierney. Mike was the Program Director at KUBE and was leaving to become a VP at VH1 (he later went on to become a VP at

Epic/Sony Records). I sat down with him before he left, at a time when I was trying to find some direction with my career. Mike gave me a piece of advice that has always stuck with me. As I look back at it, that advice in some ways has been a curse, but I guess not so much of a curse that I have abandoned it.

Mike said, "Find what you want to do and do it. Don't compromise it. If you want to work in radio "on-air" then work on-air… don't be a producer and hope to get promoted to an on-air spot someday. If you want to do news, do news… don't do something else, like sports, and hope that one day they'll move you to news, go do news. Don't leave it up to someone else. Go be who you are. Don't ever let anyone else compromise that."

At the time, it really made sense to me. It still does, kind of, but I think that is where the naive idealism started to creep in. I knew that when I quit the Sonics back in '97, I wanted to someday coach in the NBA or at an NCAA Division I school. I didn't know if I could or not. I wasn't sure if I had the ability at that point, but I knew I wanted to compete at the highest level possible. I wanted to be part of a team that played in the NBA Finals or the NCAA Final Four.

By 2006, nine years later, I knew that I had the ability to do just that.

I realized that the only thing that separated me from others who coached at those levels was really just one thing…opportunity.

I had seen enough of what other guys were doing by that point to know that my abilities as a coach were every bit as strong as any of those "names" in the NBA or Division I. In many cases, it was stronger. That isn't me saying that I'm better than everyone or they that suck and I rule. All I'm saying is that I can swim in their pool every bit as well as they can. I may not be the Magic Johnson of basketball coaches but who knows, I might be the Eddie Johnson (the good one, not the rapist)… and that's still pretty good.

So throughout the years, as I have been trying to break into this Fort Knox of careers, I continually get people asking me why I don't just take a high school job, or be an assistant at a small school, or work at the YMCA or do private lessons. All of which are noble pursuits.

My defense shields immediately go up when they ask this.

I see that question as an inference that I think I'm too good to go and do those jobs. That I wouldn't 'stoop' to those levels. But that is not the case at all.

I know that there are great, great basketball coaches who work with 10 year olds. I know that there are great coaches who work with junior high kids. I know that there are great coaches who coach high school. I know there are great NAIA coaches, great Division II coaches and great Division III coaches. That isn't the point.

Not to sound flippant, but in order to be where I want to be, I have to be where I want to be. I can't compromise or it won't happen. I can't leave it up to luck or for someone else to find me.

If I don't believe it myself, no one else will either.

When going after jobs, I knew that I could either give in to my weaknesses as a potential candidate, or I could try and turn those perceived weaknesses into strengths. I had decent (not great but decent) rebuttals to most of the primary objections to my experience and background.

I've been able to counter questions about my ability to recruit, my Division I experience, how I handle pro players, and my own playing career (or lack thereof) quite deftly.

The biggest challenge that I have faced in this search is the one weakness for which I don't have an eloquent retort. It is the grail of which I continually search to overcome.

Simply put… no one has ever heard of me before.

I am a total and complete "no-name".

Bob Whitsitt, the former GM of the Seattle Sonics, Portland TrailBlazers and Seattle Seahawks, told me once that for me to get a coaching job in a "big time" league (like the NBA or NCAA-D1) would be like winning the lottery, with the odds being about the same for both. He went on to say that no GM or AD would risk their own job on a guy they have never heard of. It would be career suicide for them, he told me.

"But what if I 'beat his goddamned door down' and told him how much I REALLY wanted the job?" I would rhetorically say to myself.

I have a ton of respect for Bob and what he has accomplished in his career. He has been a great sounding board for me and always made time for me to get together and talk hoops. While I have to admit being somewhat discouraged by Bob's words, I also used them as motivation and just added him to the growing list of people who have told me that I can't do this.

***

Armed now with at least partial knowledge on how and why I think the way I do about some of this coaching stuff, I feel like I can show you how it has manifested itself in between various ABA seasons and two CBA false starts.

In the spring of '06 I was in Southern California when I heard that Pepperdine University had fired their head coach, Paul Westphal. Coach Westphal was the former head coach for the Sonics and I was very familiar with his style and ability. Lorenzo

Romar was also a former head coach at Pepperdine and I was extremely familiar his style and ability having spent a year with him at UW. I felt like my own style and abilities were no less adequate then at least two of the men who had held the head coaching job at Pepperdine previously and that after trying it with a former NBA All Star and head coach like Westphal, maybe the school could be convinced to look at someone with a lesser-known profile.

I had no connection to the school, and I knew that there would be no way that I could even get my foot in the door (let alone an interview) by pursuing traditional methods. In fact there weren't going to be too many jobs where I could get my name in the mix because, as I said, I was (am) a "no name" in this business. I felt like my only slight sliver of hope would be to take matters in my own hands.

Since Pepperdine is a Christian school, I would go "beat the doggone door down" as opposed to my dad's more colorful option. I put on my suit, tied my best tie and drove to Malibu. My plan was to get a meeting with the school's athletic director, Dr. John Watson. Once there, I'd knock his socks off with my passion and enthusiasm for the position. He'd HAVE to hire me... Right?

Pepperdine is a spectacularly beautiful campus located on a hill above the city of Malibu, right outside of Los Angeles, overlooking the Pacific Ocean. As I wound my way up the hill toward campus in my rental car, the day couldn't be more perfect. There wasn't a cloud in the sky and the temperature was in the mid-80's. The wind was surprisingly calm and I couldn't help myself in hoping that this plan could actually work. As I drove, I fantasized of taking the Waves to the NCAA tournament with my assistant coaches, Russ, Harold and Omar by my side. I daydreamed of how I would repay the school by showing loyalty to them for taking a chance on me and how I would stay there when other suitors came calling to hire me away after our success. I thought about my recruiting plan, my academic plan and my basketball philosophies, all of which I had put together in a 50-page pro forma that I would present to Dr. Watson. I drove into the parking lot near the athletic department offices around 2 p.m. The lot was surprisingly empty for that time of day and I was a bit concerned that the school may be closed.

In fact, it was.

It was spring break at Pepperdine and the campus was closed. I walked up to the athletic department doors and pulled. They didn't budge. They were locked. I peered into the window to see if there was anyone inside.

No one.

I started back toward the car and then turned back around toward the building. I paused and turned around back to the car, took two steps and then again turned back to the building. I wasn't sure what to do. I had come a long, long way and didn't want to leave empty handed. I stood there for a moment contemplating my next move.

All of a sudden the door swung open. Out came a student wearing a Pepperdine Soccer t-shirt and shorts. I hurried to grab the door before it locked shut once more.

I was in the building.

Most of the lights inside the building were turned off. I could see cracks of light coming from underneath a few closed office doors. As I continued down the corridor, there was one door noticeably open with light emanating into the hall, illuminating my path like runway lights guiding home a pilot in a storm. The placard on the wall outside of the office read:

Dr. John Watson
Director of Athletics

I stepped inside to find a women sitting at a desk outside Dr. Watson's office. She greeted me warmly.

"Hi, I was wondering if I could speak with Dr. Watson. I don't have an appointment but only need a few minutes of his time." I tried to sound confident yet non-threatening.

"He's in a meeting off campus right now, I'm not even sure if he'll be returning today" she explained.

"No problem, I'll just wait outside in case he does get back shortly, if that's okay with you" and I pointed to some chairs out in the hallway.

She shrugged and said that would be fine, so I camped out in the hallway of John Watson's office, hoping he'd decide to come back to campus after his meeting.

I sank down in one of the fake leather chairs sitting in the hallway outside the office. I grabbed a copy of Pepperdine's student newspaper, The Daily Graphic, which was sitting on a table next to me. I got caught up with what was going on around the school, including their search for a new basketball coach... and I waited.

I flipped through my 50-page coaching packet just to re-familiarize myself with the contents and I practiced what I would say to Dr. Watson upon his hopeful return... and I waited.

I continued to fantasize about life in Malibu and how to divvy up various coaching responsibilities with my assistants... and I waited.

I took out my cell phone and played Minesweeper... and I waited.

Nobody knew that I was there. I never told anyone (friends or family) what I was doing. If it's possible, I was simultaneously brash about my own ability, yet meek about expressing it outwardly… I continued to wait.

The long wait seemed to actually settle my nerves as opposed to making me more nervous. I found myself unusually focused and intent on the task at hand.

Shortly after 5 p.m., a middle-aged man wearing a gray suit came walking down the hall and toward the office door. It looked like the picture of Dr. Watson that I had seen on the Pepperdine website but I couldn't be positive. As he approached the area where I was sitting, he looked down at me waiting there in my suit and asked if I had been helped.

"I'm here to see Dr. Watson" I told the man, feeling more and more confident that that man was him.

"I'm Dr. Watson" he confirmed.

I shot up from my chair and reached out my hand.

"Dr. Watson, my name is Rick Turner. I was wondering if I could just get 10 minutes of your time to talk? I know I don't have an appointment. I'm sorry, but I won't take long." I eagerly asked.

"Yeah sure, just give me a few minutes to get settled and you can come right in."

My mind raced.

"Uh-oh… It's on." I thought to myself. "Here we go…"

I tried to collect my thoughts and pull myself together as Dr. Watson checked in with his assistant and got settled in his office. I knew that I only had one big swing at this and I had to make it my best.

The assistant came out to invite me into the office. I walked in. His desk sat in front of the back wall facing the door. The walls were lined with framed diplomas and various team photos. Pictures of his family sat close by and a bookshelf behind the desk was filled with professional handbooks, NCAA binders and an assortment of team media guides. There were two chairs on the wall opposite the desk. Dr. Watson invited me to sit down in one while he sat in the other.

"What can I do for you?" he asked as he leaned forward slightly.

I paused and took a deep breath through my nose. I silently exhaled.

"I want to be your men's basketball coach."

Dr. Watson leaned back and smiled. I wondered what was going through his mind. Is this a joke to him? Is he put off by this waste of his time? Could he be impressed with my moxie? I'll bet he originally thought that I was some kind of a salesman.

I continued before he could say anything to stop me.

I told him I'd be brief.

I told him where I had been coaching.

I gave him my packet of philosophies and plans.

I told him why I would be the best choice.

I could feel my face and neck on fire as the blood rushed to my head. I was slightly distracted knowing that my face was all blotchy but I kept going. I was attempting to speak strong and confidently. I think I was doing okay until I said something along the lines of...

..."In the end Dr. Watson, it's just basketball. It isn't life and death and it certainly isn't brain surgery" (Or something like that)

For the first time in my rambling soliloquy, Dr. Watson interrupted me. The look on his face changed and he noticeably didn't like what I had said.

"Well actually, here at Pepperdine, we take basketball quite seriously." He informed me.

This knocked me off my game. He had completely misinterpreted what I said. I was trying to convey a thought that might have been too nuanced for that conversation and from that point on, it was over.

I understood at the time, as well as now, that the chances of me getting that job were probably less than one percent. Actually, more like one percent of one percent. But if you are trying to win the lottery, you can't do it unless you buy a ticket.

I have to say that Dr. Watson was extremely gracious with how he handled my ambush of him that afternoon. It could have gone a number of ways and he was great about even meeting with me. I left the Pepperdine campus that night and drove back toward LA. I had no regrets and even felt recharged in my pursuit.

I felt like I had the balls to do something that not many others could say they've done. If nothing else, I got a good sense of what to do the next time a situation like this comes up. I'll be more prepared for it, I'll know what to expect and I will enjoy a more peaceful level of comfort for the experience.

On a side note to that, as I drove away, I turned on one of the LA sports radio stations in the car. They were reporting that earlier that afternoon, Pepperdine had offered their men's coaching job to Larry Krystkowiak.

Now I knew where Dr. Watson was before I met with him. I couldn't help but feel a little foolish.

***

I continued to try and hone my approach to making myself a candidate for various coaching jobs. There was obviously no correct formula but I was looking for the most reliable way to insert myself into the conversation. The prospects of me being able to "beat the goddamned door down", was unrealistic because I couldn't afford the travel costs of that approach. I started sending out pretty aggressively worded emails to school presidents, athletic directors, general managers and owners. Some would respond with a polite note that they would keep my information on file; others wouldn't respond at all.

As I became more in tune with the system, I found better ways to navigate within it. I researched and targeted search committee members if that was a school's approach to hiring. I used my old media contacts to find out information on a search. I even once drove to Cheney, Washington and knocked on the door of the President of Eastern Washington University at his home, while he was eating dinner and watching a Seattle Mariner game on TV. None of it led to a job but it somehow continued to fuel my fire.

A job came open at University of California at Riverside in the spring of 2007. While researching the job, I discovered that the AD was a former basketball coach named Stan Morrison. I didn't know Coach Morrison but I knew of him. I sent him an email that appealed to the basketball coach in him and hoped that he could possibly identify with my plight. He wasn't just another administrator who had no basketball background. He understood the business. A few days after I sent my email, I received an incredible handwritten letter from Coach Morrison thanking me for my interest in the position but nothing more. It was a classy touch on his part and made me feel good about myself (sometimes the simple things can mean a lot to someone).

The next week, I was on vacation at my dad's winter home in Palm Springs. After going back and forth with myself about whether I should do it or not, I decided to pick up the phone and call Coach Morrison in Riverside, who had yet to hire a coach. The phone rang and his assistant answered.

"Stan Morrison's office this is Kathy, can I help you?"

"Hi Kathy! Is coach around?" I tired to sound like Coach Morrison and I were old friends.

"No, he's not right now."

I think she bought it.

"Can you just pop me into his voicemail then?" I asked my new pal.

"Sure, no problem…"

She connected me to Coach Morrison's voicemail where I left him a message.

"Hi Coach, this is Rick Turner. I'm in your area and wanted to see if you could carve out some time to meet with me. I know you are busy but I can meet you at anytime that works for you. Give me a call back and let me know your schedule. My number is…"

I guess my assumption was that he would recognize my name from the over-the-top, aggressive email that I sent him the week earlier. Since he had responded with a handwritten note, I figured that he might have been impressed with my approach.

My phone rang a couple hours later and it was the 951 area code of Riverside. I knew it was Coach Morrison. I took a deep breath and answered.

"Hi Rick… Stan Morrison." The voice on the other ended said to me.

"Hi Coach. I'm here in Palm Springs for my daughter's spring break and wondered if you had anytime that we could get together?"

"You know, it's just a really busy time right now and I'm all jammed up in meetings and appointments the rest of the week." He politely explained.

"We could do it anytime. I don't know what time you get in each morning but we can meet before that for coffee or even breakfast. We're both going to eat breakfast anyway aren't we? Why don't we just do it together?" I tried to jokingly ask.

"I'm usually here at 5:30 each morning and I don't drink coffee but give me a minute and let me think…" My attempt at humor landed with a thud.

He continued, "You know, I leave Sunday for Indianapolis and the only free time that I have would be Saturday morning. I could meet you across the street from campus for breakfast at seven on Saturday. Will that work for you?"

"Absolutely it does, I'll see you on Saturday at seven…"

It was Thursday afternoon and I had just over a day to prepare for my meeting. Since I was down there on vacation, I was ill-prepared for any kind of professional meeting. My white v-neck t-shirt, cargo shorts and flip-flops probably wouldn't make the best first impression. The next day, I went out to the mall late in the afternoon to get something a bit more appropriate to wear for the meeting.

As I pulled into the parking lot at the Westfield Mall in Palm Desert, CA, my phone rang. It was area code 951 again, Riverside. I figured that it was Coach Morrison calling to cancel our meeting the next day. I didn't answer it. I waited to check the voicemail that he left.

"Yeah, Hi Rick. Stan Morrison, from UC-Riverside. You know… I'm really sorry. I know we have a meeting tomorrow but I have no idea who you are. When we spoke yesterday I thought that you were Ron Turner, Norv Turner's brother. I was expecting a call from him. I realize now that you are not and I just wanted to know what we were meeting about tomorrow so I can be prepared. Thanks Rick. Please give me a call back on my cell phone tonight. 951-…"

Ugh.

This was awkward. First, I thought he knew who I was. Obviously, he didn't. This was disappointing to begin with and slightly embarrassing. Second, if I called back and told him who I was and what I wanted, he'd probably cancel the meeting.

I really had to think about how to handle this one.

I remembered that Coach Morrison knew a friend of mine named Jim Marsh who I shared an office with at the Sonics when Jim was the Community Relations Director. Coach Morrison was Marsh's assistant coach when Jim played at the University of Utah. I decided to call coach back and drop Marsh's name with him. I tried to stay nonspecific in what I wanted with a meeting and Marsh's name seemed to be enough for him to go ahead and move forward with it.

My plan worked and our breakfast meeting was still on for the next morning.

We met at Coco's near the University. I got up at 4:30 a.m. to make sure that I left myself enough time for the drive from Palm Springs to Riverside. It is just over an hour but I didn't want to take any chances.

Shortly after seven, Coach Morrison walked through the door at Coco's. He's not hard to miss. Standing at about 6'8" and wearing a UC-Riverside sweat suit, Coach Morrison could cast quite a shadow. I introduced myself to him and we were escorted to a table on the far end of the restaurant. As we began to talk, we immediately hit it off. He is a very easy man to talk to and just as nice as he is tall. We started realizing that we had many mutual friends and acquaintances. I started to feel very comfortable in the conversation but knew that I had to lower the boom on him and tell him why I was there. When there was a natural lull in our discussion, I moved in.

"Coach, I know you have an opening with your men's basketball team. I wanted to tell you that I'm interested in the job and think I would be a great choice for the position. I brought some materials with me that outline my philosophies and goals for the program… and I have a proven plan that I think will bring Riverside basketball back to prominence in the Big West." I explained as I handed him my portfolio

Without hesitation and very directly, he responded.

"Rick, that's just not going to happen."

It could have ended right there rather awkwardly. However, Coach Morrison and I continued to sit there and talk for almost an hour. It was one of the most genuine conversations that I had with someone for quite awhile. We talked a lot about hoops, where he's been and where I've been. He has a fascinating story and seemed to be honestly interested in mine. We left that breakfast agreeing to keep in touch and we have ever since. He has been a great resource for me in my ongoing search, as well as a strong advocate to have in my corner.

As corny as it may sound, although I didn't come away from that meeting with a job, I feel like I may have got something better; a good friend for life.

***

The list of "no's' continued to pile up as my search resumed around mid-April. Every year, current coaches would be fired or leave for greener pastures and someone would have to step in to replace them.

Why not me?

Well, it seemed as if there were lots of reasons for why not me. The growing theme however, was my "name" and more specifically the lack thereof.

I met with an owner who, along with a group of other fellas, owned three different D-League teams; a nice enough guy who is actually now a General Manager for an NBA team. The meetings and conversations always ended the same way. "I really like you. I like your experience, I like your passion and what you've done, but you don't have a big enough name." His exact quote in an email that he sent to me was:

> *"thanks, rick. the persons i'm considering for the head jobs right now have higher profiles. we have to be mindful of name recognition. i hope you understand. i will be happy to make certain the head coaches, when hired, have your info…"*

I lost out on another D-League job because the GM had the "once in a lifetime" opportunity to hire Sam Vincent (who had just been fired as the head coach of the NBA's Charlotte Bobcats).

Really???

I'm not knocking Coach Vincent but was he really such an amazing 'get' for them? They finished that season 15-35 and then immediately folded shop.

I spoke to a pretty influential coach in the D-League during that same off season as I was continuing to knock on doors to get a job in the league. He told me that the NBA told D-League teams that they were hiring too many white coaches. In his words, it would be pointless for me to try and get a job that season because the league wanted them to hire more black coaches and former NBA players.

An excellent job in the CBA opened up in Albany, NY. If you're going to work in the CBA, this would be the place. Albany was a well-organized operation with a great, great tradition; two of their former coaches being George Karl and Phil Jackson.

For that job, I was passed over for our good pal Vinny Freakin' Askew, who was later fired under some nefarious circumstances.

A friend of mine offered me an assistant coaching job at a Division I school. It was a pretty good situation but it only paid $12,000 per year. I asked him if I could have a couple of days to try and figure out how I could make it work. I called him back two days later and said that if he could put me up in a dorm room there at the school, I could do it. He told me that he found another guy for the job, whose sister lived in the town, so he could go live with her and work for the $12,000.

The rejections go on and on. But look... I understand that is part of the business.

If it sounds like I'm whining, I'm sorry. I'm not trying to come off that way.

Anyone can have any reason they want for hiring whomever they want. I get that. Name recognition, skin color, playing experience, who you know, blah, blah, blah; it's just the way it goes. It can be frustrating but I understand it.

But it doesn't mean that I have to agree with their choices. Obviously, I didn't. This is a tough business, and the only way a coach is ultimately judged, is on their ability to win games. When I finally do get the job that I want, I know that I'm going to get it over someone who thinks they should have gotten the job instead of me. That's just the way it goes.

My number one, main objection throughout this process though, is that I firmly believe that no one buys tickets to games because of who the coach is. I will never be convinced of it and you can argue about it with me forever. People go to the games to watch the players and see winners... not coaches. My lack of name recognition would quickly be trumped by my ability to win games for someone. That is fact.

I bring all this up, not to complain or to throw myself a pity party, but just to show that I have been out there, doing my best to hustle for jobs and not just sitting around waiting for my phone to ring. Also, to point out that my interest has been to move forward, not back, in my career in an attempt reach goals and benchmarks that I had set for myself.

After exhausting all options in the off season of 2007, it seemed as if the '07-'08 basketball season would be my first, in nearly 20 years, without a basketball job; whether that was coaching, scouting or front office work.

However, I wasn't putting all my eggs in one basket. I wasn't married to solely being a basketball coach. I had a strong background in sales, marketing and management and could do more than just coach basketball.

I went out and got a sales job with a tech company that specialized in multimedia marketing. More specifically, they put text messaging programs together for companies and even provided the platform for American Idol's text voting system; the largest program of its kind in the world.

I liked the job, it was something completely different, and I was starting to find a comfort level in it when my whole division was laid off. The company was going to be sold to a French firm and the sale fell through. About 40 people were let go and I was again, back in the job market. I found part-time hours where ever I could. The basketball season started without me and I figured that my upstream swim had finally met its end.

PART IV:

THE BLOSSOM

13

Albany

Stop…
Only old and wise with clouded eyes…
You can't see what I can, cause' I…
Blindly throw my faith, to the face…
Of the next good thing to come my way

- Dave Matthews "**Granny**"

I was surfing various basketball websites in late November of 2007 when I came across a press release.

Apex sells Great Falls Explorers

By The Standard Staff - 11/28/2007

Apex Sportstainment of Butte, headed by Joe Clark, has sold the Great Falls Explorers Continental Basketball Association team, it was announced.

West Coast Sports, LLC (WCS), a Seattle-based investment group headed by former KONG-TV President and General Manager, Michael Blackmon, bought the Explorers, the CBA announced.

WCS also owns the Vancouver Dragons of the CBA and the market rights to an expansion franchise in the Arena Football League (af2) for Everett, WA (2009). Apex will continue to own the Minot Skyrockets and Butte Daredevils.

"We are very pleased to welcome Michael and West Coast Sports, LLC to the CBA," said CBA acting Commissioner Jim Coyne. "Michael will make a great owner and CEO and I feel confident that the Great Falls Explorers and their fans will be happy with this new ownership group. Michael is an accomplished businessman and a welcomed addition to the CBA." "I am pleased to add Michael to the CBA as an owner," said CBA President of the Executive Committee Ben Fernandez. "Michael will do an outstanding job in Great Falls and we are glad that he has purchased the Great Falls franchise."

(Montana Standard)

Ha!

I laughed out loud when I read this. I went to the Great Falls Explorers' website and saw that their head coach was Scott Wedman, the former NBA All-Star who also won

- 189 -

two championships with the Boston Celtics in '84 and '86. He was perfect jock-sniffing fodder for Blackmon. It would be high comedy to follow that team or to be a fly on the wall when Blackmon and Wedman were together.

Blackmon was quite a ways away in my rearview mirror by that point but I couldn't help but feel a little disappointed that he finally got into the Continental Basketball Association, and I was still on the outside looking in. As I mentioned before, one of my main goals after I left the Sonics was to eventually coach a team in the CBA. I had mixed feelings because obviously I knew where the Explorers' train was headed with Blackmon at the helm; but again, if I could somehow get "in there", I could navigate my way around within the league in hopes of advancing my career.

The Explorers really struggled out of the gate that season. By the time Blackmon "bought" the team (although I still question that term), they had dug themselves a pretty deep hole. By Christmas, they were 3-14; hemorrhaging money with no relief in sight. On Friday, January 4th I was up at my daughter's school and got a phone call from a 406 area code. I didn't recognize the number or the area code but I instinctively knew that it was Blackmon. I didn't answer it. I let it go into voicemail but I had a pretty good idea of what he wanted. I waited until I had a good moment to call him back. Of course, when I called him back I got his voicemail. I left him a message and waited for his return call. The return call came as I was walking out of the **Bee Movie** with my daughter.

We exchanged the requisite pleasantries and Blackmon tried to catch me up on what he had walked into when he took over the team a few weeks earlier. By this point, I had a honed a pretty strong BS detector with him, and I was able to siphon off the parts of his story that seemed legit from the parts that I knew were exaggerated, or just flat out false. By reading about the Explorers online and following the team through the CBA website, I was more up to speed on the situation than I let on. I kind of played dumb as he talked about what was happening over there in Montana.

After dancing around for a bit, he finally cut to the chase. He told me that he fired Wedman and wanted me in Great Falls the next day (Saturday) to take over the team before they headed out on the road for an East Coast road trip.

He told me that I would get the same deal that Wedman had: $12,000 per month, my own car and a furnished apartment. I had to hold back the laughter. In the 36 months or so that I knew him, he hadn't paid me a total of $12,000 put together. Now he wanted me to believe that I'd get paid that each month?

Frankly the pay wasn't important. As long as I didn't have to spend any of my own money, I was up for just about anything. But I wasn't going to drop everything for this guy. For someone else, I might have. I told Blackmon that I had a commitment on Saturday that I couldn't change, but I would consider coming after that. Actually, my commitment was six Seahawks playoff tickets that I had with some friends and I didn't want to miss the game to insert myself into Blackmon chaos that may or may not be real. He said okay and that we'd talk on Sunday. As per normal, it turned out that Blackmon hadn't fired Wedman yet, but that Saturday night game in Great Falls was where all things there came to a head.

I never heard from Blackmon on Saturday. He finally called me late Sunday morning around 11 a.m.

"I have a flight for you that leaves Seattle at 1:00 this afternoon. You'll meet the team in Pittsburgh and play two games on Monday and Tuesday. Then you'll go to Albany for two games on Thursday and Friday before the All-Star break when we'll regroup. I'm really sorry for the late notice with all this but you know I'll take care of you if you can just make this happen for me. I'm really depending on you Rick. This is huge. You don't even understand. I'll owe you big time for this."

We hung up and I still wasn't sure about doing it. I went back and forth in my mind as to whether this was a good idea or not. I wanted to coach in the CBA but something just didn't feel right about this. It wasn't the way that I envisioned it happening.

The clock was ticking though and one way or the other I had to make a decision. I was still 45 minutes from the airport, I hadn't packed yet, all my "first team" clothes were in the washing machine, and the flight was to leave in less than two hours.

"Screw it, I'm just gonna go for it," I thought to myself "I don't have anything better to do over the next week anyway… Right?" I justified my decision to go by committing to coach the four games back in Pittsburgh and Albany and then re-evaluating at the All-Star break. Besides, call me a coaching geek, but I really wanted to see the armory in Albany where Jackson and Karl had coached.

Like I said before, the only thing I wanted to be sure of was that I wouldn't be spending any of my own money. Food was one thing, I was going to eat no matter where I was, but I didn't want to have to pay for any hotels, rental cars or anything else out of the ordinary. Time was running out for me though. I took all my wet clothes out of the washing machine and put them in a bag (still wet). I grabbed my suit, three shirts and three ties and threw them in a garment bag. I hopped in my car and raced to Sea-Tac airport. I still had to park and take a shuttle to the terminal before I could check in. It was going to be t-i-g-h-t.

I have always been comfortable moving my way around airports. I have never been one who gets panicked, hurried or stressed out about traveling, and my nonchalance could have cost me here. For the first time ever, I missed my flight. It was a connecting flight through Chicago and there was no other way that I was going to get to Pittsburgh that night if I missed it. I was supposed to meet the team in Pittsburgh first thing in the morning. What a great first impression this would be. I felt like a fool. I was speaking with the ticketing agent when she noticed that the earlier 10 a.m. flight from Seattle to Chicago still hadn't left because of a mechanical problem. I caught a break because I could get on that flight and still make my connection in Chicago. The first bullet had been dodged. The only question was, how many more would there be?

I was oblivious to what was happening on the ground in Great Falls. It was extremely difficult for me to find out what actually happened between Blackmon, Wedman and the team (more on the reasons for that in a moment). Everything I heard about the situation, I heard from Blackmon. I was reading the Great Falls Tribune online, which colored in some gray areas, but I still couldn't be sure. Coaching changes happen all the time. The team's record wasn't good but I didn't think that was the reason I was asked to come in.

The best account of what happened that I could ever get was from an article published in the Kansas City Star on January 18, 2008.

Scott Wedman has interesting experience in the minor leagues

Scott Wedman's departure as coach of the CBA's Great Falls (Montana) Explorers two weeks ago will no doubt be a story he'll tell for years to come.

By his count, he was fired at least twice by Great Falls owner Michael Blackmon. Or maybe it was three times. Whatever, Wedman is back in Kansas City these days after coaching the team for less than half the season.

More than half the team's roster also was fired because of ongoing battles with management over not getting paid, Wedman said.

The final straw came the night of Jan. 5 when Wedman said he told Blackmon he and the team wouldn't play anymore until money matters got resolved.

"That's when (Blackmon) said 'Well, I accept your resignation,' " Wedman said. "I haven't spoken to him since.

"The whole money issue was a constant problem. Checks were bouncing and in my case, I could survive all that. But the players were living off these promised checks and had apartments and there were evictions. It was a mess."

There was one night when Wedman and the team actually were on a bus ready to leave for an out-of-town game when they were waiting for their weekly check from management. But instead of getting $500 checks, they were handed $250 checks, Wedman said. The players agreed they'd had enough and decided not to make the trip.

"That was the first or second time we all got fired," Wedman said. "(Blackmon) just came on the bus and said 'You're all fired.' So I called the owner of the team we were playing to tell him we weren't coming and why we weren't coming, and he said 'Hey, I've got $2,000, come and play anyway.' The players liked the idea. It was like barnstorming.

"And 20 minutes later as we were ready to pull out again, (Blackmon) came on the bus and said 'You guys can't play that game' and I said 'Why not? You fired us. We're free to do what we want.' Then he rehired us."

Blackmon's version of events is different. He told the Great Falls Tribune that he fired Wedman because of "poor coaching" and has since hired Rick Turner to coach the team...

I arrived at Pittsburgh International Airport at 1:00 Monday morning. Blackmon told me that there would be a Pittsburgh team representative there to meet me and bring me to the team hotel. There was no such person there waiting for me. I turned on my cell phone and called Blackmon to see where to go. I didn't even know where the team hotel was. His phone was turned off and my call went directly to voicemail.

"Fffff (udge)!" I thought to myself

It's 1 a.m., I don't know where to go, who to call or what to do. I felt like Judge Reinholt falling for the "banana in the tailpipe" trick again from Blackmon. All I wanted to do was not let this trip cost me any money. I'm in Pittsburgh only 20 minutes and already facing a $100 night at a hotel.

I waited for my bag of wet clothes to come through baggage claim. And I waited. I was the only person still standing in the baggage claim area when the conveyor belt stopped. My bag was no where to be found. I turned to look behind me in case someone had taken it off the belt by mistake… nothing. I walked around to the other side to see if was on the floor there… nothing. I filed a report with the baggage agent and by 2 a.m., I was ready to find a place to sleep.

I couldn't help but have a little smile on my face as the adventure of this whole thing got my blood pumping again. I was comfortable in the chaos of the moment and continue to question myself as to why I operate so adroitly under those circumstances. It seems kind of sick to me actually, but I knew that regardless of however many days of this drama and chaos were ahead of me; it would definitely be an adventure.

There is a Hyatt Hotel adjacent to the Pittsburgh airport. I grabbed the garment bag and backpack that I carried on to the plane with me and walked to the lobby of the hotel. Before I went ahead and got a room, I asked the night desk clerk if I could use the guest computer in the hotel's business center.

I took a wild swing and went online to check the Pittsburgh team website for any mention of a hotel. I scoured the site. On the very bottom of some obscure page, there was one little line that read: Holiday Inn with a phone number next to it. I called the number and sure enough, they were expecting me. I asked the woman on the phone if there was an airport shuttle. She laughed and said no. I asked her the best way to get there. She told me that it was "only" a $60 cab ride, and at that hour, it was really my only option.

I grabbed a cab and checked into the hotel. I was greeted with a big gift basket from the Pittsburgh team upon my arrival, and as she handed me my room key, the woman at the desk asked when the rest of the team would be getting there.

"Aren't they here already?" I asked.

"No, I haven't seen them yet" she answered.

"I'm at the right hotel, right? They couldn't be somewhere else could they?"

"No, this is the right place."

We shrugged our shoulders and I headed up the elevator, to my room. I was finally in bed by 3:30 a.m. I laid down and shut my eyes, excited about the prospects of what lie ahead.

I awoke later Monday morning to the vibration of my cell phone and a call from Michael Blackmon. He was all business and seemed to be highly engaged in the moment. I say this because he can often get aloof during certain situations and completely shutdown, like he did in Little Rock a couple years earlier.

I asked him where everyone was. He told me that he either cut everybody or that they all quit the day before, I can't remember which. He was still trying to talk one of the players into going on the trip and he had another guy flying in from Florida to meet me and play that night. I was supposed to go pick him up at the airport at 3:30 and then go to the arena. He went on to say that Scott Wedman "stole" the uniforms and the Pittsburgh team would provide us with their road uniforms to wear for the next two nights. He gave me the number of an assistant coach with the Pitt team and told me to call him about finding players in the local area who could play that night.

Be careful what you wish for I guess.

I had finally made it to the CBA. The league that had produced so many great coaches, a league that had launched the careers of so many, many good and productive NBA players, and a league with history, tradition and a great amount of respect within the basketball landscape.

I made it.

Phil Jackson, George Karl, Jerry Sloan, Bill Musselman, Flip Saunders and now add…Rick Turner.

Yes, I had made it.

The only problem now was that I had no uniforms, no money and no players.

The assistant coach for the Pittsburgh Xplosion assured me that he would round up enough guys for us to play that night. They would be all local area players who had tried out for the Xplosion early in the year but had been cut. I couldn't help but wonder two things: how good could they be if they were cut by the team we were playing and what kind of shape would they be in?

The good thing for these guys was that this opportunity to play, over the next two nights, would be like a tryout. It was their chance to make our new roster, from which we were now starting to rebuild from scratch. While all of this was going on, I was on my phone with agents and coaches that I knew; looking for good, legit players that could join us on a more permanent basis and right away. It was proving to be a challenge.

The challenge wasn't finding players. I had players coming out of my ears. The challenge was finding players who would allow us to compete and win, particularly "big" men. Guards are a dime a dozen but good 'bigs' are tough to find.

The Xplosion had a van for visiting teams to use while they were in town. They kept it parked at the Holiday Inn and I was able to pick up the keys at the front desk. Right before I left to head back to the Pittsburgh Airport to pick up our one and only player, my luggage arrived from the night before, after the airline delivered it to the hotel. I was so busy, I had almost forgotten about my missing luggage. I guess the airline decided not to dry, fluff and fold my clothes as they were still wet, heavy and wadded up in my Nike bag as they had been for at least the last 24 hours.

I drove out to Pittsburgh International to pick up Marlyn Bryant. I met him at the bottom of the escalator leading down to baggage claim; precisely where my odyssey began just a few hours earlier. He had a deer-in-the-headlights look to him as we got back in the van but how could I blame him? He really didn't know what he was getting into. He knew less about the last 72 hours in GF Explorers history than I did, but what he did know came from a couple friends that he had on the team.

Marlyn had hurt his shoulder in training camp and hadn't played a game yet that season. He was rehabbing in Florida and ready to come back. He had been talking to both Wedman and Blackmon about his return and he decided to join us despite Wedman's departure. All Marlyn wanted to do was play. Like me, who just wanted to coach, Marlyn didn't care about all the drama; he was just itching to get back on the court.

Marlyn played college ball at the University of South Florida where he battled injuries throughout his career. He was 25 years old, 6'4" and played the 2 guard. He was a good shooter but a bit streaky. He had a knack for scoring and a great motor. He was a high-energy guy who was fearless to the basket and went to the free-throw line a bunch. He could also defend. He had long arms, good instincts and again, a high effort level. He was also the type of guy who always wanted to guard the opponent's best player. As far as an NBA prospect goes; he wasn't a consistent enough shooter yet, his handle was suspect and he was just average size for that position. He was Dwayne Wade-esque for our level, but there was nothing that separated him from a ton of other guys who played the 2 spot. He was a borderline guy for the NBA but not quite there, although he was quite good.

The two of us drove to the Mellon Arena to meet our new team. Mellon Arena was the home of the NHL's Pittsburgh Penguins, and as far as I'm concerned, also the home of the Pittsburgh Pisces from the movie **The Fish That Saved Pittsburgh** (which to me was pretty cool). It also housed the Pittsburgh Xplosion and that was our opponent for the next two nights

The Xplosion's assistant coach was very nice and welcomed me to the league when we arrived at the arena. He introduced me to the guys that he had brought in to play that night and gave me the names of a couple agents who he thought might have some players for later in the week. He handed me the Xplosion's yellow "away" uniforms, pointed us toward the visitor's locker room and we were off and running.

I don't remember much about the game. It was a blowout from start to finish. Nothing remarkable about it and we were never really competitive. I do remember an unusual sense of accomplishment though, that I strangely felt while sitting on the bench as the game began. A peculiar peacefulness fell over me as I was finally coaching in the CBA.

Despite the bizarre circumstances, I had achieved one of my goals.

The final score was 133-110. Marlyn had 29 points and some guy, who I don't remember at all, named Kevin Menifee, had 23 points and 11 rebounds for us as well.

The next day we added two more guys, both of whom had ties to the former coach of the Explorers. The first was Mike Peeples, who was cut in training camp, but had been added to the roster in the last couple of weeks. He wasn't playing much and I think he was glad to be rid of Wedman in hopes that his playing time would increase.

Mike was a 6'7", small forward from Fairleigh Dickinson, who was still just 21 years old. He was a scary-explosive athlete, whose game was still very raw, but his athleticism could fill in some of the gaps. He was a pretty quiet guy and tough to get a read on when I first met him. He was fiery and competitive on the floor and I liked that about him.

The second guy that we added was Nate Green. Nate had been with the Explorers all season and was one of their best players. It didn't take long for me to realize that in lieu of sucking Wedman's jock, Blackmon took a real shine to Nate. It was quite understandable though, because Nate 100% looked and acted the part of a pro athlete. If you didn't know any better, you'd think he was a multi-millionaire NBA All-Star just by how he carried himself. As some might say, he was on the All-Airport First Team. He looked great walking through the airport but couldn't play.

Nate was 6'9" and very skilled for his size. He was 33 years old and played at Idaho State University but had been playing professionally for 10 years. He could shoot the three, as well as score in the post, but he preferred to float around the perimeter. His focus and effort level left a lot to be desired, and even though he was a skilled player, he was exactly the opposite of the type of guys who I liked to work with.

He was a strange dude who was extremely sensitive and needed to be coddled. You can make that work when you are REALLY, REALLY good, but not in the CBA. Unlike Marlyn and Mike who just wanted to 'ball', Nate was caught up in the day-to-day drama of the team. Mostly because Blackmon called him to talk multiple times per day, but also because I think he was close with Wedman, as both of them were from Kansas City.

The results were no different with Marlyn, Mike, Nate and the seven dwarfs on the next night in Pittsburgh. We lost 128-101. Peeples led the way with 22 points and 14 rebounds. We handed back Pittsburgh's uniforms, said a quick thank you to the guys that filled in for us, and left first thing in the morning for Albany, NY. However, we did decide to bring a couple guys with us to Albany. One was a 6'6" forward from West Virginia named Melvin Garrett, who didn't make our final roster and the other was a five foot nothing, point guard from Robert Morris University named Maurice Carter.

It's not the size of the dog in the fight; it's the size of the fight in the dog… That sums up Maurice Carter quite well; a diminutive point guard, who would back down from no one, even to his detriment. He took and made big shots when we needed it at times but had more of a scorer's mentality then I would normally like from a point guard. The biggest problem with his approach was that his size didn't allow him to create for himself like he could in high school and college. He had a difficult time adjusting and constantly banged his head against the wall, making the same mistakes over and over. But he had a huge heart, was ultra-competitive and was a great foil for his teammates. You have to have someone around who can handle being the butt of many jokes and he was a great target for the guys. Mo also played for legendary high school coach, Morgan Wooten, at DeMatha High outside of DC, whose record was something like 1,143-170 when he retired. He took great pride in his high school alma mater and spoke of it often… very often… very, very often.

Mo had a friend who played at the University of Virginia named Jason Clark, who was looking for a job. I made a few calls on him, and got some really good feedback so we had Jason meet us at our connecting flight between Pittsburgh and Albany, which happened to be right in his back yard at Reagan National Airport in DC.

Jason was the type of player that was right up my alley. He was a "junkyard dog". Country strong, he worked hard and knew his limitations. His strength was rebounding and that's what he did. He didn't care about "getting his shots". He knew that his would come off offensive rebounds, put-backs and free throws. He was listed at 6'8". I'm not sure he was even that tall, but he played like he was 6'10". He wasn't a disaster offensively, he made his free throws and could knock down the random 12-footer, but he worked hard on defense and was the type of guy who you need to have if you like to win.

We also brought in Pele Paelay from the Baltimore area, who met us at Reagan National as well. Pele was a kick (no pun intended). This was his first pro experience and it was fun to see him soak it all in and enjoy it. He went to Coastal Carolina where he was the Big South Conference player of the year his junior season, beat out for the award by his own teammate in his senior season.

Pele was just 23 years old but another superior athlete. He was extremely explosive and could score in bunches. In high school, he was an All-State soccer player in Maryland (along with basketball) and I've always thought that being a good soccer player gives you a great head start in becoming a good basketball player. Pele was a bit of a momma's boy but not in a terrible way, just still maturing. He was a combo guard for us and still somewhat of a 'tweener. Good but not great at either the 1 or the 2 spot yet. Not a good decision maker and he had lapses of focus quite often. He was a great kid who just needed to play and continue to improve.

We arrived in Albany around 5 p.m. after one of the scariest flights I've ever been on. It was windy and the turbulence was frightening at best. The woman sitting to my left on the plane was in tears, and asked if she could hold my hand as the plane rocked and rolled. I honestly thought that it could all end right there as we bounced and jostled our way through the un-friendly skies. I don't know if it was unusually bumpy or not but if it gets worse than that, I don't want to know.

The GM of the Albany Patroons was at the airport to pick us up and ferry us to the team motel. Traffic was unusually bad that night in Albany because the town was on its ear for the Hannah Montana concert happening downtown. He avoided much of the traffic snarls by taking some back roads to get us there in about 40 minutes. He dropped us off at the motel and left me with the keys to the van. He told me that both teams would have to share the van as it was the only vehicle that the Albany team had (even though they were supposed to provide us with our own transportation). There was a system for leaving the keys at the front desk when we were finished using it so the other team could get it when we were done. It was obvious that the Albany players used the van quite a bit because it was all beat to shit, barely started and ran like crap. The inside was a mess, with food wrappers and Gatorade bottles all over the place and it smelled disgusting.

And speaking of disgusting, the motel they put us up in was that and more. It was right out of a horror movie. There were five separate buildings on a sprawling campus. We were in the back building furthest from the office. If anyone came back there to kill us, it would have been weeks before anyone discovered the bodies. In order to get to our building, we had to exit back onto the main street and then drive to a separate entrance into an unlit, empty parking lot of one of the other hotel buildings which was totally abandoned; with windows boarded up by plywood, weeds overgrowing through the broken pavement and graffiti written on the side of the walls. A single parking lot light dimly illuminated the entrance to our building. The glass surrounding the bulb was grimey; covered in mold or engine oil exhaust, or something else that made it dark gray and provided very little light to escape. The building itself looked more like a brick dormitory from the outside, with dirty windows and a sign on the front door that read:

"Make sure that door closes
& locks behind you"

We each grabbed our things and headed to our rooms. As I got to my room, I inserted the 'credit card-like' key to unlock the door. Of course, I got a red light. I tried again. Again, a red light. There was no lobby phone to call so I had to go back to the front desk and have them reprogram my key. I don't know about you, but to me this is one of the most frustrating experiences that you can have after you've been traveling all day.

I decided to take my life in my own hands and walk back to the front office instead of drive the crappy van. I left all my sh-tuff sitting outside my motel room door and set out to get a new key.

My heart pounded as I made my way through the darkness, across the parking lot that featured a combination of dirty snow, ice and sand. I made my way traveling from one island of light to the next. I was about 100 yards from the main building when I came to, more or less, a dead end. A huge, deep puddle of water blocked my path. Squinting through the darkness, my eyes traced around the puddle to a spot of higher ground where the curb met dirt. It looked like they were putting in a sidewalk but it wasn't complete yet. I tiptoed around the perimeter of this lake, through the shallowest part of the puddle, keeping the majority of my feet dry while my toes remained submerged in the muddy water. My fat and formally athletic body would now have to make a leap to the impending sidewalk construction and hopes of dry land; a feat that would defy all of nature's laws.

My age and physical prowess no longer allowed me to move with the nimbleness and dexterity of my younger self. This leap to dry land, and an unobstructed path to the front desk, would require an effort and focus that can only be appreciated by someone of my advanced age. Ten years earlier I would have made this entire trip in about 30 seconds; moving with cat-like quickness and legerdemain. Instead, I was forced to think about this leap, take a deep breath, and wildly swing my arms back and forward, while letting out an audible grunt.

Instead of landing heavy-footed with a solid thud, like most non-athletes would, the future sidewalk greeted me with a soft, wet squish. My feet sank ankle-deep into the mud and the dirty goop covered my shoes completely. Resignation with what had just happened, lead me to abandon all attempts to stay dry. With a figurative shrug of the shoulders, I walked the rest of the way to the office, right through the large puddle; cleaning off the mud as I went. The guy at the desk gave me a new key and I headed back toward my room, hoping that no one had stolen any of my stuff sitting outside the door.

I got back to find everything still there. That was a relief. I put my new key in the door...

...another red light.

AAAARRRRGGGGHHH!!!

When I finally got a key that worked, I fully expected to find a group of rats sitting around the night stand playing poker. I'd walk in, they'd look up for a second to see who it was and then go right back to their game. I wasn't too far off. I got into my room and found it to be just simply gross. I'm not a high-maintenance guy when it comes to these things so I don't feel bad in saying that. It didn't help that I had recently watched a 20/20 report on TV about how disgusting hotel mattresses really are. Bugs, pee stains and (ahem) 'other' stains. Bacteria, mold and spit from slobbering sleepers.

I tried to put it all out of my mind but it was tough.

The bed spread was grungy, the curtains were tattered, the carpet was (for lack of a better word) icky; there was no remote for the TV and the heat didn't work. I didn't want to burden anyone so I didn't say anything about it. After the first night of little sleep, a nightmare about having snakes in the room and waking up freezing; I finally asked to switch rooms.

The new room was in another building and much better. It had a remote control AND heat. I cranked up the thermostat to about 80 degrees, laid back and flipped channels around... just because I could. I felt soooo much better now.

I wondered why they couldn't get it right the first time. Why would they put anyone in that other room if they didn't have to? The Albany players lived at the same motel that we were staying. I couldn't help but wonder what their accommodations were like. Hopefully they were better taken care of than their visiting guests, because I would surely feel bad if they had to live in that squalor.

Shortly after we got all checked in and squared away in our rooms, we left again to have our first real practice together as a team at 8:00 that night. There wasn't much time to try and get on the same page, with only that night to practice, and an early shootaround the next morning; before we would play later that night.

We piled into the van and armed with directions from MapQuest, I somehow steered us to the Albany Armory building where the Patroons played their home contests. Waiting for us there to open the gym was CBA commissioner Dennis Truax. Dennis greeted me with a handshake and we spoke while the guys got loose. He thanked me for taking over under difficult circumstances and expressed the confidence he had in Blackmon to make things work in Great Falls.

I put on my diplomatic hat while we discussed some of the events of the last week. Dennis mentioned the empathy that he felt for Blackmon as he took on the challenges of this team while continuing to fight his contentious divorce. He talked about how Blackmon told him that his money was tied up in his bitter and ugly divorce. Once that issue is resolved, things (i.e. money) should open up for him.

As Dennis said the word "divorce", I was taking a drink from my Aquafina bottle. I choked as I tried my best to hold back the laugh as the water nearly came through my nose. Dennis asked if I was okay. I told him that the water went down the wrong way as I continued to cough and regain my composure.

I wasn't going to tell Dennis that Blackmon wasn't (and had never been) married. I didn't know him well enough yet, and it didn't feel right to throw Blackmon under the bus at that point with the league commissioner.

We practiced until 10 p.m. and were cleaning up around the gym when Nate Green walked up and asked me if I knew what time Blackmon would be there tomorrow. I looked at him with a puzzled expression.

"Huh?" I said.

Blackmon had told Nate Green that he would meet us in Albany for the two games before the All-Star break and bring paychecks for everyone. I think it was part promise and part threat. He told Nate that if he wanted any of the back pay that he was owed from the previous few weeks of missed payments and bounced checks, he had to keep playing or forfeit all of it. Nate felt hung over a barrel, so he came on the road trip instead of just walking away like the rest of his former teammates did. Blackmon mentioned at one point to me that he might be coming to Albany to meet us, but I never thought of it again. I hadn't spoken to him since the night of our last game in Pittsburgh.

For all I knew, maybe Blackmon actually was en route to Albany.

The Washington Avenue Armory was the home for the Albany Patroons and had been for the better part of 25 years, since the team started playing there in 1982. It had been built in the 1890's. It wasn't the Boston Garden or Chicago Stadium but it certainly had a character that those two venues shared. In a high tech world, where everything has to be new and shiny, the Armory remained a conduit to history. New and shiny was replaced with... I don't know... not new and not shiny? The interior had been renovated to remain current but still kept the character that defined its charm. Dark stained wood floors lined the hallways as well as the understated foyer that greeted visitors upon their arrival. Pictures adorned the walls, chronicling the history of the building, as well as photos of some of the events it had hosted including sporting events and concerts.

The gym itself is about 38,000 square feet and seats just over 3,500 for basketball. It's nice and bright inside with good lighting on the floor for basketball, and it has a huge big screen for fans to view replays. The visitor's locker room was located downstairs, underneath the gym floor. In order to get there, you had to walk from the floor, down two flights of steep and narrow stairs, out a door that lead to a small, about 10-car parking garage; across the parking lot and into your locker room. I pictured Phil Jackson and George Karl, roaming the NBA sidelines in their $5000 suits and had a difficult time picturing either one of them grinding it out in the bowels of the Washing ton Avenue Armory.

We met in the lobby of Motel Hell at 5 p.m. to leave for the game. It was a little strange because we had to take one of the Albany players with us, who would then drive the van back to the motel to pick up their team. It was odd to have one of 'the enemy' with us that close to game time. As we all piled in the van, Nate again asked me if I had heard from Blackmon. I said that I hadn't. Nate said he hadn't either but was trying to call him all afternoon. I was indifferent but it was obvious that Nate was a tad distracted by this.

We unloaded at the Armory and walked into the gym where we found the Patroon's GM Dave Bestle. Bestle was the guy that I had spoken to about the Albany head coaching job earlier that summer before they hired Vince Askew. I took a subtle shot at him on the phone when he called to let me know they had gone with Askew instead of me.

Upon getting the news that I wasn't getting the job I said, "Okay, thanks Dave. I appreciate your consideration. Obviously character wasn't an issue that you were concerned with, and that makes Vince an obvious choice since he played for the Patroons. I understand. Please do me a favor and keep my number handy when… I mean if… things don't work out like you planned."

I was diplomatic and conciliatory in my tone, so I don't think Bestle was actually listening to my words on the phone that day, which is what I had hoped. It was completely out of character for me to talk like that, but by that point, my frustration level was at an all-time high and losing out on the job to Askew just rubbed salt in my wounds. I took an unprofessional verbal swing at both Bestle and Askew but I think it went un-noticed. When Dave met us at the airport, and then again that night at the gym, I was pretty convinced that he either had no recollection of our conversation, or he didn't put it together that I was the same guy. It helped ease my embarrassment but it also was a shot to the ego that he didn't remember me.

Nevertheless, Bestle escorted us down the stairs and through the garage to our locker room where we had the Albany Patroon away uniforms waiting for us to don. Some guys dressed early, some guys waited. Some went upstairs and got shots up and others sat in their locker listening to their iPod. A couple of guys needed to get taped and I searched for how to address our pre-game talk, with very little knowledge of our own personnel and completely zero knowledge of our opponent.

I wanted to shove it up Askew's ass but I knew that probably wouldn't happen in these first couple games. I had to temper my expectations and not worry about eating a little dirt. The Albany Patroons had some northwest flavor to them; as Askew brought with him Rashaad Powell and Jamaal Miller. The last time I saw Rashaad he was going for 30 on us in Bellevue and talking smack the whole way. The last time I saw Jamaal… well actually, I never saw Jamaal because he snubbed me with the King County Royals, and never showed up after assuring me that he was going to play for us. Jamaal and I didn't really have much of a relationship but the whole night was still a little bit awkward, especially when you added the Rashaad and Askew angle to the mix.

Since I'm not big on confrontation, I was a little apprehensive about seeing Askew at first. I wasn't sure how I should act and didn't know what to expect from him. After all, less then two years earlier, he had stolen my players and basically forced our team to fold. In doing so, he had said some pretty negative things about me to my players as he was trying to recruit them away and he had been the catalyst for Blackmon choosing to fund the Tacoma team over Bellevue, despite our previous success. Beyond that, he beat me out for the Albany job that I really wanted and it just sucks when good things happen to shady people. I couldn't ignore him, but I wasn't sure how to handle it.

As Askew walked into the gym with just under an hour before game time, I was sitting on our bench just watching guys get loose, listening to music and taking in the atmosphere. There was no avoiding it now. The two of us were on a collision course with the only doubt being how bad the carnage would get. He walked passed me and over to the scorer's table to put some names on the will call list. One of the Albany players walked up to him and they talked for a couple minutes, standing at mid court. Then Dave Bestle came over to grab the will call list from Vince and the two of them spoke. Dave pointed at me while he said something to Vince and walked away. We caught eyes. Askew smiled.

Vince walked toward me and my greatest fears were realized. It was uglier than I could have imagined. He walked closer and my heart started beating hard in my chest. His right hand had been in his pocket and as he approached he took it out to free up. I was prepared for just about anything… anything but what would happen next…

"Hi, I'm Vince Askew, nice to meet you." he put his hand out for me to shake.

"Uh-um-uh-um, yeah, umm I'm Rick Turner…" I stammered while shaking his hand.

WHAT???

This mother-sucker had no freaking idea who I was!?!

Really???

That's even worse!

I had spent almost two years being pissed off at the guy and he doesn't even know who I am? What a waste of time. What an embarrassment. Anything but that. Not only was there the Bellevue/Tacoma/Blackmon connection but I was with the Sonics for nine years, traveling with the team while he was a player for them.

C'mon Vinny… really?

That just pissed me off more. Now, I really wanted to beat them.

The starting five was Mo Carter, Marlyn Bryant, Mike Pepples, Nate Green and Jason Clark. Not a bad group but they had never played together before that night. They all had a little chip on their shoulder about something, whether it was Mo, who had been cut by Albany earlier in the year; Marlyn, who was coming off injury; Mike, who just wanted some minutes; Nate, who just wanted to get paid or Jason and Pele, who needed someone to give them an opportunity. They all (with the exception of Nate) felt like they had something to prove and that they were the rejects no one wanted. It was easy to appeal to that "us against the world" state of mind with these guys. We were thrown together quickly under chaotic circumstances and the expectations for us were beyond low.

We put in some simple sets but not much more than that in the short time we were together, and we would have to just hope that good effort and smart play could keep us close. After the first quarter, it was tied 21-21. I remember thinking that we were playing just about as well as I thought we could but we were still only tied as we went into the second quarter. We were getting all the loose balls, we were getting good calls from the referees and we were making shots. Albany wasn't. I was worried that after all that good fortune, we still didn't have a lead. Things were bound to go in the other direction.

In fact they did. We fought hard to remain close but Albany took a 54-49 lead into halftime. When we went downstairs into the locker room at halftime, I think we had surprised ourselves a little. No one was quite sure what to expect from the guy next to them but I think they were surprised to find out that their teammates were pretty good. We came out of there with confidence for the second half. The third quarter of that game was when I first started to get excited about the job and really started feeling like this could be a lot of fun, despite Blackmon.

A couple plays in that game stand out.

Pele had struggled in the first half. He had some early foul trouble, seemed lost within our offense, forced some bad shots and looked bad doing so. I questioned whether or not he was a good pick up for us. He pouted a little on the bench in the first half and the start of the third quarter. I think he was pressing to try and impress me as well as pissed off that he wasn't playing as much as he was accustomed to. I spoke with him before I sent him back in and basically told him to relax and just play. No heroic pep talk or anything, just some words in hopes of calming him down. When I put him in, Albany had extended the lead on us a little bit. We were in jeopardy of letting them get out of reach. We needed some energy.

Pele checked in for Mo at the point guard spot. First trip down the floor he brought the ball up against Jamaal Miller. He was doing a bit of a side-saddle dribble with his back turned toward the defender, placing himself between Jamaal and the basketball in order to protect it. He dribbled across half court while the wings were being overplayed by the Albany defense, making it difficult to enter the ball to them to start our offense.

Pele kind of shook backward, like he was going to spin and then wheeled back around on Jamaal. Jamaal went right and Pele went left; straight down the middle of the lane. He took one dribble and exploded from the dotted line. He rose up and cocked the ball behind his right ear. With his feet tucked up underneath him and leaning slightly forward, he soared to the rim. Up to that point, it all seemed to happen in slow motion until he reached the pinnacle of his leap; then it detonated into a ferociousness that belied Pele's 6'1" frame. When Albany's 7'0" center, Amal McCaskill, came over to help, he was too late and got "posterized" on Pele's lifetime highlight reel as the young kid absolutely delivered a sledgehammer all over that big man's head.

Even the Albany crowd let out an audible "oooooh" as Pele unleashed his thunder on the Patroons. Mo and I looked at each other on the bench almost like Macauly Culkin in **Home Alone**.

As if to say, "Okay… so that's how it's gonna be."

That got us going. It got Pele going as well. Pretty soon the jumper was flowing and he was playing by instinct instead of over thinking. Our defensive intensity picked up while Albany still seemed to be knocked on their heels. A couple of minutes later, Marlyn picked up a loose ball steal and started up the right side of the court. Just over the mid-court line, he spotted Mike Pepples running down the left side of the floor. Marlyn let loose a 40 foot alley-oop pass to Mike who was running in stride. Mike had big-time bounce but I didn't know how big time until I saw this play. There is no way that my description can do it justice but I'll do my best.

Marlyn's alley-oop pass to Mike was short and behind him. As Mike leapt for the ball, he had to adjust in mid air. He jumped and was gliding toward the rim when he had to turn back and reach for the ball behind him. He grabbed the ball while he was in mid air, behind him to his right and below his waist with one hand, with the rim off to his left. All in one motion and all with one hand; he caught, adjusted and flushed the ball through the rim as he ducked to make sure his head didn't hit the back board. He made it look so easy that the crowd was stunned, almost shell-shocked.

Not his teammates though.

Pardon the expression, but they went ape shit.

Askew exploded off the Patroon bench and called timeout as we took the lead for the first time in the game. I tried to remain calm, like it was the sort of thing that I expected all the time. Cripes, I spent 10 years watching Shawn Kemp. It was tough for dunks to impress me anymore. But this was something to see. Even so, I acted like it was just another two points and tried to get us refocused. There was a lot of game left and we didn't want to get ahead of ourselves.

Albany's Jamaal Miller banked in a three-quarter court desperation heave at the end of the third quarter to pull the Patroons to within two points at 81-79.

We stayed solid in the final period, and although the score was close, we never felt too threatened. We made our free throws down the stretch and held on for a 105-100 victory. Nate Green led the way with 28 points and 11 rebounds. Marlyn had 19 points, Pele had 17 and Mike had 15. Mo had 14 points and 7 assists while Jason pulled down 11 boards including a big offensive rebound near the end to seal it.

Don't feel too bad for Amal McCaskill after Pele did him like that. As Russ Schoene would often say, "If you haven't been dunked on, you haven't played". Amal finished with a game-high 29 points and 19 rebounds for the Patroons but he had to walk around with the word "**gnidlapS**" imprinted on his forehead for the next couple days.

It was a sweet win for me personally on many levels. First, I was really proud of our guys and how they seemed to come together in a very short time. The atmosphere in the locker room after the game was like we had won something other than a mid-January, nothing game between two middling teams in the CBA. The guys were pumped up and excited about it, which made it a lot of fun as we sat around in the locker room afterward eating crappy pizza that our hosts provided. Secondly, it was my first CBA win as a coach and as you know by now, I held the league in high regard and was proud of the accomplishment. Thirdly, it was against a team that had spurned me as their head coach just a few months earlier and of course lastly, it was against Askew, who was p-i-s, pissed off about the loss, big time.

He unloaded on his team for about 15 minutes following the game. So much so that we could hear him yelling at them from our locker room. So I savored that win for the rest of the night before we had to try and do it again the next.

As we loaded up the van to head back to the motel, Nate asked if Blackmon was here yet. I said that I hadn't seen him, so Nate tried to call him. He didn't answer. Nate said "It went straight to voicemail, maybe he's on a plane"

Uh, yeah Nate… sure.

We went to our shootaround the next morning and the league commissioner, Dennis Truax, was there to speak to each guy about their travel arrangements during the All-

Star break. He went to each of them and asked where they wanted to fly to from Albany after the game.

This was when I figured out that all the team travel expenses were taken care of by the CBA league office.

Each team paid into a large travel pool at the beginning of the season and worked through the league travel agency to book any trips. The light bulb came on for me, as I now understood how Blackmon was flying us around everywhere.

In fact, he wasn't.

The previous owner had already paid into the pool for the season and we were drawing off of that payment. Marlyn flew back to Florida; Mike was driving back to Buffalo with his brother following the game; Nate was going to Yakima for the All-Star game and the rest of the guys were going to the D.C. area. When he asked me, I told him that I wanted to fly to Green Bay, where I would watch the Seahawks play the Packers in the NFC playoffs; in the snow at Lambeau with my high school buddy Brad, who now lives in Chicago.

I figured that I'd hear from Blackmon after he heard about our win, and in fact, he finally called me the next afternoon. The call came around 2 p.m., just a few hours before we were to leave for the gym.

Blackmon was still living in Seattle and had spent very little time in Great Falls up to this point. He was planning on coming to Great Falls after the All-Star break and after we had completed our 10-game road trip.

After our final game in Albany, the whole league would take a week off for the All-Star break.

Blackmon talked the league into naming Nate Green to the All-Star team, even though his numbers (and game) may not have warranted it. It was a continuing effort that Blackmon took on to appease Nate and keep him from quitting.

After the All-Star game, we were scheduled to play two games in Texas, two games in Kentucky and two more games in Butte; before returning back to Great Falls for our first home game since the Blackmon/Wedman debacle of January 4th.

Blackmon told me on the phone that he wasn't coming to Albany (big surprise), but he worked out a loan from the Albany owner so I could at least pay the guys some per diem. I didn't really care what the arrangement was; I just wanted to get some money into my guys' pockets. Blackmon congratulated me on the win the night before and I said that I would call him after the game that night. A couple of hours later, it would be time to leave again for the arena.

I sat behind the wheel of the dirty, dumpy, dented, white GMC 12-passenger van with the Albany Patroons logo painted on the side; in the driveway of Motel Hell, waiting for everyone to emerge from their rooms to head for the game. One by one, the players started climbing in the van. I knew Nate was jonesing to talk with Blackmon and I wasn't sure if I should tell him that we spoke or not. If the two of them hadn't spoken, it would only piss Nate off to hear that I did. I remained noncommittal when he asked me himself.

"Did you talk to Mike?" Nate asked me. Nate often called Blackmon, Mike.

"Uh, did you?" I answered his query with a question of my own

"Yeah, he called me this afternoon. I can't believe what happened. I hope he'll be alright."

"What do you mean?" I asked

"He told me about his emergency open heart surgery a couple of days ago and how the doctor told him that he couldn't fly. That's why he wasn't able to make it out here." Nate explained empathetically

Good gravy! This guy has no shame does he? His bulls*** is endless. I thought to myself with an internal eye roll.

"Oh yeah, right. He should be fine in a few days though." I went along with the story just to keep Nate's head in the game.

We got to the arena and it continued on there. I saw the Albany owner.

"Hey, I spoke to Mike and he told me about his angioplasty. That's scary. He wanted me to give you guys some money for per diem. Hope he's feeling better soon." And he handed me a wad of cash.

It was $400 and I gave each guy $50. It wasn't much, but at least they could eat now and most of them saw it as a good-faith gesture on our part. They were promised paychecks in Texas a week later (by Blackmon not me) and at least that little bit of cash kept them going for now.

The second game in Albany wasn't as good as the first. The Patroons took a five-point lead into the fourth quarter and never looked back, winning 100-83. Mike Peeples led the scoring for us with 19 points, but as a team we only managed a 34% field goal effort for the game and could never get it going. We would leave Albany 1-1.

I had left my house last Sunday afternoon for Pittsburgh, PA. Here it was, only Friday, and I felt like I had been gone for a month. So much had happened in five and a half days, it was hard to believe that it was real. I would head back home, re-group and figure out what might lie ahead in the coming weeks. Blackmon would use the All-Star game to make an appeal to the other owners to help him get through the season. I would wait to hear what my next move would be.

We all left for the Albany airport the next morning at 4:00, putting Motel Hell in the rearview. We would go our separate ways for now as I was headed back to Seattle, but not before I took a little detour to the frozen tundra of Lambeau Field.

14

Kentucky

Now super's all the things that I can feel;
Now here's to the future that seems real;
But if you think I'd ever sit here and settle for less…
well open wide,
open wide!

Because this, wants to be;
something real, close to me;
happiness, 1-2-3;
because there's more to this
than our eyes can see

- Goodness "**Superwise**"

Much like the month of March, my Seahawks came into Lambeau Field like a lion but left like a lamb in the 2008 NFL playoffs. The weather forecasters called for a trace of snow but once it started in Green Bay that afternoon, it never stopped. I wasn't at all prepared for the cold and snow, arriving at the last minute directly from Albany but the experience at that game was one of those once-in-a-lifetime moments. I had my picture taken in the snow next to the Vince Lombardi statue outside the stadium; I ate cheese curds with the natives at a pre-game tailgate and screamed myself hoarse after the Seahawks jumped out to a 14-0 lead in the first four minutes of the game.

It was all downhill from there however, as the legend of Brett Farve further solidified itself and the Packers came back to win handily, 42-20. The Seahawks were outscored 42-6 after the deliriously delicious opening four minutes. After a thorough beat down like that, Brad and I had no choice but to congratulate the Lambeau partisans and join them in their post-game celebration.

Oh goodness, I have to stop for a minute and go off topic. As I write this, I'm sitting at a coffee shop in downtown Kirkland. I am completely distracted from the task at hand right now by the guy sitting next to me who is bugging the pee out of me as he eats his freaking lunch. He is smacking his food, slurping his soup, talking to himself and even laughing out loud. There is nowhere in here to move so I'm stuck, grossed out, having to listen and put up with this tool.

He is dressed in head-to-toe denim with his mousse-laden coif dragging up against the collar of his faded jean jacket. The wet-head mullet he is rockin' represents the pomposity that he greets the plus-sized woman who just sat down next to him as he moves his empty plate out of her way.

"Rob?" she asks.

"Lisa?" he responds.

"Nice to meet you" they both say, 'jinxing' each other as they shake hands. Looks like they are on a blind date; meeting safely for coffee.

She has obviously put a lot more effort into this coffee meeting then he has. She's wearing nice jeans, shiny half-boot-like looking shoes (black) and a black t-shirt with no collar; cut kind of low to make sure Rob can sneak a peek. She has feathered blond hair that has a bit of a 'rocker-chick' vibe to it.

Rob can not be more obvious that he is unimpressed with Lisa as she sits down. He's a total ass. I wanted to lean over and whisper, "Bad body language, Rob. Bad body language," but thought better of it.

"So…" Lisa jumps right in "…tell me about Rob," she says.

Rob is ill-prepared for this question. He freezes. He stammers. He stalls. He stammers again and turns to his open laptop that he was working on before Lisa sat down.

"You going to type it out for me?" she tries to joke as he shows her the screen.

"This is me," he tells her.

Well done Rob. You knocked it out of the park with that one.

"I'm a voice coach. I work with singers all over the country. This is a news story that a TV station did on me."

"Very cool" Lisa says, trying to bail him out and make him feel good.

He goes on about himself, telling her about his work as a vocal coach and the new motorcycle he just bought. Obviously, this isn't Lisa's first rodeo. She knows that if she stands any chance with this guy, who is so blatantly not into her, she has to get him talking about himself. It works for a minute but then there is a really, really awkward silence. It lasts about five seconds. That's a long time under these circumstances, before Lisa says, "So what's the last movie you saw?"

Good grief. This is painful but I can't turn away. I have to pee really bad right now but I can't tear myself away from this conversation. I get up and pretend to get something so I can get a better look at these two from a different angle. I didn't want to get caught staring at them, plus it was my only chance to sneak-my-own-peek on Lisa's ample cleavage. I sat back down. Rob is sending all the worst nonverbal cues. I think Lisa realizes that this is going nowhere but is too polite to embarrass Rob. She tries to gut it out.

"Sorry you couldn't make it last night." She says.

Sounds like they had this meeting set up for the night before but bad boy Rob bailed on her. "What were you doing at 9 p.m.?" she asks.

"Ahem, well actually, I was on a date," he may as well have shit in her mouth.

Her voice gets higher as if to imply that she doesn't care and insincerely tries to sincerely ask, "Really? How was it?"

This opens the door for Rob to continue his "honesty" bent and he then launches into how he's not looking for anything serious, he wants to keep things casual and sometimes sex can just be sex. Lisa disagrees and starts talking about her teenage son. By this point, Rob has totally disengaged. In fact, he starts typing on his laptop but says, "Keep going, I'm listening," as he types away.

Lisa gets the point and says "Well, speaking of my son, I need to go pick him up from school. Want to walk me to my car?"

Rob pauses but reluctantly obliges. The two of them get up, go out the door and walk past the window in front of me where I'm writing. Rob's pace is almost at a jog as he tries to run her back to her car and finally be rid of Lisa. He's back in a blink and sits back down next to me. He gets on his computer and starts chatting online. I visually "eavesdrop" on him and his laptop. I see that he has gone back to work on Match.com, trying to set up the next coffee shop meeting. Hopefully with someone a bit more attractive and a whole lot looser.

***

Blackmon came away from the CBA All-Star game with a confidence that he could make it through the season with the Great Falls Explorers. Whether they were real or misinterpreted assurances from the league and its owners, somehow he felt like pressing on. I think the league gave him an immediate loan of $20,000. The reason I believe that to be true is first, because Blackmon told me they did; but secondly, because he all of a sudden had some money.

I had a lot of fun with the guys on our trip to Albany and was excited about the team we were able to quickly assemble. We needed a couple more pieces but thought we could be okay. That is why I agreed to coach the team for the remainder of the season. I told Blackmon that I would do it for $4,000 per month, a third of what he was "supposedly" paying Scott Wedman, but I wanted the money upfront, like Harold had done a couple of years earlier. He said he couldn't do it, and I of course, relented. I told him that instead I wanted to be paid at the beginning of each month. He said that would be okay. I stood firm that I wasn't going any further if that first check didn't go through.

As is always the case when dealing with Blackmon, everything happens at the last minute. On Thursday night, I agreed to meet the team in Texas for two games with the Rio Grande Silverados on Saturday and Sunday. I was to leave the next day, Friday. We had to gather everyone from around the country and it was up to Blackmon to get contracts worked out with the players.

As I recall, we had everyone who was in Albany come on the Texas trip but Pele. His agent wouldn't let him go until he had a signed contract. The other guys were more of the pushover type, like me. They decided to come with nothing but a promise of a contract later. In lieu of having Pele, Nate Green recommended a friend of his named Tim Pledger. In typical ball-licking fashion, Blackmon was all over Nate's suggestion, thinking that Tim would be the next Gary Payton. The problem was that the only thing Tim had in common with Gary was his age.

Tim had been bouncing around in basketball for 10 years and was in his mid-thirties. He was listed at 5'9". That's what he was listed as. If he was a breath over 5'7", I'd be shocked. Don't get me wrong, Tim was a nice guy and a good player, but a team can only support one midget and ours was Mo Carter. The two were pretty indistinguishable actually, but I felt some loyalty already to Mo. Nonetheless, Tim came with us to Texas and our two point guards, if laid end to end, were no longer than a gimmie putt for Tiger Woods.

Before the trip, I met Blackmon in Seattle to get money for myself and the guys. He signed and handed me eight blank checks as well as a credit card to use for food. He told me not to fill out and distribute checks until I spoke with him first to make sure the money from the league got deposited in to his bank account. I packed two bags this time. One was of (dry) clothes for myself and the other was the uniforms of the now defunct, King County Royals. I didn't want to wear the opposing team's away uniforms anymore. It was embarrassing, unprofessional and I didn't like the way it could affect the mentality of our team. The Royals' uniforms played right into the bunker mentality that I had successfully cultivated throughout my career, by giving us something that was uniquely "ours". I didn't tell Blackmon that I was bringing the uniforms though, because I figured he would want to use them for the rest of the season and that made no sense at all. They were fine in a pinch and for short-term mind manipulation but the Explorer's couldn't go all season wearing jerseys that said "Royals" across the front. That would have had the opposite affect on our team. Blackmon had to shell out the dough and get new uniforms.

I caught a flight from Seattle to McAllen, Texas via Houston. McAllen is about as far south as you can go in Texas before needing a passport. It is a city of just over 100,000 people, but amazingly enough, it had two minor-league basketball teams; one in the CBA and one in the NBDL.

It was mid-January and when I got off the plane the temperature was in the lower 70's; just what the doctor ordered. We had everyone there from the Albany trip minus Pele but adding Tim Pledger.

For whatever reason, Nate Green decided to be a petulant poop on this trip and this is where our relationship started to unravel. With our lack of size and experience, we needed him to play and come up big; literally and figuratively. Jason Clark was our only other player 6'8" or taller, but instead, Nate spent the weekend pouting about not getting paid by Blackmon and thus playing like he didn't care.

The Silverados exposed our lack of size and beat us up inside for a win on Saturday night, 114-98. I had to have a heart-to-heart with Nate. I knew it, but I didn't want to. I wanted to just get rid of him but Blackmon didn't want to hear that. In a surprising moment of reason, he talked me into speaking with Nate one-on-one, to try and get to know him better and figure out a way to use him more effectively. I think he had the same conversation with Nate because shortly after getting back to the hotel after the game, Nate knocked on my door and asked if we could talk.

Throughout my coaching career to that point, I had never really tried to find middle ground with a player. The voice of George Karl kept whispering, "your players have to hate you" over and over to me. It wasn't that I was unapproachable; it was more that I had a way of doing things and expected players to do them that way.

Given my circumstances as a college and minor-league coach, I could have a "my way or highway" approach. If we couldn't get along, they could go along. I never needed to compromise. But I started thinking that if I ever hoped to one day coach in the NBA, I would have to learn how to deal with petulant players; because in that league, you can't get rid of a player very easily. The contracts are guaranteed and when all is said and done, the player usually wins over the coach… in the NBA.

But this wasn't the NBA. These guys weren't good enough to be irreplaceable. Especially this guy, Nate. If we were going to lose games with him acting like a turd, we may as well lose with a different guy who actually gave an effort, and was a good teammate. At least those guys are fun to coach. Nevertheless, I used Nate Green as more of a lab experiment for open communication and future preparation for an NBA job than anything else. I knew that my instincts about him were correct but I tried my best with this different approach.

We had our "talk" in my room. As I already knew, he had an incredibly inflated sense of his own ability. This is the part that is difficult for me, because it works on my mind in two ways. First, I am not, and have never felt comfortable crushing someone's ego or self image. It is extremely common to have players who don't have a realistic view of their own abilities. It's exactly like watching the auditions for American Idol during the first few weeks of each season. The people that get cut always blame the judges for not knowing what they are talking about. They can't hear themselves to realize that they are terrible singers; it's the judges who are idiots. It's the same in basketball. It doesn't matter what level you are coaching, there are always guys that think they are better than what they really are. With that said though, I have yet to find the ability to channel my inner Simon Cowell when explaining what is missing from their game. I unfortunately, lean more towards the soft, Paula Abdul approach when delivering a blow. Because of this, it usually ends up as an argument about whether or not I'm right, or a groveling by them for clemency. Both of which are very uncomfortable. Maybe I should split the difference and try to Randy-ize them instead.

The second thing that makes these conversations extremely difficult on me is sensation of having a mirror held up to my face when having them. The player is either telling me how wrong I am or pleading for a second chance and I can't help but think that the person I am talking to is really me.

"Is that who I am?" I ask myself.

Am I the guy that has no realistic vision of his own ability? Am I an untalented joke in the eyes of others and can't see it for myself? I think that is why I try and avoid these confrontations with players and find it difficult to speak honestly to them about their ability. Maybe it's because I am speaking to myself. I don't know. I hope that is not the case. But it sometimes makes me wonder.

I understood Nate's frustration. I couldn't understand how he allowed it to manifest itself. He liked being a "pro basketball player" and he certainly looked the part. I think he would have been happy to go through the motions, play games, collect a paycheck and tell other people that he played pro basketball. Winning seemed secondary to being "a pro" for him. He had done it long enough that he felt he had paid his dues as a veteran player; like he didn't have to do everything I asked him or the things that younger players had to do. He needed a big time reality check. This was the CBA Nate. Not the NBA. This team was in total chaos and we were 'all hands on deck' in an effort to right the ship. We only had seven players. Without him pulling his weight, we really only had six. That is a tough way to compete. He had the size, talent and experience to be an impact player for us, but he was more concerned about paychecks and touches. I just wanted to win and his worries didn't register with me at any level.

I did my best though to bend a little. I tried to empathize with his complaints about money without throwing Blackmon under the bus. I told him that I had paychecks with me and that I would be handing them out before the trip was over. I explained to him what I was looking for in a player. I played my NBA card with him and talked about my experiences with the Sonics and tried to impart to him how our team success would lead to greater individual opportunities for him. I told him that I would help him find a job overseas that would hopefully pay better; but for now needed him to try and get onboard with what I expected. It was a good talk. I did feel better about things (him) afterward, but I knew that in essence, you can't shine a turd. Ultimately, things would end badly with Nate and me. I knew that.

The next night was a little better for the Explorers and we beat Rio Grande 98-88 to salvage a split on the road trip. Blackmon called and he told me that the money he was promised from the league was finally deposited and that I could write checks to guys. The rub was that I could only write them for half of what they were owed. This included my check. I started doing the math in my head and I knew that $20,000 from the league wouldn't last long.

I handed out checks before we left for home. A quirk in the schedule gave us another week off. I was going back to Seattle to pack some things for Great Falls and the final two months of the season, but before I made any hasty decisions I wanted to make sure my check cashed. We had an hour and a half layover before our connection in Houston.

Upon arriving at Bush International Airport in Houston, I grabbed a cab and went to the nearest U.S. Bank. U.S. Bank was the bank that the checks were written on. I figured that if there was truly any money in the account, U.S. Bank could cash it for me on the spot, so I wouldn't have to risk depositing it my bank and having it bounce later.

I wrote myself a check for $2,500. I wasn't sure it would work. The checks he gave me were like counter checks with no address in the upper left hand corner. His signature was inconsistent from one check to the next and very sloppy. It was obvious that the person who signed the check and the person who wrote it out were two different people.

It took about 15 or 20 minutes to find a U.S. Bank. Once we found it, I asked the cab driver to wait in the parking lot for me. I walked in and went over to the counter to endorse the check. I looked for the friendliest teller and walked up to that window. I handed her the check and my ID and waited. I felt like I had been dipped in guilt, as if I was doing something wrong. She did a few keystrokes on the computer, ran it through some machine and said, "Can you wait right here Mr. Turner?"

"Uh-oh," I thought to myself. She walked away and spoke to another one of the bank employees who seemed to have more authority. She started walking back toward me.

"I just need to have you put your thumbprint on here," and she pushed an ink pad over next to me. I rolled my thumb through the blue ink and pressed it up against the check. She took it from me, placed it in a drawer and counted out 25, $100 dollar bills. Then she recounted them out to me in full view like a deck of playing cards.

"1,2,3,4,5,6,7,8,9, one. 1,2,3,4,5,6,7,8,9, two. 1,2,3,4,5, twenty-five hundred dollars. Is there anything else that I can do for you today Mr. Turner?"

"This is mine, right? I mean, there's no way that this check could bounce, correct?" I had to make sure.

"Nope. All the funds are there. You're good to go."

I breathed a sigh of relief and hurried back to my cab, which was waiting for me in the parking lot. Even though it was only half of what I was owed, I felt a lot better with money in my pocket. It could sustain me now for a little while but I needed to get back to the airport before I got left in Houston.

So far we had played two games in Pittsburgh, two games in Albany, two games in McAllen, TX and still only had one practice. We had eight days until our next game in Pikeville, Kentucky but I still felt like we needed more (and better) players.

The plan was that I would take a day in Seattle to get some things together after returning from Texas. Blackmon and I would try to solidify the roster and I could get some practice time with the guys before we left for Kentucky. At this point we had six players: Marlyn, Mike Peeples, Jason Clark, Mo Carter, Nate Green and Tim Pledger. We agreed that we needed eight.

***

I walked off the Horizon Air flight from Sea-Tac Airport in Seattle to Great Falls, Montana at midnight on Tuesday, January 29th. It was minus 16 degrees when as I stepped out on to the stairs leading down from the plane's front door. I had never felt cold like that before. On top of that, it was windy which made it feel like it was minus 40. I loved it though. This was the adventure that I had signed up for. I loved the unknown aspects of everything surrounding this trip. I loved that I didn't know anything about Great Falls. I loved that I didn't know where I was staying. I loved the extreme temperatures. I loved being anonymous there. I loved the challenge of putting this team together, and I especially loved the idea of winning games when you're not supposed to.

Believe it or not, Blackmon actually showed up on time to pick me up from the airport. He had just driven his brand new dealership car from a holdover team sponsor back from Seattle to Great Falls. It was a beautiful brand new white Ford Explorer with a big Explorers magnet logo on each door.

I threw my bags in the back and as I hopped in the front passenger seat; he had a big smile on his face and said, "Welcome to Great Falls, the arm-pit of the west." I was so tired, all I could manage was I weak smile and he drove away toward the arena. Instead of going back to the hotel, he was all jacked up and wanted to show me the team offices. When he "bought" the team (if that's what you want to call it) he inherited a bunch of 'stuff' from the previous owner that he never had before with any of his other teams. A real office being one of them; along with team merchandise, office equipment, marketing materials, company cars and other swag. All I wanted to do was go to my room, go to bed and start fresh in the morning, but I rolled with the punches and went to see the office at what was now, almost 1 a.m.

The Four Season's Arena was where the Explorers played their home games and was also where the Explorers offices were located. It was on the site of the Montana State

Fairgrounds and as we drove into the parking lot, as you would expect at 1a.m., the place was dark and empty.

From the outside, the building looked like it was pretty nice. We parked the car and got out. Instead of walking toward the arena, we walked toward what looked like a mobile home parked off to the side.

This was the office of the Great Falls Explorers.

Blackmon was like a kid in a candy store as he showed off 'our' offices. I could understand why he was excited about it, since he didn't have to do any work to procure it, but the office itself was a total s***-hole. The front door would stick shut so you really had to lean into it in order to force it open. There was junk scattered everywhere and a crappy metal desk off to the right when you walked in. Behind that desk was a door that led to Blackmon's office. The walls inside were bare and stark. There was a desk, a chair and a phone, but nothing else in the room. To the left of Blackmon's office was a door that led to a coach's office. There was a desk in there and a big white board on the wall with a bunch of player's names written on it. Otherwise it was cold and austere. There was a brand new copier to the left of the front door that was probably obtained through trade, as well as another small office (maybe it was a closet) that looked more like storage. If it was minus 16 outside, it couldn't have been much (if any) warmer inside that office.

Blackmon looked at me and could tell that I was under whelmed by the whole thing and really just wanted to get out of there. So we got back in the white Explorer and headed back to the Extended Stay America hotel located right off the Missouri River, near downtown Great Falls. I was finally tucked in at my new temporary home shortly after 2 a.m., wondering what the next day, the next week, and the next few months were going to bring.

Blackmon called me the next morning and wanted me to accompany him on some errands that he needed to take care of. A couple of the players were already in Great Falls but a few were still going to be trickling in that day. Our first stop was with the manager of the hotel where we were staying. She needed to get Blackmon to sign some sort of credit form before she released the rooms to us but he hadn't gotten her the forms yet. They were gracious enough to put us up on a handshake agreement but the manager's patience was running short. She really needed to know how they were getting paid.

Blackmon and I met in the small lobby and he walked to the front desk to ask for the manager. I assumed that we would be going to a conference room to meet but they didn't have one there. She and Blackmon would duke it out right there in the lobby.

I knew it was going to be bad right from the get go.

Blackmon greeted her warmly and unusually friendly for him. He immediately introduced me as the new head coach of the team and I think he hoped that my being there would somehow impress her, or at least deflect some of the animosity she was showing toward him. It didn't. She was visibly not happy with him. He tried to win her over.

"First of all, before we get started, let me just apologize for my behavior last night. I was completely out of line and you didn't deserve that. I was tired and had been driving all day and night from Seattle. All I wanted to do was check in the room and I just behaved badly... I'm sorry."

"I have never had anyone speak to me like that before. I called our district manager and told him about what happened and he said we should just walk away from your business..." She went on about the episode from the night before and the demands that the hotel would have in order to let us stay there.

I was so uncomfortable and embarrassed that I stepped away from what was being said. I could only imagine the vile that spewed from his mouth the night before when confronted about a contract. Flashbacks of the American Airlines agent and the phone call following the Hall of Fame luncheon came rushing back to me.

Less then 12 hours in Great Falls and it was the same ol' stuff. Blackmon wanted to pay as we went on those rooms. I think the hotel wanted a line of credit established. Blackmon couldn't give them that and his behavior throughout (and especially the previous night) made the hotel reticent to want to work with him. They went back and forth for a few minutes before Blackmon turned and walked out the door. Leaving me and the manager looking at each other wondering where he went.

Our next stop was the office where Blackmon had a meeting with the sports editor for the local newspaper, The Great Falls Tribune, a fella named George Geise. George was doing a story about what was happening with the team since the drama of three weeks ago involving Blackmon, Scott Wedman and the players. It was Blackmon's plan to eviscerate Wedman in the paper, let everyone know that the ship is now righted, and try to get fans excited about the new roster. As we drove to the office to meet George, I tried to talk Blackmon down from his bent of ripping on Wedman. I told him that it was unnecessary, made him look small, and would force people to choose sides. Most would choose Wedman. I also told him that the pettiness of that would diminish him in the fans eyes. He finally relented and said that he thought I was right. He would tell the story without ripping Wedman.

We walked into the empty Explorers' office (there was no staff working?) that was just a bit warmer than the night before but not much. Blackmon looked at the Jim Rockford-type antique answering machine that sat on the desk and saw that there were close to 100 messages on it and full. He picked up the phone. There was no dial tone. The bill had not been paid. I poked around in the coach's office to see if there was anything there of interest. There wasn't. Some names were left written on the white board. It looked like it had been there since training camp. I saw Marlyn's name and Nate's name but no others that I recognized. Soon, I saw a car drive up from out of the window. It was George Geise, there to do the interview.

George walked in the meat locker of a trailer and Blackmon invited him to sit down back in his office. I pulled in two chairs so George and I could sit. We met and shook hands, exchanged a few pleasantries and George turned on his tape recorder. It didn't take long before Wedman's name came up.

"Scott Wedman is a thief. He is nothing but a low-life thief and if he ever comes back to Montana, I'm going to have him arrested for grand larceny. Not only is he a terrible coach but he stole money and equipment from me worth over $500, which is a felony offense and I will have him arrested."

So much for taking the high road.

Blackmon couldn't help himself. He had no filter. He had no ability to finesse any situation. He love, love, loved being interviewed and appearing in the newspaper. It was like main-lining adrenaline to his ego. I always got the sense that he knew what he was saying though. It wasn't like he slipped up and said things that he regretted. But calling him manipulative would be giving him too much credit; it seemed to almost reach that level, but not quite. You have to be really smart to be manipulative. He tried to be more intimidating with what he said. If manipulation was continued body blows in an effort to wear down your opponent, then intimidation was just a punch in the nose. It stuns your opponent for a second but they quickly shake it off and fight on.

We sat and talked with George for about 45 minutes before he left. I waited, trying to prepare myself for whatever the next meeting would have in store. George left the office at about 12:45 and Blackmon's one and only salesman was supposed to come at 1 p.m. to meet with us. Blackmon specifically said that he wanted to have me sit in on the meeting so I could give him my impression of this new salesman, who Blackmon described as "a strange guy".

His name was Brian and he was a former marine who was a total "yes sir", "no sir" type of guy. This is what I think Blackmon thought was strange about him; that Brian called him "sir". He was highly organized, respectful and formal, but my first impression was that he didn't have the schmooze factor of your typical salesman. He wasn't unfriendly but he didn't come across as particularly friendly when I first met him. He walked in the office and we shook hands as Blackmon introduced the two of us. He didn't seem to be in the mood for small talk and was "all-business" as we walked back toward Blackmon's office. As the three of us walked in, Brian looked at me and said, "Mr. Turner, if you don't mind, I'd like to speak with Mr. Blackmon alone." I was happy to oblige although he had such a pissed off and vacant look in his eyes that I half expected Brian to shoot Blackmon dead right there in the office.

I went back into the coach's office and played solitaire on my cell phone while I waited for the gun shot. I couldn't quite make out what they were saying. I know Brian expected to be paid and Blackmon expected him to sell something; neither of which had happened to this point. I could tell that it was getting a little heated but no one raised their voice. I could hear Blackmon pleading poverty and imploring Brian to go out and make a sale. I could hear Brian telling Blackmon that he had a family to support and they needed some money for food. The back and forth didn't go on for very long before I heard footsteps, the front door open, then slam shut and Brian drive away in his rig (they drive rigs in Montana). I walked into Blackmon's office with my palms held up and shrugging my shoulders as if to ask what happened.

"Do you think your friend Giles would want to move to Montana and sell sponsorships for the Explorers?" Blackmon asked sarcastically.

It looks like Brian had quit.

Shortly after Brian left, another guy drove up to the office. It was the Explorers' PA announcer. He was looking for some money also. It seemed that he hadn't been paid either. He was taking his family to Disneyland and wanted the money that he was owed before the trip. This guy actually looked like he could be a pretty friendly guy, but like Brian, seemed to be really pissed off. He had a distinct look of distain on his face for Blackmon, like he could barely stomach sharing the same air. I couldn't help but think that he had taken a bad approach to Blackmon for someone that was looking for money. A little honey might work better then vinegar in this situation. Blackmon tried to be empathetic and told the guy that he could have the money tomorrow but the PA guy said that they were leaving first thing in the morning and needed it today. Again, they went back and forth and that guy too, went storming out of the office. Blackmon and I got back in the Explorer and headed for lunch.

"Holy geez…" I remember thinking to myself, "… these people loathe him in this town."

He had no chance to succeed here in Great Falls. It was so bad that I immediately suggested that we move the team back to Seattle and finish the season there. It was somewhat of a selfish suggestion on my part, but it actually did have some merit. There was nothing keeping us in Great Falls. Blackmon had the Bizzaro King Midas touch working for him in Great Falls where everything he touched there turned to crap instead of gold. It would be less expensive in Seattle since we each had homes there already. Each of us knew the lay of the land better in Seattle, and we had established relationships that we could rely on to at least get through the next two months.

"We gotta get out of here," I turned and told him. "I've got a terrible vibe about this place."

We went to the McKenzie River Pizza Company located next door to our hotel for lunch. We walked in a saw Mo Carter, Jason Clark and Tim Pledger having lunch. We sat down in the booth next to them and started making phone calls. Our immediate needs were uniforms and big men. Blackmon's first call was to order the uniforms. I described to him what I wanted and he relayed that to the guy on the phone. We turned to the booth where the guys were sitting and asked them what numbers and sizes they wanted. Blackmon ordered 10 blue, road uniforms for immediate delivery. He said that he would order the home, white uniforms later. I knew that he never would.

Tim went back to the hotel and Mo and Jason hung around in our booth for a bit as Blackmon bought them dessert. The subject of big men came up and Mo suggested that we try and get a guy that he knew in Virginia named Junior Burrough. Jason emphatically agreed and we asked Mo to get a number for Junior.

Thomas "Junior" Burrough was a 6'9" power forward who played at the University of Virginia from '91-'95. He was the 33rd overall pick in the NBA draft, by the Boston Celtics, in 1995 and he played one season for the Celtics before going overseas where he played all over Europe, Asia and South America with tremendous success. He was home in Virginia, without a contract, and trying to hook on somewhere.

Junior could play with his back to the basket but also had a nice mid-range game and could step out to 18-20 feet. He was a leader and a calming veteran presence that had been playing professionally for a dozen years by this point. He kept himself in excellent physical condition and didn't just talk the talk with other players, but walked the walk. He was the anti-Nate Green, extremely professional, good-natured, a hard worker and a really good player. He was exactly what we needed.

Blackmon got a hold of Junior and somehow convinced him to join the team. I think it took some arm twisting from Mo and fellow UVA alum Jason Clark, but Junior finally decided sign up with us and he would meet us in Kentucky a few days later.

The next guy that we signed was Lamont Arrington.

Lamont was a 7'0" center who played two years at the University of Colorado. I don't remember how we ended up with his name, but nevertheless he came to us and after a few phone calls to some coaching friends, we added him to the roster. Lamont needed more experience. He was still raw but had the tools to be a successful player. When you have that kind of size and skill, the only thing holding you back is you. Guys like that (7 footers) get every opportunity to find the light switch and some can, while others simply can't. This was a good situation for Lamont, where he could get some great experience without the pressure of being heavily relied upon. He had physical guys like Junior and Jason to beat on him in practice to help get him better, and now he just needed to work hard for the final eight weeks of the season and see what happens. He could block shots and had a decent touch around the basket. Another plus was that he was a really good guy who was easy to be around and didn't cause problems. He fit in nicely as a big man coming off the bench.

With two big men taken care of, my next project was to lobby Blackmon to bring back Pele. Somehow Pele's agent had pissed off Blackmon and he wasn't inclined to try and work it out. Plus, Pele would have been the ninth guy and we were only going to carry eight on the roster. I told Blackmon that we needed to dump Tim Pledger and sign Pele. He was reluctant to do it, but he finally gave in after I gave him all the reasons why we needed this to happen.

Finally, we had our roster set and it was as good, if not better, then any team in the league.

Maurice Carter – point guard
Pele Paelay – combo 1/2
Marlyn Bryant – 2 guard
Mike Peeples – combo 2/3
Nate Green – 3/4
Jason Clark – 4/5
Junior Burrough – 4/5
Lamont Arrington – 5

We had size, we had flexibility, and we had talent. Now we just needed time to play and practice together and that was running short.

Blackmon told me that the team had a trade deal worked out with the Peak Athletic Club in Great Falls for use of their facility. The club had all the nice amenities of your typical health club, as well as a gym where we could practice. The only problem was that no one had followed up to maintain the account, or as they say in the biz… fulfillment.

The previous owners had made sponsorship deals that Blackmon then inherited when he took over the team. Much of his problem though was that he made no effort to see that those deals were met. He took their end of the deals; courtesy cars, restaurant meals, fitness club memberships, but he never followed up to see that his end of those contracts was fulfilled.

The Peak Athletic Club was one of those deals.

When I took the team to the club the next morning for our first practice in Great Falls, I had to essentially save the deal from blowing up right there on the spot before they would let us in the door. The staff at "The Peak" were great to us but they definitely wanted to make sure they weren't getting taken advantage of. I did my best to assure them that all the contract requirements would be met but I really had no way of making this happen. I didn't want to be disingenuous, but at that moment I needed to get a practice in, so I said whatever I had to in order to get us through the front door.

We had three days of practice at the Peak. We were still without Junior and Pele so we couldn't do anything more than 3-on-3 and 5-on-0 work at the small gym of the club.

On top of that, the club wouldn't close the gym for our practice, so if one of their members came in to use it, they could, regardless of what we were doing. They were adamant about us not infringing on their members when using the facility so we really had to walk on eggshells while we were there.

According to Nate Green, Wedman had given away all the team's basketballs to the former players on their way out the door and the only CBA ball we had to use was the one that Wedman had given to Nate. The only other balls available were the torn up, crappy balls that the health club had, scattered around off to the side of the court for their members to use.

Six players, one basketball and a half a basketball court…

I was livin' the dream.

***

Blackmon had talked the East Kentucky Miners into housing us for a couple of extra days before we were to play them; so we left for Pikeville, Kentucky on the Saturday before the Super Bowl to play two games on Tuesday and Wednesday.

As you could probably guess by now, we all had to check out of the Extended Stay America before we left because Blackmon didn't want to pay for rooms that we weren't using. That obviously meant that we couldn't get too comfortable in our rooms because we needed to be able to pack and get out of them at any time. As strange as this may sound, with no space to call your own, or no place to hang your hat so to speak, you feel like you are constantly traveling. It wears you out.

We flew from Great Falls to Salt Lake City and then from Salt Lake City to Cincinnati where we met up with Junior and Pele and then from Cincinnati to Lexington, KY. Once we got to Lexington, it was 142 miles to Pikeville or about a two and a half hour drive. We were met at the airport by a young assistant for the Miners by the name of Mark King. Mark had a 12 passenger van there to pick us up. We had nine big guys, all of our belongings (remember we had to check out of our hotel in Great Falls), including multiple bags for Junior and Pele who came packed for the rest of the season in Great Falls, the uniforms and we had no room for any of it.

We shoved ourselves into that van like Rosanne into skinny jeans. We had to take a collective deep breath just to get the doors to shut. We headed east on I-64 for the two and a half hour drive to Pikeville, bulging out from every crevasse of that van. Young Mark, the driver, cranked up the Kanye West CD "Graduation" and soon I was imploring Mark to drive faster through Kanye's lyrics

> "N- n- now th- that don't kill me
> Can only make me stronger

I need you to hurry up now
'cause I can't wait much longer..."

We eventually arrived at the Heritage House Hotel (or the Triple H as no one called it) in Prestonsburg, KY after the longest 142 miles on record. This was a part of the United States that I had never seen. It was coal mining territory and we were "in country". I half expected to hear the **Deliverance** dueling banjos playing as we finally burst from the van. We were deep in the Appalachians and the squirrels outnumbered the resident's teeth 2-to-1.

The front desk receptionist at the Triple H was such a cliché, I hesitate to even tell you but it's absolutely true. She was pregnant, missing one of her front teeth, had a slight beard and was holding a chew in her bottom lip. The lobby reeked of cigarette smoke from the karaoke contest going on in the adjacent lounge and a spurt of blue smoke along with a few notes from one of the local's version of "Black Velvet" would escape from the lounge every time someone opened the door into the lobby.

There was nothing near the hotel; I mean nothing. We were as isolated as the Torrance family in **The Shining**. No cell phone reception and no nearby restaurants for the guys to walk to when hungry. We weren't there on vacation but we were there for an unusual amount of time for just two games. An idle mind is the devil's playground, so I tried to find us things that could occupy our time for the next seven days. It wasn't easy.

It was shocking to see the beautiful new arena that the East Kentucky Miners played in. It was a 7,000 seat, state-of-the-art arena located in Pikeville, KY which has a population of only 6,500 residents. The building hosted big time concerts and other large events, and the Miners had drawn a near sell-out crowd in their previous game a couple days earlier.

One of the Miners co-owners was Jay Fiedler, the former QB for the Miami Dolphins among a couple other NFL teams, and the Miners' GM was Kyle Macy, the former University of Kentucky All-American and seven-year NBA star. It was a well run organization.

We won our first game in Kentucky by the score of 109-108. In poker terms, it was a suck and re-suck sort of situation. The Miners hit a prayer, running-fall-away-off-balance-bank in three-pointer to tie the game with .7 seconds left. We called time out and drew up a play for our own desperation shot. We were fortunate to get a crazy foul called against the Miners on the inbound pass with .3 seconds left. Mike Peeples missed the first free throw but made the second and we escaped with a great road victory. The Miners coach wasn't too keen on the call:

"This is professional basketball and this is probably one of the most inconsistent seasons that I've had as a basketball coach," said Miners coach Kevin Keathley. "We tie the ball game with 0.7 and they called a foul 25 feet outside the basket. You just don't make that call. You let players win basketball games. The outcome

shouldn't be determined by outside forces. I'm just disappointed and that call should never have happened."

He was quoted as saying that in the Appalachian News Express immediately following the game.

I'm not sure if he was pissed about the outcome, playing games with us, or was just a jerk, but he wouldn't let us practice in the arena the next day at any other time but 8:00 in the morning. There was no way that I was going to make our guys get up that early the next day and make the 40 minute drive back to the arena to practice at 8, so I made other arrangements at a local junior high school nearby where I traded some tickets for gym time. It worked out great. The kids at the school came out and watched our practice, cheered us on, got autographs afterward and became instant Great Falls Explorers fans. The principal of the school emailed Blackmon later that same day.

February 5, 2008

Mr. Blackmon,

My name is Jack Goodman and I am principal of Adams Middle School in Eastern Kentucky. Your team practiced at our school on Feb. 5. I felt obliged to allow this to happen because our gym was vacant at the time your team needed to practice. However, what I found out most important about your team's coach and players was that they were so gracious to have the opportunity to use our gym to help them prepare for the East Ky Miners. I was proud to have them at our school, not to show off their talents or make our school look like something we aren't, but for the simple reason these guys were just great individuals, role models, guys our kids need to be around more often. Please take time to tell Coach Turner and the players how much we appreciated how hospitable they were today. Most of the times, players of this magnitude will tend to turn their noses up to kids and others in a place such as we live.

If your team is ever in our area again, please inform Coach Turner to contact me at school (606-8xx-xxxx) or at home (606-4xx-xxxx) or cell phone (606-7xx-xxxx). Good luck tomorrow night and the rest of the season.

PS: If you could send an autographed picture or anything for our Special Education students' classroom, it would be very much appreciated. It was their gym time that I gave to your team. They came to the gym to watch, very little, but didn't complain at all since they thought it was helping someone. These kids have many issues you wouldn't imagine. If you can't do anything like this, don't worry. Again, thanks for you time.

Thanks,

Jack Goodman, Principal
Rebecca Hicks and Tommy Poe, Asst. Principals
The Staff and Students
2520 South Lake Drive
Prestonsburg, Ky 41653

He was right. We had some outstanding young men on our team; men of character and determination. It's hard to put your finger on it, but even after just a few days, I knew there was something special about this group. They showed it at Adams Middle School in Kentucky. They were thankful, affable and approachable to all the staff and students. They didn't hide underneath their headphones and hooded sweatshirts. They just generally made me feel proud to be their coach. We met some good, good people during our week in Kentucky; completely shattering the image we had built upon our arrival in town. With the exception of the coach for the Miners, everyone was very friendly and accommodating. They are basketball crazy in that state and this is no exaggeration. They go nuts for all forms of Kentucky basketball. It was a cool experience to bear brief witness to at least a little of that frenzy in the short time we were there.

The next game didn't go as well for the good guys. We lost to the Miners 118-112. Mike and Marlyn each had 22 points while Junior pitched in 21, but it wasn't enough. I had decided to bring Nate off the bench in that second game. He was versatile and could score which meant that he could come in at a variety of positions and provide us some scoring punch off the bench. He didn't like this idea at all but Junior needed to start. I didn't start Junior the first night because he had just joined us and I didn't want to just throw him in there. He understood that; but he was brought here to play and had earned the benefit of the doubt throughout his career. He provided leadership on the floor and he needed to be in there. Jason Clark gave us a physical-ness that I liked to establish the game. He didn't care about scoring, he really wanted to rebound. Nate could then sub in at the 3, the 4 or the 5 spot. It gave us some flexibility and it just made more sense to bring Nate in off the bench.

Nate came in and played just 'okay'. His body language was terrible though and everything he was saying and doing told me that he was more concerned about himself then the success of the team. It isn't uncommon at that level, but it's every bit as destructive to the rest of the players as it would be in high school or college. For whatever reason, some guys at the pro level think this behavior is acceptable (sometimes even expected) simply because they are "pros". Maybe they see NBA guys grouse and bitch and get their way but they don't fully comprehend that they themselves are a long, long way from those perks. Not to mention the fact that it's cruddy behavior anyway. To this point in my career I had handled these situations swiftly, and frankly, pretty callously.

It was a little different with Nate though, because Blackmon wouldn't let me just cut him, which was my immediate reaction to do here with him. "Reaction" is the operative word though, because in hindsight, I think my emotions surrounding this situation (and maybe some others throughout my career) could have been a bit reactionary.

What makes it tough is that you don't want negative situations around your team to linger and fester. I always tried to act without hesitation to end the problem as well as send a strong message to the other guys about my commitment to them, my commitment to "team" and the consequences of not getting on board. At the same time, maybe I could have been more patient. I don't know… but by Blackmon not allowing me to do anything with Nate, it forced me to deal with him directly, which in turn, made me a better coach.

A split on the road in Albany, a split on the road in Texas and now a split on the road in Kentucky.

Not a bad start for a team who was still learning each others names.

We headed back to Montana where we still had two more games on the road to play in Butte before finally playing our first home game.

Butte, Montana was the home of Evel Knievel, and as such, the nickname of Butte's CBA team was the Daredevils. They played at the 6,200 seat, Butte Civic Center which was a nice building, but it looked more suited to a rodeo than basketball because of its length and relatively low ceiling. It looked like a big barn.

Normally, the team (or league) would arrange a bus for us to travel in from Great Falls to Butte but the day we were to leave, the bus never showed up. It seemed as if no one called to schedule it. Blackmon must have thought that a bus would magically show up on its own. Besides that, the previous bill that Blackmon had with the bus company had not been paid. We had Blackmon's Ford Explorer along with a minivan that was provided to the team by a different local car dealer (that was the "car" that Blackmon had promised me before my arrival). This was all we had to get us to Butte.

Five guys drove with me in the minivan and three guys drew the short straw and rode with Blackmon in the Explorer. We took off, south on I-15 toward Butte, 157 miles away in the cold and snow of Montana. I was white knuckling it the entire way, afraid of hitting a patch of ice and slowing to a crawl as we passed through waves of blinding snow showers. I was mentally wiped out by the time we got to Butte and checked into the hotel.

It was early afternoon on Saturday and we had our first game with Butte later that night. We needed to get some rest. I felt like the travel was starting to catch up with us… at least it was with me.

Six players in double figures, led by Marlyn's 26 points, and the Explorers dealt Butte their 12th loss in a row, 110-103, in front of a small but boisterous crowd at the civic center. After two weeks on the road, this was Blackmon's first chance to see his new team play. Rather then sit in the stands or courtside like most owners would, Blackmon decided that he would sit at the end of the bench and get water and Gatorade for guys as they came out of the game; essentially making him our water boy. I have to give him credit though; he didn't interfere at all or say anything negative to anyone during the game. He was mostly a positive cheerleader.

Honestly, I think he was pretty blown away by how good our players were. I don't know that he expected it. His jock sniffing respect for this group kept his penchant for insults in check. From a pure talent stand point, we were way, way better than any ABA team that he had in the past and much, much better then the team that dissolved in front of his eyes just a month earlier in Great Falls. I think he was pleasantly surprised with what we had built in such a short time.

After the game, Blackmon and I went to dinner. Even though he had just had a pretty decent game from a numbers point of view, I still was lobbying to do something with Nate. I didn't have a great plan in place (I was working on that) but it was such a drag on our team, I was afraid for it to continue much longer. Under different circumstances, it could have been dealt with more deftly.

The problem that I saw was that it had a potential to quickly divide us when, to this point, we had been pretty strongly united. I think Blackmon was so sick of listening to Nate complain about money, that he was starting to move off his commitment to him. He wasn't ready to altogether punt on Nate but at least the wheels were in motion. Now I would just have to find a good plan on who to bring in to replace him.

After the game, I was so tired at dinner that I almost fell asleep in my Moons Over My-Hammy. Whatever we were going to do about Nate, it wasn't going to get worked out tonight. We had a game tomorrow that he would play in, so we could deal more with it afterward. Just get me back to my room. The sooner I could crawl into bed, the better.

We went back to the hotel and I slowly shuffled back to my room, keeping the exertion of my journey placid and composed so I wouldn't wake myself up too much on the walk. My plan was: start unbuttoning my shirt a few steps from the door of my room, undo the final shirt button as I put the key card in to unlock the door, push open the door with my right hand while (neglecting to turn on the light) simultaneously unbuckle my belt and unbutton my pants with the left. Operating completely hands free now, I would walk toward the bed leaving a trail of first, my shirt by shaking it off with a slight shoulder shimmy, and then continuing to walk, right out of my pants, leaving them behind in a crumpled mess, crotch up as an overnight monument to salute the days accomplishments.

As I stumbled closer to paradise, I would fall face first into the bed wearing only my black dress socks pulled up just under my knee, and my favorite camouflage boxers. Arms at my side, cockeyed on the mattress, and slobbering contently on the hotel's pillow; my rapidly moving eyes would battle my oxygen-deprived snore for that night's supremacy. Later, I'd crawl under the covers sometime in the middle of the night after waking up cold, snuggle back in, spoon the dry pillow and fall back asleep one more time.

It was the perfect plan.

There was one problem however...

There to greet me upon my arrival back to my room was a smelly, stinky hefty bag of sweaty uniforms that needed to be washed before tomorrow's game.

I had forgotten all about it.

A conciliatory sigh exited my body as I looked down at the torn up plastic bag. It was time for a personal pep talk which I quickly delivered to myself and then set off to find the nearest laundromat. There, I spent the next two hours fluffing and folding; dreaming about the day when I wouldn't have to wash the uniforms or drive the crappy van overnight and through white-out snow storms. Would it ever happen? Will it ever happen? Am I paying my dues or am I just a fool?

Sometimes it's the small battles that will win a war. Rather than coaching the Sonics, or coaching in the Pac-10, or coaching in the ACC; right now I just wanted to coach where someone else would do the laundry.

The next night we snapped Butte's 12-game losing streak. Trailing the entire way, we lost 94-86. Upon arriving at the gym before the game, Marlyn got a text message from a friend of his in Great Falls who said that the newspaper was reporting that the County Sheriff had gone to the Explorers team offices and placed locks on the doors. It turned out that there was a balance of $16,000, outstanding from games played at the Four Seasons Arena earlier in the season, that hadn't been paid; and as Blackmon claimed, it never would be.

That mini-drama created a buzz among the guys during our pre-game and further shined a light on what they already knew; things with Blackmon weren't exactly as he would lead you to believe. There is definitely an excitement to being in the middle of this chaos. Something that strangely energizes you for a short time. Just about the time you get bored with the latest drama surrounding Blackmon and the team, something new takes its place. Like bumping from one high to another; part of what feels good is that sense of being on the edge and just a little out of control. You never knew what would happen next.

Nate, of course, continued to be a turd bird in the second game. He had a hard time integrating himself socially with the new guys which isolated him from the group. He had a hard time with his role as "sixth man" which was a haymaker to his ego, and his patience with Blackmon was wearing extremely thin. It was a trifecta of poop soup that was difficult for Nate to digest.

Blackmon kept making him promises that he never followed up on, mostly involving money. A part of me really felt for Nate, while another part of me was disgusted by his inability to buck up and get over it. His 2 of 11 from the field and 4 of 9 from the free-throw line that night wasn't nearly as bad as his own complete indifference to it all, including the loss. Blackmon finally got to see for himself what I had been talking about for the past two weeks.

He actually came up with a good idea though. Instead of just cutting Nate like I wanted to do, Blackmon suggested that we try and trade him first. This wasn't a bad idea. He had good size, good skill, was a CBA All-Star that season (thanks to Blackmon pleading with the league) and definitely passed the eye test. I told Blackmon to go ahead and pursue a trade, but either way, Nate Green had played his last game for the Great Falls Explorers.

On our way out of town, Blackmon took us all to dinner at the Butte location of the McKenzie River Pizza Co. Big men, big meals and a big bill. I guess I don't have to tell you whose credit card didn't work after all the plates were cleaned. This time, Blackmon didn't lose his cool on the staff of the restaurant; however I could feel that it was dangerously close to happening. Rather than allow my guys to watch the meltdown unfold before them, I decided to quietly escape before we found ourselves washing dishes. I got my group loaded up in the minivan and took off before the bill dispute ever got resolved. I'm still not sure how he got off the hook. My guess is that he either wrote them a bad check or promised to pay them when we got back to Great Falls. Whatever the case, it was obvious that the noose was tightening around Blackmon's neck. The next couple of weeks would soon deteriorate into a circus that I could have never predicted.

15

Great Falls

The fix with Nate had to be done. We were an extremely fragile team at that moment; balancing on the precipice of greatness (that might be an exaggeration; maybe good-ness) or complete implosion. I think the guys realized that we were pretty good, but at the same time, they weren't getting paid like they were supposed to. While we were playing with confidence, it was a delicate balance to keep them focused and motivated; while not being distracted by Blackmon and money. Each new day I could tell that their enthusiasm was waning and the excitement of the challenge put in front of us had dulled. We were able to keep the bunker mentality edge and remained close, but instead of "us against the world" it was turning into "us against Blackmon". I had to work hard everyday to play three difficult and distinct roles to everyone involved.

1) Empathetic
2) Neutral
3) Loyal

Whether it was with the players, the owner, or various people within the community; I attempted to express empathy for their plight, remain neutral in taking sides and maintain a loyalty that would not diminish my integrity. It would've been very easy for me to kick Blackmon around when talking to players, and other people within the league and around town. I did my best not to, for a number of reasons. One, I thought that it made me look small. Two, I didn't want anyone to think that I was weak enough for him to have the ability to affect me in any way; and three, I had a very vivid memory from the Sonics that I wanted to avoid.

During the last couple of years of my time in the front office at the Sonics, people would come into my office to complain and bitch about stuff on a daily basis. My office became a revolving door of impromptu therapy sessions and my-job-is-worse-than-your-job contests. I always kind of liked it though; partly because it made me feel good that they would trust me with their gripes and partly because it made me feel like the popular guy in the office.

They'd come in, sit down and we'd gossip, and whisper and complain and generally hate on anyone and everyone. Misery loves company and I loved being in the mix of everyone else's problems. Each day it made me become more and more disenchanted with where I was; to the point that I was miserable in a job that was actually pretty perfect for me. I didn't realize how destructive those daily "union meetings" were until I had a few years of separation to look back on it. Once behind me, and without the distractions of co-workers in my life, I could see how cancerous those situations can become and wanted to avoid putting myself in middle of that ever again.

It was tough watching my players go through this and even tougher to try and keep them motivated. Usually the checks were late. No actually, the checks were always late. When Blackmon did pay them, he wrote checks for less then what they were owed. It ended up being a race between all eight guys to try and get their checks cashed first before the account was overdrawn.

One or two guys would usually get their checks cashed first, leaving the others in the dust. This created some unneeded animosity and acrimony among the players. I know that Jason Clark deposited his check once and made a withdrawal on his account before it cleared. That left him owing money to his bank along with all the fees that went with it. He wasn't too happy about it. When Jason confronted Blackmon about it, Blackmon tried to blame the bank for screwing up. It wasn't just players that weren't getting paid though. Blackmon left a slug trail of red ink with everyone he came in contact with.

The thing that put us over the top and sent us into our ultimate, unrecoverable tailspin was his dispute with the Four Seasons Arena. Even though he looked really bad, and even though I didn't agree with his assessment of the situation, he actually made a pretty decent public argument and spun it as best as anyone else could under the circumstances.

Blackmon's point of view was that the previous owner of the team, a guy named Joe Clark, agreed to a lease with the Four Seasons Arena before Blackmon took over. The lease, however, was never signed by Clark. Blackmon claims that on the night of the first game, the arena manager (a guy named Bill Ogg), gave him the lease and said the game would be cancelled unless he signed it. Blackmon claimed that he didn't like the lease terms, but agreed to sign it under duress, and with the stipulation that they could renegotiate it after the first home stand. According to Blackmon, he and Ogg had a gentlemen's agreement to revisit the lease when there wasn't the immediacy of a game staring them in the face. The Arena had to have a signed lease for liability reasons, in order for anyone to play there, which was why they went ahead with the lease that Clark and Ogg had worked out.

My guess is that Blackmon never followed up with Ogg and the terms of the current lease continued to remain in place. Blackmon was living in Seattle, the team sucked, no one came to games, and by the time the January 4th Great Falls massacre happened, the team had mounted a $16,000 bill. With the uncertainty of the team, the wild stories in the newspaper surrounding Wedman and previous players not getting paid; it raised the awareness of Blackmon's troubles within the management offices of the Four Seasons Arena. The urgency of settling the current bill became a priority. Blackmon's inability to promote diplomacy further drove a wedge between himself and Bill Ogg. Soon, Blackmon was trying to win, in the court of public opinion, and negotiate through the local newspaper. He puffed his chest and made all sorts of threats about playing elsewhere. He told anyone who would listen that he'd never pay them a nickel and he constantly disparaged the arena management staff.

On the other hand, Bill Ogg remained quite diplomatic with his responses in the newspaper and expressed his interest in getting the situation resolved amicably. I don't know where the truth actually was, but from a public perspective, Ogg came off as cooperative and Blackmon looked petulant.

Tuesday, February 12, 2008
Publication: Great Falls Tribune

Four Seasons pulls plug on Explorers' home games

The Great Falls Explorers won't be playing a scheduled Continental Basketball Association game Wednesday night at Four Seasons Arena because the team owes back rent at the county-owned building.

Bill Ogg, who manages the arena for SMG, said Monday that Explorers owner Michael Blackmon failed to pay the bulk of his lease fees last week, so the basketball court remains in storage at the fairgrounds. The amount of rent in question is between $12,000 and $16,000.

"There won't be any game at the arena Wednesday," Ogg said. "We had dirt from the monster truck (show) in there, and we could have hired extra crews to get the facility ready for Wednesday ... right now (Monday night), our court isn't down. We didn't invest in that extra crew because we haven't been paid, and at this point it would be very expensive (labor costs)."

Blackmon said he fully anticipates playing two scheduled games against the East Kentucky Miners, probably at one of the city's two major high schools, either Great Falls High or C.M. Russell High.

"I have a meeting Tuesday with Gary DeGooyer (athletic director of Great Falls public schools) and we have about four options," Blackmon said Monday night.

"We're done with Four Seasons," he added.

Blackmon also mentioned Paris Gibson Learning Center and Great Falls Central as alternative sites, but both of those gyms have District 8C high school tournament games those days.

"Ogg presented me with a bill of $16,000" Blackmon said. "I said I don't owe it, and there was no attempt to negotiate.

"They gave me an ultimatum, to pay $13,000 by Friday, and I said I'm probably not going to do that."

Ogg confirmed he met with Blackmon last Wednesday to discuss the Explorers' bill with SMG, which manages the arena under contract with Cascade County. Blackmon, who bought the team from Apex Sportstainment just before the CBA season began, claims the previous owner left him with a bad arena contract.

"I felt we had a fairly productive meeting," said Ogg. "We compromised significantly off what he owes us on the contract. He was supposed to have paid us by Friday at 4, but I didn't even get the courtesy of a phone call. I feel like we've bent over backwards to keep this guy alive, in hopes he can pay us and other retailers some funds we are owed," said Ogg.

Blackmon said he offered to share revenues with Four Seasons management for the remaining 13 home games, but was turned down.

"I made a presentation to Bill, and said let's tear this lease up, get some people in the building, and split revenues 50-50," said Blackmon. "I think that was a very fair way to do it. I did it by their rules the first half, and it obviously didn't work."

Blackmon said the team, which has a 4-4 record under new coach Rick Turner. Has a chance to make the CBA playoffs.

Once we got back to Great Falls after our two week, 10-game, five-city road trip; it was as if Captain Kirk said "Lt. Sulu, take them to warp speed," and the craziness level intensified exponentially.

We had no where to play our games, our players weren't getting paid, and the team's financial woes were on full display in the local newspaper as each day another business would come forward with an unpaid bill.

There was no time to breathe because the East Kentucky Miners were due in town in two days for the first of six games in six nights, and we still needed to find a place to play. It was like the famous episode of **I Love Lucy**, when Lucy and Ethel Mertz went to work at the candy factory. The candies kept coming down the conveyor belt faster then they could wrap them. Pretty soon, Lucy was shoving them in her pockets and putting them in her mouth just to try and keep up. No matter what they did, the belt went faster and faster.

Our situation wasn't quite as funny as Lucy and Ethel's but it was strangely entertaining nonetheless.

We had Monday and Tuesday to find a place to play our home games now that the Four Seasons Arena was out. Not only was it out but for some dumb reason, Blackmon had a bunch of his clothes in the office at the Arena which we were now locked out of. I remember that he had to go to the mall just so he could have some clothes to wear that week. We had just spent the last couple of nights in Butte, and I think when we all had to check out of our so-called "apartments", Blackmon took a bunch of his stuff to the office to store it for a few days until we got back. Now we were locked out and he couldn't get to his clothes.

The options for gym space were pretty limited because of the high school district playoffs being held at numerous sites around Great Falls that week. I drove around town from school to school trying to find a place for us to play.

The University of Great Falls was unavailable because of its own home games at that week. We had to widen our net and start looking outside of Great Falls but neither one of us knew anything about the area.

Late on Tuesday afternoon, Blackmon called to tell me that he found us a place to play. It was at Cascade High School in Cascade, Montana, about 30 miles outside of Great Falls. Cascade had a population of 773 people and the school actually housed kindergarten – 12th grade. The gym was small, with bleachers on just one side and the court was 18 feet shorter then a regulation-sized floor. It seemed like about two steps in from half court and you were in three point range. Our guys just wanted to play though and we didn't care where or who.

I'm proud of the way my guys handled the situation. A lot of players, and frankly other coaches, would have complained and found excuses as to why it was such a bad scenario to *have* to play at a little high school in Podunk, Montana; but not my guys. They stayed positive and rolled with the punches quite well. In fact, the Eastern Kentucky jack-ass coach tried to get the league to call off the games and make them forfeits because he thought it was "too dangerous" for his players to play on a small court. He said the walls were too close to the baskets, the lines on the court weren't NBA lines and there were no shot clocks (we had to keep time manually with a stop watch and an air horn). He lobbied the referees hard to get them to cancel the game, and was on the phone with the commissioner practically up to game time, demanding that we forfeit. The commissioner told him to play us at Cascade or forfeit the games himself; so we played.

* * *

Blackmon had told me on my first day in Great Falls about all the great local support from the community. There were the car deals in place which provided his Explorer and the minivan; the team actually had a local booster club which helped promote the team and do nice things for the players; there were rabid season ticket holders AND he said the local Tony Roma's Restaurant would provide a pre-game meal to the team before every home game. He told me about this arrangement with Tony Roma's on my first full day in town but I never thought about it again since. Either I chalked it up to typical Blackmon exaggerated bull s*** or I just forgot about it.

I was out and about trying to get last minute things done before the first home game in over a month in Great Falls (well actually, Cascade) and my first home game in town period; when Blackmon called me at around 2 p.m. He said he was at Tony Roma's and wondered where I was; as if I was supposed to be there. He told me to round up the guys and get them over there for their pre-game meal. I had already eaten lunch and I suspected most of them had as well. It might have been a little too early for a pre-game meal but I did what I was told and called everyone to meet at Tony Roma's.

When we got there, Blackmon was just leaving. He welcomed us in like he owned the place and told us to order anything that we wanted off the menu. Knowing what I know about these players, I had to double check.

"Are you sure we can order anything?" I asked.

"Yeah, whatever they want, it's all taken care of," he repeated.

"Okay," I shrugged and conceded but something didn't sound right about that. I told the team to try and police themselves a bit and don't take advantage of the generosity; be polite, gracious and don't be foolish.

The wait staff and the manager seemed to be pretty excited that we were there. They were very friendly and I think at least somewhat awestruck by our guys. Remember... this group of players was completely different from the last time the team was in here for a meal back in early January. Plus, there had been quite a few positive articles written about the players in the local paper; so I think the staff was happy and anxious to have them in the restaurant. Beyond that, they looked impressive when they walked in. They were big, strong, lean and athletic men who were on their way to becoming celebrities in small, little Great Falls.

I would hate to have seen what they would have done if I hadn't told them to take it easy with the menu because these guys went nuts; appetizers, ribs, steaks, sandwiches, desserts... on and on and on. They were boxing stuff up for after the game, for breakfast tomorrow and probably even for lunch the next day. I can't say that I could blame them. It seemed like they were trying to take out their unpaid wages in Tony Roma's ribs. Goodness, these guys could eat. They put a fat guy like me to shame with their caloric intake. It was simultaneously impressive and embarrassing.

About 90 minutes later, we were ready to get back to the Extended Stay, relax or for some, get a quick nap in before the game. All the guys had their white styrofoam to-go boxes ready to go and were transferring the pitchers of lemonade remaining on the table into paper cups that they could carry out. The manager came by the table to thank us for coming in, wished us luck in the game later that night and told me that Ken wanted to meet me.

Ken? Who the "sam h" is Ken? I wondered to myself. The way the manager said it to me, it was if I should know who Ken was. In typical fashion, not wanting to expose my ignorance, I just went with it.

"Yeah sure, that sounds great," I told the manager.

As our waitress came by to assess the damage we caused at the table before calling in FEMA. I grabbed her and whispered to ask who Ken was. She looked at me kind of funny and told me that Ken was the owner of Tony Roma's and one of our biggest sponsors.

Duh...!

I have to admit, my ample ego allowed me to think that Ken wanted to meet me because I was the new pro basketball coach in town and he wanted to rub elbows with me. As Coach Romar would say, I was wearing my "cool jacket" when I was met with a friendly ambush by Ken Hatzenbeller, the owner of a number of restaurant franchises throughout Montana, Idaho and the Midwest, his son Lance, VP of the family business, and the Tony Roma's manager, whose name escapes me.

We shook hands and they took me to a back booth in another part of the restaurant that was closed at the time. I thought we were going to talk hoops, the new players, the prospects of making the playoffs, upcoming games and so on. I was prepared to heap praise upon them for their support as big as the portions of food our team just enjoyed. I was looking for a five minute meet and greet so I could get the players back to the hotel. Instead, what I got was a 45 minute semi-friendly tongue lashing about what an idiot Blackmon was. I say semi-friendly because Ken and Lance were very calm and professional in their approach with me, but they had been disrespected and pushed to their limit by Blackmon. They were extremely frustrated and had not been able to vent. Lucky for me (wink-wink) I was there for them.

I was blindsided by the meeting. I was unprepared, ignorant to the history, had no background on the relationship, and had myself, just finished taking advantage of their generosity. In fact, I probably still had barbeque sauce on my face. My lifelong pursuit of living blissfully ignorant would not serve me well at all during this summit. Blackmon had led me to believe that this was one of the few relationships in town that was actually working and that Ken was, in Blackmon's words, "one of my best friends in Great Falls".

He actually told me that.

The four of us sat down in the corner booth. I slid to the inside next to one wall and facing another. The restaurant manager sat next to me and Ken and Lance sat opposite of us. As I mentioned, Ken wasn't confrontational but we definitely weren't there to talk about how we were defending the pick and roll. In fact, there were just a few gratuitous comments before Ken cut to the chase.

"We're concerned," was how the conversation started.

I nodded.

I was now wearing a hat that I was very uncomfortable with. It wasn't that I was unfamiliar with customer relations, or sponsorship fulfillment or even moderating grievances. That wasn't what made me uncomfortable. I was just pissed that I had been put in this situation at all.

All I wanted to do was coach this team. I understand that there are things that go along with the job that you often have to do beyond coaching your team. I get that. In fact, my ability and willingness to handle those periphery things is one of my uniquely strong qualities as a coach. My broad background in sales, marketing, administration, broadcasting and management; sets me apart from many other coaches who have never set foot in an office nor held the acumen to navigate through a meeting such as this. The difference here however, was that given my background with and knowledge of Blackmon; I wanted to steer clear of any of these ancillary duties. I wanted people to see us as completely separate. I didn't want his stink on me. Now, sitting there with the management team of the Great Falls Tony Roma's, I felt like I was in a precarious position. I had to act as an agent of the team, but at the same time, these guys were totally "preaching to the choir". I did not like having to defend Blackmon.

Ken told me that first off, Blackmon would not return any of his phone calls. He said that Blackmon was avoiding him (which I found strange since just two hours before, Blackmon was in the restaurant). He told me that many (if not all) elements of their contract were not being satisfied. There were in-game promotions not happening, free tickets not being provided, a VIP area at each game wasn't set aside as called for in the contract; signage that wasn't being displayed and PA announcements that weren't happening. There was an expectation of fan attendance and Ken expressed concern that we were now playing at Cascade High School which was first, too far away to appeal to his potential customer base and second, would impact attendance and the number of potential eyes seeing his advertising (albeit currently nonexistent anyway). We were not living up to any of our obligations to the contract, yet we were totally taking advantage of restaurant's obligations.

Ken tagged his son Lance to step into the ring and now it was Lance's turn to take a flying elbow smash at me. Lance said that the agreement was for the team to come in for pre-game meals and order one item and a drink from a special menu that consisted of mostly sandwiches, hamburgers and chicken.

"Dog gammit," I thought to myself and internally shook my head while externally listening intently, "I knew it".

For whatever reason, this piece of the ownership's discontent made me feel foolish. Common sense would say that these players can't just walk in and order whatever they want off the menu or as much as they wanted. That's just dumb. Yet I let Blackmon tell me otherwise. I cussed myself out. I should have been on top of this and confirmed with someone else before we ordered. It was an obvious and egregious error on my part. I thought I was smarter than that. This one had me backpedaling a bit.

I offered to pay them for that afternoon's meal but they graciously refused. Not only did the team come in and decimate the menu before each game, which had gone on since the previous coach, Scott Wedman and all of our predecessors earlier in the season; but as Ken and Lance told me, they never even left a tip for the wait staff who had to accommodate this large group of large men that acted as if this meal was their manifest destiny. The tip should have been around $50 or more to the staff each time the team came in. That's a significant amount to the people who worked the table. It was embarrassing. What was Wedman thinking? Thank goodness for us, I had already collected money from each of our guys to leave for the wait staff at the end of our meal that afternoon, but it didn't soften the blow of humility for the organization.

Both Ken and Lance knew that they were talking to the wrong guy but more than anything, they just needed to be heard. I think they appreciated that I sat there and took it as diplomatically as I could. Every fiber of my being wanted to throw Blackmon under the bus and pile on by dishing all the dirt that I had on him to my interrogators. But I couldn't do it. I listened earnestly, tried to reassure them that we'd do a better job but ultimately knew that for all intents and purposes, our relationship with Tony Roma's was over. There wasn't going to be anymore pre-game meals and they had no interest in continuing to do business with Blackmon.

Any association with Blackmon was starting to reflect on those people within the community and Ken's business was too important to allow this idiot from Seattle to have a negative impact on his livelihood. He tried to explain it finally by showing me an email that had been forwarded to him by another one of the team's sponsors.

I was told it was from a guy who owned a furniture store in Great Falls that had sent Blackmon an email.

The business community in Great Falls was pretty small. Everyone knew everybody else and once this email made the rounds among these business leaders around town, Blackmon's goose was pretty well cooked.

It read as follows:

> Mr. Blackmon:
> The record of poor payment of salaries and expenses incurred by the Explorers is just poor business. When I read that now you are not paying for the facility the team was contracted to, I was dumbfounded. Bad arena contract or not, when you bought the team, the contract was already in place and I assume you knew that. If not, you didn't complete any due diligence. Your organization is giving Great Falls a bad reputation with your failure to meet your financial obligations. I, for one, choose to not do business with an organization that has such low ethical standards. So, I won't be buying any tickets nor will I be sponsoring your team in any way.
> (signed)A disappointed fan

As I'm sure you can practically guess by now, Blackmon's response to one of his own sponsors was less than courteous and pretty much sealed his fate among the business leaders of Great Falls…

Yeah, thanks for your two cents, pal, but you don't have the slightest fucking idea what you're talking about.

Joe Clark BEGGED me to take this franchise off his hands. NO ONE wanted to undertake this mess so late in the year. The only reason I did it was for the sake of the CBA. If Great Falls folded it would have made an unbalanced league of 9 teams instead of 10.

I was told that there was $125,000 in receivables from sponsors and season tickets when I bought the team, and that there was a group of local investors willing to buy 20% of the franchise if someone would take the majority. When I first read the lease Joe had negotiated, I knew it was obscene… $2,500 a night and nothing from concessions.

I got into Great Falls for the first time on the evening of November 19th. I called Ogg the next day, and left another message for him a week later. The first time I ever met him was on opening night, December 4th, when he walked up to me in the arena and shoved the lease under my nose and said, "You need to sign this or you can't play tonight." With the CBA Commissioner, Dennis Truax, sitting next to me, I told Ogg I'd sign the lease, but that I wanted to re-visit the terms at his first opportunity. He agreed. I'm supposed to get a settlement sheet within 48 hours of each event. Ogg took three weeks to get me one for the first 7 games. He demanded $9,000 in addition to what they took in. SMG manages the building. They control the box office and all the revenue. They take their rent right off the top, and after paying their other expenses, I get what's left. Let's do the math together, pal. After eleven home games, I owed them $16,000, including $3,000 for ticket stock ordered by the idiot general manager from the previous ownership. That's TEN FUCKING years worth of tickets!

In summary, I played 12 games at Four Seasons. I paid $14,000 in rent and owed them $16,000 according to lease terms I never fucking agreed to!!!

Get it, moron? I'm sick and fucking tired of being dragged through the mud by the people and newspaper of this town who are saying I haven't paid rent. Without me this team would not have played a single fucking game. It's now mid-february. I have not received a single fucking dime in revenue. Nothing from ticket sales, nothing from sponsors. All that money went to Joe Clark before I arrived.

Last Wednesday I met with Ogg and his two stooges. They told me that I needed to get them a cashier's check for $16,000 by close of business last Friday or they wouldn't set up my court for this week's games. When I failed to deliver the check, they changed the locks on the Explorer's office. My luggage is in there. My garment bag with six suits, a dozen shirts and all my clean underwear, not to mention two computers with all the financial dealings of the franchise, a $12,000 copy machine and $3,000 worth of Explorers merchandise has been locked inside all week.

My only choice now is to barnstorm around high school gyms for the rest of the month playing for whatever gate receipts we can generate. Under my guidance, we've now played 33 games. Every cent has come out of my personal checking account to the tune of $195,000. Could you do that, bigshot? Nope, you're not as dumb as me, I'll give you that.

This is not my town. I've been living in a hotel for three months. I had heart surgery on January 2nd in Seattle. Pissing away hundreds of thousands of dollars on minor league sports like CBA and arena football has cost me my marriage. I have put together one of the best teams in the league. We will absolutely have a playoff series in Great Falls this season, and who knows what could happen then? I don't need to be worshipped. I don't even need to be thanked or liked for that matter. But, it's pinheads like you who make me wonder why I bother.

I'm just stupid, I guess. That's my excuse anyway. What's yours?

Michael Blackmon
President and CEO
West Coast Sports, LLC
www.GreatFallsExplorers.com

Absolutely quintessential Michael Blackmon. I have to admit, he always made a pretty decent argument if you could set aside the crassness of his response. Just take the Tony Roma's deal for example: that contract was negotiated and completed before he took over the team. He didn't get any of the revenue yet still had to meet the contractual obligations. As you and I both know, that is just part of the deal when you take over a business; you assume its liabilities, but Blackmon obviously never saw it this way and had no desire to live up to other people's agreements. Since he didn't see any of the revenue, in his mind, it wasn't his responsibility. Not only that, but his complete lack of tact, contrition and editorial discretion was awe-inspiring and continually left me amazed at his ability to offend and insult anyone in his path.

With temperatures in the teen's and plummeting further, and with snow beginning to accumulate on the roads; Blackmon, the seven guys remaining on our roster and I, headed south on I-15 toward Cascade. Nate was left back at the hotel, waiting to see if Blackmon could find any team to take him. Regardless of where he was, Nate was done playing for the Explorers. We had rented a 15 passenger van for the visitors to use over the course of the next six days. East Kentucky would have it for two days; Atlanta, who came in next, would have it for two days and then Oklahoma would finish out the home stand.

Like Yogi Berra said, the game at Cascade High School was "déjà vu all over again". Just like our very first game in the ABA at Renton High School a couple of years earlier, Blackmon and the school were ill-prepared to host a pro basketball game. Just like at Renton, the floor needed to be relined with the appropriate CBA markings; and just like at Renton, they ran out of tape before the job was complete. Just like at Renton, Blackmon had no staff to man the scorer's table and he had to rely on the school's athletic director to help him out. Just like at Renton, Blackmon decided that he was the best choice to do the PA announcing and just like at Renton, he was a total embarrassment. First, by once again forgetting the words to the Pledge of Allegiance (not cool anywhere but especially in a place like Montana) and second, by doing a running play-by-play throughout the contest.

An estimated 221 people attended the game on that snowy Valentine's Day night of 2008. The Explorers weren't able to overcome a 40 point effort from East Kentucky's Boo Jackson as the Miners got the first win of the brief two-game series 111-103. The crowd was small but vocal and the ones who were there seemed to be quite excited to have professional basketball in their small town. Other then the expected Keystone Cops routine with Blackmon before the game, it all came off relatively smooth. The gate receipts put some money into Blackmon's pocket and he was able to keep the players at bay by giving them a little cash.

The Great Falls Tribune did a good front page article about our game in the morning's sports section and we were hoping for a bigger crowd for game two. The article didn't dwell too much on Blackmon's dispute with the Four Seasons Arena and was actually much more positive then even I thought we deserved. Finally, it seemed like the local media was back to focusing on the basketball and highlighting the team as opposed to its dysfunctional owner.

Game two was much better for the hometown seven. With all seven guys scoring in double figures, led by Pele's 27 and Mike Peeple's 26, we put our best game of the season together and beat East Kentucky 126-108. Actually it wasn't even as close as the score would indicate. At one point in the third quarter, we led by 36 as things started clicking for us on both ends of the floor. Coming into town next was the only other team that might have been able to challenge us in the dysfunction department.

The Atlanta Krunk (yes, that's Krunk) started the season with former NBA and Georgia Tech great, Kenny Anderson as head coach. By the time they rolled into Great Falls, Montana in mid-February; the team had no coach. When I say they had no coach, that's exactly what I mean. They didn't have a player coach; they didn't have an assistant coach who was stepping in, and they didn't have an interim coach. They were out on the road all by themselves playing because they loved it.

None of the Atlanta players had been paid all season long; they played in a gym with no heat, were down to just six players and found themselves 9-27 on the season. They had a 5'5" team manager who traveled with the team, and when one of their players came up sick after they got to Great Falls, they had to suit the manager up as well.

We followed the same routine as the previous two nights as we made our way out to Cascade for our third game in three nights. This time the Krunk team followed behind us so they didn't get lost. Mike and Marlyn rode out to Cascade with Blackmon and they were already there by the time we pulled up to the gym.

There seemed to be a problem, however, as both teams and the referees pulled in to the parking lot. The gym was dark and locked. Blackmon had forgotten to reserve the gym that night and just assumed that the school's AD would be there for us.

He wasn't.

The AD was 90 miles away at the Cascade girls team playoff game. There was no way that we would be playing that night at Cascade High. In fact, there was a wrestling match scheduled at the school for the rest of the weekend and the gym would be inaccessible to us for the next three days. We still had two games with Atlanta (actually one after that night) and two games with Oklahoma. Now we had to find another gym. It was over the course of the next 72 hours when things got to be just too much.

***

The cesspool of chaos began later that night at Boston's Pizza when Blackmon took us all out to dinner after the game was cancelled. All the players grabbed a table in the bar but I didn't feel comfortable infringing on their "team time", so I sat by myself at the bar, waiting for Blackmon to join me. He was out in the parking lot on the phone with a variety of people (mostly the CBA commissioner) trying to get the next few days figured out. I ordered the Chipotle Chicken and Bacon Salad and a diet coke while I sat and watched the NBA slam dunk contest from All-Star weekend in New Orleans. As I waited for my food show up, Blackmon came slowly strutting in from the parking lot where he had been on the phone and walked over to me.

"Hey grab a seat, I just ordered. Are you eating?" I asked him, trying to remain upbeat and positive.

He looked at me disgusted and scoffed, "You just don't get it do you? It's over Rick. We're done. This team is finished as of tonight." Then he turned and slowly walked away, back out the door from which he came and out into the parking lot.

I turned back toward the TV, took a long suck out of the straw resting comfortably in my diet coke just in time to see Dwight Howard's "Superman Dunk" on the big screen TV hanging above the bourbon section of the large bar. I wasn't going to be bothered by Blackmon's theatrics that night. He had made these definitive declarations before only to renege after he had time to think it through.

Sure enough, about 20 minutes later, he came back in, sat down next to me at the bar and started talking about tomorrow's game as if his previous episode just a few minutes earlier had never happened. As Blackmon and I were brainstorming solutions to our current pickle, the female bartender came over to see if Blackmon wanted to order some food. She seemed to be really outgoing and had a great personality in the short time that I had been sitting there. She was friendly and good at her job.

"Hi, what can I do for you?" she asked Blackmon as she placed a coaster on the bar in front of him.

He looked at her with distain.

"What can you do for me?" he sarcastically repeated back to her as she stood in front of him smiling.

He pointed to the other end of the bar.

"You can walk over there, get the f*** out of my face and mind your own god damned business. That's what you can do for me."

Good grief. Not again, I thought to myself.

I couldn't sit there and listen to that anymore. I finally confronted him about it.

"What's wrong with you? You can't talk to people like that."

"Like what?" he asked.

"What do you mean, like what? Like that! You can't cuss out the bartender just because she was doing her job trying to help you out. You're an asshole. Why do you act like that?"

He didn't say anything. He sat there for a minute. Then he got up and walked to the other end of the bar where she was standing there, in tears, talking to one of the male bartenders.

I couldn't hear what was being said but I could tell that Blackmon was apologizing. The guy bartender looked pissed off and said something back to Blackmon but the woman wouldn't even look at him. He sauntered back to his seat, sat down and started right back in on what we were going to do about tomorrow's game. For the rest of the night we had a new bartender.

During the telephone tag on Saturday night as Blackmon tried to find a gym for us to play in on Sunday, many of the people who turned him down had suggestions of places that might be able to accommodate us. That call would lead to someone else and so on until finally, Blackmon somehow came up with a place for us to play.

As it turned out, the next stop on our barnstorming tour of the greater Great Falls area would be Fairfield High School, this time 30 miles northeast of Great Falls, in the opposite direction of Cascade.

Fairfield was a town of 615 people, but the gym at the school was a little larger than Cascade's, and they seemed to be even more excited to have us there than Cascade. The AD at Fairfield was much more organized and had a staff in place to run the game operations for us. This enabled me to talk Blackmon out of doing the PA and leave it for someone who knew what they were doing. We avoided any embarrassing "Pledge" mishaps and instead he would just sit at the scorer's table and do stats; staying totally out of the way.

I was awakened in my room on that Sunday morning by a phone call. I had yet to find out that our games would be played at Fairfield by this point. I answered the phone and it was Tim Schmidt, the AD at Fairfield. I had never heard of Tim Schmidt or Fairfield High School. I had no idea who he was and I didn't know that we would be playing there later that night. As we spoke and he explained the situation, I started to piece things together. I didn't want to sound like an idiot so I never let on to him that I didn't know what he was talking about. He said that he had been calling Blackmon on his cell phone and in his hotel room for the past couple hours but he wasn't answering. Imagine that, I sarcastically thought. He told me that if he didn't have some proof of insurance faxed to him within the next hour, there was no way that we could play there tonight.

I wrote down his fax number, his cell number and told him that I would take care of it.

With absolutely no idea of how to take care of it, we hung up and I tried to clear the morning cobwebs and hurriedly think of a solution. The best that I could come up with was to call CBA Commissioner Dennis Truax and dump this problem on his plate; which is what I did.

The CBA did not want to cancel games for two obvious reasons: 1) they were difficult to reschedule and 2) it made the league look bad and they were extremely image conscious. Dennis was willing to do whatever he could to ensure that the games went forward and he personally called Fairfield's AD to work out the insurance issue. About an hour later, Dennis called me back.

"We've got another problem," he told me. Blackmon still wasn't answering his phone and by now Dennis realized, that in spite of my relationship with Blackmon, I was actually reliable.

"Uh-oh. What is it?" I asked, feeling the adrenaline of being needed.

"When Blackmon called me last night and said that you were ceasing operations, I went ahead and sent the referees home. They each got on flights this morning. I can't get them back for the game. Can you find some local referees?"

"I'm on it" I said, accepting the challenge but having no idea on where to even start to find people on a Sunday afternoon just about six hours before game time.

I had the number of a local Great Falls high school coach who had helped me out on some practice space a couple of times. I gave him a try. I got a hold of him and he gave me the number of a college official who lived in Great Falls. I called that guy who wasn't home but his wife gave me the number of a friend of his who was also a referee in town. I called him. He was unavailable for that night also but he gave me the name of the referee assignor for all the high schools in the area. He didn't have the number offhand, so I looked the name up in the white pages of my hotel room. Thank goodness Great Falls was still small enough that people had their home phone numbers listed in the local white pages. I called the assignor and he said that he would do his best to find me two strong officials. By 4:00 p.m. we located two referees for our 7 p.m. game.

While all this was going on, Dennis called me again. The Oklahoma team had landed at the Great Falls airport but there was no one there to pick them up.

What???

I didn't even know that they were coming in today. I was pretty sure that Blackmon didn't either. With the high school basketball regional playoffs in town, I wasn't even sure if the hotel had any rooms for them. Our team and Atlanta's team were already there taking up rooms in the hotel. I didn't know if they could accommodate a third team.

I knew Blackmon was going to freak out when he found out that he had to (theoretically) pay for two teams in town at the same time, because let's face it, he couldn't afford one.

Dennis told me that we needed to go pick the Oklahoma team up at the airport. "We" meant me. Blackmon was still not answering his phone and there were no other options for them to get to the hotel. I tried to take the 15-passenger van that we had rented for Atlanta, but they were gone somewhere with it, and I didn't have any of their phone numbers to call and ask them to return it. My only choice was to take the minivan up to the airport.

Oklahoma was a real team. They had 10 players, an assistant coach, a team trainer and a radio guy (their head coach was at the NBA All-Star game). With 14 guys and all their bags, I was going to have to make three trips back and forth to the Great Falls airport in order to shuttle them back to the hotel in that minivan.

So, while Blackmon was MIA, holed up in his hotel room sleeping all day, I was scrambling to make this game happen in six hours, getting proof of insurance to the school, searching all over Great Falls for two referees with enough experience to officiate a professional game, holding our game day shootaround at the Peak Athletic Club, making three trips back and forth to the airport to pick up and shuttle our opponent for the next two days, securing their rooms at the hotel, and buying basketball shoes for the 5'5" Atlanta manager who would have to suit up that night for the Krunk who only had five players because one was sick.

And my compensation for all of this and more…???

Try zero, or as Jon Gruden would say "Z-E-R-O". Not a dime, not a red cent, bubkiss, nada, and any other word you can think of to describe a guy who was completely being taken advantage of. At least that's the way I was starting to feel. The basketball part of it was fun, but if I was going to have to actually work, then I wanted to get paid.

I hadn't been paid since the Texas trip when I took the cab from the Houston airport during my layover to cash my check. That's not entirely true. Blackmon had written me two checks since then. One was for half of what he owed me and the other was for a quarter of what he owed me; each time he promised to make up the difference later.

Both checks bounced.

Like I said before, I wanted to get paid, but it didn't really matter because I was getting something out of this experience that was at least of equal value in my eyes: an opportunity to coach very high-level players in a league with a very high level of play. The money would have been nice but it wasn't (and has never been) a motivating factor for me. As such, I tried my best to stay out of all the front office stuff. To this point I had been relatively successful, but as I suspected, as soon as I was thrust into having to do Blackmon's job as well as my own... the fun was quickly sucked out of the experience.

I was mentally spent by the late afternoon leading up to the game Sunday night. I needed a little pick me up and that's exactly what I got with a phone call from Marlyn. Marlyn was a fan favorite who had played in Great Falls the previous season, and he knew people around town. He stayed with a family in town, rather than the hotel where everyone else stayed, and he was kind of dialed into the pulse of the community surrounding the team.

Marlyn called to tell me that there was a rumor that Blackmon was going to have his dealer car repossessed during the game. Apparently the dealer who loaned the car to Blackmon was based in Fairfield. Either his dealership was there or he lived there; one of the two. Somehow the dealer had heard that Blackmon was driving back and forth from Seattle with the Explorer. The agreement, I heard, was that he had to keep the mileage under 1,000 miles. Each trip to Seattle alone was 700 miles one way, and he had made at least two and maybe even three trips back and forth. Not to mention the trips to Butte (150 miles each way) and the three trips to Cascade (30 miles each way). He was supposed to use the car just for driving around town. Blackmon had already put over 5,000 miles on the brand new, white Explorer, and on top of that, he wasn't returning any of the car dealer's phone calls. Essentially, in the dealer's eyes, he had stolen the Explorer. Marlyn told me that the owner of the car dealership was going to show up during the game in Fairfield with a second set of keys for the Explorer and just take it back.

As much as I hate to admit it, the thought of this really tickled me. Call me devious, disloyal or just plain deceitful; I really wanted to see how this would play out. This got my blood pumping again, and all of a sudden the frustration of my Sunday leading up to that point, was replaced with the excitement of having another melodrama to witness.

I HAD to see what would happen.

I asked Marlyn to keep it to himself and let me handle it. My way of handling it would be to do nothing and wait to see Blackmon's reaction to his "stolen car" being stolen back. I couldn't wait.

The atmosphere at Fairfield High School was much better than that of Cascade High School. Much of that was due to the school's athletic director who was much savvier about putting on an event like this. He had a willing staff on hand that was extremely helpful and the sheer number of staff that was there made things run much smoother.

The Atlanta team was a decimated and demoralized group. I felt bad for them but we needed to win games in order to make a push for the playoffs. We couldn't afford to let our guard down with a wounded animal. Besides, I couldn't bear to tell my friends that we lost to a team called the Krunk. They had six guys who made the trip, losing two games to Yakima before coming to Great Falls. One of the players was "sick" but I really think he was more like "sick of...". He stayed back at the hotel and they suited up their diminutive manager who had played in high school, but as he would soon find out, this was a whole different level entirely. They had five players plus one, but at the same time, we only had seven, so I didn't think it was too huge of a disparity.

Unfortunately, this was not your father's Krunk. This team was beat down and hurting. Our team, on the other hand, was just coming into its own. Despite two 40-plus point performances from Bilal Simmons (44) and Terrance Hunter (40), Atlanta got krunked by the Explorers' **173**-120. Yes, you read that right; <u>one hundred</u> and <u>seventy-three points</u>! It was the second most points scored in the 62-year history of the CBA. Marlyn had 42 points, Mo had 40 and Pele had 32 in the onslaught. The crowd, as you could imagine, loved it. The operation of the game itself went off without a hitch. The referees showed up on time and worked out just fine; and best of all, Blackmon stayed away from the microphone. The biggest disappointment of the night came after the game when we all left to go back to the hotel. With great anticipation, I walked out to the parking lot expecting to see a now empty space where Blackmon's white Explorer had sat just a couple of hours earlier. Instead, there it was; parked right where he left it. Maybe the recovery effort will take place tomorrow…???

16

Purgatory

If everything could ever feel this real forever
If anything could ever be this good again
The only thing I'll ever ask of you
Got to promise not to stop when I say when

- Foo Fighters "**Everlong**"

Michael Ray Richardson was the head coach of the Oklahoma Calvary. If you really want to read something salacious, just wait until his biography comes out. He is a one-of-a-kind character with an incredible background. I will try and provide the Cliff Notes to his story.

Michael "Sugar" Ray Richardson was the fourth pick overall in the 1978 NBA Draft, selected behind Mychal Thompson, Phil Ford, Ricky Robey and two spots in front of Larry Bird. Ironically, he went to school at the University of Montana, where he was recruited by Jud Heathcoat, and was arguably the greatest player in the history of the school.

Coming back to Great Falls to coach was a bit of a homecoming for him.

Richardson led the NBA in steals and assists in just his second year in the league and went on to become an All-Star for the New Jersey Nets. In 1986, after various drug-related issues, Michael Ray Richardson became the first person to be banned for life from the NBA. He went on to play in Europe where he had an excellent career in NBA exile for 14 more seasons.

Just one year earlier, in 2007, Richardson was the coach of the CBA's Albany Patroons. He ended up in quite a bit of hot water after some comments he made to the local Albany newspaper.

From ESPN.com, March 28, 2007:

> *Former NBA All-Star Michael Ray Richardson appeared to be getting his life back on track after his league suspension in 1986 for drug use. He was coaching in the Continental Basketball Association and had led his team, the Albany Patroons, to the playoffs. But as they say: What goes up, must come down.*
>
> *The Patroons have suspended Richardson for the rest of the CBA championship series for comments made to the Albany Times Union on Tuesday.*

Before Tuesdays game against the Yakima Sun Kings, Richardson made anti-Semitic comments to two reporters in his office when discussing the contract general manager Jim Coyne had offered him Monday to coach his team in the CBA and USBL.

"I've got big-time lawyers," Richardson said, according to the Times Union. "I've got big-time Jew lawyers."

When told by the reporters that the comment could be offensive to people because it plays to the stereotype that Jews are crafty and shrewd, he responded with, "Are you kidding me? They are. They've got the best security system in the world. Have you ever been to an airport in Tel Aviv? They're real crafty. Listen, they are hated all over the world, so they've got to be crafty."

And he continued, "They got a lot of power in this world, you know what I mean?" he said. "Which I think is great. I don't think there's nothing wrong with it. If you look in most professional sports, they're run by Jewish people. If you look at a lot of most successful corporations and stuff, more businesses, they're run by Jewish. It's not a knock, but they are some crafty people."

And the offensive remarks didn't stop there.

According to the Times Union, Richardson told a fan who heckled him early in Tuesday's game, "Shut the [expletive] up." And near game's end, he shouted at another heckler, "Shut the [expletive] up, you [derogatory term for gay men],"

Assistant Derrick Rowland will coach the Patroons for the reminder of the series. Richardson will not be allowed into the Washington Avenue Armory during practices or games.

"It's terrible and I don't think it's fair," Richardson told the Times Union regarding the suspension. "But I want to make an apology if I offended anyone because that's not me."

Richardson, the fourth overall pick in the 1978 draft, is best known for an embattled NBA career that ended because of drugs. He joined the NBA out of Montana and played eight seasons with the New York Knicks, Golden State Warriors and New Jersey Nets. He was the subject of a 2000 film "What Happened to Micheal Ray?" documenting his troubled life.

In his second year, Richardson became only the second player in NBA to lead in both assists and steals. In 1986, the four-time NBA All-Star was banned for life after he violated the league's drug policy three times in what David Stern called "the hardest thing I've ever had to do as commissioner."

Richardson began his comeback in 1988, joining the ranks of ex-NBA players in European leagues where he played for 14 years. His right to play in the NBA was restored that year but he stayed in Italy, where he was a leading scorer and fan favorite.

Richardson failed two cocaine tests in 1991, though he disputed the results.

This guy was a true piece of work. He was let go by the Patroons at the end of that season and hired by the Oklahoma Calvary to be their new head coach for the '07-'08 year. On December 16, 2007 he was fired by Oklahoma, only to be reinstated as their head coach eight days later, on December 24th.

The Monday following our Sunday blowout of Atlanta was President's Day. For some reason, the Fairfield gym was only available to us in the afternoon of that Monday. I think it was because their boys basketball team had a playoff game that night somewhere else and there would be no staff available to work the game. We decided to try and play the game at 3 p.m. instead of the official time listed on the CBA schedule of 7:30 p.m. It turned out Michael Ray was flying to Great Falls from the NBA All-Star Game in New Orleans and his flight wouldn't be arriving to Great Falls until 6:00. When he found out that we intended to move the game up to 3:00, he went ballistic and threw an absolute conniption fit. Just like the East Kentucky coach, he wanted a forfeit because we were changing the game time. He accused the commissioner of racism and said that because Blackmon was white, the league was allowing us to play around with the schedule; if he tried to do the same thing, they wouldn't allow it because he was black. He was totally freaking out.

The commissioner was fit to be tied. He wasn't sure what to do. Both teams were there, we had a gym; the only thing holding us back was Oklahoma's coach who was crying racism. It was his choice to go hang out in New Orleans for the weekend, and he should have known the risks of cutting it so close with scheduling a flight that was due to land an hour and a half before tip off anyway. Besides that, he had a good assistant coach, Greg Graham, who was definitely capable of stepping in and was there and ready to go.

To add further stress to the situation, I was having a difficult time finding two referees to work our game that night. One of the guys from the previous night was available but we couldn't find anyone else to partner up with him. Between Blackmon, Richardson and the referees, my "volunteer" work for the Great Falls Explorers was rapidly losing its appeal.

The commissioner and I finally decided to punt on the Monday game and concentrate on getting organized for Tuesday.

***

On Tuesday morning I got a call on my cell phone from Oklahoma assistant coach Greg Graham. I had met Greg on Sunday night when the team got to town and I told him that if he needed anything while they were there, to give me a call. Greg seemed to have a pretty calm demeanor much like me and he was a nice guy to talk with. He played a few years in the NBA and we knew some people in common, so we hit it off right away. I saw the unfamiliar area code pop up on my phone when he called and I was curious to see who it was.

"Hello?" I answered.

"Hey coach, its Greg. Do you know where our van is?" he calmly asked me.

"Uhh? What do you mean?"

"I think our van got stolen last night. We parked it right outside and this morning we went out to go to breakfast and it was gone. I have the keys with me right here."

What? I wondered. What could possibly go wrong next? Who would steal a 15-passenger van?

"Okay, let me figure it out and call you back." I told him and hung up.

I called the Enterprise rental car company up the street where we rented the van to ask them how I should handle the situation.

"Hi, this is Rick Turner from the Great Falls Explorers. We rented a 15-passenger van from you last week and I think it may have been stolen" I explained to the young guy who answered the phone.

"Oh no. We came and picked that van up this morning. The credit card that you gave us was declined and we tried calling Mr. Blackmon but he never returned our call. One of our employees saw it parked at the hotel this morning on his way into work, so we went and picked it up."

What next? I wondered.

I called Greg Graham back to let him know what happened. As I was talking to Greg, my call waiting rang. It was Tim Schmidt calling from Fairfield High School to ask why his staff never got paid on Sunday night. I clicked back over to let Greg know that I'd call him back and then clicked back to Tim. A couple of minutes later, as I was talking to Tim on the phone, there was a knock at my door. With my cell phone up to my ear, I asked Tim if he could hold on a minute while I answered the door. I opened the door to find Greg Graham standing there. With the door handle in my left hand and holding my phone to my ear with my left shoulder, I looked up at the 6'5" Oklahoma assistant who seemed to be oblivious that I was on the phone.

"Coach wants to see you" he told me, referring to Michael Ray.

With an exaggerated bug out of the eyes as if to say, "Can't you see that I'm on the phone?" I gestured toward the phone with my right hand, then held up my hand up like a stop sign, shook my head and said, "Okay, give me a couple minutes"

I closed the door and went back to my conversation with the Fairfield AD. I was assuring Tim that his people would be paid and that Blackmon was probably just waiting to pay them all at once later that night. As I was explaining that to Tim, there was another knock on my door, not even two minutes later. This time I sat the phone down on the bed and went to answer the door. With a frustrating emphasis on the defenseless door handle, I whipped open the door; this time to find Michael Ray, who I had yet to have the "pleasure" of meeting.

With a finger in my face he started in…

"W-w-where th-th-the f-f-fuck i-is B-B-B-Ba-Blackmon?" Sugar Ray spoke with a stutter "I-I-I'm g-gonna k-k-k-kick his m-m-mutha ffu**in' a-a-ass" he screamed in my face.

Stunned, a tad concerned and a ton embarrassed, I remembered that Tim was hearing all this at the other end of my cell phone. I turned back to grab the flip phone that was sitting on my bed with the Fairfield AD, Tim Schmidt, listening on the other end.

"Umm Tim, I'm going to have to call you back." I said while simultaneously flipping the phone closed.

I turned back around to a crazed Michael Ray Richardson, who had followed me in, and was now standing in the middle of my room. His stuttering rant continued. It was so irrational, so out of nowhere and so comical to see and hear this guy; who I only knew as "the guy who was banned for life from the NBA", deliver this Tony Montana diatribe, while using Porky Pig's voice, it was hard to keep a straight face. I watched in fascination, almost as an outside observer as this meltdown happened; even though it was me that was suffering the brunt of it.

I half expected him to finish and say "T-t-that's all f-f-folks".

I did my best to remain calm and tried to diffuse the situation but he was going nuts. I was going to tell you that I don't ever remember seeing anyone snap like that so strangely out of the blue, but then my mind returned to Blackmon, whose meltdowns I routinely witnessed.

I finally got Michael Ray out of my room but he wasn't finished. He continued down the hallway of the hotel, pounding on every door he walked by and screaming "B-B-Blackmon, wh-wh-wh-where a-a-are y-you? G-g-get th-the f-f-f-fu** out h-h-here and f-f-face m-m-me l-l-like a m-m-man!"

With the debacle of the previous day, and the antics of that morning, this game tonight with Oklahoma was shaping up to be something very interesting. Richardson was telling anyone who would listen (including our players) that we were garbage and that they were going to "kick the sh** out of us" that night.

Blackmon did his best to avoid any confrontations with Michael Ray, so the Oklahoma team had to go out and rent their own van in order to get out to Fairfield that night.

Oklahoma was pretty good. They were 20-14 on the season but had won nine in a row coming into the game. With Montana's own Sugar Ray Richardson in town, a full day to get the word out, and an impressive win two days earlier; we turned out a nice crowd at Fairfield on that Tuesday night. They were loud and really into the game.

It turned out that Richardson was as much of a jackass on the sidelines as he was in person. As queer as this sounds for me to say; his demeanor was too unsportsmanlike for my taste. It was actually to the point of embarrassing and his theatrics on the sidelines distracted from what was a good group of players. I know, I know… many people find guys like him entertaining. They smile, shake their heads and say things like "Boy, that Michael Ray is a real character" or "Ha-ha, he's worth the price of admission, ha-ha"… I just think he's an embarrassment to the game of basketball and has been now for almost 30 years. I find him, and guys like him, to be nothing but a joke… but maybe that's just me.

This game with Oklahoma was one of the stranger games that I have ever been involved in. In the locker room before the game, Marlyn told me that he was leaving the next day to join a team in Puerto Rico. Junior was working on his own new gig in Europe and told me that he was close to a deal. It seemed as if the sand was quickly running out from this team's hourglass.

We jumped out to an 18-2 lead right away on the Calvary and I think led at one point, 28-6. Sugar was definitely sour as he ranted and raved up and down the sidelines. Oklahoma came back to go on a 15-0 run to end the first quarter, and the game went back and forth from there with each team taking big swings at the other. The Calvary had a huge second quarter and we came back with a big third quarter. In the fourth, we just didn't shoot as well, and they got an unforeseen boost from their 10th guy coming in off the bench, who rarely ever played, and lifted them with two big 3's down the stretch. In the end, we fell to the Calvary 112-106. I hated losing to jackasses like Richardson. I usually dealt with losing okay, but this one stung a little more because he was such a jerk.

To add insult to injury, the threat of repo'ing Blackmon's Explorer never came to fruition in the Fairfield High School parking lot as I had secretly hoped. I didn't even get the satisfaction of seeing that whole scenario play out which I know would have been great fun.

Feeling worn out and defeated, both literally and figuratively, I sulked my way back to the minivan and got ready for the 45 minute drive back to Great Falls. Junior climbed in front, all seven feet of Lamont crawled into the far back with Mike Peeples and Pele, while Mo and Jason sat in the middle seat. We were crammed into that van as we headed back to town.

Not even 10 minutes down the road, a large SUV passed me in the other direction. As it passed, I noticed out of my sideview mirror that it had pulled a quick u-turn in the middle of the highway. I immediately looked at my speed. The posted speed limit was

70 and I was going about 73 or 74. Soon I saw the cherries on this unmarked SUV light up. I pulled over so he could pass. Instead of passing me and racing off to where I thought he must have been being called to; he pulled up behind me.

I was confused.

He couldn't be pulling me over for speeding, could he? I was barely over the limit.

As the patrolman was getting out of his car to come to my window, Blackmon went flying past in his (essentially) stolen white Explorer. He never bothered to stop and see if we were okay. I turned off the rap music that was reverberating throughout the van, reached into my front pocket to pull out my driver's license, and rolled down my window. The cop shined his flashlight directly in my face rendering me temporarily blind, as I put my hand up in an attempt to block out the aggressive brilliance. His wandering beam briefly found Junior in the passenger seat before exploring the back, where it found five large black men with their knees up to their chins just hoping to get this whole thing over with so they could unfold themselves out of their Chrysler-induced misery.

"Good evening, do you know how fast you were going?" he asked me in a very business-like tone but not unfriendly.

"I think I was going 71 or 72?" I answered him as affable as I could, making my voice raise up at least two octaves.

"I had you at 74. The speed limit here is 60."

"Oh man, I thought the sign back there said that it's 70" I retorted trying not to come off as argumentative.

"It's 70 during the day, but 60 at night" he said flatly.

What? Is this guy messing with me? I've never heard of anything like that before.

"Really? I didn't know that. We're not from here" as if the six black guys in my car didn't already give that away, up here in B.F. Montana.

"Can I see your license, registration and proof of insurance?"

Junior rifled through the glove box looking for the van's registration… Nothing. We each looked above our respective visors. Still nothing. I handed the cop my license.

"This isn't my car. I don't know where the registration is and I don't have my insurance card on me" I told him meekly.

"Wait here please" and he walked back to his patrol car.

This was not what I needed right now. To get a speeding ticket when I wasn't even thinking that I was speeding, in a car that I have know idea who owns, doing a job that doesn't even pay me. It would be the straw that finally broke this already very wobbly camel.

It was pretty quiet in the minivan as we awaited our fate. Then Junior mentioned that this had all the feel of a DWB (Driving While Black) which according to him, happens all too frequently where he's from in Virginia and the D.C. area. Jason and Mo agreed. I scoffed at the thought. They tried to tell me that if one of them had been driving, they'd be spread eagle on the hood being searched right now. I couldn't tell if they were joking or being serious. I think it was a little of both, but I did pick up a very real and palpable distrust of the police by them that was foreign to the white middle-class cocoon that had blanketed me for 40 years.

As I have mentioned before about other meaningful situations in my life, this was a 'moment' for me. The conversation started out kind of funny as each of the guys would tell me what would've happened if they'd been driving; handcuffs, full body searches, kissing the pavement, a random tasing and rides in a paddy wagon would have been their fate they joked. It remained relatively light, but there was a somberness to it that let me know that to the guys in the car, this was no joke.

It was strange because, as the patrolman was sitting in his car figuring out what fate he would brandish upon me (and us); I was gaining access to the unadulterated emotions of black youth and their fragile relationship with the police. There was no bravado, no bluster and no spurious claims. No one was trying to channel the Black Panthers as we sat there in the van. To them, it was as plain as the nose on their face; just a matter of fact. I resisted the urge to take sides. I realized that my ability to relate was like a dog trying to fly like a bird; it was just never going to happen. I wasn't going to sit there and say "yay black kids, boo the fuzz" or vice versa; I knew that I had no credibility. But to me, something that had always been a specious claim, started to sprout wings of validity.

The trooper opened his door and started walking back to our car. He handed me back my license.

"Mr. Turner, did you know that this vehicle has no tabs and no visible license plate?"

"Uhh... no I didn't. Like I said, this isn't my car."

"I'm going to give you a warning on the speeding violation, but I am going to cite you for your back passenger who isn't wearing a seatbelt, and tell you to get the licensing on this vehicle taken care of immediately. The seatbelt violation is a $20 infraction and you can pay that to me directly right now if you'd like or send it in with the ticket later."

I gave him a $20 bill, he gave me a receipt and we were free to go. I carefully turned on my left blinker and merged back on the highway. I could see Junior staring at me out of the corner of my eye. I looked over at him and smiled.

"What?" I asked. He kept staring back at me. I laughed. "What?" I repeated.

"Okay coach, let me get this straight. You were speeding, had no registration, no insurance, no license tabs, no license PLATES and the only ticket you get is for the black guy not wearing his seatbelt?... Sheee-it..."

The van exploded in laughter as Junior reached back down to turn on the music. Soon we were back to the heavy bass beat of Jay-Z's "Oh My God" from the Kingdom Come album. The bitterness of the loss to dumass Michael Ray's team quelled but the sour taste of the past 72 hours would not.

This was not fun anymore. I told myself a long time ago that if this ever stopped being fun, it would be time to move on. I wasn't going to compromise. I could justify some of it if I was getting paid, was under contract, or even if I had someone (an assistant coach) to help and at least share in my misery, but I had none of that. I was feeling more alone and isolated than I had ever before. I was not going to forego what (if anything) was left of my reputation by further doing Blackmon's bidding. If people were going to disrespect me or think that I was an idiot, I wanted it to be because of my own doing and not because of my proximity to him. I didn't want to drive his getaway car just because I needed a lift across town.

My mind was made up and I wasn't going to second guess it. When we got back to the hotel, I packed my bags. I called Horizon Air and got on the first flight out of Great Falls the next day. It was a 6:15 a.m. flight to Seattle. I didn't want any drama so I didn't say anything to anyone. I wasn't quitting. I had just decided that I wasn't going to work anymore for free. If Blackmon wanted to pay me what he owed me, I would've immediately come back without hesitation. I took the uniforms to the laundry room at the Extended Stay where I stayed up until almost 1 a.m. getting them washed and dried for the final time.

I set my alarm for 4:30 a.m. I gathered all my belongings and shoved them into my oversized luggage. I could barely get it all zipped in as the bag was bursting at the seams. I hopped in the minivan and drove it to the Great Falls airport. I parked in the long-term parking lot, put the key under the driver's side floor mat and left the door unlocked. I would call Mo later, after he woke up, to let him know where the van was for them to come pick up.

Shortly after I arrived at the airport, I was upstairs reading the newspaper, waiting for the TSA agents to arrive that morning and open the security checkpoint that led to the gates. Coming up the escalator, I spotted Marlyn who was making his way out of town as well. He was going to Salt Lake City, then on to Miami before catching a flight to Puerto Rico. It had only been two months, but I had grown very close with these players in a short time. I didn't want it to end and I don't think they did either. We all wished the circumstances were better because we felt like we had a special group, a special team.

Marlyn and I said our awkward "guy" goodbyes. I think he appreciated the opportunity that I provided for him and the confidence that I showed in him, at least I hoped he did. I certainly appreciated his commitment and high level of effort through difficult conditions. I couldn't help but think about when we first met in Pittsburgh as this brief but eventful journey started. He was the first guy that I met, and in a weird way, it was like we had built the team together. Now, he was the last guy that I'd see as I left Great Falls forever. I knew that I'd probably never see Marlyn again. I hoped that somewhere along the way, I could try and repay him, and all the other guys on that team, for the commitment and loyalty that they showed me over the previous two months. As much as I tried though, I never really could.

I guess my timing was right with my decision to leave. The six remaining guys (Junior, Mo, Jason, Pele, Lamont and Mike) went to the club the next day to work out. When they got back, their room keys didn't work. They went to the front desk to check what was wrong and the hotel told them that Blackmon hadn't paid his bill and they had to get out.

The staff at the Extended Stay was always great to me and the players. It was Blackmon who they couldn't stand. After some pleading, they agreed to allow everyone to stay in one room for the night as they each tried to figure out their next move. So everyone packed up all their stuff and moved it into Junior's room where the six of them spent the night.

Refusing to go down without more of a fight, Blackmon convinced the remaining six guys to go to Butte the next night for a game with the Daredevils. If nothing else, at least they'd have a place to stay, provided by the Butte team. Blackmon sat on the bench and acted as the coach even though he did nothing. He emailed me a picture of his "coaching debut"

The Great Falls Explorers beat Butte that night 115-101 in what would be the final game for the franchise.

The now vagabond team traveled back to Great Falls and checked into a hotel which apparently hadn't heard of Blackmon yet. Junior got a relatively lucrative contract from a team in the Ukraine, but Blackmon refused to do the paperwork to release him, and the window of opportunity for the job there closed for him.

Blackmon told the players in the final days that he had no money to send them home and they would be on their own to get where ever they needed to go. Many of these guys didn't have the money for last-minute plane tickets to the east coast and they weren't sure what to do. They contemplated putting all six guys in the minivan and heading east on I-90, dropping guys off at their homes along the way, and leaving the van someplace for Blackmon to have to deal with later. Luckily, it never came to that. The CBA commissioner stepped in and bought everyone plane tickets home.

***

Coaching in the CBA confirmed something for me, that for whatever reason, I still needed validation. It confirmed for me that I was good at this coaching thing. It was just my timing that wasn't. I had hoped to parlay my CBA experience into something new and better but I was running into problems. Some of those problems were very familiar, and there were others I didn't anticipate. After years of chasing down a CBA job and finally landing it, the league was on extremely shaky ground, and the stability and reputation wasn't what it had been for the past decade or longer. The NBDL had become the preeminent U.S. minor league now and its rise had, in effect, moved the target that I had been shooting at. I had sacrificed and compromised myself to finally get in a position where I could navigate around with more ease and confidence and let my work and abilities speak for me; but instead, it was as if I had finally bought a CD player when everyone else had moved on to iPods.

It was okay though, I thought to myself. Even though the goal had shifted a bit, everything about it was still pretty much the same. The players were the same and many of the people involved now in the NBDL were the same after trickling over from the CBA for the past couple years. Plus, I counted on the wild card that I held over some other coaches who were trying to land D-League jobs; my nine years of service within the NBA itself while working at the Sonics.

Continuing in the CBA was a losing proposition. It would have been like buying stock in a company that made typewriters. I turned my focus to the NBDL and college basketball.

For the next four months after leaving Great Falls, I knocked on every door that I could think of in hopes of finding some stability. The tail that I had been chasing since leaving Bellevue Community College in 2004 was getting seemingly more elusive. Every time I thought I was close or was making inroads, I'd get knocked back again. It all finally came to a head in July when I got turned down once again for a head coaching position in the D-League.

Part of the GM's excuse, when telling me that I wasn't the right guy for his team, was that I didn't "know" enough people in the NBA and that I wasn't "connected". This comment really bothered me. I didn't know how to respond. How would he know who I know? I'm not a name-dropper type of guy and never wanted to be one. And besides, who are the "right" people to know anyway? I walked out of his office extremely disappointed; feeling thoroughly defeated and also really pissed off.

"Oh yeah? I don't know anybody, huh? I'll show you…" is what I thought as I drove away from our meeting.

In a move that teetered on desperation with a hint of immaturity, I decided to essentially empty my rolodex on this guy.

I pulled over in a local shopping mall parking lot and called or texted everyone in my phone who I thought might be "someone" to this guy, and asked them to make a phone call to him on my behalf. It was a knee-jerk reaction and one that I wasn't all that comfortable doing, but I looked at this as my Waterloo.

I had taken coaching as far as I could and it looked like I had reached a dead end. I had nothing to lose now but the small residue of pride still left in the Mason jar of my ego, and if this was it for me, at least I'd go down swinging. I opened up my contact list and started dialing.

I called or sent a text to all these guys asking for help. Some did, some didn't...

George Karl, Head Coach, Denver Nuggets
Nate McMillan, Head Coach, Portland Trailblazers
Lenny Wilkens, NBA all-time winningest coach
Jack Sikma, Assistant Coach, Houston Rockets
Bob Whitsitt, former GM of Portland and Seattle
Wally Walker, former President of Seattle Sonics
Rick Sund, GM of the Atlanta Hawks
Dwayne Casey, Assistant Coach, Dallas Mavericks
Quin Snyder, then-Head Coach of D-League Austin Toros
Chris Grant, then-Assistant GM of Cleveland Cavaliers
Sam Perkins, Assistant for the Indiana Pacers
Rob Palinka, Agent for Kobe Bryant

I list those names only to illustrate what I did in response to my D-league rejection. I don't know if these are some of the "right" guys to know or not. If nothing else, I felt it was a good list to start from.

Regardless... my impetuous response to the accusation of poor NBA connectivity had all the impact on this D-League General Manager of a Playboy Magazine to a blind man.

Absolutely none.

I failed to convert on third and long; and now it was time for me to punt.

When I finally gave up my fight for a coaching job, a tangible feeling of peace and calm enveloped me. I refused to look back and feel sorry for myself. I did everything that I could but realized that I was never going to be "in". I started as an outsider and would ultimately finish (appropriately I guess) on the outside. I had completely given in to that outcome and was ready to move on to the next new challenge. The only question was: what would that be?

I was continuing to do part-time work at a small regional airline in the Seattle area called Kenmore Air as I waited for my great epiphany. The shifts were 14 hours long and I could knock out almost 30 hours of work in just two days. After one of my days at Kenmore Air, I got in my car where I had left my cell phone for the day and saw that I received a call from a number that I didn't recognize. I checked the voice message. It was from Bob Weiss.

Bob Weiss had been either playing or coaching in the NBA for over 40 years, since he was drafted by the Philadelphia 76ers in 1965. He had been a head coach for four different NBA franchises (Seattle, Atlanta, San Antonio and the LA Clippers) and an assistant for many years as well. I knew Coach Weiss from when our paths crossed at the Sonics when I was there from '89-'97. He was there as an assistant to George Karl and others from '94-'05, so there was a three-year overlap. I knew him but I don't think he remembered me.

He called to tell me that he had just been hired to coach a team in China and asked if I would be interested in coming along as his assistant. I asked him how he got a hold of me, and he said that I was recommended to him by Dallas Mavericks Assistant Coach Dwayne Casey, who was a good friend of his. I guess my petulant name-dropping stunt a few weeks earlier actually did pay off.

Coach Weiss and I met at a Tully's coffee shop in Madison Park to discuss the situation and see if it would be a good fit. It was a strange meeting because I already felt like I knew him; but I could tell that he didn't really remember me at all from my time with the Sonics. In essence, I was meeting with an old friend and he was meeting with a complete stranger. It was tough for me to adjust to that dynamic. As such, I thought that it was a terrible meeting, at least for my prospects of getting the job. I think I reeked of desperation and wanted the job so bad that I couldn't put an intelligent thought together. Plus, I had been facing so much rejection over the past few years; I think my lack of confidence was embarrassingly exposed. I knew it while it was happening, and I could feel it while we talked, but I still couldn't do anything about it.

I showed up to the meeting with the impression that I might have been his only option. When Coach Weiss told me that he still had a couple more guys to talk to about the job, I left the meeting fairly convinced that I wouldn't be getting it.

I was half right. Although I wasn't his first choice, and maybe not even his second, at least I was THE choice, and I ended up accepting the position as Bob Weiss' assistant coach after at least one other guy (and maybe two) turned it down.

I was ecstatic on so many levels. 1) It was an opportunity to work with Coach Weiss, who had a great reputation and had played, coached or coached against every single one of the best players in the history of basketball. He had seen it all. 2) It was an opportunity to live in China and see the country in a way that most don't ever get to see. 3) It was an opportunity to keep coaching when I thought that my time in the game had expired and 4) It was an opportunity to make some money, which I hadn't done for far, far, far, far, far too long.

PART V:

THE HARVEST

17

China

I was taught a month ago; to bide my time and take it slow
But then I learned just yesterday; to rush and never waste the day
Well I'm convinced the whole day long; that all I learn is always wrong
and things are true that I forget; but no one taught that to me yet

- Phish "**Character Zero**"

We were hired to coach the Shanxi Zhongyu, a team in the Chinese Basketball Association, located in Taiyuan, China, a small town of just three million people located 300 miles south of Beijing. The Chinese are crazy about basketball and the Chinese Basketball Association is their version of the NBA. It's a big deal over there.

The team we took over however, was miserable. The year before, they only won five games but two of them were by forfeit when their opponent used an ineligible player, so really they only won three games on their own volition. Neither Bob nor I knew much about the league itself going into the season but we knew that the NBA had just started a division called NBA China, which was trying to explore ways to tap into the rabid basketball market over there. NBA China launched in January of '08 and both of us thought that our timing, going to China when we did, was ideal. Growth seemed eminent with the involvement of the NBA as well as the upcoming 2008 Beijing Olympics.

Coach Weiss left for China just a couple of days after offering me the job as we couldn't get the paperwork together in time for me to leave with him. With the Olympics going on, I would have to wait almost three weeks before I could get a visa and get over there. It turned out to be a good thing though, because I think his accommodations were pretty spartan before I got there. Bob didn't like the hotel where they originally were going to house us and talked the team into moving us to a better place before his wife and I arrived.

One of the strange things surrounding the job started in a question that Coach Weiss asked me during our original interview. He wanted to know if I had any experience running a strength and conditioning program. I did have some experience with this but it certainly wasn't at the level that he had been accustomed to in the NBA.

Coach's entire professional life was spent in the NBA where money was never an object, budgets were bigger than the GDP of a small country, and the staffs were highly specialized. I came from a background where I was the defensive coach, the offensive coach, the strength coach, the team nutritionist, the bus driver and uniform washer. I had developed weight programs for my teams but it would be unfair for me to claim to be a professional strength and conditioning coach.

Coach Weiss told me that he told the GM and owner of the team, that I could develop and run a strength and conditioning program for the Zhongyu. I think this was part of his sales pitch to them to convince them to allow him to bring an assistant coach.

I spent the next two weeks cramming, trying to learn as much as I could about biomechanics and physiology. I talked to a number of friends who were strength and conditioning coaches on the phone, and I went to meet with Seattle Sonics strength coach, Dwight Daub, right before I left. They all had great suggestions which I would later try and incorporate for our team.

One area of consensus that they all shared was that I should be careful about over doing it with the 'squat' exercises. Unless I was totally sure that I could teach the proper technique on how to perform them, I should tread lightly when doing squats. All of them told me that there is high risk of injury for basketball players if not done properly and that squats (although helpful) can be very hard on your body. I wasn't very comfortable in my ability to teach a proper technique and as I will explain, this would come in to play later.

The CBA (Chinese Basketball Association) season usually started around the end of October or the first of November, but because of the Olympics, they pushed it back to begin at the end of November. There are 48 games in the season and each of the 18 teams in the league can have two foreign or non-Chinese players on the roster. Everyone else on the team had to be Chinese (or from Taiwan).

While I was still in Seattle waiting on my visa, I made contacts with various American players who Coach Weiss and I thought could be good in that league and for our team.

Not only did these American players need to be good but they also would have to possess a demeanor that would allow them to survive and thrive in an unknown foreign country, where the language, culture and simple things like food choices are very different from what they are used to.

Once I got over there however, I realized that all my legwork locating players during the three weeks leading up to my trip was a complete waste of time.

My visa finally came through in the first week of September and I was scheduled to leave for China on September 10th. I was just rolling with the punches on this whole experience; there was never really much of a plan for my arrival beyond just meeting up with the team's interpreter in Beijing and figuring it out from there. We never made specifics arrangements about when and where he would pick me up, I had no back up plan in case he didn't show up, and I wasn't sure what to do if there were any last minute mix ups. I didn't have a contract, so I was taking a leap of faith that I would be paid what we agreed on, and I didn't have a return ticket home in case things didn't work out. I trusted Coach Weiss though and I had been in contact with him over the previous few weeks, so that gave me faith that things would be okay.

I struggled to fight back the tears as I said goodbye to my daughter Scout, before boarding the 12-hour flight to Beijing. I was excited and anxious about the trip and the unknowns that waited for me behind the Great Wall but I didn't want to leave her behind.

I couldn't distinguish between whether I was pursuing a noble effort or just continuing a pattern of selfishness. I was worried that I was being a bad father by electing to leave. It would be easy to say that I had no choice but really I did; and I chose me. That seems pretty selfish. Thank goodness the world has shrunk so much with technology and we discovered Skype, which allowed us to have a video call every day.

I ended up feeling much better about the situation, when after a while, I think she got kind of bored talking to me everyday. I think its harder when you can't see someone, but when you have the video element of the phone call, it eases the separation. After a couple of weeks, she seemed to adjust just fine, probably better than me.

I was a little surprised at how small the seats were on the Hainan Airlines direct flight from Seattle to Beijing. They certainly weren't built for big guys and the fella sitting next to me gave me quite a challenge in the girth department.

I don't think that I had ever been that uncomfortable on a plane before and I was staring into the face of remaining that way for the better part of half a day. Not only was I squished up against the window of the plane with 42 inches of fat ass spilling over into the seat next to me and an arm rest buried into my muffin top; the jackass in the seat in front of me put his head rest in my lap, and my knee caps crushed into the seat back. The temperature in that plane also had to have been 160 degrees. At least it felt like that; and there was no air coming out of the little air hole above the seat. I looked at my watch. Whew… Only 11 hours and 45 minutes left before we get there.

I was anxious to get there; extremely uncomfortable in my seat and sweating like Chris Farley as a Chippendale dancer. It was a trident of confluences that no one should experience. I decided to pull my chute early and reach for my suicide pill. I quickly popped two Ambien in my mouth and swallowed; using only my own spit as a chaser. I woke up shortly before the plane touched down on the Beijing tarmac with my mouth wide open, drool on my little airplane pillow (that hundreds of others had drooled on before me… gross) and my big ass practically in the lap of my seatmate (sorry guy).

We left Seattle at 2 p.m. and arrived in Beijing at 4 p.m. the next day. I walked off the plane, quickly got through customs and strolled into the airport terminal not knowing what to expect or who to look for. The team interpreter for Shanxi Zhongyu was a guy named "Joe". Actually his name was Guanjie but he went by Joe Kwan. He was the only connection in China that I had to this point (other than Coach Weiss) and Joe was supposed to be there at the airport to pick me up, but I didn't know what he looked like. I found nothing and no one. I stood there, looked around and tried to be as conspicuous as I could in hopes that Joe would spot me. I continued to wait, not wanting to venture too far from the spot where I was standing, while other people from the flight were exiting and being met by friends and family. Pretty soon, I was the only guy left there. Still waiting, alone and unsure about what to do. I had my cell phone with me but it was my intention to not use it because of the high costs of international roaming charges. Even though I didn't have a phone number for Joe, I turned it on anyway, in case he was trying to call me.

The first place I saw as I walked out into the terminal was Starbucks. It was both comforting and irritating to see. I had been boycotting Starbucks since Howard Shultz, the CEO of Starbucks and owner of my Seattle SuperSonics, sold the team to the dick-holes from Oklahoma; who then stole the team out from under us and moved them to Oklahoma City. To me, Shultz had become Lord Voldemort, He-Who-Shall-Never-Be-Named, or more specifically, He-Whose-Coffee-I-Shall-Never-Drink-Again. Yet there I was, 6,000 miles from home, 45 minutes into this epic adventure into the unknown reaches of the Far East, and the first thing I see is the exact same Starbucks that I can find every 150 yards or so in Seattle. Like I said, it was irritating yet strangely comforting at the same time.

I walked into the coffee shop to check it out and see how different it was from one in the States. It wasn't different at all. Everything in there was exactly the same and the person at the counter spoke very good English. I broke the promise to myself and ordered a tall, iced vanilla latte. Little by little, the guilt I felt from betraying my boycott washed away with each small sip of that sweet caffeine-laden nectar. Shortly after, my phone rang. It was Joe.

I met Joe out in front of the KFC, right next to the McDonald's and two shops down from the Starbucks I had been sitting in.

So far, China was underwhelming me.

He asked if it would be okay for us to drive the 300 miles back to Taiyuan instead of flying, since he needed to get his car down there from Beijing. Joe was living in Beijing before getting hired by Shanxi and he accompanied Coach Weiss to Taiyuan a few weeks earlier. He had left his car behind. I had no expectations to fly and I certainly wasn't going to create any problems within the first hour of my trip. For some reason I kind of expected that we were going to drive anyway, so I told Joe that I was game for anything. We got on the road a couple of hours before dark. By the time we got out of Beijing, I definitely realized I was somewhere entirely different.

The drive from Beijing to Taiyuan was one of the most harrowing experiences I've ever had and that is not hyperbole. We headed south on the Jing-Shi Expressway and a few things stood out, especially after it got dark. The first of which is that even though there may be a speed limit (still not sure); it is definitely not observed on either the slow side or the fast side. You can have a guy pass you going 100mph and soon come up on a small truck going 15mph. The second thing that stood out was that there weren't any discernable lanes that people drove in. It was a total free for all. In general, driver's stayed to the right, but it wasn't uncommon to have someone coming at you in your lane, counting on you to get out of the way first, like Kevin Bacon playing chicken on a John Deere. The other thing that was a killer was the many, many cars and trucks that had no tail lights. We'd be driving down the unlit highway with our own crappy headlights and all of a sudden, we would come right up on someone in front of us who we couldn't see ahead of time. I was in the passenger seat constantly pushing on the invisible brake on my side of the car, white-knuckling the dash board in front of me, with my hands out pushing, while trying to look like I was unfazed by the whole thing.

I hit a wall of fatigue at one point, a few hours into the drive, and I was so tired I could barely keep my eyes open. But at the same time, I was so worried that we were going to meet our fate and frightened by this experience, I was afraid to close them. I didn't want to sleep through the circumstances leading up to my impending demise. It was a rough, rough drive and by the time we pulled in to the parking lot of the Longcheng Hotel at 2:30 a.m., almost nine hours after we left Beijing, I was wiped out (with an exclamation point).

Coach Weiss called me at 7:30 a.m. to check in with me and make sure I made it in one piece. He was excited to have me there if for no other reason than to have someone to talk to, but I also knew that he was ready to get to work with me and start this thing for real. He suggested that I skip the morning practice, get some rest and we'd have lunch together before our afternoon practice where he could get me caught up on things. As much as I was ready to dive in, I welcomed this plan and went back to bed for a couple hours.

Taiyuan has a cold, semi-arid climate. In other words, it's very hot in the summer and very cold in the winter and it rarely rains. On this early September day, it was very hot when I went down to the lobby to meet Coach Weiss. The elevator doors opened and the first thing that hit me was a wall of cigarette smoke that was trying to escape its entrapment in the hotel lobby.

The lobby was bustling with business people filing in and out of the revolving door in the front of the building and the buffet lunch was buzzing with hungry customers. I must have looked like a deer in the headlights as Coach Weiss took me outside to walk around the neighborhood and show me a few things, most notably the nearby grocery store.

We walked about two city blocks to the grocery store where, once inside we were met with a smell that was quite displeasing to the ol' olfactory system. After a few minutes you kind of adjust and get used to it, but as I think back on that odor now, I can almost force myself to smell it again.

The first floor of the market had the produce and seafood; the second floor had other meats, a deli and most of the canned and dry goods. The third floor was more like a department store with clothing, home furnishings and electronics. We grabbed some fruit, nuts and water and headed back to the hotel before we were to get picked up for practice that afternoon.

Foreigners are not allowed to drive in China (thank goodness) and as such, we had a driver who picked us up and drove us to and from practice everyday, twice a day. His name was Mr. Wong and he didn't speak one teensy-tiny bit of English. In fact, we were hard pressed to find anyone in Taiyuan who spoke any English at all. It was much different than Beijing where you could move around quite effectively without having to know Mandarin Chinese. Here in Taiyuan, it was virtually impossible to communicate with the local people.

The practice facility was about 10 miles from our hotel but with traffic, we rarely ever made it there in under 45 minutes. The facility itself was better than I expected, but then again, my expectations were pretty low. It was a far cry from similar facilities in the States in terms of its plushness and aesthetics, and although it was quite pedestrian in appearance, it was functional and worked just fine for our needs.

It was located out in the corn fields, not far from the city itself, and growth was quickly infringing on its remoteness. Each day that passed, it seemed as if the city was inching closer and closer to the site, which not only had a large gym with two full-sized basketball courts, but also housed a dormitory for the players as well as the team's offices. The other building on the property had a huge coal-burning furnace that would later supply the heat for everything on the campus as the weather turned colder.

Coach Weiss asked me if I wanted to have a weight session with the guys after practice. I asked if we could wait a day so I could get a look at the equipment that they had and design something accordingly. He agreed and we walked into the gym for my first look at our new squad.

The first thing that stood out to me, as I watched us play on that first day of practice, (at least first day for me); was how terrible we were. They were fumbling and futzing with the ball, and throwing it all over the gym. It was immediately apparent why they were so bad the season before. I also remember feeling very awkward about knowing exactly the best way for me to compliment Coach Weiss as his assistant.

I hadn't been an assistant coach for seven years or so, and the dynamic of the job is much different than that of the head coach. On top of that, it was my first time working with Coach Weiss and I didn't want to be teaching things that he didn't agree with. I wanted to jump right in and show him that I was a good choice to bring along to China, but I also felt like I should lie back and get a feel for him and the things he likes to do first.

By the end of that first practice, I wondered how we were going to win any games, let alone match last year's record of five wins. I couldn't help but wonder how bad the teams were that we beat the season before must have been.

I was sitting on the sidelines after that first practice, digging something out of my backpack before we left for the hotel. Most of the guys were still milling around the gym, gathering up their jackets before heading back to the dorm, or stretching or changing shoes. One of the guys came down and sat next to me with a big smile on his face. His name was Jin and he was a five-foot-nothing point guard with a great personality but a hair-trigger temper. A few days before I got there he had chased one of his teammates around the gym with a brick after they had got into a scuffle during practice. I think among some other issues, Jin maybe had the Chinese version of a Napoleon Complex.

He sat down next to me and wanted to try out some of his English.

Very slowly he started with "Heh-row…"

"Hello" I said back smiling.

"You… hhav… barry… broot-ti-fer… eyesh" and he pointed at my left eye.

"Uhh…?" I looked around to see if other people were watching and maybe laughing at me. I didn't know how to react. I was a little uncomfortable. I had never had a man tell me that I have beautiful eyes. I don't think I ever had a woman tell me that either but that's beside the point.

"Umm…thank you" I responded, not knowing if I should be weirded out or flattered.

"Yes, yes" he nodded.

I smiled and knew right then that this was going to be an interesting trip.

***

----- Original Message -----
From: Rick Turner
To: Friends and Family
Sent: Tuesday, September 16, 2008 5:30 AM
Subject: china

My body clock is finally adjusting. I've been up at 3a everyday until today (I slept in until 6a) too early to tell how its going to be but i know it will be a unique experience. three things stand out after a few days… smog, traffic and the helplessness of not being able to communicate. In what will be a number of "firsts" for my career… for the first time, i had a player tell me that i have beautiful eyes. Besides that fact that i do, it struck me as a bit odd…

Coach Weiss and I are struggling with the "management" of the team about getting Americans over here. We want a guard and a big, they want two bigs. We've given them some names but they don't seem to trust our judgment of talent. I think there are a few people in the states that they trust and if those guys don't know the player that we're talking about, our management dismisses them as no good. It's a bit frustrating but I think there will be many frustrations along the way.

im staying in a hotel. nothing special just an ordinary pretty nice hotel. at this point, I couldn't imagine anyone coming to visit. its hard to explain just how difficult it is to do ANYTHING w/o speaking the language and NO ONE here seems to speak english. I haven't been in search of or even heard of any nightlife. With that said, Im sure it will get better as I get a feel for everything but right now im kind of in lockdown.

Its now 8:30p and I just had dinner for the first time since ive been here. Yes... I havent had dinner yet since thursday (unless you count apples).

The players are not very good. We knew that coming in but they are worse than I expected. They were the worst team in the league last year so I guess there is nowhere to go but up. We really need to bring in some good Americans. My teams at BCC would beat these guys.

68 tv channels and there are all run by the govt... one channel is in english. I was up at 4a on Sunday to listen to the Huskies and 4a again on Monday to listen to 'hawks on the computer... what a waste of time...

More later, your boy...
rt

About a week after I arrived in China we played in a preseason tournament in a city called Foshan, in the Guangdong Province, on the southeastern corner of the country about 1000 miles from Taiyuan. Bob's wife Tracy had joined us by now and so did two American players, James Lang and Damon Brown. I knew a little bit about James Lang because he played in the ABA in 2005 and we played against him. I didn't know much about Brown and Coach Weiss and I would get our first look at him in Foshan since he had no practices with us leading up to the trip.

It doesn't really matter where you are, what level you're coaching, or what league you play in; basketball stays relatively consistent as far as team dynamics, what it takes to win and just your everyday preparation. All the stuff between the lines is surprisingly similar whether you are coaching 30-year-old pro players or high school junior varsity. It's all the stuff outside of the practices and games that differ from one level to the next, not the basketball.

Essentially what differentiates it all is money and budgets. The Chinese Basketball Association was NBA "Light" in terms of the ancillary stuff outside of basketball. Perhaps because of the recent partnership with NBA China, or just through their own aspiration to emulate the NBA's marketing model, the ChBA was putting a lot of effort and money into simulating the NBA experience as best they could. At risk of exposing my own superficiality, this made my experience in China a lot of fun.

While my passion is, was and always has been the coaching; I have to admit that the outside stuff was quite self-indulgent and something that I didn't want to take for granted. As I search for ways to describe what I was experiencing at the time, I can't help but feel embarrassed or maybe even guilty by the emotions that this evoked in me. I'm reluctant to even tell you, but there was so much that I liked about not having to do everything.

Saying that makes me feel weak, soft and lazy but it was true (if I can't tell you, who can I tell?). This first trip to Foshan shone a light on those feelings.

Frankly, it was fun to have a staff.

Our team driver, Mr. Wong, who drove Coach Weiss, the American players and me to practice everyday, also drove our team bus.

It was a real bus, not a 12-passenger van that we all had to squeeze ourselves into. It had a space down below for luggage, the seats were plush, there was lots of space for guys to stretch out, move around and best of all, I didn't have to drive it. He picked us up and took us all to the airport for that first trip. Joe, our team interpreter, got us all checked in at the airport and took care of everyone's ticket. Once we arrived at the Guangzhou Airport, there was another bus to pick us up and drive us to the team hotel. Once we got to the hotel, there was someone else to get us all checked into our rooms.

For Coach Weiss, who had been in the NBA for the past 40 years traveling like a rock star wherever he went, the travel experience in China probably seemed like amateur hour. For a grinder like me, it was miraculous. For once, I wasn't the guy herding cats on a team road trip, but for whatever stupid reason, the sense of satisfaction that I felt from being taken care of left me guilt-ridden. I started feeling like I didn't deserve this. Every time I started giving into feeling good, I had to check myself and temper my enthusiasm.

I don't know what your impressions of China are, but I was continually shocked by how new, modern and up-to-date many things were; which I didn't expect. I think that I half expected to be transported back a few decades or even centuries upon my arrival, but it wasn't like that.

Actually… in a lot of ways it was like that… but in many others it wasn't.

There seemed to be an extremely wide spectrum between the influences of old and new; much more so than in the States. In the U.S., you don't really see too many cars on the street more than 10 years old; in China it was common to see a brand new Range Rover flying down the street past a tiny, 40-year-old, three-wheeled pickup truck sputtering down the road. Or you might see a big, beautiful new 50-story office complex sitting right next to a rundown, two-story brick building that was built at the turn of the century.

That is why I guess I was so surprised to see how large, new and modern the airport in Guangzhou was when we landed. We gathered our luggage and headed toward the bus that would take us to the hotel. As we walked out of baggage claim to the concourse the first thing that I saw was a 7-11, again, not something that I expected. The next thing I saw were palm trees lining the airport drive. It was a little humid but otherwise very comfortably warm. We were definitely in a different part of the country. My enthusiasm meter went up another notch.

To me, Foshan had a feel similar to the U.S. East Coast and especially in the area where our hotel was located. The streets were narrow and bustling with people and food vendors. The hotel itself wasn't particularly nice, by western standards. There was no grand lobby entrance, fancy elevators or big meeting rooms. It was clean, reliable and mature. It was something of a throwback. The elevators were slow moving and you could tell which floor it was on by the dial at the top of each door. It was usually faster to take the stairs than wait for the elevator. The doorways were small. My guess is that they were seven feet high which made all of us feel like we had to duck to walk through them. I flopped on the bed once I got into my room and almost had the wind knocked out of me because it was so hard; which I actually really like but just wasn't expecting it. Everything in the room, and I mean everything, was covered in 1950's looking cherry red wood paneling; which really helped give it a dated feel. The shower head pointed at my chest which meant I had to shower in the Utkatasana yoga pose if I wanted to wash my hair (good thing I'm in such great shape).

There was no internet available in this hotel and the only English-speaking channel on the TV was showing a **Clifford the Big Red Dog** marathon. We had an 8 a.m. shootaround scheduled for the next day so I went right to bed after we all got settled into our rooms around 10 p.m.

Coach Weiss took an early morning walk the next day and found a nearby McDonald's where he brought me back an Egg McMuffin and hot chocolate before our shootaround. I powered them down in the bus on the way to the gym.

Normally, you do a shootaround at the gym where you are going to play later that night, but I guess the gym was booked with something else so we went to a nearby rec center that morning to shoot and go over some plays. I actually think the facility might have been a table tennis (ping-pong) academy because adjacent to the gymnasium was a room, with what looked like 100 ping pong tables inside. There was one lone Chinese guy in there practicing his serves and let me tell you… he was a bad ass server. He was fun to watch.

The gym itself however, left a little to be desired.

We walked into the small gym with our NBA-esque pro basketball team; strutting in with a little swagger like we were better then the 5-35 record from the season previous. Maybe our guys were filled with confidence now that they had a former NBA head coach to lead them, or maybe they were just being typical cocky athletes but whatever the case, we were quickly humbled when we sauntered in the gym.

As some of my former players would say, that gym was "toe up". One rim was bent; the other one was low. There were no nets on either rim (which always bugs the pee out of me). The wood on the court was rotting, and along with a bunch of dead spots in places where someone would dribble, there were a couple of sizable holes in the floor that were showing exposed dirt. There was no ventilation and the morning sun had already hit the windows of the building, rapidly heating it up.

Couple that with the humidity of the area and the temperature in that gym was hot… real hot… sticky and uncomfortable. The mosquitoes didn't seem to mind though as my sweaty arms and legs provided an unexpected breakfast smorgasbord of fat, white guy that they probably didn't get a lot of in them there parts.

The smell inside the gym was difficult to decipher and even more hard to take. It seemed to be the perfume of rank animal touched with a hint of sewer. I knew that if I just dealt with the smell and took it all in, it would quickly tattoo itself on the inside of my nostrils and soon I wouldn't notice it.

Coach Weiss didn't seem to be fazed by any of this, and it was so early into our relationship that I didn't want him to see that I was struggling. It was game day and he appeared to be pretty focused at the task at hand while I was distracted by crappy hoops, a chaffing crotch from the heavy humidity, and an insect feast happening on my ample epidermis that threatened to give every mosquito in Foshan a coronary.

I did my best to try and contribute in a meaningful way during the shootaround and again, prove to Coach Weiss that I was a valuable Tonto and that he didn't make a mistake by bringing me to China. But I have to say, all I wanted to do was get out of that gym. I left there really praying that this wouldn't be the norm. Thankfully it wasn't.

I neglected to mention that there was another assistant coach for the team and his name was Coach Xia. X's are pronounced as 'sh' in Chinese, so his name was said as "Coach Shia". He was an older man who I never learned too much about but he had been coaching for years and years over there. To what success, I don't know. He could have been the John Wooden of China for all I knew or he could have been something much less successful. Whether it was out of respect for Coach Weiss, or because he was intimidated by him, or maybe because he didn't like him; Xia seemed to stay in the background quite a bit. He didn't really contribute at practices and never tried to speak with either one of us about basketball or the team.

As we got back to the hotel from the shootaround, Joe told Coach Weiss and me that we would <u>have</u> to have a pre-game meeting at 4 p.m. later that afternoon. We both figured that our pre-game meeting would happen before the game at the arena, but Joe told us that this was the "Chinese Way", and something that we had to do. We would hear quite a bit more about the "Chinese Way" as the season progressed.

On the third floor of the hotel there were some private dining rooms. This is where we would meet for our mandatory pre-game talk. Everyone gathered in the room shortly before 4 p.m. and Joe looked at Coach Weiss as if to say "okay, here we are, what do you want to say?"

It wasn't that Coach Weiss wasn't prepared but I could tell that he really didn't have all that much to say. We didn't know anything about our opponent. It was the first game of the season (albeit a pre-season game) and we didn't know what our own guys could do yet. He muscled through about a 10 or 15 minute talk, pausing every so often to let Joe's Chinese interpretation catch up with him… and then he made a big mistake.

He asked Coach Xia if he wanted to say anything.

Unfortunately, Coach Xia did. He talked and talked and talked and talked and talked. About 20 minutes into Coach Xia's talk, Joe just finally quit translating. Coach Weiss, Big James, Damon and I sat there listening to this old Chinese guy rambling incoherently until I thought my ears would explode. He literally spoke for almost an hour and only stopped talking because it was getting close for us to leave for the arena. It was miserable. In fact, it was so miserable that it started to be funny. I would catch Coach Weiss looking at me from out of the corner of my eye. I couldn't look at him because I thought I would break out into laughter, or at least appear to be disrespectful to Coach Xia if I did, so I avoided any and all eye contact. Coach Weiss finally interrupted Xia and said that we needed to go; otherwise I think we might still be there. Unfortunately for us, this scene would repeat itself for the next two games as well.

We left the hotel at 5:30 p.m. for the 8:00 game. None of us knew where we were going, and apparently the games were spread out in various outlying arenas, not just in Foshan. It seemed as if our bus driver didn't know where he was going either because soon he got lost. We had to pull over three different times and ask for help; we were driving in circles as well as getting stuck in heavy evening traffic.

It took us two and a half hours to get to the arena!!! It took us only about 45 minutes to get back, that's how lost we were… two and a half hours!!!

We were playing the defending champions from the previous season, the home town Guangdong Tigers. We finally got to the arena and pulled the bus in next to the television truck parked outside the building. This game was being televised locally. Since we were late, we walked into the arena and right out onto the floor to get warmed up. The players had already dressed at the hotel instead of waiting until we got to the arena, which was another new one for me.

Again, if it wasn't 85 degrees in that arena I would have been knocked over with a feather. It was a hot mess in there and I felt bad for the guys to have to play in it. The Guangdong Dance Team was practicing in the middle of the floor when we came out, and with all due respect, left quite a bit to be desired.

Good grief.

Unshapely, unattractive and untalented was their unfortunate trinity. I wouldn't say they were fat, but they all had spare tires around their waists. The teeth were neglected from the orthodontia that their American brethren found commonplace and their rhythm rivaled that of Navin R. Johnson. They were an extremely underwhelming group.

Even though it took us two and a half hours to get to the gym, the Guangdong team that we were playing that night still hadn't arrived by the time we walked in the arena. I got the feeling that no one was too concerned about what time the game would start. Our opponents finally showed up shortly after 8:00, the game staff opened the arena doors and let the crowd file in. The clock started counting down toward tip off and the familiar, dulcet tones of NWA's F*** the Police was pounding throughout the building. No one in this place, save Coach Weiss, his wife, James, Damon and me knew or fully understood the filth that was spewing from Easy E's microphone as the players warmed up on the floor in front of them. It didn't stop with just that song however. There were probably 5,000 people in the arena and the only music they were "treated" to was **uncut** American rap music with all the mf's, bs's and n's left in it. They had no idea what was being said and ate it up.

As we took the floor for our pre-game warm ups, Joe informed me that it was the assistant coach's job in China to oversee the team's warm up routine. This seemed to be another spoke in the "Chinese Way" that Coach and I were quickly learning about. This wouldn't have been any problem at all if either, Coach Weiss had asked me to do it, or if I had been given a heads up before hand. Neither of which happened.

My philosophy on a team's pre-game warm ups was simple.

It is a player's thing.

In other words, this is their time to get focused and loose (stretched and warmed up) before a game, and with only those two goals in mind. How they want to achieve getting focused and how they want to achieve getting loose is really up to them.

I looked over at the Guangdong team on the other side of the court, and their assistant coach was running them through various drills. I looked over to Coach Weiss and he kind of shrugged his shoulders and rolled his eyes; so I went to our basket with Joe to try and run us through some drills.

I am the sort of guy who likes to be really prepared, and under normal circumstances, we would have practiced our pre-game warm up at least once before, at a practice or shootaround. Because I had no idea that this would be falling on my shoulders, I wasn't at all prepared.

Since I've never concerned myself with pre-game warm ups before, I wasn't even really sure what kind of drills to put them through. On top of all that, the drills I did have in mind needed some explaining, which meant that I would have to tell it to Joe in English and then have him translate to Chinese. We ended up spending more time on the explanation on how to do the drills then actually doing it; totally defeating the purpose of the warm up.

As the "hot shot" American coach, I felt pressure to come up with some kind of spectacular warm up routine that the Chinese guys would be impressed with and recognize what an amazing coach that I was. At the same time, I wouldn't say that I was disinterested, but I just didn't fully buy in to this aspect of the "Chinese Way"; and it probably showed. It was an agonizing 20 minutes as I was continually explaining what I wanted them to do and then stopping them to re-explain and correct things; while all I really wanted them to do was find their focus for the game and get warmed up to play.

Whatever we did in the warm-ups must have worked out okay because we went out and beat the defending champs that night in our first pre-season game. The team that took the floor and the team that I had been watching practice for the last week and a half were two, totally different teams. It helped that Guangdong was missing a few of its best players, who were currently playing with the Chinese National Team but we still played well.

James Lang played very well and put up some big numbers but Damon Brown left a bit to be desired. We gave him the benefit of the doubt since he was still so new but his leash was pretty short.

James Lang was a 6'10" post player who went straight from high school into the NBA draft in 2003. He was drafted by the New Orleans Hornets in the second round of that year's draft, but he could never really stick with any team, mostly because of weight and conditioning issues. He was a skilled offensive player who had soft hands and great footwork, but tended to be challenged on the defensive end, again mostly because of his wind. He had been bouncing around the NBA, the NBDL, the ABA, the USBL and Spain before he hooked on with us in China. It looked like he was serious about getting his game right and doing what he had to do in order to get back in the NBA.

That is the basketball breakdown. Off the floor, he was a gentle giant and just a sweet and friendly guy to be around. I know Coach Weiss really liked James and felt like he had the ability to help the big fella get to where he wanted to go; which was to the NBA. I think James also understood the opportunity that he had to have someone like Bob working with him everyday. In those first three pre-season games down in Foshan,

James put up some big, big numbers both scoring and rebounding. It looked as if he would be a force in this league, and now we just needed to find the right guy to pair him with as our second American player.

Damon Brown was a 6'9" forward from Syracuse who was also a second-round pick in the NBA Draft, but in 2001 by Philadelphia. He was much quieter than James but seemed to be a pretty nice guy nonetheless. To me, he didn't have the demeanor to excel in a situation like this which I think calls for someone with a bit more of an outgoing personality. Regardless of his personality, if he could play, it wouldn't matter.

Unfortunately, his quiet off-court demeanor carried over to be a quiet on-court demeanor. Damon was a good player when surrounded by good players, but I didn't see the aggressiveness needed to, as they say "hang numbers" in this league. I could understand his reluctance to just come in right away and impose his will on the team but he only had a short window to show what he could do. He didn't have time to work his way in slowly and I think this is what ultimately hurt him. Damon didn't last long before the team cut him and started looking for a replacement.

We won the first game in Foshan but lost the next two. Even though we lost, we still played better than I expected and we basically got no help from Damon. I felt like if we could get another good American to go along with James, we might be okay. We also had another ace in the hole. Since we were one of the bottom four teams in the league the previous season, we had a special exemption for a third foreign player. The only stipulation was that he must have an Asian passport; so Coach Weiss and I went to work on finding another good player to add to the roster.

In the meantime, the owner of the Shanxi Zhongyu joined us for our second and third games in Foshan (you know, the ones we lost...). I had not met him before but I had heard some people say that he was kind of crazy.

Crazy?

I scoff at that thought. If anyone knew what a crazy owner was, it was me. I knew there was nothing that this guy could do that would shock me. No matter how 'crazy' he was, it would be junior varsity foolishness compared to the varsity insanity that I had witnessed over the past four years.

I wasn't sure what others had meant when they called the owner of Shanxi Zhongyu crazy, but it didn't take long for me to find out.

As I question my own sanity and reflect on this path I have chosen, I recognize that one of my lesser refined qualities is my utter lack of ability to kiss ass. Believe me, I say that without any sort of pride attached to it. I wish I was better at sucking up to people since it is probably the single greatest liability that has held me back professionally. For whatever reason, I am really bad at it; more so than any of the many other faults that I put on regular display. Knowing this, I really tried hard to make a positive impression on our team owner when I met him.

Actually, to more accurately state it, I tried really hard not to make a negative impression on our owner; a subtle nuance in my effort.

The owner's name was Mr. Wang, pronounced like 'Vong' with a soft v, almost like an f, sort of in between an f and a v. He was a short guy who made his money in steel and seemed to have a working-class background. He wasn't an "elite" who grew up in money. He was new-Chinese wealthy and came across as pretty unrefined socially. He was also a basketball junkie who watched a ton of NBA games on TV and thought he understood the game better than anyone else on the planet.

As is the case with many owners of professional sports franchises, this team was just a really expensive toy for Mr. Wang. If he showed up for practice both Coach Weiss and I knew to throw the practice plan out the window because something strange was about to happen. Often, he would show up in the middle of practice, everything would stop and he would grab a few guys on the team to play 3-on-3 with him. This happened quite a bit. Anytime that he showed up at the practice facility and wanted to play a game, anything that was happening at the time would cease so he could get his workout in.

One time he pulled one of the Chinese players out of practice and made the player give him a massage on the side of the court while everyone else continued working out. At another practice, he stopped us while we were in the middle of going over some defensive rotations, and he divided the team up into two squads. He took the five best players and said he wanted to scrimmage the others. He would coach the first five. Coach Weiss coached the second five.

Coach Weiss' team beat the piss out of Mr. Wang's team. Afterward, Mr. Wang said that his team should be made to "push a ball up and down the court with only their noses". I wasn't sure if this meant something other than what it appeared to mean on face value (which was that they should push a ball up and down the court with their noses) or whether the translation had been somehow messed up; but either way, Mr. Wang did not like losing.

Coach Weiss was Shanxi's fourth coach in the last 12 months and Mr. Wang had no problem firing anyone who disagreed with him. Mr. Wang showed up to our second game in Foshan, and although he actually sat right there on the bench with us during the game, for the most part he thankfully stayed in the background.

At least until after the game; when he delivered a scathing post-game rebuke to our team. Whether it was out of respect, fear or just the infamous "Chinese Way"; Joe wouldn't ever translate what Mr. Wang was saying while he was talking. He would give us a synopsis of what he said afterward, but never while it was happening, so we would have to sit there and listen to his lengthy diatribe with no clue as to what was being said. After that second game, Mr. Wang berated the players for about 20 minutes in the dressing room. After our third and final game in Foshan, the verbal beat down lasted nearly 45 minutes. If you're having a hard time conceptualizing that, trust me; it's a really, really long time for one guy to chew your ass.

***

We cut Damon Brown when we got back from our trip and spent the next couple of weeks bringing in players for tryouts. I use the term 'we' loosely because Coach Weiss and I had very little say about who came and went. It was a parade of American players for the following weeks after returning from Foshan. We hosted a team from Romania for two games, and along with James Lang, we added Donta Smith, a 6'7" small forward who went straight from junior college to the NBA as a second-round pick for Atlanta, Sean Lampley from the University of California and Jeff Varum from Washington State University.

Big James continued to play well and put up some big numbers in the two games against the Romanians but it was hard to say which, if any, of the other guys should stick. Varum just wasn't good enough for this league, he was undersized and couldn't shoot well enough; that was a no brainer. But both Lampley and Donta were intriguing. Both of those guys had a good feel for the game and both guys made their teammates better by their play. Donta however, was more aggressive looking for his own shot, at least right off the bat.

It had to be tough for these guys though because everyone that was brought in to tryout was usually brought straight from the airport and thrown into practice; or in the case of Donta and Sean, they literally walked straight out of a taxi and into the game. A 12-hour plane ride, body clock disruption, lack of sleep, language barrier, strange culture and a new environment does not provide for the optimum recipe when trying to impress a potential employer within the first 24 hours of meeting them. Ultimately, they kept Donta around for another week and let Lampley go because he didn't score enough right away.

What was shocking however, to both Coach Weiss and I, and frankly pretty confusing and irritating, was when the team decided to release James Lang without ever consulting Coach Weiss.

----- Original Message -----
From: Rick Turner
To: Friends and family
Sent: Friday, October 10, 2008 7:21 AM
Subject: Two pics and update

A couple pics with a story to each...

First is the workers of the bank that is attached to our hotel. Every morning at 7:45a they are lined up outside in the parking lot doing stretching and calisthenics coordinated to loud music. When they are finished, they get an "inspiring" speech from the bank manager before they tackle the day ahead. (afterward, a least half have a cigarette before they go in to work)...

Next, is a very common sight around here. You'd think that it was just one kid that we saw but really, it's all...
The toddler aged kids walk around with holes cut in the crotch of their pants. Its either because the parents don't want to buy diapers or they can't. But the kids basically "relieve" themselves anywhere at any time. Usually right there on the sidewalk. It's lovely...

As far as an update on the team...

I wish it was better news. It's difficult to describe how the people over here think. They hired Coach Weiss and me to bring an American style of coaching to the team/league but yet they keep telling us that we need to understand the "Chinese Way". Apparently the Chinese Way is to completely overwork and berate your players to the point that they can't think on their own, get no recovery time and have every minute of every day planned for them. On Monday they more or less demoted Coach Weiss to "Team Consultant". They brought in a Chinese "head coach" to crack the whip on the team because they thought Coach Weiss was too soft on them. The interpreter told me that if Bob was the head coach (in title), the owner would be shamed if he wanted to fire him later or if Bob wanted to leave. As the 'consultant' he can leave at anytime without it reflecting on the owner... strange people. So this now leaves me as the Consultant's Assistant??? I don't know how much longer they'll want to pay me for that. So we literally do NOTHING at practice. We drive an hour each way, twice a day to go to practice and sit on the sidelines watching a bull**** practice.

Morning practice is warm up (dribble up and down the floor), stretching, ball handling drills for <u>an hour</u>, 3-man weave for <u>a half hour</u>, individual shooting (sometimes we get to be rebounders) and weightlifting.

Afternoon practice is warm up, stretching, passing drills for 45 mins, defensive slides, scrimmage and brutal conditioning. The daily schedule is as follows:

7:30 – Breakfast
9a – 11:30a – first practice
Noon – Lunch
3p – 6p – second practice
6:30p – dinner
8p – 9p – free throw shooting (3rd practice)
9p- 10:30p – fill out daily journal
10:30 – lights out

We still have over 30 days before our first game!!! I don't know what's going to happen...

We can sign 2 Americans. We are about to sign one American named Donta Smith. He was drafted by the Atlanta Hawks a couple of years ago out of a JC. He's pretty good, especially over here, and even more important he's a good guy to be around. That helps. We are still trying to get a big guy. They want to sign Olumide Oyedeji who was drafted by the Sonics a few years ago and played a year with them. He played in China last year and led the league in rebounding. Hopefully we can get him over here.

Because the team was so bad last year, they get an additional foreign player exemption but it has to be a player with an Asian passport. So we can get someone from Japan, South Korea, etc... but I don't think they have any idea who to sign. Coach and I are trying to convince them to get a good point guard (ours are terrible) but I think they want another big... they don't seem to heed our suggestions.

I joked with Coach Weiss today after he got to be a passer in a shooting drill that he has to be the highest paid passer in China to which he figured to be about $450 per pass. I also found out that I can take my sweatshirt on and off about 200 times and that will kill an hour of practice time... it's the little things that keep you going.

So as I said, not real exciting but at least I'm getting paid for the time being so I can't complain too much. I'm cramming on my language lessons in case I have to leave sooner than expected...
Who knows???
Stay tuned...

Rt

18

Taiyuan

Upon our return from Foshan was the bombshell that our owner, Mr. Wang, had hired another Chinese coach to come in and help instill "discipline" on the team. It was very confusing and neither Coach Weiss nor myself could get any straight answers as to what was happening and why. They kept assuring Bob that he was still the head coach, but when the new coach came, we were relegated to watching from the sideline. At least for the first month or so, while we were still training for the start of the season, it seemed as if Coach Weiss was just a figure head. This left me without a role completely.

The new coach's name was Liu Tia (we called him Leo). He was relatively young and had never been a head coach; although he was an outstanding former player in the league. Like many former players who are new coaches, he was cocky and arrogant. There was only one way... his way, and I have to say, if they wanted more discipline, they got it with Liu Tia. As I said in my email back home, Coach Weiss and I did a lot of watching from the sidelines during practice. The only time I was ever really able to get involved was when I refereed our scrimmages. Once in a while, Liu would ask me to rebound in one of our shooting drills which just had a demeaning feel to it.

Liu always showed Coach Weiss great reverence, but for whatever reason, never gave me an ounce of respect. I could never figure out why. I always treated him respectfully but maybe my disgust for what was happening to Coach Weiss and I was more obvious than I realized. He never asked for my opinion on anything, never sat down with me to talk hoops, and actually never talked to me at all. He had no idea if I knew anything about the game and had no interest in finding out. I tried to kiss ass, but as we all know by now, I just don't know how. I, for sure, made an effort to ingratiate myself to Liu but he just never took to me. As I have since tried to piece together what might have happened between Liu and me, there are two factors that I keep coming back to that I can't help but think were contributing causes. The first of which, was this stupid strength and conditioning program.

The more I have talked to Coach Weiss about it, and the more that I thought about my observations of the Chinese staff while I was there; the more I started to figure out that I think they brought me over to China as a strength and conditioning coach... period and nothing else.

I think Coach Weiss convinced them that they needed a strength and conditioning guy but it was really his way to get himself an assistant coach over there to help. However, in the eyes of the Shanxi staff, a strength and conditioning guy was all I was. I don't think that the owner, GM or anyone else with the team knew that in actuality, I was a basketball coach and a damn good one.

In many respects, I think they saw me as Coach Weiss' valet.

A couple of things worked against me in my charade as a Chinese Strength and Conditioning Coach for the Shanxi Zhongyu. The number one thing was my own "strength" and "condition"; which was "weak" and "lacking". I've known a lot of real S/C coaches and none of them rock the undefined, pear-shaped, fat ass like I do. I'm a walking diabetes diagnosis just waiting to happen, so I didn't exactly imbibe the persona that I was attempting to portray.

The second thing that was much more tangible in nature was the fact that, all these Chinese mother suckers wanted to do was squats!

If the workout didn't include squats, it was a bulls*** workout in their eyes. In hindsight, I don't know why I just didn't have them do the squats that they wanted and be done with it, but for whatever reason, I tried to steer them away from that exercise as I had been told by the NBA strength and conditioning coaches that I spoke with before I left.

I should have known better when I saw their weight equipment on my first day there.

They didn't have a separate workout room. What little equipment they did have was shoved off to the side of one of the courts.

They had one set of dumbbells, two bench press racks and FOUR SQUAT RACKS!

And that was it!

Because of our time constraints, I couldn't do individual routines. I had to develop something that we could do as a group. We lifted three days a week, usually after our morning practice. I tried to incorporate what little equipment they had and still do something that could be beneficial. I decided to combine some various strength and conditioning techniques and create something of our own. It was part circuit training, part super-sets and it worked arms, legs and core. We had seven stations, I had them partner up, and we did three sets of as many reps as they could do in 30 seconds and then rotated stations.

Stations were:
1) Bench Press/ Box Jumps
2) Backward Leg Lifts/ Leg Curls
3) Bicycle Crunches/ Side Lunges
4) Tricep Curls/ Dumbell Curls
5) Leg Raises/ Shoulder Shrugs
6) Frog Jumps/ Forward Lunges
7) Flys/ Leg Circles

I knew that we wouldn't be building a lot of muscle but this wasn't the time of year to be doing that anyway. This workout accomplished a few things. It met the logistics that we had to operate with, but it also worked on tone, flexibility and most importantly, cardio conditioning. I was kind of proud of it really, given the tools available to me. I never could tell what Coach Weiss thought of it (if anything). I thought the players felt challenged by it but I was quite certain the Chinese staff was unimpressed. They wanted squats, bench, sit ups and more squats.

I don't think they ever got on board with me as a strength and conditioning coach. And ultimately, I think that led to my undoing. Once Liu started coaching, we did my routine one time. After that, he incorporated his own strength program that was heavy lifting on bench and squats. That was it. Apparently, that's all they wanted. They were doing eight (yes I said eight) sets of squats every other day (not to mention four sets of bench) and this wasn't just during the pre-season, it was all season long. I feel quite comfortable saying that Liu's workouts, at a minimum, led to a bad back injury to our best power forward and took the legs away from our best shooter.

The second thing that I think may have contributed to the erosion in my relationship with Liu Tia was a situation that happened at a pre-season practice with one of our American players, Donta Smith. It didn't help that Donta and Liu constantly bumped heads. Donta felt some loyalty to Coach Weiss and didn't like what had happened with the insertion of Liu Tia. What Donta had going for him was that he had some leverage because he was a really good player and thus he was given a longer leash. Donta was also a really good guy but he was young, just 23 years old. He quite often ended up in a battle of wills with Liu on a number of issues, and more often than not, he ended up winning. Coach Weiss would find himself acting as a buffer between the two and did the best he could to help the relationship between Donta and Liu remain workable.

Donta injured his ankle in our final pre-season game in Changchun, the capital city of the Jilin Province in Northeastern China. It was still three weeks before the season started, but Donta had done a number on that ankle and had to sit out for awhile. As he was beginning to come back, I was asked to help him rehab the ankle and get him ready to play. In part, I think they asked me to do this just to give me something to do but I took it on as a challenge to show them that I actually could contribute more than refereeing scrimmages.

One afternoon, as Donta was almost all the way back and ready to play, the team finished practice and went on to go lift weights. Donta still wasn't practicing full speed with the team and afterward, he refused to lift weights with them, claiming that he couldn't do it because of his ankle. Instead, he asked me to work with him on some shooting and individual offensive drills on the side. "On the side" in this case meant right in front of everyone on the team who was lifting weights on the sidelines of the court.

I have to say, that on that day, Donta and I had the best individual workout that I have ever been involved with. It wasn't a great workout because of anything that I did or because we were doing any special drills. It was a great workout because of how hard Donta worked. It was at least 45 minutes long (maybe longer) and he really worked his ass off. While everyone on the team (including Liu Tia) watched nearby, all eyes in the gym were on us.

It was unintentionally very conspicuous as it was happening. I could tell that his teammates were impressed with the workout because a bunch of them later came and asked if I could design something like that for them. When the workout was finished, I knew we had made an impression on everyone in the gym. For one of the few times ever, Liu Tia called me over to talk with him. He asked me who came up with the workout. I couldn't tell if he was asking because he was impressed or if he was pissed off. I told him that Donta and I had worked on it together. He told me it was okay but would have been better if Donta would have worked harder.

HA!!!

I had never seen anyone work harder in an individual workout before or since. What a joke Liu's comment was. The only problem was that he wasn't joking. I don't know if he felt like I, Donta, or both of us had shown him up in that workout, but ever since that day and for whatever reason, my relationship with Liu was very chilly.

***

----- Original Message -----
From: Rick Turner
Sent: Thursday, October 23, 2008 7:33 AM
Subject: China update

Ni Hao Goomers,

Thought I'd give you an update on what is going on in China. In part, because it continues to be semi-entertaining to witness and also because I need something to do. Hope this doesn't bore you too much. I don't have many pictures to send along because Bob's wife is home in Seattle for a couple weeks and she has been our chief pho-tog.

A few have asked me if I'm going to start a blog. I've considered it but not sure if it would be very interesting or not. For now, I'll just continue to send these un-interesting updates...

Going back to last week:

While continuing to negotiate a contract with Olumide Oyedeji, the team brought in some other Americans to tryout (although I think they each thought they were coming to sign a contract). Tyrone Washington, a 6'10 F/C from Miss. St who has been playing professionally for quite some time and Larry Turner (no relation) a 6'11 Center from Tennessee St.; came to us early last week. Tyrone is a guy who Coach Weiss recommended to the team quite a few weeks ago but they blew him off. Turner was a guy that they asked each of us about. Neither of us had much background info on him so Coach W called some NBA guys to check on him. They told us that Turner "had bad hands, wasn't a scorer, couldn't defend or rebound and doesn't block shots" (other than that... he's great). Coach W gave the team that info but apparently they didn't believe him because they brought him in anyway.

Washington had played in China before so he was pretty familiar with how these teams operate. As such, he decided on his own that he would not participate in any of the stuff in practice that might make him look bad. In other words, pretty much anything but scrimmaging. As he put it, "I'm here to play basketball, not go through all the bullsh**". So while Larry "No Chance" Turner worked his tail off during practice, TWash looked on from the sidelines waiting for the time to come in practice where he would wear Larry out. And he did. When Tyrone finally did play, he drug Larry up and down the court.

On Tuesday night, **Oct. 14**, we got word that they finally worked out an agreement with Olumide (pronounced o-LOO-mi-day). Lot's of money, a 4-bed room apt, his own driver and a personal trainer. Seemed kind of excessive to me but ???, more power to him, I guess...On Wednesday morning, we go out to meet the van and we have ANOTHER new American player that no one ever told us about, waiting to get a ride to practice. It's kind of awkward to see a guy in the morning that you had no clue was going to be there and trying to act like you did, which is what Coach W and I had to do. His name was Norman Nolan, a 6'8 forward from UVA. So now we are bringing 3 guys to practice that think they are trying out for a team that actually has no openings now that Olumide is signed. We go through the same routine only now, TWash watches both Larry AND Norman work out for over an hour before he decides to finally lace 'em up and join in the scrimmage.

By Thursday, **Oct. 16**, all the new Americans have heard about Olumide's signing but they are also hearing that he is having second thoughts because OO's heard what a circus that it is here and that Coach W has been essentially "demoted". So now, the 3 Americans think that they have a chance to get that last roster spot and the team is scrambling to assure OO that Coach Weiss is still the head coach and this current situation with the new Chinese coach is only temporary until the season starts. OO verbally agrees to a bigger contract in Iran and goes back to our team with his concerns about the coaching situation. Coach Weiss gets on the phone w/ OO to let him know what's going on from his perspective and somehow or another it all gets worked out by Friday and we get a signed contract. On Saturday, we send the 3 Americans home... but first...

I neglected to mention that TWash brought his own interpreter along with him. He's a young kid named Garrison who actually used to work for our team a couple years ago. A great guy and very good interpreter. Garrison stays with TWash during his

- 290 -

stay here in Taiyuan and they share a room. On Friday night, Garrison discovers that he has $900 missing from his wallet. He asks TWash about it who offers to give him the $60 to help him forget about it. Garrison smells something fishy. He calls the police. The Chinese PoPo show up at their door and they start talking to Garrison in Chinese about what happened and keep looking over at Tyrone as they speak. Before anything else can be said, Tyrone panics, goes and gets the $900 and tries to explain that he was just playing a joke on Garrison. Thank goodness for TWash, Garrison just wanted his $$ back and nothing happened beyond that. There would be no caning of TWash and no international incident. I couldn't help but feel a bit of disappointment about that.

Saturday, Oct 18 finds us on the team bus heading up a mountain on a one-lane, winding road with no shoulder. We are traveling up Sky Dragon Mountain to get in a workout. We get to the top of the Mt and find a big parking lot. The driver starts heading back down the mountain. We go a ways back down before he pulls the bus over and we look back at where we came from. There we see the hillside with many Buddhist Temples sprinkled all over it. Quite a sight (this is where I wish that I had better pictures). We get off the bus and we start walking back up the hill but not on the road. We walk up steps that lead from the road back to the parking lot and wind through all of the temples. As we stop to look inside each one, there are monks and incense burning throughout. But let me just say that this isn't a leisurely walk up a hill. They were stone steps; uneven and STEEP! As coach Weiss put it, "The escalator must be broken".

Once we get to the top, the Chinese coach (Coach Liu), had us go back down about 100 yds or so. Then he says that we need to sprint back up the steps 3 times. I actually do it and don't pass out which is a miracle in and of itself so I'm thinking there is something about the Buddhist shrines around me that is allowing this to happen. To answer your question, Bob waited for us at the top (bad knee). By the third one I'm am d-o-n-e, done; but Liu sends the players back down again. Now, he has one guy get on the others back and they climb the stairs with a guy riding piggy back. They each do this once and he sends them back down AGAIN! This time they have to "fireman carry" their partner up the steps.

Finally, the madness ends and we head back down the mountain. It actually was a good team building experience and a great memory to take home. As we wound our way back down the mountain, our American player Donta Smith was scared to death because of the sheer cliff on the shoulder of this narrow, winding road and the speed of which our driver chose to descend. He kept yelling "Slow Down Mr. Wang!" but of course Mr. Wang couldn't understand and we didn't have our interpreter with us for the trip. I noticed Coach Weiss was pretty quiet on the way down the mountain and he later told me that he was certain we would have a blown out tire because of how fast we were going and he was planning his exit strategy out of a burning bus.

Sunday, Oct 19 we finally got a well needed day off. I spent the morning listening to the Huskies not almost win another one against a NW rival. At one point I thought that the announcers, Bob Rondeau and Chuck Nelson were going to get in a fist fight in the booth but I quickly lost interest (as they did too) and I headed to breakfast faster than you can say "Let's send it down to Elise".

We can't just have a day off however.

Of course, we have to attend an 8p meeting at the practice facility; which is an hour each way and at least 90 minutes of meeting, where Coach Liu (and only Coach Liu) talks about the previous week of practice and the upcoming week of practice. It's like sitting in an Economics 201 lecture only the professor is speaking Chinese. In other words, it is beyond boring.

Highlights of the lect... I mean meeting...

Coach Liu instructed the players that it is bad for them to cover for each other. He told a story about when he was playing; one of his teammates went out drinking the night before and didn't show up for practice. The coach asked where the player was and everyone said that they didn't know. Apparently, the player had got drunk, walked in front of a taxi cab and was killed. We're still not sure how letting the coach know where the guy was the night before would have helped him, but that was the story. As Coach Weiss later said, there is nothing that helps team morale quite like encouraging teammates to "rat" each other out. Later, Coach Liu told the players that they need to do a better job keeping their journals. He read them and noticed that they were not sharing enough of their feelings about practices, only writing about what they did. He wanted them to know how the things that they are doing in practice are affecting them spiritually and emotionally. This prompted me to create my own faux journal entry in my notebook as I continued to endure this torturous meeting. It read:

> *Dear Diary,*
> *Today I watched as we dribbled up and down the court for 45 minutes. This makes me feel terribly bored. So much so that if I have to go though another day of this, I will attempt to gouge my eyes out with a spoon.*

I made the mistake of showing this to Donta in the middle of the meeting. His soda nearly came out his nose. Real mature stuff, I know, but you have to find ways to keep yourself mildly entertained... About 45 minutes in to the meeting, the translator quit translating what was being said and started making jokes instead. He still acted like he was translating though. For example, as Liu is talking, the translator is saying things like, "Coach, you talk too long and your stories are boring us all", "Coach, you are like a machine gun, I can not keep up with you", all the while acting as if he is translating. Liu is none the wiser. The meeting finally ended and we got back to the hotel at 10:30p; up again at 7a tomorrow for practice... So much for a day off.

Monday, Oct 20. Three days before the roster deadline and there is a problem with Olumide's passport. Olumide lives in Atlanta but we find out that he can't get a visa in the US. He has to go to the Chinese Embassy in Nigeria in order to get the visa. These things are never easy and it isn't like he just buys a plane ticket to Lagos, walks in and says "I'll have a visa please", and then leaves. There is a bunch of paper work to get through and on top of all that, we get word late in the day on Monday that the Beijing team who he played for last year might still have his rights. This is when I witness first hand why they call it a "Chinese Fire Drill" (whoever 'they' are). This is the point where we lose our translator for the rest of the week as he attempts to work on the Olumide Situation... which is not unlike the "Bonnie Situation", but without all the little pieces of brain. So Bob, Donta and I have been going to practice all of this week without a translator and with no clue as to what is being said at anytime. We also have no way to communicate ourselves to any of the Chinese. We are rendered useless, powerless and helpless; three "-less" words that no one wants to be straddled with. The second practice ends on Monday night and after a long a kind of stressful day, I looked forward to going to bed early with the remote control in my hand and nothing more then sleep on my mind.

Just as I got out of the shower at 8p, my phone rang. Bob is the only one who ever calls me so I was quite surprised to hear a Chinese voice at the other end of the line. It was Ren, the guy that took us to Pingyao a couple weeks ago. He called to ask if I wanted to go have a drink with him.

I didn't.

His English is just barely better than my Chinese and I knew it would be a painful night of trying to communicate. Plus, I was super tired, kind of grumpy and had to be up for practice at chi, I mean 7a. However, I thought that if I didn't take him up on his offer, I might not get another invite out; and I did want to see more of the city than just my room and the road between the hotel and practice. So I agreed to go for a quick beer.

He picked me up about a half hour later. He said he wanted me to go see his friend sing. Immediately, I'm thinking Karaoke. So... not only am I not wanting to go out, I definitely don't want to go listen to Chinese Karaoke. As it turned out, he took me to a really nice club. It was pretty cool inside and surprisingly classy. When we first got to the night club there were just a few people sitting around at tables. I'd say just a handful of people. We went and sat down with a couple of Ren's friends. A guy named Anya (probably not spelled that way but that's how it was pronounced) who Ren had known since they were kids growing up and Anya's girl friend whose name I did catch on to.

As we sit down, the waiter comes over and pours a fifth of cognac and a small (I mean a small) bottle of iced tea in a pitcher. Anya asks if I'd like some of his "wine". I tell him that I'll just have a beer and he laughs at me and tells the waiter that I want a Budweiser. "Why don't Americans like wine?" He asks. "They always want beer", he says. I try to tell them that I have to be up early for practice but I don't think they understand. Ren isn't drinking because he is driving (I was happy to hear but surprised at the same time) and Anya and his girl start in on the Cognac "wine".

A few minutes pass and the place starts to fill up a bit. Pretty soon the waiter comes back with my Budweiser... and 17 MORE!!! He sets 18 beers on the table. There are 4 of us, one of whom isn't drinking and two of which just cracked open a 5th of cognac. Who is going to drink 18 beers? The sage wisdom of my friend Greg Hunter enters my mind   immediately... "Drink the first, sip the second, refuse the third" he told me once. Before I can say "Let's send it down to Elise", I find myself in a game of Rock, Paper, Scissors with Anya, Ren and the girl. But this wasn't your fathers Ro-Sham-Bo. First you had to 'fire' to the beat of the music and second of course, if you lost... you drank.

The happy ending to this story is that I was home by midnight, all the beers somehow got drank and I was no worse for wear the next day. I'm thinking that wasn't the case for Anya and his girl...

Tuesday, Oct. 21 had to be the most boring of any of the practices I've been to at this point. No ability to communicate and nothing to do but watch from the sideline. The thing that turned my frown upside down though was that we got paid that day and it didn't seem to be quite as bad after that. We went back to the hotel after the morning practice and Bob called me to let me know that we had pictures to take after practice later in the afternoon and to bring a coat and tie. Since they were only headshots, I didn't need pants. I think you know where this is going...

After practice, we find out that along with head shots they are doing a team photo. Of course, I grabbed my pants earlier before we left, only to put them back saying to myself that I won't need them. Why would you not bring your pants??? Why not bring them just in case? So stupid. It would have taken 5 extra seconds. So out I walk into the gym for the team photo wearing my coat, tie, gym shorts and basketball shoes. I looked like an idiot. It was quite a sight. Luckily they were able to hide me in the back row, so hopefully it can't be seen... what a dum ass...

As far as the afternoon practice went... I decided to chart turnovers as a way to keep myself busy before we scrimmaged (I referee the scrimmages). We had 31 turnovers in the drills leading up to our scrimmage. This was in the drills alone, with zero defense playing against us. We're in serious trouble.

Wednesday, Oct 22 started out like any other day with the Shanxi Zhongyu. We got to the gym at about 8:45a for our 9a practice. Just as practice was about to start, a very large African American gentleman walked into the gym. I didn't think that they could have got the Olumide Situation figured out that quick and as he walked closer, I started to recognize him. It was Robert "Tractor" Traylor, who played at Michigan and was an NBA first round pick for George Karl when he went to Milwaukee somewhere around '99 or '00. Bob, Donta and I looked at each other and wondered, what the heck was going on? I went and introduced myself to "Big Trac" and he told me that he just signed a contract with our team and was just getting here from the airport. There was a very awkward, "uhhhh?" uttered by me and we tried not to let on that anything was wrong. Then the interpreter appeared after 3 days of exile and got Bob, Donta and me together. He told us that the GM asked that we don't tell Tractor anything about Olumide and that they were still working on his visa but needed a backup plan because the deadline is the next day. Tractor went back to the hotel to get some rest and we stayed for practice.

Tractor came back with us for the afternoon practice but he didn't suit up because there was a "problem" with his contract. He didn't know what the problem was and we didn't want to say anything because if the Olumide thing went T.U., we wanted Big Boy to play for us. So it was a weird afternoon. On a side note... 9 turnovers in our first 11 possessions of our scrimmage that day.

Thursday, Oct 23. Today... Robert is still here, although we haven't seen him today. The GM went to Beijing to register our foreign players with the league and we are assuming that Olumide Oyedeji will be one of them. Practices were rough. Players tired and still no interpreter...

Stay tuned...

rt

After Tyrone Washington was cut, our GM Zhang Bei Hei (ZBH), decided to keep Tyrone's interpreter Garrison around with us to act as a second interpreter for the team. I think it was, in part, because Liu didn't trust our current translator Joe, and he wanted his own guy in there who was young and more easily pushed around. I could never tell what ZBH thought of Joe because he spoke about him out of both sides of his mouth. When Joe wasn't around, Zhang Bei Hei would tell us that he didn't trust him, yet his actions toward Joe spoke much differently.

ZBH charged Joe with finding our third foreign player, the exemption that we received from the league for being so bad the previous season. The requirement was that the third foreign player had to have an Asian passport. He couldn't have dual passports; it had to be only Asian. Coach Weiss asked me to help find a good player that we could plug into this open roster spot and I reached out to various scouts, agents and coaches that I knew who could help get me a line on someone. I found about a dozen guys who fit the bill and sent emails to both Coach Weiss and Joe about the guys that I found. The team did nothing to act on any of my recommendations. Besides, what does a strength and conditioning coach know about talent evaluation?

Joe's mother-in-law lived in Kazakhstan and I think he was just angling for a trip to go see her because he (they? the team?) wouldn't look at anyone outside of Kazakhstan. I think that was because of Joe's influence.

ZBH sent Joe to Kazakhstan for a week to go scout players. In the meantime, a friend of Coach Weiss' told him about a Jordanian point guard who played college ball in the U.S. and was a very good player. His name was Sam Daghlas and he was a 6'5" point guard who was probably the best player to ever come out of Jordan. On a side note, in the eyes of FIBA, the international governing body of basketball, Jordan is an Asian country.

This was perfect. We had Donta already, a 6'7" wing who was super athletic, could score, defend and was a great 'team' guy. We were close to signing Olumide, who led the CBA (Chinese Basketball Association) in rebounding the previous season in Beijing, and now we had a third foreigner, which other teams couldn't have, who was an excellent point guard. It was just what the doctor ordered for our team who lacked athleticism, size and basketball IQ. The only problem was that (pardon me), Joe f'ed it all up.

I am fairly certain that Joe cut a deal with an agent in Kazakhstan that would pay him a portion of the commission on a kickback from any player that we signed from there. I think Joe was somehow working on ZBH to scare him away from signing Sam Daghlas. If that's not what happened, it at least appeared that way because the guy that we ended up signing from Kazakhstan was a total joke. His name was Ruslan but everyone called him Big Russ. He showed up fat, out of shape and had a much greater self-image of his game than what was actual reality. In my advanced age and debilitating lack of conditioning, I was only slightly worse than this guy. If I held an Asian passport, it would have taken me two weeks to get in enough shape to drag this guy's ass up and down the court. That's how bad he was.

When ZBH went to the league meetings in Beijing to officially register our team with the league, he was somehow convinced that Sam Daghlas held two passports, Jordanian and American. Coach Weiss was assured by Sam's agent that he only held a Jordanian passport, yet for some reason our GM, Zhang Bei Hei, refused to believe it and registered Big Russ instead of Sam. The only guy who ever supposedly saw Russ play was Joe, who later told us that he didn't actually get a chance to see him play; he just went off what some other people told him... So then why did we send you to Kazakhstan Joe?

Whoever was at fault, the fact that we didn't take full advantage of our third roster exemption was a crime. I don't know if ZBH waited too long to get serious about signing someone, if he was getting bad information from outsiders or even insiders (Joe), or whether it was just simple incompetence, but that should have never happened. The guy we ended up with was the worst player on our team; a team that had some pretty bad players.

***

----- Original Message -----
From: Rick Turner
To: Friends and family
Sent: Saturday, November 01, 2008 7:58 AM
Subject: another week in China...

Ni hao goomers,

In case you're wondering, they don't celebrate (is that the right word?), Halloween here in China; at least not in Taiyuan. I thought that they might of last week when I went to Pizza Hut. Yes, there is a Pizza Hut not too far from the hotel. It's about a 15 minute walk and the pizza is pretty good. It's not like a typical U.S. Pizza Hut though. It's more like a TGI Fridays without the wait staff wearing "flair". The thing is though, whenever you walk in the door, no matter what time it is, they say "Good Morning"... to EVERYONE! Not just fat, white guys. I should have known better about my assumption that they were gearing up for Halloween by hanging the Halloween decorations last week though; because in order to put up the Halloween decorations, they had to take down the Christmas decorations... no joke.

So I started taking notes a couple weeks ago. Things got so crazy before my last email that I wanted to make sure that I remembered as much as I could. That is what prompted me sending my last update. Things have not been nearly that entertaining over the last 10 days, for a number of reasons but we leave tomorrow for a 5 day trip and I didn't want to get too backed up with filling you in on things. We are going to play a couple of practice games in Jilin Province. I don't know much about it but have been told it's very cold.

I mentioned last time that the roster deadline was on Oct. 23rd. Our GM had to go to Beijing to register our foreign players with the league office. Each team can have two foreign players. We have Donta Smith and Olumide Oyedeji. The bottom four teams from last season, of which we were one, also get a third foreign player but that player must hold an Asian only passport. The rules here are a little confusing so I won't get bogged down in explaining in its entirety but this gives us an extra bullet heading into the season.

This player also needed to be registered on the 23rd and we had not done much in recruiting anyone for this spot. We were afraid that if we didn't have someone on the 23rd, we'd lose the roster spot. So the GM sent our main interpreter, Joe (more on this later), to Kazakhstan to find a player. Our league is starting a month late this season because of the Olympics, so most, if not all of the other leagues around the world have already started. This means that any "Asian" player that could really

- 296 -

help us is probably already under contract somewhere. So while Joe is in Kazakhstan looking for a player, Coach Weiss ends up finding a guy that played in the states, fits our need of a point guard perfectly and is Jordanian (considered Asia for our purposes). The guys name is Sam Daghlas and he is a 3-time MVP in Jordan and a member of their national team. Sam grew up in San Diego, so he speaks English and has some NBA experience, albeit in the D-league. Coach W gets word to the GM on the 22nd that Sam is available and wants to come. They spend the next 24 hours working out a contract. We are assured by Sam's agent that he is not a dual citizen (against the rules) and holds only a Jordanian passport.

So the GM gets to Beijing on the 23rd with everything worked out. We have Donta Smith (or as the Chinese call him, just... "Smiss"), we have OO locked up and we have the Jordanian point guard. Perfect...

One problem

As he registers Sam, the CBA tells our GM that he is a dual citizen of Jordan and the U.S. We have been assured by his agent that he isn't but the GM doesn't want to risk losing the roster spot by registering an illegal player. So he gets on the phone with Joe in Kazakhstan and asks him for a name of a guy. Joe ends up getting another big man that none of us have seen, including him, and he won't get here until late next week. We are pretty sure that he doesn't speak Chinese but also don't know if he speaks any English??? So it could be quite an adventure with this new guy. We'll see???

That was the excitement of the roster deadline. Now we're just waiting for OO, who got his visa yesterday and the unknown Kazakhstanian to get here so we can finally practice with our complete roster. Tractor left last Saturday. He went back to Detroit before apparently heading off to a team in Turkey sometime soon. He was so bored though, he kept coming to practice until and including the day he left. I think it was just so he could play cards with us on the van ride over to practice. It was a good move on his part too because they ended up being lucrative trips for him... much to our disgust.

On Sunday, Oct 26th
Coach Weiss went to Beijing for CBA coaches meetings. He's been gone all week and is meeting us in Jilin tomorrow.

Monday, Oct. 27th
The temperature was in the low 30's. The gym wasn't much warmer if at all. I wore a stocking cap throughout the whole practice, in part because I didn't bring any sweats to China (im not a "sweats" guy anyway). A couple weeks ago, one of the two major shoe companies over here (called Anta) sent Coach W and I, two big boxes of gear. Lot's of it. Sweats, shirts, shoes, shorts... the works. Great stuff. But they sent me size 4x... It fit like scuba gear. It is completely un-wearable. The shoes were too small as well. So I froze my tail off on Monday morning. On a side note, we passed a truck on the way to the gym that day. It was parked on the side of the road and had a bon fire built underneath it. I'm afraid to use my cell phone at the gas station, yet here was a guy that built a bon fire UNDER his pick-up truck. Funny.

Not much happened differently in the afternoon practice but afterward I got a new box of 'stuff' from Anta. Brought it back to the room, opened it up and found size 7x waiting for me. Now it's all too big... but at least I can wear it, so I won't be sending it back. They did however send the exact same size shoes which I will be sending back. (don't I sound ungrateful?)

Tuesday, Oct 28th

In Taiyuan, as in many places in China, the city's heat is centralized. So, until the gov't fires up the coal-burning boilers, there is no heat for almost everyone in the city. On Tuesday, they fired them up. Now I understand why the air quality is so bad here. I'm not saying that it worries me or anything but I did find it odd when I discovered my pet canary dead on Tuesday morning... go figure.

It doesn't matter now though because at least I have sweats to wear. Right? I slide on my 7x sweat pants and head to practice. Everyone comments that I'm not wearing shorts today. For whatever reason, the players were always concerned that I was too cold. I never had been too cold until the previous day before but it never mattered... wouldn't you know it though, on this day, it must be 85 degrees in the gym! It feels like a sauna in there as they try and get the heaters adjusted after firing up the coal plants for the winter. I didn't wear shorts under the sweats so I was stuck there; sweating like Jack Tripper during a Mr. Roper drop-in, wearing my 7x sweats and big heavy sweatshirt shirt watching another day of monotony as our players dribble up and down the court for 45 minutes straight.

My mind wanders during this time...

I've never seen a more loogy-hocking, nose-picking, snot-rocketing people in my life. I'm referring to the Chinese, not our team in particular, although they too fit in just fine with this description. I know it sounds terrible but it's true. Maybe it's the coal filled air or the dry climate, I don't know, but it makes me want to throw-up in my mouth multiple times a day as I watch it. In fact, the ashtrays in the hotel lobby have more spit than butts in them and the sidewalks are teaming with "pavement oysters" that I continually dodge daily on my morning pilgrimage to McDonalds for a hot chocolate and egg mcmuffin, 'bu dan' (or 'no egg' as we say in Chinese).

It may sound like an exaggeration but I promise I wouldn't say it if it wasn't true. It was one of the first things that I noticed when I came to China and it has been un-relenting ever since. If I don't see a dozen people with their fingers two and a half digits up their nose everyday... I've never seen one. So it occurs to me as I'm sweating my ass off, watching practice, grossing out on players' loogy-ing on the court, that if I ever do write a book about this experience the title will be:

Coaching in China... Drowning in a River of Spit

The rest of the week was pretty uneventful; especially without Coach Weiss there and no interpreters until yesterday. I say plural interpreters because it looks as if the team has hired Garrison now as a second interpreter. Who knows what was behind that move but we'll see how it works out.

It was kind of awkward yesterday though because they were each at practice. I never know who I should listen to. I feel like if I listen to Garrison, I'm 'cheating' on Joe.

It's weird. It's also tough though because Joe has a (I don't know what to call it???) "wisdom hair?", that is growing out of the side of his cheek. It is literally 6-7 inches long, pure white and a total distraction. It is definitely in a place where he could shave it if he wanted to, but for whatever reason doesn't. Did you ever see Uncle Buck? Remember when Buck has to go see his niece, Maisy's principal because she is too much of a dreamer and a silly-heart in class? Remember the big, huge mole on the principal's face that was a total distraction to Buck? He introduced himself to her by saying, "Nice to meet you, I'm Buck Melanoma... Moley Russell's wart. I mean uncle. I'm Maisy Russell's uncle."? That is what it is like talking to Joe. I always feel like I'm staring at it and afraid I'll slip up and ask him what "Coach Long Hair... I mean Liu" just told the team.

Smiss and I were laughing hard though yesterday because Coach Liu had his regular talk to the team after practice. Joe was there to interpret for us. Coach Liu was telling the players that they need to stay calm while they play. Play hard but keep their head and remain calm. At least that's what we assumed he meant because Joe was telling us that the players should stay clam while they play. Remain clam, stay clam and play clam. It gave me and Donta a few chuckles on the way home...

Enough for now I guess. Off to Jilin tomorrow. I'll let you know how it goes. I'd offer an opportunity to unsubscribe to these emails but I suppose you're only a delete button away as it is anyway...

Stay tuned
rt

Shortly before our trip to Jilin for our final two pre-season games, I started to hear some rumblings that made me extremely uncomfortable. Joe started asking how I would feel about coaching the Shanxi Zhongyu junior team. I am normally a pretty good team player but started feeling like that easy going quality also made me susceptible to getting run over by people. I decided to try and stand my ground on this issue. If Coach Weiss would have asked me to coach the junior team, I would have done it in a heartbeat but, he didn't, and that wasn't why I had come all that way over to China.

The junior team consisted of twelve, 15-18 years olds who also lived there at the practice facility but they never played any games. All they did every day, three times a day, was practice; separately from the senior team. When Joe brought it up with me, I tried my best to ignore it in hopes that it would just go away.

I knew I needed to figure out a way to make myself valuable to Liu, ZBH and Coach Weiss.

I spoke to Coach Weiss about various things I could do to carve out a role for myself that Liu could get behind. Bob wanted me to remain with the team but he was still trying to get a clearer idea of how he, himself was fitting in. We realized that no one in China was doing much in the way of video work to help coach their players and scout their opponents, so I decided to take on that roll. I had actually planned on doing something like this all along, but now Coach Weiss would have to try and convince Liu that it was a worthy pursuit.

We left for Jilin and two pre-season games, but instead of being on the bench, next to Coach Weiss as we had both anticipated; I was in the stands holding a video camera. It wasn't what our original plan was, but at least I was still there doing something.

Before I left for China, I purchased my first laptop. Unbeknownst to me, at the time that I bought the laptop, was that it had a video editing program called Microsoft Movie Maker. I had also brought over with me some equipment that would allow me to download video on to my computer. It was a process that I probably made more complicated then it should have been, but I was proud of myself for getting it figured out without having the resources there in China (namely the language barrier) to help me.

The process was to videotape the game, then go back to the hotel or apartment and transfer the video to the computer. This had to happen in real time so just getting the video transferred took a couple of hours. If a game ended at 10 p.m. and we went to eat before we went home, the transfer might take until 2 a.m. Once the video was downloaded, then I could work on putting something together. I wanted to be as thorough as I could; in hopes of not only impressing Coach Weiss but also the Chinese staff.

I would log every single play and then build individual videos for different players as well as team breakdowns of offense and defensive sets for the coaches. Once I had everything built, I would burn individual DVD's and hand them out to those who needed them.

We were in a place called Changchun, the capital of the Jilin Province and it was flipping cold. Really cold. I woke up early our first morning there and set out to find a McDonald's so Coach Weiss and I could continue our morning ritual of hot chocolate, OJ and Egg McMuffins. I piled on multiple layers of clothes and headed outside in a light flurry of snow in search of the Chinese version of the infamous golden arches. As I walked down the slippery sidewalk away from the hotel, I got lost in my thoughts.

With my mouth closed, I used the back of my tongue to suction out some milky yellow mucus from the back of my throat leading up from my sinuses. The warm, slippery substance filled my mouth with a satisfaction that the impending expectorant would fly far and fast. I used the front of my tongue this time to consolidate the package with help from the roof of my mouth. I pursed my lips and simultaneously inhaled deeply through my nose. The cold air burned as it filled my lungs. I cocked my head back and picked out a target. It was the trunk of a small cherry tree that had lined the road that I was walking on. With a violent push, I forced the cool Changchun air from my lungs and returned it from where it came, sending the tightly formed mucus parcel along with it. The DNA bomb hurdled toward its intended interceptor tumbling over itself as it attained maximum velocity. As it approached its deciduous destination, this blue-ribbon loogy veered wide right like a Scott Norwood field goal and landed abruptly on the unsuspecting street below. The unpleasant sound that it made upon impact fell somewhere between a thud and a splat; and was loud enough to quickly wake me up from my waking disconnect. What am I doing? Have the Chinese mores gotten the better of me? Do I now feel like I have carte blanche to just hock loogies wherever and whenever I want?

I was immediately thrust back to my old neighborhood and Jean Hawkins, who lived four houses down from us when I was a kid. Ralph and Jean Hawkins had two kids, Chad and Amy, who were older than me but who I really liked to play with. Chad was

- 300 -

three years older than me and Amy was one. I liked to spend time at their house and did so quite often. In fact, it was in the Hawkins' backyard swimming pool where I, along with most of the neighborhood kids, learned to swim.

On my way home for dinner one warm summer night when I was about six years old, I walked out their door and headed back toward my house. As I walked through their yard, I hocked a loogy in their driveway. I never thought anything of it and continued on to my house, getting closer and closer to the promise of mom's tuna casserole. I reached my house and readied myself for dinner. Shortly thereafter, we heard a knock at the front door. It was Jean Hawkins. She explained to my mom that I had spit on their driveway and that she thought it was disrespectful and uncalled for. I remember her saying that it was tantamount to me leaving a banana peel in their yard. My mom made me get a paper towel and some household cleaner and go clean my spit off the Hawkins' driveway. I never did anything like that again. I still spit, don't get me wrong, but I just did it when people weren't looking and where no one would step in it. It seemed as if the Chinese had broken me and I was quickly becoming one of them. I mentally slapped myself to try and (as Eminem would say) "snap back to reality".

I eventually found the McDonald's that I was looking for, about a mile away from the hotel, where I bought a bag full of caloric goodies to share with Donta and Coach Weiss. Three Egg McMuffins, two Sausage McMuffins, two hot chocolates, two hash browns, two OJ's and a coffee. I timed my adventure perfectly because I got back to the hotel just as everyone was getting on the bus to go over to our morning shootaround at the arena. I handed out my bounty to the appropriate recipients and shortly thereafter, the bus crawled away from the hotel parking lot, en route to the site of our game later that night.

I remember having an internal struggle with myself as I sat alone on the bus ride over to the building. I was trying to remain positive while I was, at the same time, questioning what was going on around me. There was a twinge of paranoia as I wondered if anyone actually wanted me there. I would fight off that paranoia by reminding myself that I was being too narcissistic. Not everything was always about me. I tried to remember, while I was worried about what they (the Chinese staff) were thinking of me, the fact was probably that they weren't thinking of me at all. I mean that in a good way. I questioned why Liu didn't like me, when in all likelihood, I probably didn't even register on his radar. As we sat on the bus on our way to shootaround, I couldn't help feeling lonely and isolated; hopefully this Egg McMuffin could help fill the void, because as we all know, nothing cures loneliness like food (obviously I've been lonely a lot).

I was anxious to see how Liu ran a shootaround and I was surprisingly impressed with what we got accomplished that morning. Liu asked Coach Weiss about installing a press breaker which we hadn't done yet to that point, and Coach Weiss asked me if I had one that we could use. I did. It was a simple but effective play that I learned from Ed Pepple at Mercer Island High School almost 15 years earlier; one that Coach Pepple called "3 Across".

I showed it to Coach Weiss and then he showed it to the team. Liu was impressed with the play and told Coach Weiss that he liked it, thinking that it was Coach's play. Bob told Liu that I had given the play to him, I think in an effort to help ingratiate me to him. I don't think it worked though because Liu seemed completely unmoved by this news. When Liu had a question about it, he asked Bob instead of me. Then, Bob would have to ask me. I would answer him and he would tell Liu. Add one or two translators in the mix and it became a veritable game of Chinese Telephone. I am not trying to say that Liu wouldn't talk to me. My point is that I think there was a protocol that Liu followed that was kind of like a military chain of command. Bob and I were oblivious to it at the time, and more often than not, came away from Liu just shaking our heads, baffled by what was going on. I think if someone would have just explained the custom or protocol to us, it would have made sense and we would have been fine with it. While it was happening though, it just seemed silly.

After installing my press breaker play and now feeling buoyed by my new found contribution to the team; I thought that I would turn my frown upside down and make a more concerted effort to get involved. During the walk-through of one of our opponent's plays at the shootaround, I asked Liu how he wanted to defend a certain portion of the play, just to clarify it for everyone. Liu answered and we moved on. I never thought about it again until a couple weeks later when Joe told me that I wasn't supposed to ask Liu questions in front of the team. When I did this, Liu thought that I was shaming him in front of the team and thus I made him "lose face". To me, the question was asked to help our team, not make him look bad. And in fact, he didn't look bad when he answered it.

How would we have known something like this if no one ever told us? If I would have asked any other American coach the same question they would have answered and moved on, never thinking twice about it. They would have appreciated the question for trying to make us a better team, not an attempt to embarrass the coach. I was starting to think that no matter what I did, I couldn't win with Liu.

I understand that there are cultural differences, and I never expected that everyone should adapt to Bob and I, but I thought there should have been a bit more understanding on their part.

I also found out later that day in Changchun that Liu had a rule about no eating or drinking on the bus. Earlier, I had come strolling on to the bus, loaded to the gills in Micky D's, completely oblivious to any rules that Liu had about food. It must have appeared like I was taking a pee in his eye. No wonder this guy didn't like me. But again, how would I have known if no one ever told me?

Our first game in the Jilin Province was against the Liaoning Dinosaurs, the CBA championship runners-up from a year ago. We all met in Liu's room before the game where he went over the scouting report of Liaoning. It was an hour-long meeting that felt like four. At one point in Joe's translation he said that the Dinosaurs had a player who "was almost 7'0" feet tall, I think he is 6'12", he told us. I looked up at Donta when Joe said it and we each smiled knowingly. I couldn't help but think that there were only 51 more of these pre-game meetings left.

My random thought of that day came earlier at lunch.

When we were on the road, all the team's meals were prepared by the hotel where we were staying and served family style to us in one of their private rooms. We would sit around two or three big, circular tables with a Lazy Susan in the middle of each. The staff would bring out these great dishes of Chinese food which usually had a culinary influence of the region we were in at the time. The food was "da bomb" and there was lots of it. What was funny though, was the way our guys ate.

I quickly discovered that Emily Post held no influence among the Chinese. When our food was delivered, our guys attacked it like lions feeding on an impala. It was served family style yet there were no serving spoons. Everyone used their own chopsticks to take food out of each bowl or plate. They reached across each other, stabbing at their kill and quickly shoveling it back onto their plates so they could swiftly attack it once again. They would hold their bowls up to their mouth and loudly slurp any noodles or soup that the chefs had provided for their enjoyment. Any piece of meat would go into their mouth and they would render it clean before spitting the pristine bone back onto their plate, where it would collect with others, nearly re-creating a skeleton of their prey.

Every single meal, not once in a while, but every single meal, I thought of the **Seinfeld** episode when George was accused of double dipping at the wake of his girlfriend's Aunt Clarice, as Timmy told George, "It's like putting your whole mouth in the dip".

Every time they went back for second helpings, with their fouled chopsticks, I felt like they were putting their whole mouth back in the dish. I had a decision to make. I could either be disgusted by it and allow it to ruin my meal, or I could join the Romans. I chose the latter.

Our first game on that pre-season trip to Jilin was pretty interesting because there were a lot of dynamics happening at once. It was Liu's first game with us, it was Bob's first game since Liu's arrival, Olumide was supposed to be there at some point for his first game with us, I was relegated to videotaping the game from the stands, and the owner was there to sit on the bench.

I quickly went from feeling like a part of the team to feeling like somewhat of an outsider. It was a very familiar feeling. It brought me back to my time with the Sonics and stirred up many of the same emotions that nudged me toward leaving back then. I didn't like the feeling of being an outsider. I wanted to contribute. My vision of sitting next to Coach Weiss all season and helping him help us compete for a CBA championship had been kicked out from under me. I found myself oozing cynicism and contempt while I secretly rooted for Liu to be a bust. I tired to figure out a scenario where our players could be successful but Liu would implode. I didn't know if that was even possible.

I took my walk of shame up to some empty seats, opposite the team's benches, and set up my video equipment. My semi-OCD meticulousness drove me to try and film the perfect video. If I wasn't going to be allowed to sit on the bench and coach, I wanted to at least show these guys that I was the best videographer of all time.

Midway through the first quarter, Olumide arrived at the arena straight from the airport, came out from the dressing room and joined our team on the bench. He had a bunch of built-in respect from our Chinese players because of his previous success in the league with other teams. His presence provided an immediate lift to our boys.

Liu had installed a zone defense that he called "the best zone in China". Coach Weiss and I hated it because we thought it was too over-extended. Much to my surprise, the zone looked pretty good when Liu decided to put it on midway through the second quarter. It actually was the thing that got us back in the game when it looked like we might get blown out early.

I was worried about Donta as it seemed like he was starting to wear out his welcome with Liu and the Chinese. It's one thing to be high maintenance when you're playing well but when you're not; that routine can wear out quickly. Donta was coming off a groin injury, and although he played a good all-around game, he didn't shoot it very well and I know they were depending on him to score. On top of that, this was the game where he badly sprained his ankle. I started thinking that he might get cut.

The team went in at halftime trailing by eight points. Mr. Wang was not happy with their performance and chewed them out for the entire 15 minute halftime and then some. As the buzzer sounded to start the second half, our team was no where to be seen. The referees and our opponents didn't even notice that we were still not out of the locker room. They all looked at each other, shrugged their shoulders and wondered where the heck we were. I could see from my perch way above the floor, that one of the referees had gone back underneath the stands to go fetch our team. It was a full five minutes later before we came out of the dressing room, fresh from a verbal beat down from Mr. Wang to start the second half (without a warm up).

Wang's venomous inspiration was no help as we went on to lose a close one; in a game that we essentially gave away. Liu's game management at the end was a train wreck, but I was later told that the owner was really the one who was calling the shots. I think it was a little of both. One good thing that came out of the game was our first chance to get to see Olumide. In just over one half of play he pulled down 14 rebounds. It was obvious right away that he was going to help. He really had a knack for rebounding.

That may have been the only good thing to come out of it. Along with the injury to Donta, and the unknown time that he would miss because of it, I was observing Coach Weiss from afar. For the first time in the two months we had been in China, he looked like he was hating it. His normally happy-go-lucky spirit looked as if it was taking a beating and the fun of this adventure overseas was being slowly sucked away. As upset and frustrated as I was with the situation, I could tell that he was even more so. As dumb as this may sound; all of a sudden, I didn't feel so alone.

We stayed for the second game that followed ours that night between Jilin and Xinjiang. We were scheduled to play Jilin the following night and I stayed up above to tape it while the team watched from down below. My plan was to do a really detailed and extensive scouting report to include video; which would again, try and showcase my value to the team. With about four minutes left in the game, I looked down to see that everyone from our team had left. No one came to get me. I had no idea where our hotel was or what it was called and no way of telling anyone if I did.

I gathered all my stuff, my backpack and video camera, and headed out to the frigid night air as all the other spectators poured out from the building after the game. I had a general idea of what direction the hotel was in but I wasn't sure. I started down the street that I thought looked vaguely familiar from our bus ride earlier when I spotted two young guys trying to hail a cab. Even from the back, they looked kind of familiar. As I got closer, I could see that it was two of our players, Wei and Zhai who had stuck around to watch the second half of the game, after the rest of the team had left. It was a fortunate bounce in my direction that I found them; otherwise I could still be walking around Changchun, looking for that hotel.

I jumped in the taxi with them and we headed back. I would be up until 2 a.m. editing a video package for tomorrow's opponent. I finally called it quits and went to bed shortly before 2:00, intending to get up early the next morning to complete it. When I got up the next day, I discovered that I somehow screwed up how I saved the project on my laptop. None of the work that I had done the previous night was saved anywhere. I would have to start the whole thing over.

19

Dalian

I'm writing you to catch you up on places I've been...
and you held this letter probably got excited, but there's nothing else inside it...
Didn't have a camera by my side this time
Hoping I would see the world through both my eyes
Maybe I will tell you all about it
When I'm in the mood
To lose my way with words

- John Mayer "3 x 5"

We had been in China for over two months and we still had another 10 days before the regular season started. As the road opener approached, I was doing my best to fly under the radar and avoid getting assigned to coach the junior team. The monotony of the daily routine was starting to get broken up with a spate of public appearances that we made around the city as the build up to the first game kicked into high gear.

This was all very new to me and I was a little embarrassed to even be partaking in any public appearances. Coach Weiss was a bit of a rock star in Taiyuan because of his NBA background. The team and the league did a great job of promoting him and people recognized Bob when we went to various places around town. Many wanted to shake his hand or have their picture taken with him when they saw him. When the team scheduled us for a couple of autograph signing functions, I was a little leery as to whether they wanted me to go, or if they were just asking me so as not to offend Coach Weiss. You know, with me being his valet and all.

I didn't want to be embarrassed by going and finding that no one wanting my autograph. As a disclaimer, I don't think anyone <u>should</u> have wanted my autograph. I was a nobody there anyway, who didn't play in the NBA and really had no previous career or background to admire. Beyond that, I've never understood the whole autograph thing anyway. I guess it is just proof that you met somebody famous but I certainly didn't fall into the "famous" category. I just didn't want the embarrassment of feeling even more left out than I already did. Despite my reservations about the whole thing, I felt like I had no choice but to go to these public appearances.

Our driver picked up Coach Weiss, Donta, Olumide and me. We met up with three other of our Chinese players at a local university while the rest of the team and Coach Liu went to an appearance at different school across town. It was far more organized than I anticipated. When we arrived at the school, there were actually quite a few people already there waiting for us as we drove in.

Since we couldn't read or understand the language, we never actually knew how or if the team was promoting us. We didn't know what was being written in the local newspapers and we had no idea if there were any advertisements about our upcoming games on radio or television. All we could do is judge it by results and this was the first opportunity that we had to see if anyone actually cared about this team.

We drove up to an outdoor basketball court at the school and got out of the van to see and hear about 200 people cheering loudly for us. We were ushered over to a long table where there was some really nice, big and glossy team posters of which, to my surprise, I found myself featured prominently. We didn't know anything about the posters and had never seen them before. The posters had a red and gold background with I think about seven of us photo shopped together in various poses. There was Coach Weiss, Coach Liu, Donta, Wei, Zhai, Olumide and me. They handed out these posters along with ones of the entire team, gave us each a black Sharpie, and let loose the hounds.

We were mobbed.

I could tell that Olumide and Donta were kind of going through the motions after a while and quickly became bored with the whole production of it all. However, I came at this from a different place. I had never signed an autograph before and had spent years watching pro athletes get put off by these people who idolized them; failing to understand that without these fans, they would have no job playing this simple game.

I always remembered my first year as an intern at the Sonics back in 1989. We played at the old Seattle Center Coliseum and were playing the Detroit Pistons. This was in the glory days of the Piston's "Bad Boys" run; with Isaiah Thomas, Bill Laimbeer, Joe Dumars, Dennis Rodman and "The Microwave", Vinnie Johnson.

After that game in early December, which the Sonics won 120-95 (Ellis had 30, X had 26 and 10), I had to go back to the visitor's locker room to deliver something to someone there. As I was walking back out of the Piston's locker room toward the court, I was moving at a brisk pace. Bill Laimbeer was in front of me, walking slowly, with a bag over his shoulder. He had a pretty crappy game that night with just two points and three rebounds; and as we all know, he was a pretty competitive guy. As he was turning left to go get on the team bus, I had caught up to him and was now walking by. Just as this was happening, a young kid of about 10 or 11 years old, walked up to Laimbeer, held up a pen and paper and said, "Mr. Laimbeer, can I have your autograph?"

The 6 foot 11 inch, 245 pound forward from Notre Dame looked down contemptuously at the young boy who barely came up to his waist and snarled, "F*** you kid" and coldly walked away toward the bus.

I never forgot that.

Even though I've never had and never will have the same success or fame that Bill Laimbeer and 1000's of others have enjoyed; I'll never be put off if someone asks for an autograph. I could have sat there all day signing for people, and I have to admit, I was pretty stoked that the team had included me on the poster. It made me feel like they thought a little higher of me than I was thinking they did.

Later that same day, we found out at the last minute that we were moving out of our hotel and into some apartments that were located at a different hotel. By now, I had become accustomed to where we were living, had my routine together, and was getting to know the staff there quite well. I liked where we were. Coach Weiss had his wife there, and the accommodations for them were just too small and Olumide was now with us and he was contractually promised a three-bedroom apartment; so Coach had been working on getting us all moved. I give him a lot of credit because he was pretty persistent about it and the place we moved to was one of the few five-star hotels in the city. The staff there actually could speak a little English; there was a health club and spa right there and the televisions received channels like ESPN and HBO.

It was called the World Trade Hotel and it was modeled after the New York towers of the same name.

Beyond the small inconvenience of moving, the comparison between the two places was night and day. The World Trade Hotel was much, much nicer; but we had one problem.

Donta refused to move.

To me, this was Donta's weakest moment of the trip. He had been with us for over a month, putting up with some questionable Chinese coaching philosophies, and was probably a little tired of it all. He had just watched Olumide come in and be treated like the second coming of Bill Russell and he probably had a little resentment because of that and as we found out later, his mom was dealing with some health issues back home that worried him and probably put him a little out of sorts.

Regardless of the reasons, he was behaving like a petulant child and acting totally out of character from the guy we had grown to know so well over the past few weeks. After all the hard work that Coach Weiss had put in to get us moved to this nice place, Donta just flatly said no. I have to come clean on what could have been another major factor in his refusal; he also found out that he would be sharing an apartment with the new guy from Kazakhstan... and me.

Admittedly, I wasn't super excited about living with a couple of 24-year olds either, but at that point, I was just happy to have a job and was not going to do anything to cause any waves. It was the night of November 13th and we were leaving for our first regular season game early the next day. We had to get everything moved out of the old hotel and into the new one that night.

Later on, sometime around 9 p.m., Joe would be picking up the new Kazakhstan player from the airport (who we had yet to meet or even see play), and delivering him to the new apartment. I felt bad for Coach Weiss though; because he seemed to be so excited about getting us all moved to the new hotel and yet Donta was totally harshing his buzz.

After a little "man-to-man" chat with Coach Weiss back at the Longcheng Hotel, Donta finally acquiesced, and he too packed his things for the move across town. Once we got there and got all of our stuff moved in; Bob, Tracy, Donta and I did a tour of our new digs and stopped to have a drink in the piano/lobby bar before going back to our rooms to pack for our trip to Dalian the next morning.

We raised our glasses to what lay ahead. The 70-plus day grind of the seemingly endless pre-season was finally over. We could now look ahead to what we ultimately came here to do: win a CBA championship. It seemed like we had packed about two years of practicing into the last two months and now the fun part was finally going to start.

***

Side bar: You may notice on my emails home that I start with a greeting of "ni hao goomers". It was done somewhat tongue-in-cheek but as most of you know, "ni hao" basically means hello in Chinese.

"Goomers", first of all, isn't spelled right. I couldn't find anyone who could tell me how to spell it so I just wrote it out the way it sounded (sort of), but it essentially means "my very good friend". If you say it with a hard G like the word "gum", it is intended for a man. If you say it with a soft G, like "germ", it is intended for a woman...

----- Original Message -----
From: Rick Turner
To: Friends and family
Sent: Saturday, November 15, 2008 8:49 PM
Subject: Shanxi Zhongyu- The Musical

Ni hao goomers,

I currently sit in a hotel room in Dalian, China, getting ready for our opening game of the season tomorrow night against the CBA runner-up from a year ago, the Liaoning Dinosaurs. It's been a couple weeks since I updated you so I thought I'd give it a try before the season got underway. I also thought that before the script plays itself out here this season, I should introduce you to some of the cast...

Before I do however, I'll pause to let you know a couple things that are on my mind currently.

Number one is a music tip. Try the new Ray LaMontagne disc, **Gossip in the Grain**... Wonderful, just wonderful.

Number 2?

About 20 minutes ago I unknowingly ate donkey at the restaurant's buffet. My gag reflex has taken over and I am seriously considering a new vegan lifestyle. I'm not happy about it. They had some really good sweet and sour pork and a great chicken dish (boneless no-less) which gave me the confidence that it was a pretty tame spread. I let my defenses down. They had another dish that looked like big strips of bacon with some vegetables mixed in. Everyone knows that anything with bacon is good so I loaded up on it. With about two bites left, I found out that it wasn't bacon, but donkey. Not good times, bad times...bad times.

There has been lots of stuff going on over the last couple weeks but in hindsight, none of it seems all that entertaining or interesting. Last time I told you about one of our interpreters named Joe, this time I thought I tell you about some of the others involved here on a daily basis.

Coach Weiss (or as the Chinese call him Boba Wee-sah) is the head coach but there has been a Chinese coach brought in to "install discipline" to the players. I think I mentioned this a few weeks ago. His name is Coach Liu. He is a former player in the CBA who I heard had a very productive career and is well regarded as a former player (not unlike me). He is among the top 5 scoring leaders in CBA history and I'm told there was even a book written about him. As a coach, he is still green. His playing career just recently ended so he doesn't have a lot of coaching experience. But that doesn't mean that he is short on confidence. As a player, he played many years for the "Bobby Knight of China" on the Chinese Red Army team. So... he is no nonsense, very sure of himself, as well as the right way of doing things.

Curfew at 10:30.

Lights out at 11.

That means no talking after 11. Not to your roommate, not on the phone; nor to yourself. No going out after a game. Phone calls to your parents or girlfriends after the game must be brief. No talking during stretching or weight lifting. If you want to chat, go to your teammate's room after practice. There was a rumor going around this week that Gary Payton was going to sign with this team.

Uhhhh...right.

I would have loved to see Gary's reaction to Coach Liu. High, high comedy.

I don't think this is an attribute unique to Coach Liu but, man, can he talk. I think most Chinese coaches are pretty long winded but you never get used to it. He seems to gives at least 3-4 "inspirational" speeches per day. If we get any more inspired, we'll be building a rocket and racing the Russians to the moon. It is incessant. Usually there are references to soldiers, war or great moments in China's history but sometimes it is just a story to motivate. I jotted down some to pass along:

"Everyday, the zebra wakes up thinking he must run all day to avoid being eaten by the lion. The lion wakes up everyday thinking, today I must catch a zebra" - a reference to the fact that even though we are working hard in practice to "avoid being eaten", other teams are working hard to eat us.

"Every great war is followed by terrible disease" - saying that we should never quit fighting... I think. Not really sure.

"Often, just one step can be the difference between being great and being a loser" - talking about working on details. This is a consistent theme.

"To fill up your mistakes, you must learn from your shames" - don't think that was translated correctly but essentially telling them to play smarter.

"Don't be a flower in the greenhouse. Be a mighty tree in the forest" - they can't stay protected from the elements forever.

The funniest thing about Coach Liu to me is one that hits close to home. Every time he demonstrates something at practice, he does it at 200mph. It reminds me of working for my dad when I was in college. One day, I was digging a ditch for a sprinkler system. My dad drove up to the job site, saw me shoveling and didn't think I was working hard enough. He came over and said "That's not how you dig a ditch son, gimme the shovel". He jumped in the ditch and shoveled dirt as hard and as fast as he could for about 10 seconds. He jumped out of the ditch, completely breathless, hair all messed up and ready to pass out... threw the shovel at me and said "Now that's how you dig a ditch". That... is Coach Liu

Our second Chinese coach is Coach Xia (she-AH). He is like your stereotypical older Chinese man. If you put a pair of Dorothy Michael's glasses and some suspenders on him, Coach Xia would be the Chinese Larry King... "Foshan, hello?" He has one of the best smoker's voices of all time and a long career as a coach in China. He is well respected around the league and most important I think for him, has the ear of the owner. Before Coach Liu arrived, Coach Xia was the only Chinese voice on the coaching staff. He didn't speak often but when he did, he spoke forever. 40 minutes straight would not be unusual. With the new coach here though, Xia has really taken more of a back seat and mentoring role for Coach Liu. One day at practice when we had 3 Americans here (I think it was Donta, Monty Wilson and Sean Lampley), Coach Xia showed up wearing a full sweat suit but with dress shoes on instead of court shoes. The guys thought that was hilarious and ever since that day, the players have called him "Wingtips"... unbeknown to him of course. He seems gruff at first but I think he is a very good man who I hope to get to know better as the season continues.

I mentioned last time that we have hired a second interpreter. I don't know if both will be with us all season but it is kind of nice to have a second person that can help in translating. I told you about Joe. The other interpreter is named Garrison (english name). He is young, in his early 20's, and thus can relate better to the players because he is their age. He is a good interpreter and even though he is young, has been working with basketball teams for a while. He is a basketball and pop culture junkie who sings American pop songs and dresses like he just stepped out of Tiger Beat magazine. I don't envy him or Joe because they take a lot of crap from all sides and they are stuck in the middle having to do everyone else's talking. However it is funny when they mess up the language and say something like "stay clam" instead of "stay calm" or when one of them said about a player, "he's almost 7'0 feet tall, I think he is 6'12..." or instead of players that need to "focus" telling us that they need to "fuckus". It's always good stuff. Garrison always slips in his own lingo though which makes the interpretation more interesting. He has told us many times while Liu talks that Coach said the players "must chill". In my description of Coach Liu, can you imagine him ever saying the word chill?

The owner of the team is Mr. Wang. He made millions with a steel company that he owned and millions more when he sold it. He is a very unique person to say the least but to this point I don't really know how best to describe him... Others have described him as crazy (5 head coaches in the last two years), eccentric (sits on or behind the bench berating players from the sidelines and during timeouts) and tempestuous (excruciatingly long tirades during practice, at halftime and after games). Earlier this week, he came to practice. As soon as he walked in the gym the whole vibe of the practice changed. Players were on edge, afraid to make a mistake and everyone else got very jumpy. We had just started a good drill where we were breaking down our offensive sets and trying to refine our execution when he stopped the drill (about 3 minutes into it) and said he wanted us to scrimmage instead. He divided the teams up and said that he would be coaching the red team and Coach Weiss would coach the black team. The red team got smoked by the black team and I knew this wouldn't end well. At the end of the scrimmage he brought the team together and ripped their backside for about a half hour. The classic line was when he said... "If a player makes a mistake, he must come out of the game. If he makes the same mistake the next time, he must be punished. He must be forced to do something like push the ball up and down the court with his nose".

The next few weeks should be very interesting as the season begins tomorrow. I hope and expect that we will get off to a good start with 3 of our first 4 games at home but for some reason if we don't start off well... I'll either have great stories or be asking you to pick me up at the airport.

I told you about the guy we signed from Kazakhstan, right? He finally got here yesterday. His name is Ruslan or Russ for short or Roose if you are Chinese. Speaking of which, he is a spittin' image of my friend Russ Schoene. The only problem is that he can't play like Russ. At this point I am reserving judgment. But let's just say first impressions aren't always the best impressions. He had a long day of travel, doesn't know the plays yet and is grossly out of shape... he'll be fine, right? At this point my main fuckus has been to get him to say "I must break you". Haven't asked him yet but I think I will at shootaround tomorrow. As I've said before... it's the little things.

Olumide Oyedeji (or O-da-jay as the Chinese say) arrived in the first quarter of our exhibition game almost two weeks ago now. He is a funny guy. Both funny in a 'ha-ha' way and funny in a strange way. So much so that I could almost devote an entire email just to the crazy stuff he says and does. I will say this though... the man can rebound. Off the airplane, no practice and running on only adrenaline, he had 21 points and 14 rebounds in his first game with us and 12 points and 21 rebounds the next night. He has played in China for 3 or 4 years so he has picked up some language and knows the league pretty well (just ask him). He'll be good for our team.

The last week and a half we have done some public appearances at schools, had a season opening press conference and changed hotels. I am now living with Smiss and Roose in a 3-bedroom apt at a 5 star hotel. Nice digs but quite a change of pace to be living with a couple of 24-year olds. I guess I better learn how to play Playstation and surf MySpace.

I'll be happy to answer any questions now or take comments, either written or by phone at my new number 425-296-xxxx. It's a free call from anywhere but please note that I am 16 hours ahead on the west coast and 13 hours from the east.

The season starts tomorrow. Who knows what's ahead... but in the meantime, I'll try and lay off the donkey.

With the season now staring us in the face, I think the owner got some cold feet with Liu. Mr. Wang (through Joe) told Bob that he would be the head coach again, which by now, I'm not so sure was a bus that Bob wanted to throw himself in front of. Don't get me wrong, Coach Weiss wanted to coach this team but the operative words here were COACH WEISS. I think he knew that no matter who was holding the title of head coach, whether it was him, Liu or even the infamous Chairman Mao for that matter; Mr. Wang would be calling all the shots. This sort of situation would be appealing to no one (including The Chairman).

The script had flipped and now it was Liu that was more or less getting the demotion. For the first time since he came onboard, Liu was showing signs of humility. I think the shared distain of the owner had now actually brought Liu and Coach Weiss a little closer together.

To me, Liu seemed to be in a little beyond his depth. I give him credit for being able to get a team in great condition and the fear factor that he uses to install discipline; but his technical skills and preparation left quite a lot to be desired.

We went to shootaround at 10 a.m. on the morning of the opener. We had one hour on the floor to walk through our sets or talk about any new plays we felt like we needed to put in. Instead, we spent 50 of the 60 minutes doing passing drills. It was a complete waste of time and Bob, Donta, Olumide and I all thought that it was way too intense physically, for a game day practice. Olumide was especially pissed off about it. I can still hear him, with his thick Nigerian accent, slowly and emphatically saying "I have had e-NUFF of dis boo sheet. I am NOT doing dis sheet eva a-geen!"

Speaking of Olumide, he and I had a talk at dinner the night before; it was the same night that I accidentally was feeding on ass. He had spent the last few seasons playing in China and therefore was familiar with the cities and hotels where we were staying. He told me about the spa at this hotel and the great massages that we could get there. He said that they were cheap, long and just very good. We had talked about getting one later that night (no, it wasn't a couples massage) but he forgot to come get me when he went. I saw him the next day before the shootaround and asked him about it. He said that it was great and that I should do it sometime later that day before the game.

As it turned out, there was a problem that day with the hot water in the hotel and the showers in our rooms were only spitting out cold water. I had heard that the hot water in the spa was working, so I decided to kill two birds with one stone. I would go get the massage that Olumide had told me so much about as well as gain access to a hot shower before the game. This would work out perfectly.

I sent an email home that described my experience.

***

----- Original Message -----
From: Rick Turner
To: Friends and family
Sent: Monday, November 24, 2008 1:30 PM
Subject: Week 1 in the CBA

Ni hao goomers,

Rather than watch another mixed doubles badminton match on ESPN International, I thought I'd hit you with a report from Week 1 of scintillating CBA action as the first snow of the season begins to fall here in Taiyuan.

Two things before I do however...

First. Pizza and movie night at the Weiss' last Saturday. Tracy got "**Lars and the Real Girl**" for us to watch. If you haven't seen it yet... do. Wonderful, just wonderful.

Second. Last weekend Olumide convinced me to get a message at the hotel where we were staying in Dalian (the one with the donkey a la o'range).

It just can't ever be easy.

He told me that it was about $10 US for a 45 minute massage and that it was pretty good. "Just go down stairs where the spa is and they will take care of you" he told me. So I thought I'd give it a shot. Even if it was a crappy massage, it would be worth the $10 just to check it out. So I walk in to the "spa" (it kind of looks like a Gene Juarez spa) and tell the woman at the desk that I'd like to get a massage. She has absolutely no idea what I am saying. They try and locate the one girl in the hotel that speaks a little English and she is no where to be found. So I give her the international sign for massage which I'm thinking is fingers moving, as you rub a pretend back. She nods as if she understands and hands me a small washcloth, keys to a locker and gets two guys to escort me to the men's locker room. So far, so good.

We find locker #152. The locker room attendant opens it up and points to my shirt. I don't know what he's wants so he grabs a hanger to let me know that he will hang up my shirt. I give him my shirt. He then points to my pants. I give him my pants. Now, I'm standing there in my socks and "un's" when he grabs another hanger. It happens in slow motion as he points to my boxers. A meek little "um, no" comes from my mouth but in my head it sounds like when Will Ferrell takes the dart in the neck in **Old School**. "Noooooo!!" I'm screaming in my mind. He has a puzzled look on his face. "No, that's okay" I say again. But he is insistent. I think for a minute. Now, there is this guy and 3 other locker room attendants there waiting for me to get with the program. Finally, I think, "what the heck?" and reluctantly give him my shorts. On a side note, this is exactly why I would never last in prison. I'm a pushover.

Off come the boxers (he, for some reason, hangs them on a hanger) and the socks. Now I'm standing there buck nude, two raisins and a cheeto; with 4 Chinese guys checking to see how the American is hung... I feel like the reputation of all American men is at stake. Where is Dave Weston when I need him?

At this point, me and my Chinese motorcade walk through the length of the locker room. Like the hallway in **The Shining**, the walk gets longer and longer. No towel, I'm holding just my little washcloth and they bring me to the entrance of a big room.

Immediately in front of me is a huge hot tub. Its really more like a swimming pool that you'd find at a nice resort but shallow like a hot tub. Behind that is a sauna. A steam room is off to the left along with a big sink area where naked Chinese guys are shaving and brushing their teeth; there are showers to my right. The locker room attendant gives me some size 6 sandals to put on and walks me over to the showers. Now I'm thinking that they want me to shower before I get the massage which (from my limited massage experience), doesn't seem all that unusual. The hot water in the hotel had not been working and this was the first shower that I had in two days, so it felt great. I soaped up, shampooed and even conditioned. Just what the doctor ordered. I turned off the water expecting someone to be there with a towel for me but no such luck.

Still holding my now wet and tiny washcloth, I looked around... no towels. Now what do I do? and where do I go? Since I was there, I thought I may as well get a shave.

I shuffle over to the sink area in my size 6 sandals that pretty much cover the balls of my feet with my toes hanging over the edge and my heels trailing far behind. A different attendant hands me a razor and places a dollop of shaving cream in my hand. I walk over to the sink and realize that the only way to get this done is by sitting down in front of the mirror because it is too low for me to stand. But EVERYTHING in this big room is soaking wet; the floor, the counters, the walls and of course the seats. "This can NOT be a healthy environment" I whisper to myself. I look at the seat and contemplate my next move. With no towel in sight to lay on the chair, I decide to just go for it. I sit on the very edge of the seat with as little skin as possible touching and get my shave on.

I finish shaving. Looking and feeling great, I find the attendant to ask where I go to get my message. I say "Massage?" and shrug my shoulders with palms up? He has no idea. I again bust out the international sign for massage that seemed to work so well last time. My fingers wiggle. The light bulb goes off over his head and he nods and says "okay". He walks me over near the back of the room and says something to 4 older men who all scramble. The oldest of the group grabs me and takes me into a room that connects to the "pool room". There is a massage table in there but something doesn't seem right. The room is tiled and there is no door. It is more like a big shower with a table in the middle of it. He points at the table and gestures for me to get on. At this point, I am a tad bit more comfortable in my nakedness but still extremely aware that I was completely bare pickle.

The table is soaking wet as I hop up on it. I was hoping for a woman to do this massage but at this point I just wanted to get it over with (sound familiar ladies?). I swing one leg up on the table like I'm mounting a horse and the guy says "no-no". He wants me to lie on my back! George Costanza goes racing through my head. Now, a brief moment of panic sets in.

"What have I gotten myself in to?" I thought.

But I lay down anyway. Completely nude, eyes wide open and every muscle in my body clenched. He wraps his hand with something. I can't see what it its. He comes to the head of the table and goes to work...

Starting with my neck and shoulders, this guy rubs me down with what felt like an SOS pad made from broken glass. There was nothing pleasant about this as he moved down to my chest and stomach. As he started scrubbing my sides, I tried to scream but nothing came out. It was if I was being dragged behind a pick up truck down I-5 at 60 mph. Down my legs, between my toes and back up. Then it happened...

It was brief, but nonetheless shocking in its audacity. He quickly grabbed my "stuff" and scrubbed "downstairs". I coughed in case he was checking for a hernia but the pain made it sound more like a hiccup. Then he gestured for me to turn over and the process started all over again on the other side. To answer your next question, yes, he got up in there too. Again, thankfully brief but still, no less appalling.

Like Hurricane Hugo, it was over as quickly as it started but the damage was devastating. As I lay on my stomach, nude; on this totally un-sanitized table and breathless from the events of the last few minutes (actually it could have been hours, I'm not really sure)... he holds a package in front of my face and asks if I want it. My hope is that it is some kind of salve and I agree. He opens it up and starts rubbing it on me. It feels fine and actually more like what I thought I was signing up for in the first place but at this point, I am so tense and stressed that nothing can relax me. He rubs it all over my back and legs and then... he instructs me to turn over again!!! NOOOOO!!! I slide back to my back like a beached whale fighting for its last breath. He goes to work on my front while my back burns as it makes contact with the table. As the lotion hits my skin, it's like Father Merrin hitting Regan with the holy water in **The Exorcist**.

He finishes with the lotion part of our show and tells me to sit up. I do. Dazed and worn out like a super heavy weight that just went all 12 rounds, I reluctantly stand. He helps me slide on my baby sandals and then escorts me to the sauna. Nude, covered in lotion from head to toe, I shuffle over to the sauna like Tim Conway's Mr. Tudball, expecting to slip and fall on my raw, bare backside at any time. I finesse my way in to the sauna. Just me and my postage stamp washcloth.

Four Chinese men are in the sauna, telling jokes and hocking loogies as I walk in. Exhausted and totally defeated, I slowly sit down. All eyes turn to the American covered in un-rubbed in yellow lotion. Still unsure if this is all a prelude to my impending massage or a cruel unfortunate misunderstanding, I wait and wonder what is next.

And I wait.

And wait.

"Is someone coming back to get me or am I on my own now?" I ponder as the lotion and sweat combine to create a septic solution that would make e-coli blush. One by one, the Chinese guys leave the sauna. I find myself alone again; sitting on my life raft of a washcloth, timing how long it takes for a Chinese loogy to dry in extreme temperature and breathing in perspiration fumes that have a distinct and disturbing smell of donkey.

I finally realize that no one is coming to get me for my "massage appointment" and I slowly make my way out from the sauna. As I slide out the exit door of the hot box, I see them. As Bono said, "Like a needle needs a vein, like someone to blame, like a thought unchained, like a runaway train, I need your... TOWELS!!!" The tears welled up in my eyes as I went for them. Okay, there were no tears but I was pretty happy. I could only move as fast as my tiny ice skates would allow but I finally made it to the towels. Like a starving man reaching for a piece of bread, I grabbed one and immediately wrapped it around my "stuff". Another one went over my shoulders but I still wasn't out of the woods. I had to try and make it back to the showers; and with the baby steps that I was forced to take, this may still take awhile. Inch by inch, I made my way along the pool holding on to the sides in case the lotion on the bottom of my feet betrayed me.

From the back of this cavernous room to the front, where my journey began, I sought out the same shower stall that I had used earlier. With nothing to hold onto for the final 20 feet, I bravely made it back to the showers, walking the final expanse like a baby deer who was taking its first steps. I promptly turned on the hot water and attempted to wash away all the sweat, lotion, filth and guilt that I had accumulated over the last 90 minutes.

Teaming with a fruit salad of emotions, I stood in the shower and reached for the one thing that bore witness to these events. The one companion who was a consistent pillar of support as I navigated my way through this Chinese labyrinth. I reached for... my tiny washcloth...

...but it wasn't there.

In my haste to find something "bigger and better", I left my friend behind. Like Tom Hanks in Castaway I screamed "WIILLLSSON!!! It echoed throughout the locker room. "I'm sorry Wilson", I cried as the locker room attendant escorted me back to #152.

I'm still not sure what happened. It all seems like a surreal dream. What started out to be a relaxing 45-minute massage turned into something entirely quite different. The head to toe scrub down, sauna, shower and shave ended up costing me about $8 dollars US and an untold amount of humiliation, pride and contempt. It will certainly be a lasting memory from this trip. Much more so than an ordinary message would have been but; from this point forward... shall never be spoken of again.

Later that night...

We had our first game of the season last Sunday. We played a team called Liaoning who was CBA runners-up a year ago. Our team owner showed up for the game. Not with his wife, but with his mistress. She was there by his side in the locker room before the game and we were lucky enough to have her sitting on the team bench with him throughout the game.

Our team won a total of 5 games last year and 3 were by forfeit, so to say expectations were low going into this game would be a huge understatement. On the road, opening night, sold out crowd against a team that played for the championship a year ago? No chance, right? Well as they say, that's why you play 'em.

The Shanxi Zhongyu shocked the world and destroyed their hosts by 20, 94-74, getting 21 points and 24 rebounds from Olumide Oyedeji in the process.

Up 30 with about 1:30 remaining, Liaoning scored 10 unanswered garbage points to "pull" within 20 as time ran out and let's just say Coach Liu was not happy. As the players celebrated an impossible victory, Liu was steaming. He really let them know it when they got back in the locker room. It took what should have been a great atmosphere after the game and turned it somewhat tempered. Too bad for the players, because they deserved to feel good about themselves after that win.

Our next game was our home opener on Wednesday against Bayi. Bayi is like The Beatles in short pants. They have a bunch of National Team players on their squad including Wang Zhi Zhi who played in the NBA for a few years. He is HUGE over here. So it was quite an atmosphere for our game.

Coming off a big win on the road and opening night against the Beatles; needless to say, it was a sold out crowd that was fired up from the opening tip. The game itself was close all the way but the good guys lost 116-110. Wang Zhi Zhi went for 33 and Bayi's experience down the stretch was the determining factor.

Friday night we played Shaanxi. Yes that is spelled correctly. We are Shanxi with one 'a' and they are Shaanxi with two. We didn't need the extra 'a' however after giving them a 111-98 beat down. "Don-day Smiss" exploded for 38 pts, 8 rebs and 10 assists just missing the triple-double and Wei Ming Lei came off the bench to get all 24 of his points in the second half.

Last night we played Xinjiang (roughly pronounced SHIN-jon). They were too much to handle as former NBA player Mengke Bateer poured in 16 first quarter points on his way to 30 and the Brave Dragons lost to the Flying Tigers 105-79.

Just a couple of side bars:

The day after each game, we have a 10a meeting. In this meeting, Coach Liu reads the entire box score of every game for every team from the previous night. It is absolutely excruciating.

On opening night when John, Paul, George and Ringo came to town; they ended their pre-game warm-ups by doing dunks. Our crowd went nuts with Bayi dunking and our owner got pissed that they were cheering so loudly for them. The next day, our team was instructed that they had to finish up their warm-up with a 'dunk show' from now on. The only problem is that we don't have too many guys that can dunk. So at our next game right before the warm-ups ended, Liu told them to dunk. The first three guys missed. The next 4 didn't even attempt and we ended up missing a total of 12 dunks before the horn mercifully sounded to start the game.

Finally, there is a new league rule that the arenas must be at least a certain temperature at game time or the team will incur a very large fine (I think its 15 C?). Anyway, I don't think our team received the memo. Our gym is so cold on game nights, even with 5000 people in there that I can see my breath. I sit there completely bundled up; with a sweatshirt wrapped around my legs to try and keep warm.

This team also has a junior team. They just fired the head coach. The GM has told me that he wants me to coach the junior team. I'm working hard to avoid taking that bullet. Hopefully Bob can help me there... We'll see...

Stay tuned
rt

I was told that I couldn't be on the bench because the league only allowed a certain number of team personnel to sit on the bench during games. We had Bob, Liu, Xia, Garrison and the owner. Joe and I were both told that we couldn't be on the bench. Imagine how I felt at our first game, as I was sitting up in the stands with my video camera; looking down to see our owner's 20-something year old mistress sitting on our team bench. It sucked.

As I mentioned in the email, our next three games were at home. It was our first in front of the home crowd. In the back of my mind, I was still worried that they were going to move me to the junior team. I was trying my best to keep my head down.

When we walked into our arena for the home opener, the place was abuzz and had a real atmosphere of a big event. The arena was in tip-top condition and had been decorated throughout. As I walked onto the floor, I looked up to see 30-foot banners hanging from the ceiling of the building. Each banner was a larger than life picture of each of our players, Coach Weiss, Coach Liu... and me??? It made me chuckle when I saw the banner because the photo was from the picture day that I wasn't wearing any pants. I had no idea what they were taking our pictures for that day or how they were going to be used. If I did, I think I would have tried a little harder to look decent. It continued to confuse me, however, because on one hand I was feeling isolated, like I was just taking up space, while they considered moving me to the junior team. On the other hand, it seemed as if I was being promoted relatively heavily by the team, even though I had such a limited role. I wasn't sure what to think.

As shallow as this sounds; it was a lot of fun to play at home because the fans treated the team (and especially us Americans) like rock stars. After every game, we were bombarded for autographs and had to run a gauntlet of 40-50 local police officers and soldiers who lined up to create a walkway that would allow us to get to our bus without getting mobbed. The crowd was loud in our building (despite the temperature) and they loved Donta and Olumide. It was a lot of fun. The one thing that was kind of interesting though, was what would happen at halftime of every game. We would go back into the team room for our halftime chat while it seemed as if everyone in the building would light up a cigarette during the NBA-style halftime show. When we came back out for the second half, there would be a blue haze that enveloped the court; slowly rising toward the rafters and wouldn't finally dissipate until at least the fourth quarter. It was like going into a locker room at halftime from a basketball court and coming back out into a bowling alley.

***

As I look back over my notes, starting from the last two preseason games and into the first week of the season; I am finding one consistent complaint which I had forgotten about until a re-look through my journal jogged my memory. The first time that I see the note comes on November 4th, when we were in Changchun. It was written during the day in between our final two pre-season games and in my dreadfully sloppy handwriting.

It simply reads: "SITUATIONS… We need to work on situations!!!"

I find it again on November 16th in notes during a team meeting: "Situations???"

And again on the 18th :   "Things we need to work on:
                              Situations: 2 for 1, End of clock, end of game, up, down…"

November 20th : "Why can't we work on situations? How can you expect a team to execute end of game, if you don't practice it".

Obviously, Coach Weiss knew this as well, but Liu was clueless as to the importance of a team working on a variety of specific situations that they may encounter in a game or during a season. When I saw that our team had the chance to be pretty good, it was extremely frustrating when we weren't doing everything possible to prepare them properly. We had won a total of three games the previous season. This year we had already won three games in our first five outings.

I didn't get it.

At the home games, I was able to sit behind the bench because we had members of the junior team videotape the games instead of me. I took meticulous notes during the games, not only to help myself, but to also address things with Bob after the game and provide constructive analysis. From my vantage point behind the bench however; what was really interesting was observing the dynamics of the bench and watching how everyone interacted with each other.

The funniest thing was watching when we wanted to call a timeout. If it happened once, it happened a hundred times, and it never stopped being funny. In part I think, because no one ever did anything to fix it. Here's what would happen…

In the CBA, the head coach is the only person that can call timeout. Unlike in the NBA or college basketball, a player cannot call a time out. It has to be done by the head coach; our head coach was Bob.

On our team however, the only person calling timeouts was the owner, who always sat four seats down from Bob. If the owner wanted a timeout, he would tell Liu, Liu would tell Garrison and Garrison would tell Bob. Bob would jump up off the bench and yell out to the referee that we wanted a timeout. However, invariably the length of time that it took to send the word from Wang to Liu to Garrison to Bob to the referee was always too long before the team inbounded the ball and put it back in to play. They would miss the small window of opportunity that they had to get the timeout called.

It was the same routine every time, and like watching Abbott and Costello's **"Who's On First"** routine over and over, it was funny every time. The fuse would light and slowly make its way down to Bob. He would jump off the bench like a firecracker went off in his pants; making a 'T' sign with his hands and running at the referee screaming "TIMEOUT!". As usual, he wouldn't be granted the timeout. He would turn back toward the bench, turn his palms upright and shrug his shoulders with an exasperated look on his face... every... single... time...

***

My fears were finally realized after our first home stand.

Joe and I were both moved to the junior team. It was entirely something that I didn't want to do. I was there to work with Coach Weiss and experience China. With this junior team, I would be doing neither. I wouldn't be doing any traveling and I would be stuck in Taiyuan by myself while the team was on the road seeing 17 different cities in China. I tried to spin it to myself as best that I could. The positives were that 1) at least now I would be coaching 2) I wouldn't have to sit idly through the monotony of another one of Liu's practices and 3) I was still getting paid the same.

The thing that was most difficult about coaching the junior team, however, was that they didn't play any games. Just like the senior team, the junior team was required by ZBH to practice twice a day for three hours per practice. That is a lot of practice for a team who doesn't play any games. I knew that it would be difficult to keep the young guys motivated without a game schedule to look forward to.

The senior team hit the road the next week and I was left behind to coach the young kids. We practiced Monday through Saturday from 9 a.m. - noon and again from 3 p.m. -6 p.m., no exceptions. That's 36 hours of practice each week and I knew after the first day that I would need to develop something that would take some of the stress off me.

For whatever reason, I have always been stressed out about writing practice plans. I've always wanted them to be perfect and I get entirely too worked up about making them just right. In fact, they sometimes get agonizing for me to write as I try and plan them to perfection; with just the right amount of pace, instruction and competitive balance. Therefore, you can imagine how I was feeling about the prospects of creating prefect three-hour practice plans, twice a day, six days a week, for the next four months. I had to find a better way.

I decided the best thing that I could do, would be to create 12 different, three-hour plans and just repeat them each week. Every Monday we would do the same thing as the previous Monday. Every Tuesday we would do the same as the previous Tuesday and so on. I took my day off on Sunday and spent much of it designing our daily practice schedule. It actually turned out pretty good.

***

----- Original Message -----
From: Rick Turner

To: Friends and family
Sent: Thursday, December 18, 2008 4:11 AM
Subject: China - The Christmas Edition

Ni Hao Goomers,

It has been about a month since my last offering and I'm sure many of you are just fine with that. Actually, there hasn't been much to report since the season began as everyone has been concentrating on games here with the team playing 3 times a week. As I've mentioned before, this team won a total of 5 games last season and 3 were by forfeit when a team used an ineligible player; so being that we are 7-6 right now, I'd say it's a dramatic improvement. The city seems to be pretty excited about the team and last week they were on national television for the first time.

My own situation is a little tenuous but I won't bore you with the details of that. Suffice to say that I am pretty much coaching the junior team full-time right now since their coach was fired and going day to day with that. The positive of that is, at least I feel like I am contributing and have something to prepare for on a daily basis. The negative is that it is not what I came here to do and frankly isn't as rewarding, personally or professionally. I suppose things could be worse, I could be living in the States...

I don't think Christmas is really "celebrated" here as much as it is just recognized. Officially, China is an atheist country but you will find the random church here and there. But as we all know, Xmas is really about the presents anyway. There are many Christmas decorations up around the city, lights are hung and the trees are lit as well. In the hotel where we stay, Dean Martin has been singing about "Rudy, the Red-Beaked Reindeer" for a few weeks now and I'm ready for him to give it a rest already.

No email would be complete without a little drama however and after a slow couple of weeks... drama finally returned to the Shanxi Zhongyu. In previous emails, I have mentioned the owner of the team, Mr. Wang. Five coaches in 2 years, a hair-trigger temper, a penchant for eccentricity and his pre/post game rants have become legendary for their length as well as content. A couple of examples...

In our pre-game meeting on Wednesday, the owner told our starting point guard not to be nervous for this game because the other team's point guard was "just a bad as he is"... a real confidence builder. Last week he fired one of the guys on staff because he wouldn't play basketball with him one afternoon. Apparently the guy has a bad back and wasn't able to play but it offended the owner enough to fire him.

It has also become totally clear that he (the owner) is really the coach of this team. Coach Weiss and I kind of joked around about that but we are finding out more and more that it is true. He sets the line-ups, tells the coaches who to sub, who should play and who shouldn't on his whim; when to call timeouts and how/what to practice. Armed with this knowledge, it becomes easier to "let go" and just roll with the punches because it's useless to try and swim up stream against the owner's ideas.

After starting off the season 7-3, things were looking good. The team was playing with a lot of confidence, they were starting to form a bit of an identity and their new found success was pushing them to play a little over their heads... then the owner struck.

His first missed step was to bench the best Chinese player on the team against Beijing, a team that we were better than. There was no explanation, no one knew why it happened and the player (Zhai Jinshuai) was crushed. The arbitrary nature of this move (I think) had reverberations throughout the rest of the team and particularly the Chinese players, who have since seemed to be afraid to make a mistake. It also sucked some of the joy out from the good start. Needless to say, we lost the game and have been in a bit of a funk ever since.

Things really got interesting last Friday though. While the team was on a 3-game road trip, I was stuck here in Taiyuan coaching the juniors. My interpreter, Joe, said to me on Friday morning that the team signed Bonzi Wells and that he'd be here that afternoon. Immediately, I thought of my roommate and new friend Donta Smith. I don't use that word 'friend' loosely.

On a side note, when I left the Sonics in 1997 to pursue coaching full-time, I sat down with George Karl to discuss my move. One of the things that always stuck with me from that conversation was when Coach Karl told me that "Your players have to hate you". I've told that story many times and most people I tell it to dismiss it on face. However, I do think that there is some truth in what Coach said. I never took that advice literally but instead interpreted it to mean that there has to be a line between coach and player. If you're not careful, that line can get easily blurred in this kind of environment where you spend so much time together practicing, traveling and playing games with lots of emotions experienced every day. It is very difficult to be both coach and friend. Some guys can pull it off but they are the exception, not the rule. Just like being friends with your boss, its hard know where that line is drawn when the "s" hits the fan and tough decisions have to be made. With Coach Karl's words always in the back of my mind, I have continually tried to keep my players "at arm's length" and have seen them more as a son or nephew rather than a friend (as we say in the hood... just keepin' it real).

Anyhoo... since I haven't been doing much coaching with the senior team and also since we live together, I feel like the friend/coach line has been blurred a little bit with Donta. So when I heard that we signed Bonzi on Friday, my immediate concern was for Donta and his future.

My first move when I got back to the apartment was to email Coach Weiss to see if they had told Donta yet.

Unfortunately, they hadn't told Coach Weiss yet... so he was completely blindsided by the news. The rest of the weekend for the team was shrouded in uncertainty and sadness that their best player, team leader and proverbial "straw" was leaving; only no one would say anything to him to confirm this.

To try and give you a clearer image of what was happening at the time; let me first say that signing Bonzi Wells may be one of the biggest stories in CBA history. For a few reasons... 1) he will be highest NBA draft pick to ever play here in this league, 2) he has had a successful NBA career and been a major contributor on many playoff teams and 3) and maybe the biggest here, is that he used to play on the Houston Rockets with Yao Ming and most of their games are on TV here so EVERYONE knows who he is. It has been rumored that he was signing here for so long now that we all just dismissed it as rumor. When it actually happened last Friday, it became a bit of a media circus.

Everyone seemed to be in on it except Donta, who wasn't sure what to believe. He can't read the Chinese press reports , he'd been hearing this for so long now it probably was just another rumor and besides... he's KILLING guys in this league! Yet, he felt something was different. As he told me a couple days ago, the Chinese players started acting funny around him and this made him suspect that something was up. So with one foot in the grave he continued to play over the weekend. 15 points in just 12 minutes of play against the Chinese Army team on Friday (league rules restrict how much Americans can play against the Army team) and 35pts/ 8rebs/ 5 assists on Sunday before coming home to uncertainty on Monday. The team lost all 3 games on the road trip and would come home on Monday to see if in fact Bonzi was here or whether the rumors persisted.

Back with me in Taiyuan on Monday, the rumors proved to be true. Bonzi showed up at the end of my morning practice flanked by a brigade of Chinese news media. He wanted to work out so I put him through a short work out which included showing him as many of our plays that I could so he would have a head start at Tuesday's practice. I wasn't sure what to expect from him as his reputation for petulance was well documented. He came off as a pretty good guy and I wasn't sure who to feel worse for... him (coming) or Donta (going). We went back to the hotel, had lunch and I filled him in on the craziness of the Zhongyu. I wondered out loud what Donta's next move would be and Bonzi asked what I meant. I told him that each team can only have 2 foreign players and someone would have to be cut. We can't cut Olumide (he's our only big) so obviously Donta is out. Bonzi said, "Hold on, we can't cut Donta, that boy can PLAY!" I told him that there was no choice. "No, no..." he says, "...I have to talk to somebody. We can't cut Donta."

That afternoon, Bonzi came with me again to practice with the junior team and get a workout. As we walked in the gym, he went directly to the GM and told him that they can't cut Donta. The GM has no real response, in part because he speaks no English and also because he is shocked at what he's hearing.

Bonzi tells me that he hasn't played since September and is in terrible shape. I know the team, heck the entire country, is expecting him to play on Wednesday but he says he won't be ready for 2 weeks.

On Monday night, the team returned and Bob, Tracy, Bonzi, the GM and I have dinner together. Bonzi reiterates that he is no where near ready to play so the GM asks Bob if he will help talk Donta into playing one more game on Wednesday before they cut him. On Tuesday morning, all of us get on the bus to go to practice; me, Bob, Olumide, Russ (the Russian), Donta and Bonzi. Donta knows he's out but is going to anyway so he can say goodbye to everyone and get some info from the GM about his release. Everyone gives hugs and high fives to Donta as he walks in the gym. Remember, he is our leading scorer - 21ppg, he is our 2nd leading rebounder (7 rpg) to Olumide (who leads the entire league); he leads us in assists with 5 per, steals at 3 per, blocks and FT %... and we are cutting him.

He goes with Garrison to speak with the GM about his release. The GM (Zhang Bei Hai) is feeling terrible about the whole thing and tells Donta that he wants to keep him but the owner is making him sign Bonzi. As they are talking, Garrison starts to cry which is not something that you expect from your interpreter and especially not from your Chinese interpreter since the Chinese have seemed rather unemotional most of the time. But Smiss has such a big personality that everyone on the team has grown very fond of him and these "business" decisions often have deeper impact. ZBH makes an appeal to Donta and asks him to play one more game since Bonzi isn't ready and it would be a personal favor to him if he played on Wednesday. Donta agrees even though he already has three offers from other teams that want to sign him immediately.

By Wednesday morning, there is a growing concern about Bonzi. He doesn't seem too anxious to play, nor willing to capitulate. The coaches, GM and owner meet with him on Wed. afternoon before the game. He tells them that he needs more practices. The owner makes the suggestion that he "practices while he plays in games". Bonzi says no... As we get to the game on Wednesday night, there is a flicker of hope that maybe the owner will reverse his course and keep Donta but that is quickly extinguished before the game when he tells Donta to "say goodbye to your fans tonight".

With about 5 minutes before the game starts, Coach Weiss and I notice a meeting of the minds over near the bench. It's the owner, the GM and the two Chinese coaches (Liu and Xia). They call Donta over with about 2 minutes remaining before the buzzer sounds and tell him that they want him to stay in China, practice with the team but not play in games to see how it works out with Bonzi. Donta just laughs as the game is about to start.

Donta goes for 23 points in the 3rd quarter in route to 41 for the game and brings the team from down 17 to take the lead in the 4th quarter. The storybook ending didn't quite make it as we ended up losing 122-118. The crowd was electric with the signing of Bonzi; having him in attendance and Donta's performance... it was a fun night until the final score. Bonzi, Donta and Olumide were totally mobbed by fans after the game wanting pictures and autographs. Two of them loved it while the other one was less than enthusiastic. You can guess who was who.

I am writing this on Thursday night. Currently, nothing is resolved. The team doesn't want to give Donta his release even though he has no roster spot and a pending contract offer in Australia. It's a little unfair but I think both Bonzi and the team are getting buyer's remorse. Hopefully for everyone's sake, Bonzi will acquiesce and agree to play Friday so Donta doesn't miss his chance to hook on elsewhere. And one other note to the NBA people that are included on this email. Not friend Rick talking but Coach Turner... Donta Smith should be on a NBA roster without question. If you want specifics, please contact me but be assured I will be contacting you in greater detail about this later.

Four losses in a row has put everyone on edge and the Bonzi/Donta drama has tensions peaked. It will be interesting to see what transpires in the coming days as anything could happen with this owner involved.

Merry Christmas and Happy New Year. Have a great holiday and don't be shy to shoot me an email anytime. It gives me something to look forward to while I dodge theoretical bullets on the other side of the Great Wall. As always...

Stay tuned...
rt

I needed to gain some perspective. I could feel the walls closing in on me. I had been trying to meet with Zhang Bei Hei for at least two weeks but I knew that he was avoiding me. I told Joe that I wanted to go home for a couple days for Christmas and my daughter's birthday. I knew that he could run the practice while I was gone (we'd been doing the same thing every week now for nearly a month) and since I wasn't with the senior team, I wouldn't have to miss any games. Even though Coach Weiss promised me, before I committed to come to China, that the team would fly me home once or twice during the season; I was willing to purchase my own airfare. I only needed a couple days. I couldn't see the downside.

Joe warned me that if I left, the team might not allow me to come back, so I had to speak with ZBH myself. I finally tracked him down about 10 days before I wanted to leave.

He sat with me and Garrison in the lobby bar of the hotel and we talked about my trip. He was extremely accommodating and said unequivocally that it would be no problem for me to leave for a couple days. In fact, he said that I could take as many as two weeks away if I wanted. He told me that he didn't need me back until January 5th. I didn't want to be gone that long so I booked my return flight to return to China on December 29th so I would only be gone for five days. I'd be home for Christmas as well as Scout's birthday on the 28th.

Before I ended my conversation with Zhang Bei Hei (ZBH), I asked him one more time to confirm that my leaving for a few days would be okay. He laughed and said, yes, no problem. I told him that I was going to leave all of my belongings in China because I was intending to return. Again, he said no problem.

***

----- Original Message -----
From: Rick Turner
To: rickturner04@
Sent: Saturday, January 03, 2009 4:22 PM
Subject: a big ribbon

Ni Hao,

Happy New Year!

When we last left... The Bonzi (or as they call him in China, Bon-chi) and Donta drama was reaching a crescendo. In his final game on Wednesday, Donta scored 41 points and electrified the crowd in what the owner told him would be his farewell game. I sent the email out on Thursday and by Friday, it really got interesting.

For 3 full hours, from about 8p to 11p on Thursday night... the GM (ZBH), the team interpreter (Garrison) and Bonzi's personal interpreter ("Mark") were knocking on Bonzi's door; trying to talk to him about his situation. But Bonzi wouldn't answer the door. He thought they were there trying to make him let his boy "Mark" stay with him in his apartment. As Bonzi put it... "the guy stinks". So Bonzi would not come to the door, would not answer his phone and did his best to ignore their constant pounding and bell ringing. This went on for nearly 3 hours.

What they were really there to do was cut him.

The team plays every Wednesday, Friday and Sunday and the routine is: Shoot around at the arena at 9a, lunch, rest, team meeting at 4p, go to the arena right after the meeting at 6p and then play the game at 7:30p.

On Friday morning, everyone went to shoot around. After shoot around, Bob came to our apartment. Bob was pretty happy. He told Donta that he just got done speaking with Garrison and the GM. The team changed its mind and decided to keep Donta and let Bonzi go. Donta seemed to be happy with the news as well but I warned him to remain cautious and not blow up his Australia deal yet. At the same time though, I couldn't help but feel a little sorry for Bon-chi and the way that all this was being handled. He was oblivious to the new turn of events and was still lobbying for Donta to stay a little longer while he tried to work himself into shape.

Friday afternoon after lunch, the events of the previous night repeated themselves. Garrison, "Mark" and the Asst GM (Mr Chin) were the ones at Bonzi's door but again he ignored them. They went as far as to get a key from the hotel's front desk, to let themselves in, but Bonzi had locked the door from the inside as well. He still wouldn't answer his phone and the team employees were extremely frustrated. You see, this time they were there to let Bonzi know that the owner wanted to play him 1 on 1 in the afternoon before the game and he needed to leave early with them. They are so in fear of the owner that they didn't want to leave and have to go back to the practice facility w/o Bonzi. Then have to face the owner and tell him that they couldn't find Bonzi. Unfortunately for them, this was exactly what they'd have to do.

The junior team practice started at 3p on Fridays, an hour before the pre-game team meeting for the senior club; so I went out to the practice facility before everyone else. As I got to the gym, the owner was in there, dressed in his basketball gear, waiting for Bonzi.

The foreign contingent of Coach Weiss, Donta, Olumide, Russ and Bonzi got there a little bit later than normal... shortly after 4p. Bonzi went straight to the gym where the owner was waiting for him and the rest of the guys went to the scheduled pre-game meeting. Before they got there, Coach Liu had told the Chinese players that the team was keeping Donta and when they walked in the door, the team exploded in applause and high fives as they welcomed Donta back to the team.

Meanwhile, in the gym, the owner had Bonzi playing against the junior team in 3 on 3 games and 4 on 4 games which he also played in. Frankly, Bonzi did not look very good against the junior scrubs and the 5' 3" owner; but he did a great ass kissing job. You could see on the owner's face how happy he was to "get" to play with a former NBA player like Bonzi. It made me realize that it doesn't matter what team you own... whether you sell $5 coffees and find yourself in the NBA, you are a schizophrenic compulsive liar who toils in basketball's minor leagues or a steel magnate with a little man's complex in Mainland China... jock-sniffing knows no boundaries.

Nothing had been said to Bonzi as we went to the gym for the game on Friday night, a game in which we beat Qingdao (Ching-dow) 106-95. Olumide had 26 pts and 13 rebs while Donta chipped in 16 for the winners.

By now, Bonzi and Donta had become pretty good friends and were hanging out a lot together. They were making plans on what they were going to do in Beijing, which the team was leaving for the next day on Saturday. The mood was very upbeat after the win. Another huge crowd of people waited to cheer the players and Coach Weiss outside after the game as we got on the bus. Lots of people were carrying signs and telling Donta how much they were going to miss him. They didn't know that the team had changed their minds on keeping him; they thought that it was his last game.

I think in part because Bob's wife Tracy had gone home for Xmas, we skipped the normal post-game meal of martini's and bacon-cheese burgers while the Filipino duo of Lucia and Max sang the Barry Gibb and Babs Streisand hit "Guilty" in the background of the hotel's lobby bar. Instead, we all went back to our rooms. I got online to check my emails and Donta got on his Playstation where he doubled as an Army Commando. At around 12:30a we got a knock on our door. It was Coach Weiss. He had a bad look on his face and I could tell he was upset. He asked for Donta and went back to his room. He told him that the owner changed his mind again after playing with Bonzi earlier in the afternoon and they were cutting Donta. If our lives came with a soundtrack, circus music would have been playing in the background as Coach Weiss was talking.

This time it was for real and Coach Weiss realized that with the team leaving for a road trip in the morning, this would be his goodbye to Donta. He wasn't happy about it and the two of them did the awkward "guy goodbye" where each wanted to say something more but their guy-ness wouldn't allow them to get too sentimental. It was quick, uncomfortable and seemed somehow, incomplete...

Bonzi played his first game the next Sunday. He scored 48 points, had 11 rebs and 7 steals in a 107-106 win over TianJin. So far the team is 3-3 with Bonzi and he has had games of 48, 41, 46, 52, 3 and 27.

As for the star of our show and your boy, RT...

Before I came to China in August, I spoke with Coach Weiss about the possibility of getting home for Xmas and more importantly my daughter's birthday. He didn't think that it would be a problem but I started to have my doubts once I got there. After I was moved to coach the junior team, I saw an opportunity to make that happen. I spent nearly 3 weeks trying to get a meeting with ZBH (the GM). With everything going on, he was hard to pin down and I think he was avoiding me because the team owed me money and he thought I was going to complain about my new role. By now I had actually grown to kind of like it and found a good routine everyday. I really just wanted to talk about a short Xmas trip.

I went online and found a pretty cheap ticket from Beijing to Seattle. ZBH was on the road with the team so I emailed him to tell him that I was going to buy it. I got no response so I waited. Finally, about a week before I wanted to leave, I was able to meet with him. I explained my situation and he said that it would be no problem for me to go home for a few days. In fact, he said that I could stay up to 2 weeks if I wanted. As long as I was back in China by January 5th, it would be fine. I appreciated that but knew that I was in a tenuous position. I decided to only stay for 5 days. So I bought the plane ticket which had now doubled in price. My interpreter Joe, told me that if I went home for Xmas, they would not let me come back. I spoke with ZBH about this and he assured me that it would be fine. I told him that I was going to leave my things in China. He said no problem.

On Sunday night, a couple days after Donta's final game with the team, he and I were packing up to leave the next morning. We were on the same flight to Beijing, then he was connecting to Melbourne and I was connecting to Seattle. The team spent much of the day Saturday trying to convince Donta to stay for a couple weeks, be inactive and wait to see if the Bonzi experiment was going to work. He said no way. He had a better deal in Australia where he would make more money, play less games, had an American coach and a team that was in first place. And oh yeah, it is SUMMER time there!

At about 10p our phone rang and it was Joe calling to let me know that Mr. Chin would be there at 7a to drive me to the airport. I told him that Donta needed a ride as well and this took him by surprise. Donta didn't tell anyone that he was leaving. He was just going to have his agent finish all the details with the team and he was going to get out of Taiyuan as soon as possible and on a plane to Melbourne. I could tell by Joe's reaction on the phone that no one knew of Smiss' impending departure and I shouldn't have been surprised when I got a knock on my bedroom door at 1a.

I was just finishing up watching "**Good Luck Chuck**" on HBO before racking out for the night. When I heard the knock I told Donta to come in. Instead of Donta, I heard a Chinese voice say "Uhh, Rick? Could you come out here?" I threw on a tee shirt and wearing my camouflage boxer's, I stumbled out to the living room. There I saw Joe, Mr. Chin and the accountant (Du) along with Donta. They've come to take one last swing at Donta to try and convince him to stay in case it doesn't work out with Bonzi. Again, Donta says no way. He is already packed and ready to get on a plane in just a few more hours.

So they ask me write up a contract that dissolves the existing contract between the team and Donta. I have two things going against me here. First, I have no law background. The closest I've been to the bar exam is singing "You've Lost That Lovin' Feeling" with Lucia and Max a couple night's earlier. And number two, this hotel we are staying at is NOT a Holiday Inn Express.

I ripped a piece of paper out of my notebook and wrote out the terms of the agreement in English. Du, copied down what I wrote in Chinese on a separate sheet of paper. Donta and Du, signed each document and they then handed Donta 250 US one-hundred dollar bills. I'd be lying if I said my mouth didn't water as I watched Donta count out the money

As everyone was leaving and saying their goodbyes to Donta, Mr. Chin told Joe to tell me that I would have to move out before I left for Seattle. Remember, I was supposed to leave in about 5 hours. I had only packed a small bag to bring to Seattle with me and all my stuff was scattered around the apartment. Mr. Chin told me that they pay for the apartment per day and it made no sense to pay for it while I was gone because I had to move to a one-bedroom anyway when I got back. We agreed that I would get it all together and they would come back tomorrow to store it somewhere while I was gone.

I came back to Seattle, had a good Xmas and celebrated Scout's birthday on the 28th. In the short time I was home, I tried to do everything and see everyone that I missed over the last 4-5 months. I was having drinks with one of my boys, Kevin Calabro, at about 9p the night before my flight when my phone rang. It was Coach Weiss. I was excited to answer it, thinking that he had some good news for me about my return to the team or some funny story to tell me about something that happened while I was gone. I hurried to answer the phone but as soon as I hit the button, for whatever reason I got the feeling that the news would not be good.

He told me that he got a call from Joe to tell him that I would not be allowed to come back. He didn't have much more information other than to let me know that they would pack all my things up and send them home to me.

I was shocked, disappointed, hurt, angry and confused. I was supposed to be on plane in less than 12 hours and the plug had been pulled. I wondered if they lied to me or just decided change their mind. I came home to find an email from Joe:

Rick ;
i just got a call from Mr zhang he wants me to tell you that the second team and the teenage team will merge to one team and coach Zhao and me will coach this team so they don't need no more help .i hate be picked to tell you this i am sorry.
joe

It was definitely an interesting experience. I had plans to take the Trans-Siberian Railroad from Beijing to Moscow and then Euro-Rail from Moscow to London before flying back to Seattle after the season was over. I was enjoying the tumultuous adventures of the team on a daily basis and the experience of living in such a uniquely different culture from the US. Honestly, I didn't particularly enjoy what I was doing every day but I could put up with it for a few more months and wanted to see it through. Plus, I held out hope that Coach Weiss could help me get back with the senior team which I know he tried to do.

I now find myself back at square one, only 6 months older and no closer to a "real job" than I was before I left. I guess I'll throw it out that if anyone has a suggestion for me, I'll listen. Thanks for indulging me with these emails and who knows... maybe another adventure is in the offing???

Stay Tuned...
rt

***

I had packed a small bag for my trip home and left most of my things in Taiyuan. Now I was home and all my stuff was still over there. No one there seemed to be in any sort of a hurry to get me my things back. I barely had any clothes to wear. I was stuck as to what to do next and a bit of panic set in as I knew that I needed to find a j-o-b, a-s-a-p.

I answered an ad on Craigslist for a salesman at a funeral home. I thought the money might be good and I knew it was an industry that was recession proof. I responded to the listing and immediately got a response from the sales manager there, a woman named Neily Bissette. Over email, we set up an interview time for the day after New Year's on January 2nd. I was proud of myself for not wasting any time and coming up with a job interview right away.

I had a problem though. All of my varsity clothes were still in China.

I put on an old suit and it didn't fit me well at all. I had to suck in my expansive gut as far as I could just to get the pants buttoned and make sure that I practiced my best shallow breathing techniques. The coat was tight... real tight and it felt like I might rip the back out at any moment if a wrong move was made. The only shirt I had was too small in the neck. To button it all the way to the top in order to put on a tie, jeopardized my ability to remain among the living. I decided to stuff myself into the suit, but go without the tie, and hope that it wouldn't be a big deal to Ms. Bissette.

I drove up to the Sunset Hills Memorial Park and Funeral Home at 11:50 for my noon appointment with Neily Bissette. As I drove into the parking lot, I noticed that people were gathering for a funeral inside and the service was about to start in the funeral parlor. An air of gravity weighed on my disposition, and any attempts to try and lighten the mood of my interview would give way to my respect of the surroundings.

I looked like dump, which made me feel like dump. It's not the way that I recommend going into an interview. The mood was sullen, and every step I took had to have the preciseness of walking on china, because one false move could explode the entire wardrobe at any minute. I wasn't wearing a tie which made me feel guilty and lame; and because of the recent New Year's holiday, I had no time to print out a proper resume that fit the job description. All in all, I felt like crap.

I walked in the front door and immediately saw many of the Sunset Hills employees dressed to the nines as they acted as ushers for the upcoming service. Through the front doors, I made an immediate left and into the administrative offices. There was a receptionist sitting at the front desk, who looked up at me as I walked in; or should I say, as I waddled in, trying not to split my pants.

"Hi, my name is Rick Turner. I have a noon appointment with Mrs. Bissette."

"Who?" she snidely responded with a disgusted look on her face.

"I'm here to see Mrs. Bissette. Sorry, I'm not sure if it's pronounced Neely or Nelly?"

"Do you mean Mr. Neily Bissette?" she huffed and grunted.

"Oh yeah, wow… it's Mister?" I tired to lighten the mood, "I'm glad you told me… that could have been death…"

As soon as I started saying the 'd' in death, I realized where I was. What an idiot. Now I really was feeling like a turd in a punchbowl.

Go figure… I didn't get the job.

Now what?

20

Snoqualmie

Can you picture what will be
So limitless and free
Desperately in need
of some...stranger's hand
In a...desperate land

- The Doors "**The End**"

I wrote this all down for two main reasons. First… I wanted to have some sort of (at least partial) recorded history of my journey to pass on to my daughter in case my passive attempt of suicide by food actually takes. And second… I thought that getting it all on paper would provide me with some clarity as to whether or not the professional choices that I have made to this point have been meaningful or more simply put… worth it.

The food part is working. The clarity in choices however is somewhat more muddled.

My goal in writing this was just to relate some (hopefully) entertaining and (sometimes) funny stories about events that have accompanied my journey during the past few years in the pursuit of a career in coaching. As this writing process neared completion, I explained to people (friends, colleagues, agents and publishers) what I was doing. Many of them asked me the same thing. They asked what the message of the book was or the purpose that I was trying to convey.

Upon their questioning, I was stuck trying to provide an answer.

All of a sudden, I lost sight of the fact that other then my own personal hopes for clarity as a result of this… all I ever really wanted to do for you was entertain. It was never my intent to try to motivate or inspire. After all, it was only my original emails from China that acted as a punk to the fuse for this entire project and I saw this as just an expanded version of those missives. But then, all of a sudden, I felt pressure to be "meaningful", "purposeful" or even "life-changing" as I try to wrap this up and tie a bow on it all.

It was as if this whole writing exercise wouldn't have been worth it unless I somehow changed your life for the better after reading it.

I thought and contemplated and worried and consternated and pondered and reflected and generally worked myself into a frenzy trying to find a brilliant ending. Ultimately, I felt like if there was a message or meaning to any of this, each of you can find it for yourselves.

***

Coaches like to define themselves with little axioms or phrases that they can quickly pull out and use, to let other people know about the make up of their character... or the things that they believe in. As most of us know, two of the more frequently quoted coaches not only in sports but anywhere, are Vince Lombardi and John Wooden.

"Be quick, but don't be in a hurry." - JW

"Never mistake activity for achievement." – JW

"Once you learn to quit, it becomes a habit." – VL

"Success demands singleness of purpose." – VL

Those are a few of my favorites from Coach Wooden and Coach Lombardi, but there are many others. All of us use stuff like this to communicate with our players or define what we believe in to recruits, parents, athletic director's, the media, general managers and owners. Whether it's short phrases or just single words, this is an effective way to quickly effuse our philosophies.

I'm no different. I have used various little axioms to help define myself as a coach or express an attitude to my players.

I mentioned at one point earlier, that one of my all-time favorites was a quote that I stole from former Washington football coach Don James, **"Don't tell me about the pain, just show me the baby"**.

I talked about Frosty Westering's philosophy of "**Make the Big Time Where You Are."**

I told you the words that George Karl left me with as I entered into this coaching adventure on my last day at the Sonics... **"Your players have to hate you."**

In a number of job interviews, I've used three words to describe my own personal "Defining Principles" to potential employers: **Organization, Preparation and Resolve.**

Four words to encapsulate my "Mission Statement" for my teams: **Passion, Selflessness, Commitment and Courage.**

And then, three brief absolutes for winning basketball: **1) Be Physical 2) Impose Your Will and 3) Attack the Basket** or in other words… **Rebound, Control Tempo and Shoot Free Throws.**

So, I looked and looked for some defining moments to take away from this whole experience. In doing so, I kept coming back to one question.

Was it worth it?

My visceral response to that question was frankly, no. It wasn't worth it. Sure, I have done some fun things, seen a lot of craziness, visited places that I would otherwise never have the opportunity to visit and coached some great, great players; but ultimately I find myself an outsider, in an insider's world without the ability to find a foothold to place my crampon. I did reach one of my goals of being a head coach in the CBA (back when the CBA was a good league) but just like the gambler who plays at the table minimum… that wasn't enough. The $5 blackjack bet wasn't holding my interest any longer. I needed more juice on the line to satisfy my fix. I wanted more.

I want to coach in the NCAA tournament; I want to coach a team to an NCAA National Championship. I want to coach a team to an NBA Championship.

Will that ever happen?

At this point, probably not. I realize that.

The fear of being swept back downstream in this profession has been realized. There was a lot of ground to make up in a race that I got a very late start in. A race where I wasn't just trying to catch the guys in front of me, but one where I also had to constantly fend off a steady stream of newcomers who are regularly allowed to join the race well ahead, in spite of their experience (or lack thereof). Any momentum that I had built for myself quickly evaporated once I left China.

In order for me to regain some of that momentum (if it's even possible at this point), I would almost have to start over completely.

Or

As Bob Whitsitt so wisely informed me… hit the coaching lottery. The fact is, my odds of hitting the Powerball might actually be better.

***

People always talk about "paying your dues".

What are the dues? Are some "dues" better than others? Is years as an assistant coach the right "dues"? Is being a former NBA player the right "dues"? Is failing at a previous job the right "dues"? Is being the son of another coach the right "dues"? Is five years long enough? 10 years? 20 years?

My belief is that if you can coach, you can coach. There is no formula to the right hire. Can you relate to your players? Can they trust you? Can you teach? Can you bring them together to pull in the same direction? Can you manage different personalities? Are you organized? Can you be flexible? Can you handle the media?

CAN YOU WIN?

But my beliefs on this topic are inconsequential in this pursuit.

Wasn't it Ben Franklin who said that the definition of insanity is doing the same thing over and over again but expecting different results? If that's the case, then this pursuit of mine can definitely be called insane. This would then have to lead me to believe that it in fact, it hasn't been "worth it" at all. The constant rejection alone is enough to make a zebra doubt if he actually has stripes.

However (and thank goodness), a much more measured response to the merits of this journey presents itself almost on a daily basis; the only problem is that my myopic focus on advancing my own career often times gets in the way of recognizing it. Thankfully, from time to time, I get slapped back to reality by someone or some thing that drives home the fact that… yes… this really has absolutely been worth it.

Just when I think I made the biggest mistake of my life by chasing this not-so-Holy Grail; I realize that there is nothing that I would ever trade for the experience and the blessings it has given me.

I was watching a James Taylor concert on PBS (my nose goes up in the air a little as I say that) and he talked about being "discovered" by Peter Asher back in 1968, who was working in A&R at The Beatles' Apple Records at the time. During the program, Taylor said something to the effect that Peter Asher had "opened a door for him and he found his life on the other side of it". That statement really resonated with me (then he busted into "**Fire and Rain**" which is one of my all-time favs).

I realized that the residual effects of this elusive chase are bigger than me and my selfish ambitions.

This coaching door opened for me and on the other side of it, I found my life.

As I reflect on some of my former coaches and others who have had an influence in my life and career, many of whom I've told you about already: like Mike Cashman, Ed Pepple, Ernie Woods, Lorenzo Romar, Stan Morrison, George Karl and Bob Weiss; I can't help but realize that in one way or another, for better or worse, the players who I have coached have definitely been impacted by my actions, words and deeds whether they liked it or not (and I hope that they did). Even though Coach Karl told me that "your players have to hate you", I discovered that no matter what, you can never hate them (as much as they may try sometimes).

Every single guy (or girl) that you coach becomes a part of your family. You care about them almost as much as one of your own kids. You battle and fight with them like you would with your own kids. You defend them from outsiders like you would your own kids, and you want to see them with nothing but the best as they move on and move away.

When I first started coaching, I didn't put a lot of thought into the things that I said to my players. Often I said things right off the cuff and with a fairly acerbic tongue. But I can vividly remember when that all changed. A time when I realized that the things that come out of my mouth (any coach's mouth, not just mine) will hit a player with an impact that I never originally prepared myself for. I realized that the words a coach uses to teach, motivate, communicate or simply just engage with one of their athletes are not just hollow vestibules that drift off into the ether, but can land with an forceful impact (whether intended or not) that can linger for quite some time.

Luke Seidel was a guy who played for me briefly at Bellevue CC. He was a very good player at that level who was skilled, athletic and charismatic. His teammates followed him. His main problem was that he was at a time in his life where he was still extremely immature. He was making poor decisions in his personal and social life and he wasn't going to class. I had numerous one-on-one talks with Luke in my office and I had a real affinity for him. I knew he was somewhat troubled, but I thought that basketball could be a pathway for him to overcome some of the hurdles that he faced. Simply put, Luke partied too much and was blowing a tremendous opportunity in front of him.

One day Luke came in to see me before practice, and in the course of our conversation, he told me that he was an adult now and wanted to be treated as such by me, his parents and others in his life. He said that he was old enough and smart enough to make his own decisions and that we needed to trust him more.

Later that day, at the end of practice, we were running conditioning drills and it was a day where the conditioning stuff was heavy, hard and challenging. Luke, who saw himself as a leader just like I did, was doing the drills without problem but visibly not liking it. Since it was the beginning of the season, the volleyball team was using one of the courts next to ours, and the woman's basketball team was trickling into the gym for their practice that started immediately after… so the gym was full of people as our practice ended. The players lined up on the baseline one more time and I said something to the team. Luke muttered something snide under his breath. Something like, "This is bullshit".

With that, I kind of "lost it". Without hesitation, I stuck my finger in his face and at the top of my lungs yelled…

"GAWDDAMMIT LUKE, YOU SAY THAT YOU WANT TO BE TREATED LIKE A MAN? WELL THEN START ACTING LIKE A MAN!!! IF YOU WANT TO ACT LIKE A LITTLE BOY, THEN I'LL TREAT YOU LIKE A GAWD DAMN LITTLE BOY…!!!

I'll never forget the look on his face as I unleashed on him there in front of everyone in the gym. You could here a pin drop by the time my decibel level returned to acceptable norms. Whether my overreaction to his petulance was right or wrong, justified or not, is now water under the bridge. I'm not trying to say that I handled it correctly, just that I can point to that moment as the time when I realized that the things we as coaches say… have impact.

Luke had smiled and charmed his way through life to that point. He was such a likeable kid that he usually got his way with things. I don't think anyone had ever talked to him like that before. I felt kind of cruddy that I had brought our private one-on-one conversation earlier in the day into public view like that, but my frustration got the better of me.

I often will run into a former player and he'll say something to me like, "Remember that one time at practice when you said…?" or "I'll never forget when you told me…" and more often then not, I have no clue as to what they are talking about. Some of that is my own acute narcissism, but some of it is just the fact that there are many times when we say something, that seems insignificant at the time, but ends up striking a chord with the player and sticking with them forever.

I wish I could say that my Bobby Knight moment with Luke was enough to get him back on the right track, but unfortunately it wasn't. His classroom work (or lack there of) finally caught up with him and he dropped out of school. He left Bellevue hating me (Coach Karl would have been proud) and in a pretty bad tailspin. But later, he was able to recover and pull himself up. I'm happy to say that he eventually got his act together (as most finally do) and went on to finish his two-year degree at another school in Eastern Washington. He then went on to earn himself a scholarship to play at a small four-year college in Southern California where he had a nice career. And no one was more proud of Luke then I was.

He was my son.

As are all the others that have come and gone along the way.

Too many to mention each individually, but whether they realize it or not, and whether they like it or not… they will always feel like a part of my family.

So was it worth it?

I keep thinking about the couple, who hook up with each other, accidentally have a baby together, and ultimately end up hating each other. They break-up or get divorced, can't stand the sight of one another, fight for years and find themselves questioning what they were ever thinking by getting involved with the other in the first place.

Then… they take one look at their beautiful baby and know that no matter what is said or done… no matter what happens or who did what to whom…they both know… that yes, it was definitely all worth it.

Coaching and I may someday reconcile. We may get back together and try to give it one more shot. Who knows? But for right now, I think we each just need some space.

I look back on this anonymous journey of an anonymous coach and can't help but wonder how things would be different if my name was something like Phil Jackson Jr.? Would I be sitting next to daddy on the Lakers' bench knowing that with one phone call by him, I would be the next head coach of the Kings or the Suns or the Magic?

I do know this…

If my name was Phil Jackson Jr., I would have never had the chance to experience Michael Blackmon. I would have never had Michael Ray Richardson's finger in my face in a Montana motel room as he stuttered unremitting threats at me. I wouldn't have had the chance to experience China with someone as fun and genuine as Bob Weiss. I wouldn't have ever had to wash uniforms, drive the team bus or run a practice with just four players…

…and I wouldn't have had the chance to coach all the unbelievable players that I have had the great privilege to coach. Most of who, turned out to be even better people than they were players, which is really saying something.

I look back on this journey and one word keeps coming back to mind…

Surreal.

The End ?